CLAIRE TOMALIN

———————

THE INVISIBLE WOMAN

THE STORY OF NELLY TERNAN
AND CHARLES DICKENS

PENGUIN BOOKS

PENGUIN BOOKS

Published by the Penguin Group
Penguin Books Ltd, 80 Strand, London WC2R ORL, England
Penguin Group (USA) Inc., 375 Hudson Street, New York, New York 10014, USA
Penguin Group (Canada), 90 Eglinton Avenue East, Suite 700, Toronto, Ontario, Canada M4P 2Y3
(a division of Pearson Penguin Canada Inc.)
Penguin Ireland, 25 St Stephen's Green, Dublin 2, Ireland (a division of Penguin Books Ltd)
Penguin Group (Australia), 707 Collins Street, Melbourne, Victoria 3008, Australia
(a division of Pearson Australia Group Pty Ltd)
Penguin Books India Pvt Ltd, 11 Community Centre, Panchsheel Park, New Delhi – 110 017, India
Penguin Group (NZ), 67 Apollo Drive, Rosedale, Auckland 0632, New Zealand
(a division of Pearson New Zealand Ltd)
Penguin Books (South Africa) (Pty) Ltd, Block D, Rosebank Office Park,
181 Jan Smuts Avenue, Parktown North, Gauteng 2193, South Africa

Penguin Books Ltd, Registered Offices: 80 Strand, London WC2R ORL, England

www.penguin.com

First published by Viking 1990
Published with additional material in Penguin Books 1991
This film tie-in edition published 2014

002

Copyright © Claire Tomalin, 1990, 1991
All rights reserved

The moral right of the author has been asserted

The acknowledgements on page xiv constitute an extension of this copyright page

Printed in England by Clays Ltd, St Ives plc

ISBN: 978-0-241-96941-0

www.greenpenguin.co.uk

PENGUIN BOOKS

THE INVISIBLE WOMAN

'Starting out with scarcely the bare bones of a story, Tomalin
convinces by the end that she has got as near to the truth as
anyone will' Anthony Howard, *Sunday Times*

'A wonderful book . . . In telling the Dickens–Ternan story as
the story of two people, Tomalin does more than restore an
invisible woman to her rightful place in history. She gives us a
hitherto invisible man as well'
Katha Pollit, *Newsday*

'A compulsive read . . . Claire Tomalin makes the Victorian
world accessible and has a clear, unreverential approach
to Dickens himself . . . Her picture of the London theatre
is equally immediate and absorbing'
Kate Kellaway, *Listener*

'As a piece of detective work, this book is elegant and fascinating . . .
As social history it is illuminating. The careers of the Ternan
sisters make livelier reading than many a novel'
Sue Gaisford, *Independent*

Claire Tomalin worked in publishing and journalism for many years. She was literary editor first of the *New Statesman* and then the *Sunday Times*, before devoting herself to writing full time. She is the author of eight highly acclaimed biographies: *The Life and Death of Mary Wollstone-craft*, which won the Whitbread First Book Award; *Shelley and His World*; *Katherine Mansfield: A Secret Life*; *The Invisible Woman: The Story of Nelly Ternan and Charles Dickens*, which won the Hawthornden Prize, the NCR Book Award and the James Tait Black Memorial Prize for Biography; *Mrs Jordan's Profession*; *Jane Austen: A Life*; *Samuel Pepys: The Unequalled Self*, which was the 2002 Whitbread Book of the Year; *Thomas Hardy: The Time-Torn Man*; and, most recently, *Charles Dickens: A Life*.

She lives in London with her husband, the novelist and playwright Michael Frayn.

Contents

CONTENTS

List of Illustrations

TEXT ILLUSTRATIONS

For Katharine M. Longley

Acknowledgements

My first and greatest debt is to Miss Katharine M. Longley who, in an act of rare generosity, placed her own research and unpublished typescript at my disposal. She gave me her time, answered my questions, shared her discoveries and pointed me in the direction of both specialist libraries and private archives and information. She has also allowed me to use photographs in her collection, many of which have never been published before. All this she did without seeking to influence my views in any way. I bow before her scholarship, and my gratitude for both her friendship and her forbearance is partially expressed in the dedication to this book.

My next debt is to other Dickens scholars: Dr Graham Storey, who among many kindnesses allowed me access to the as yet unpublished letters of Dickens, in preparation for later volumes of the Pilgrim Edition; Michael Slater, not only for his book *Dickens and Women* and his articles in *The Dickensian* but also for several enjoyable conversations; and George Curry, who kindly gave me a copy of his *Charles Dickens and Annie Fields*. Dr David Parker, the curator of the Dickens House Museum in Doughty Street, has been constantly supportive in offering advice, providing information and allowing me to use the many excellent resources of the museum. Miss Eileen Power, at one time Assistant Curator, also gave me useful advice at an early stage; her successors Angela Brooker and most recently Andrew Bean have also been helpful.

I am profoundly grateful to the pioneering work of Ada Nisbet, Emeritus Professor of Victorian Studies at University of California, Los Angeles, whose *Dickens and Ellen Ternan*, published in 1952, made the fruits of years of patient research available in a compact and carefully argued form.

My next large debt is to Robert Cecil Esq., who most kindly allowed me to see his collection of family letters and to transcribe from them; he also made available pictures in his possession.

My thanks go to many libraries and their curators: to the British Library; to the London Library, its excellent Librarian Douglas Matthews and his always helpful staff; to Alexander Wainwright of Princeton University Library, who went to much trouble to assist me with the microfilms and photocopies I needed, as well as other kindnesses; to the late Lola Szladits, Curator of the Berg Collection, her successor Francis O. Mattson and the staff there; to the Pierpont Morgan Library; to Nancy Romero of University of Illinois at Urbana-Champaign; to Ann Caiger, Manuscripts Librarian at University of California, LA; and to the Department of Archives in Arras, France. I also appreciate help received from the staff of the Minster Library, York; the reference section of Newcastle upon Tyne Public Library; Penny Ward of Margate Library; the reference section of Slough Public Library; the Library of the London School of Economics; the Guildhall Library; the John Harvard Library in the Borough High Street; the Public Record Office; and Martin Tupper of Islington Reference Library. I am grateful to the staff of the Theatre Museum, now in Covent Garden; to the Colindale Newspaper Library; to the Imperial War Museum Library; and to the Ministry of Defence Archivists.

I much appreciate being allowed to examine the Dickens box at Messrs. Farrer & Company, and the help extended to me there by Mr R. Robertson. My thanks also go to the Keeper of Archives, The Queen's College, Oxford.

To Mrs Lillah Fields I am indebted for hospitality, information and the loan of several precious and personal family possessions.

To Mrs Ayres also I am under an obligation for sparing time and lending me papers and photographs in her possession.

I am grateful to Ron Woollacott, local historian and author of *A Historical Tour of Nunhead*, for his generosity with time and information on more than one occasion.

Mr and Mrs Harold Yexley most kindly took in a strange inquirer, entertained me, gave me a careful historical tour of Park Cottage and offered interesting information about the surrounding area. Mr and Mrs David Barker likewise invited me into their house in Rochester Villas and found the deeds for me to inspect.

In Boulogne, I am grateful for advice and help to Madame Janine Watrin and Monsieur André Beaudel, and for hospitality to Monsieur et Madame Viala and Madame Houillez, the present owner of the Chalet Dickens at Condette.

In Southsea the administrators of the Highland Road Cemetery were kind enough to search their records and to direct me to the graves of the Ternan sisters.

I had good and useful talks at various times about various topics of this book with Catherine Peters, Susannah Clapp, Miriam Margolies, Victoria Glendinning, David Gentleman and my daughter Jo Tomalin.

Professor Eric Hobsbawm gave me a detailed account of Victorian property prices and rents in north London. Dr Jonathan Miller directed me to information about treatment and charges in insane asylums in the 1840s. John Keegan told me exactly where to look for information about the army in the period of Geoffrey Wharton Robinson's service. William Feaver shared his knowledge of the artists Frith and Cruikshank with me, and both Catherine Peters and William M. Clarke gave me information about Wilkie Collins. Jo Mitchenson of the Raymond Mander and Jo Mitchenson Theatre Collection first described to me the portrait of Dora Jordan acting with her baby in her arms. To all these specialists thanks for their generous help.

Further thanks are due to Mrs Edward Norman-Butler, who kindly sought to trace the family connections of Eva Makepeace Thackeray; to James Rowlatt, who checked the Latin poem by George Wharton Robinson and provided me with a careful translation; to Dr John House, who gave me permission to quote from his mother's correspondence; and to Professor N. John Hall, for advice and assistance.

Tony Lacey has been a supportive and helpful editor, as has Chuck Elliott of Knopf: both made invaluable suggestions for improving the text.

I am especially grateful once more to Donna Poppy for the rare combination of meticulousness and enthusiasm she brings to copy editing. It has also been a pleasure to collaborate again with Susan

Rose-Smith, most knowledgeable and indefatigable of picture researchers. Thanks also to Janice Brent for her editorial work, and particularly for bringing to my attention the story of the Hull hosier; and to John Shields for finding his great-grandfather's obituary notice.

Finally, thanks to Michael Frayn for all his practical and patient help in my research, which involved much travel, driving and walking in England and abroad in quest of houses, archives, theatres, cemeteries, etc. He was the first to read my text; and his criticisms and suggestions have been adopted almost without exception.

Permission to quote from manuscripts in their collections has been kindly granted by: the Dickens House Museum, London; the Huntingdon Library, San Marino, California; the British Library, London; the Morris L. Parrish Collection, Princeton University Libraries; the Henry W. and Albert A. Berg Collection, The New York Public Library, Astor, Lenox and Tilden Foundations; and the Pierpont Morgan Library, New York.

Grateful thanks is also made to the following for permission to reproduce copyright extracts: the British Broadcasting Corporation; W. & R. Chambers Ltd; Oxford University Press Ltd; and Random Century Group (UK) Ltd.

I should like to express my special gratitude to Miss Katharine M. Longley and Robert A. Cecil Esq. for permission to quote from manuscripts in their possession; to Mr K. J. Ley for permission to quote from an unpublished article by J. W. T. Ley in the possession of the Dickens House Museum; and Mr Charles Monteith.

Was talking with Mrs Warner, who gave her opinion with some bitterness that theatrical people – players – were not lower in character, etc., than literary people. But I fear this is only the result of a mind, never very elevated, undergoing a process of vulgarization. – William Charles Macready, the actor, reporting a conversation with his leading lady in his diary for 11 February 1847

'*I suppose that most gentlemen become acquainted with some people that they would not wish all their friends to know that they knew. They go about so much more than we do, and meet people of all sorts.*' – *Emily Dunstable to Lily Dale in* The Last Chronicle of Barset *by Anthony Trollope, 1867*

No conceivable process by which the girl might grow into the middle-aged woman ever seems to have presented itself to Dickens's imagination. His heroines are . . . perennially young and pure. The fear of ageing, an ever-present horror in a society that demanded girlish women, never seems to trouble their heads at all. Furthermore, though spinsters are acknowledged to be laughing stocks, the Dickensian heroine must display no eagerness to get hold of a husband. Ideally she should be perfectly unaware of the facts of life, and will imagine that the man who is forcing his attentions upon her is really applying to become her brother or father. – John Carey, The Violent Effigy: A Study of Dickens's Imagination, *1973*

'*Marry this woman! Marry at eighteen an actress of thirty – bah, bah! I would as soon he went into the kitchen and married the cook.*' – *Major Pendennis in* The History of Pendennis *by William Makepeace Thackeray, 1850*

PART ONE

I

'N'

This is the story of someone who – almost – wasn't there; who
vanished into thin air. Her name, dates, family and experiences
very nearly disappeared from the record for good. What's more,
she connived at her own obliteration; during her lifetime her
children were quite ignorant of her history. Why and how this
happened is the theme; and how – by a hair's breadth – she was
reclaimed from oblivion despite strenuous efforts to keep her there.

She was 'N', otherwise Nelly, Miss Ellen, the Patient, the Princess, E.L.T., the Dear Girl, the Darling, the magic circle of one,
the little riddle, Miss T., Miss Fernan, Miss Terman, Miss Teman,
Miss Turnham and probably Mrs Tringham. She played a central
part in the life of Charles Dickens at a time when he was perhaps
the best-known man in Britain. The relationship lasted for nearly
thirteen years, from 1857 until his death in 1870. Her full name
was Ellen Lawless Ternan, though she was almost always known as
Nelly and will be called Nelly in these pages. She was born in 1839;
was eighteen to Dickens's forty-five when they met; and outlived
him by forty-four years.

Clearly, she could have given the world a unique account of his
character and life, and her part in it. Yet, although she was
intelligent, well educated and able to express herself in writing –
among other things, she helped her sister research and write a
literary biography in the 1890s – she never wrote a line about him.
In fact, she left no written trace, and precious little spoken record,
of the fact that she had even known him.

She was wholly excluded from the great biography of Dickens
written by his friend John Forster, who knew her well. No letter to
her from Dickens, or from her to Dickens, appears to have survived,

and there is no mention of her in the first edition of his letters, which was prepared by two of her close friends, Georgina Hogarth, his sister-in-law, and Mary (Mamey) Dickens, his elder daughter. When in 1905 *The Dickensian*, a scholarly and celebratory magazine, was founded, and its editors were keen to publish reminiscences by anyone who had actually known the great man, no approach was made to Nelly or any other member of her family; and neither she nor her surviving sister Fanny volunteered any contribution.

Nelly was not the only member of her family to be blotted out. Fanny, a remarkable woman by any standards, who had also known Dickens well, got similar treatment in the three-volume autobiography of her own husband, Thomas Adolphus Trollope. She is there but only as a very shadowy figure. This was not spite, for he was devoted to her, and she to him. It was fear of gossip, of scandal, of disgrace. Thomas, born in 1810, was the elder brother of Anthony and as prolific as all the writing Trollopes; his autobiography is a book of considerable charm, studded with famous literary names. It appeared in the late 1880s and contained a particularly pleasant account of Dickens, whom he had known well. Trollope also knew his sister-in-law Nelly well; she stayed in his Italian and English houses on many occasions; but you would not guess as much from his book. Nor can you glean from it the names of Fanny's parents and sisters, or anything about her hard-working professional past.

Nelly and Fanny Ternan were written out for two reasons. The first and obvious one is that Nelly was a blot on the good name of Dickens, and the Dickens machinery for public relations was unrivalled. Dickens wished to be, and was, generally worshipped – the word is not too strong for a person who evoked comparison with Christ at the time of his death – as a man of unblemished character, the incarnation of broad Christian virtue and at the same time of domestic harmony and conviviality. The jolly domestic part of his reputation had been acquired young, through his early novels and his notably exuberant and hospitable family life; it had been crowned by his Christmas stories and never dislodged. It came to exasperate his percipient daughter Kate, but the very fact of her exasperation shows how firmly the legend was established and sedulously kept going in the reminiscences of his more pious children. Amazing as it now seems, the break-up of his family left it unaffected; Dickens preserved his renown as the jovial keeper of hearth, home, children and dogs at Gad's Hill even as he was ridding himself of wife and children.

The public swallowed the carefully maintained domestic image, but it would have been too much to expect it to accept the presence of Nelly in Dickens's life. There is evidence that he himself wavered about this point once or twice, but his friends did not. They made him see the impossibility of any public acknowledgement of a relationship with her; they were also, as a body, remarkable for their loyal silence. Forster's decision not to name or explain her in the biography has been mentioned; it left an emptiness in the chapters covering the last years of Dickens's life which no subsequent biographer has been able to fill properly. Wilkie Collins, himself a master of the discreet irregular *ménage*, remained totally discreet about his friend, as did Frank Beard, who was doctor to both Collins and Dickens and can't have failed to know their private circumstances. So did the other younger men who undoubtedly knew something, the journalists George Augustus Sala and Edmund Yates, and Dickens's manager, George Dolby. So did Harry Wills, Dickens's assistant on his weekly magazine and his confidant in all private matters. Wills and Collins failed only in not destroying all Dickens's letters to them, some of which contained indiscreet remarks.

Dickens's large circle of theatrical friends was also staunchly reticent. The best of these, the retired tragedian William Charles Macready, should, in theory at any rate, have particularly regretted the circumstances of the case, because Macready had struggled all his life to raise the tone of theatrical life and the reputation of actors and actresses; and yet here was Dickens involving himself with a young actress, to the danger of both their reputations. It confirmed all the stereotyped views of the profession. Not only that: Nelly was the daughter of an esteemed colleague of Macready. He had known her father and acted opposite her mother through many seasons.

This leads us to the other reason for the blotting out of the name of Ternan. The Ternans were a theatrical clan. Nelly, her two sisters, her mother, her aunt and her grandmother were all on the stage, mostly from infancy upwards. They were part of a subculture of British life which, throughout the nineteenth century, was viewed by the rest of society with at best equivocal feelings, at worst alarm. 'And you knew that this person was on the stage, and you introduced her into my son's family?': the words are put by Thackeray into the mouth of a grandmother who discovers that the modest and blameless family governess was once on the stage. 'Pack your trunks, viper! and quit the house this instant,' she commands; and the governess's admirer, a respectable young doctor, drops her at the same point, with bitter words of blame.[1] Thackeray himself isn't taking sides; the governess is a victim, but she is also deceitful, and the theatre is an immoral place. He lets her marry her widowed employer, but he's a bit frightened of her cool ambition.

This jump from actress to governess to lady of the house was made in reality by Fanny Ternan six years after Thackeray's story appeared; and Dickens was in some sense the agent of her change, since it was he who recommended her as governess to the child of his widowed friend Tom Trollope. After the marriage – which took place within five months of her appointment – neither Fanny nor anyone around her breathed a word about her past career again.

Deceitful perhaps. But the point is that they felt it as necessary to practise this deceit as Dickens felt it necessary to hide his association with Nelly. The Ternan sisters effaced their theatrical past, because it was such a liability; because it prevented them from being seen in any light but a theatrical light, and a theatrical light was one that blotted out everything else, disqualified them from any other consideration. Or so they believed. It may seem extraordinary – incomprehensible – to us now. It becomes less so if we go back and examine the world in which they were raised and the assumptions made by the people they lived among. The fact that Nelly always expressed particular dislike for the work of Thackeray suggests that she may have recognized and winced at the accuracy of his picture; and actresses, ex-actresses and the children of actresses make many appearances in his pages. The dancer turned governess has shared the stage with ladies who allowed themselves to be installed in cottages in Regent's Park by rich men. Emily Fotheringay, star of the provinces, dazzles innocent young Pendennis and

6

nearly leads him astray with the help of her scheming old Irish father. Morgiana Crump is the daughter of a dancer who has been married to her aristocratic lover's valet, paid off in turn with a public house and a dowry for the child.[2] Becky Sharp in *Vanity Fair* is also the child of theatrical folk and is herself a terrific mimic, a skill she uses to ingratiate herself on her upward social path. Thackeray loved the theatre and was fascinated by it for exactly the reasons which made the Ternan sisters escape from and deny it: it existed outside the world of Victorian middle-class values of careful self-respect and dignified self-improvement. It appeared to be sexually emancipated, in that it displayed women who were willing to show themselves off, tendering a promise of sophisticated pleasure. Its market values were also more down to earth – some would say more honest – than those of the drawing room.

Thackeray, Dickens and Macready all belonged to a club named for the great eighteenth-century actor David Garrick, founded in 1831 with the particular purpose of 'bringing together the patrons of the drama and its professors' and becoming a place 'in which actors and men of education and refinement might meet on equal terms'. This was certainly one of its chief attractions for Dickens, who had a passion for the theatre and made serious preparations to go on the stage professionally himself in 1832; he was an early member of the Garrick, elected in January 1837 when he was only twenty-four years old, already a successful and distinguished writer, and newly married.

The 'professors of the drama' mentioned in the prospectus of the club were all, of course, male, although David Garrick was never averse to the company of actresses. Yet the idea of a woman member of the Garrick Club was unthinkable (and still is today). For women patrons and professors of the drama, equal terms have meant simply that the walls of the club are hung with portraits of actresses. Pictures are one thing, people quite another. 'Well, perhaps in the next world women will be more valued than they are in this,' grumbled the great Mrs Sarah Siddons. She knew exactly how equivocal was the admiration accorded even to great actresses.

Nelly's portrait is not on the walls of the Garrick, but she did at least reach the steps outside. It was on these steps of the old building that a group of members was standing together on a May evening in 1858, gossiping enjoyably. The subject of their gossip was their fellow member Charles Dickens, by then the best-known writer in England and, doubtless, in the world. Dickens had just separated formally from his wife Catherine after twenty-two years of marriage: an almost unheard-of action in high Victorian England. He had done it brutally and publicly. Catherine was not renowned for her beauty or her wit, but she was a clearly blameless mother of ten; and he had insisted on taking her children from her and keeping them under his own care and that of Catherine's younger sister, Georgina Hogarth, who was so much in thrall to Dickens that she braved her family's outrage and the disapproval of the public to remain with him. Only the eldest son, Charley, defied his father and declared he would make his home with his mother.

Dickens was now in process of quarrelling with anyone who did not accept his version of the separation without question or murmur. He attributed it to a deep and long-established incompatability between himself and Catherine, made worse by her failure to take any interest in her own children; according to his account, which was backed by Georgina, she did not love them. Dickens went so far as to say that Catherine herself had long desired a separation and that she suffered from a 'mental disorder'. This was flagrantly untrue, as anyone who knew the family could testify; but he was beyond the reach of reason at this point. Gossip had it that Georgina was the real cause of the trouble, and it was this that was being discussed at the Garrick. The idea of a member of the club so distinguished for his celebration of the domestic virtues being caught out in a love affair with a young sister-in-law was certainly scandalous enough to cause a stir of excitement.

As Dickens's fellow author and member, Thackeray, arrived for the evening, he was asked for his opinion. At once and authoritatively he denied that the sister-in-law was the cause of the trouble. He had been told the truth at Epsom races. The affair was not with her at all: 'No says I no such thing – its with an actress.' Thackeray's inner reaction, which he set down in a letter to his mother, was dismay at what such a lapse might do to the always slightly precarious reputation of literary men: 'O dear me its a fatal story for our trade.'[3]

When Thackeray's words were brought to Dickens, who was equally sensitive to the reputation of the literary trade, he sent him an angry denial. Thackeray obviously did not believe it, and the two men ceased to be friends; they had further reasons for falling out, but Thackeray made a point of being cordial to Mrs Dickens and showing her continuous courtesy and kindness; we hear of her dining at his house in later years. Dickens was left with his denial and Thackeray with the view that the man was frantic, 'half mad about his domestic affairs'. Early in June the story reached *The New York Times*. Its London correspondent reported that 'All London . . . had for some time been rife with legends concerning Dickens and an actress, with whom it was at last affirmed that the author of *David Copperfield* had eloped to Boulogne.'[4] The paper went on to say it was all a lying scandal; this was probably not much comfort to its subject.

Dickens, as is well known, published a statement both in *The Times* and in his own magazine, *Household Words* – it appeared a few days after *The New York Times* story – in which he denied all the allegations against him. He also forced his in-laws to retract their accusations as a condition for making a proper settlement on Catherine, and he never acknowledged thereafter that he had any private connection with any actress. He was so successful in imposing his version of what had happened on the world that when, sixty years after his death, it was first publicly stated that he had kept a mistress and that she had been an actress, the British public was deeply upset and outraged, and there was a general tendency to protest that it could not be true. In my own family my grandmother's distress is still remembered.

Nor was Nelly very kindly treated on her first appearances in print. From being too bad to be mentioned at all, she became mentionable chiefly to be blamed for her failure to give Dickens what he had hoped for. Wrong to succumb to Dickens, wrong in failing to make him happy, wrong finally because she said later she regretted the whole thing: this became one popular view of her. 'Mercenary' and 'cold' were two of the regular allegations made against her. Edmund Wilson, the most brilliant and influential of

Dickens's twentieth-century critics, saddled her with the character of Estella, the girl reared to torment the male sex in *Great Expectations*: he suggested Nelly was frigid, indifferent, petulant, spoiled and proud. He also wrote that money was 'one of the things that Ellen got out of her liaison with Dickens': true, though not necessarily as disgraceful as Wilson seemed to think. With a last glancing blow he added that 'it seems to be the general opinion that Ellen was neither so fascinating nor so gifted as Dickens thought her'.[5] He returned to the attack in 1952 in his Foreword to Ada Nisbet's short, scholarly study of the evidence for the Dickens–Ternan affair; this time he called her 'not very imaginative or sensitive and not very much interested in Dickens' and held her responsible for leaving him 'without human contacts', though he did concede that 'she may not have been so bad as that' in his concluding sentence.[6]

Wilson's remarks were followed by Edgar Johnson's massive biography of 1952, which has become the standard one. Johnson approached Nelly more cautiously, in flutters of rhetorical questions: 'Did he [Dickens] suspect her . . . of being calculating and mercenary? Was his tenderness . . . shot through with the bitterness of disillusion?'; he asked 'in what abyss of personal agony' Dickens learned about cold obduracy and love without tenderness or illusion; and whether the promised fictional struggle between Helena Landless and Jasper in *Edwin Drood* might refer to a real struggle between Dickens and Nelly. On some points Johnson was absolutely clear, though. Dickens had 'won Ellen against her will, wearing down her resistance by sheer force of desperate determination'; and there was no doubt that she 'failed his need'.[7]

In the scale of things Nelly is not an important person. No one would have begun to think about her were it not for Dickens, standing like a giant over the Victorian age, the creator of a dramatic language for his characters that fixes them for ever in the mind, and of great set pieces that speak directly to the reader with a verve, a confidence, a springing rhythm, an individuality no other English novelist can rival. But just because Dickens chronicled and charted so much of the life of his generation and protested against so many of its wrongs, his failures and omissions seem all the more striking. He turned his attention on to his own childhood to such good effect that the vulnerability (and resilience) of children is one of his most common and confidently handled themes; against this his difficulty when it comes to creating credible women stands out sharply. Grotesques he can do, Sairey Gamp and Mrs Gummidge; before normal female flesh and blood he falters. As his own daughter Kate said, 'My father did not understand women.'[8]

Whether Dickens understood the woman in his life about whom we know least any better than the others seemed a question worth looking into, even if the material was slender. That was my point of departure. Very soon the quest became something different, its connection with Dickens more tangential. I found, of course, that Nelly's story starts long before her meeting with Dickens and continues long after his death. It is full of surprises and, in parts, is as curious as one of Dickens's own plots. It casts light over a whole area of nineteenth-century life which is still very shadowy: first the world of professional actresses, then the world of women who knew themselves to be bad and were condemned by respectable people. These are not areas much explored by Dickens, perhaps because he felt them to be too painful, too raw, too dangerous; he knew that in fiction his readers had to be told that bad women came to bad ends. Nelly, flanked by her two remarkable sisters and her courageous mother, is a small piece of reality to set against the omissions and evasions of Victorian fiction: a complicated and resourceful young woman who was very nearly crushed by the huge weight of Dickens on her life, and who fought to save herself in the only way she knew.

Biographies of Dickens appear at a rate of rather more than one to the decade; there have been six major ones since the war, buttressed by a great many studies, two volumes of biographical reminiscences of his contemporaries, a *Dickens Index* and a complete chronology of his life. More important than any of these is the Pilgrim Edition of his letters which, as I write, has reached its sixth volume and the year 1852: a work of impeccable and exhaustive scholarship which offers not only the best key to Dickens's personality but also, to any reader who cares to browse in its thick underlay of footnotes, a rich general impression of the age in which he lived. The great man and the great writer deserve no less. Yet no one can read Dickens

without absorbing his interest in the apparently insignificant, the
lesser figures at the edge of the picture, the unknown men, women
and children inhabiting the uncharted areas of English society; the
poor and the shabby genteel, those who thronged the packed, dirty
London streets and the packed, dirty places of entertainment; those
who hung on to respectability by their fingernails, and those who
let go. One reason for his popularity was precisely this, that his
sympathies were with the little people rather than the great. It
provides as good a starting point as any for looking into the life of
the small figure of the undistinguished actress half hidden at the
edge of the Dickensian panorama, Wilson's 'commonplace' person
who has so far attracted little interest in her own right and still less
sympathy.[9]

2

'Agreeable and beautiful talents'

Nelly's history begins with a matriarchy. Her mother and her grandmother, though neither was rich or highly educated, were both independent and enterprising professional women. In each case their husbands disappeared from the scene when the children were still small; Nelly's mother was about ten when she lost her father, and Nelly herself was younger still and can have had very little memory of hers. Mother and grandmother were women who earned their own livings, organized their own careers and managed to bring up their families without the help of husbands, brothers or sons. This was something so rare in nineteenth-century England as to set them quite apart from the general experience.

The stage was virtually the only profession in which this sort of independence was possible for women at this time.[1] The microcosm of the theatre differed in almost every respect from the social world surrounding it. An actress could, for instance, command payment equal to that of a man, or better. She could make her own working contracts. Her horizons, instead of being limited to a domestic circle, were as wide as the English-speaking theatre. She could, and frequently did, flout the prevailing sexual rules. The admirable Fanny Kelly, a contemporary of Nelly's mother, bore and brought up a daughter unassisted and never married. In the same generation Fanny Kemble left her husband when she found him tyrannous, and later divorced him. Mrs Siddons arranged her life so that she and her husband were never together. Lucia Elizabetta Vestris abandoned her first husband, and Mrs Abington paid hers an annual sum to keep away. Helen Faucit, a byword for respectability in the Victorian theatre, was the child of an actress who left her husband, and Helen's early career was actually managed by her mother's lover, the actor William Farren.[2] Ellen Terry took husbands and lovers with a total disregard of what the world might say; both her children were illegitimate. Fanny Stirling, one of the finest of the mid-century actresses, separated from her husband and lived openly with another man, whom she was able to marry only at the end of her life; and so on. None of these was a wicked woman, but they lived by standards that were quite different from those of their contemporaries and much closer to those of the late-twentieth century.

Still more remarkably, perhaps, women were accepted as directors and managers. At the very beginning of the century the Rochester circuit, which had theatres in a good number of Kentish towns, was managed by the efficient and popular Mrs Baker. In the 1830s the actress Louisa Nisbett managed first the Queen's Theatre and then the Adelphi, 'with all that character of taste and propriety which Lady-Managers seem to have a peculiar talent of imparting to such things. Admirable managers they are, and the influence they possess is really extraordinary': so wrote a young theatre critic called Charles Dickens.[3] Another actress, Elizabeth Yates, also managed the Adelphi for a while in the 1840s after the death of her husband; but the best known of the women managers was undoubtedly Lucia Vestris, who described herself as 'the first of all dramatic Joan of Arcs', and brought about a revolution in staging techniques during her twenty-five years at the Olympic, Covent Garden and the Lyceum between the 1830s and her death in the mid-fifties.

The theatrical world was hierarchical, with the London stars at the top and the poorest of the provincial strolling players at the bottom of the heap; it was also relatively small and closely interconnected. The great stars depended on their earnings from regular tours of the provinces; they worked with the stock companies and got to know their managers and regular players well in the process. Equally the provincial companies were the nurseries of talent, and their star performers moved on into London. Tate Wilkinson, for example, who ran the York circuit in the last years of the eighteenth century, discovered or promoted the talents of a galaxy that included Mrs Jordan, Mrs Inchbald, Charles Mathews and John Kemble. The prompter in Wilkinson's company for many years was John Jarman, Nelly Ternan's grandfather.

The children of actors tended to follow their parents on to the stage, and there was both intermarriage and a circulation of the younger or less successful brothers and sisters around the provinces. John Kemble's brother Charles, for instance, married Marie Thérèse De Camp, bringing two great clans together and producing Fanny Kemble from their union; Miss De Camp had begun her stage career at six, as Cupid at Drury Lane, and later worked for Wilkinson. Her sister Adelaide worked as a girl on the Durham circuit with Stephen Kemble; one De Camp brother managed the Sheffield Theatre, another emigrated to America to become an actor there. Again, Charles Mathews married a clever actress called Anne Jackson, half-sister to Fanny Kelly: Anne's actor father had died, and her mother had married another actor, one of the Irish Kellys, and when this husband abandoned her she asked her impresario brother-in-law, Michael Kelly, to train little Fanny for the stage. He did it so well that Fanny was earning the family's bread by the time she was six, like Marie Thérèse.

Macready, the son of a theatre manager, first saw his wife Kitty Atkins as a child performer of nine in Glasgow and began his wooing by persuading his own father to give work to her entire family – Mr Atkins as a stage painter, Mrs Atkins good only for delivering messages or playing bit parts; Macready called her a 'female hick, or *hickess*'.[4] He made Kitty leave the stage and successfully kept his children from it, but his action was unusual. Charles Kean, son of the great Edmund, was sent to Eton to put ideas of the theatre out of his head, but he could not resist the lure of the stage and made a highly successful career as an actor-manager. The son of Charles Mathews trained and practised as an architect for some years but, again, the draw of his parents' world was irresistible; he became almost as celebrated a comic actor as his father, enjoyed a particularly successful professional partnership with Lucia Vestris, and became her second husband.

All these couples and families knew one another as fellow workers and friends, and the Ternans were no exception. Nelly's grand-parents played with De Camps, Kembles, Mrs Siddons (*née* Kemble), Mrs Jordan and Charles Mathews; her mother played with Vestris, Edmund Kean and Macready; Charles Kean and his wife gave work to Mrs Ternan and all her daughters. There were quarrels and rivalries but also a sense of solidarity; and the solidarity was reinforced by the fact that the profession was disapproved of as much as it was admired.

The theatre had its own customs, beliefs and laws of behaviour. While depending on the support of the society around, it maintained itself quite apart; and society showed towards it an intense curiosity. Actresses were the supreme objects of this curiosity. Their position was seen to be especially anomalous. They were certainly not ladies, since ladies, by definition, did not work: 'A lady, to be such, must be a mere lady, and nothing else. She must not work for profit, or engage in any occupation that can command money.'[5] Actresses worked for money and, at the same time, constantly represented ladies of the most exalted rank on stage; the decorum and polish of their representation was often held up as a model of fine, ladylike behaviour.

To pretend to be what you were not and to make a good job of it made you morally suspect. Alongside the admiration was a steady stream of abuse directed against actresses on the grounds that their work was of its very nature damaging to character. The point was made by many writers throughout the century. In Fanny Burney's last novel, *The Wanderer*, which was published in 1814, her heroine Juliet has no hesitation in preferring the prospect of starvation to a perfectly good offer of work as an actress, because she considers its very nature to be corrupting. In the same year Jane Austen's *Mansfield Park*, although it addressed itself only to amateur players, held up the most skilful and enthusiastic participants to particular disapproval: Mary Crawford's charm is part of her inauthenticity, she is a good role-player on stage because she is a practised role-player in life, and she is propelled by vanity and self-love. Three decades later Thackeray, as we have seen, uses a similar principle when he makes Becky Sharp the child of a theatrical family and herself a skilful amateur actress; her success springs in part from her ability to fake her feelings. In 1850, in *The History of Pendennis*, he went further, and drew a professional actress, Emily Fotheringay. The emphasis of this portrait is precisely on the rift between the person young Pen falls in love with on stage – a drooping, romantic, poetic heroine – and the prosaic, uneducated and calculating character of the actress offstage. Even her name is false: it is not really Fotheringay but Costigan. Pen has to learn about this rift between appearance and reality as part of his sentimental and moral education: the implication is that this sort of deception, supremely exemplified in an actress, is what men have to look out for in all their dealings with women. Fotheringay/Costigan is a symbol of the inherent duplicity of all her sex as well as a socially unacceptable member of it – socially unacceptable, that is, to Pen's family. She is, in fact, a scapegoat for her sex. And although Thackeray goes half-way to admitting that the Fotheringays of this world had little choice about how they were perceived by their admirers, he is too solidly committed to the point of view of the Pendennis clan not to treat her more harshly than he treats them.

Elizabeth Prior, or 'Bessie Bellenden', who appeared for some years at the St James's Theatre in spangles and then escaped into governessing, has already been mentioned in Chapter 1. She is Thackeray's last equivocal heroine, and 'Lovel the Widower' was written at the end of his life, when he was acknowledged as the writer who came nearest to presenting the standards of gentlemen to his contemporaries. He is markedly ambivalent about her, showing her as deceitful but also brave, hard-working, attractive and even lovable: a fighter who uses whatever weapons are available to her in a world which he knew allowed her very few. Elizabeth's past is not her fault, but it has made her a dangerous person to introduce into a conventional family. When that past is revealed, the young doctor who has been in love with her departs, sobbing with vexation: 'It wasn't fair not to tell me. It wasn't fair ... I couldn't ask a party into my family who has been – who has been ...' – and he can't even bring himself to say what she has been.

The *Encyclopaedia Britannica* had set the tone for all this with its article on actresses, in 1797:

> There are some very agreeable and beautiful talents, of which the possession commands a certain sort of admiration; but of which the exercise for the sake of gain is considered, whether from reason or prejudice, as a sort of public prostitution. The pecuniary recompense, therefore, of those who exercise them in this manner, must be

sufficient, not only to pay for the time, labour and expence, of acquiring the talents, but for the discredit which attends the employment of them as the means of subsistence. The exorbitant rewards of players, opera-singers, opera-dancers, &c are founded upon these two principles: the rarity and beauty of the talents, and the discredit of employing them in this manner. It seems absurd at first sight that we should despise their persons, and yet reward their talents with the most profuse liberality. While we do the one, however, we must of necessity do the other ... Such talents, though far from being common, are by no means so rare as imagined. Many people possess them in great perfection, who disdain to make this use of them; and many more are capable of acquiring them, if any thing could be made honourably by them.

The assumption behind these words seems to be that the exercise of any talent by a woman in public is a form of prostitution. Fanny Kelly, who was seven at the time the article appeared and, as we have seen, already working to keep her family fed, expressed her just fury with it later; and her determination to change such an attitude lay behind her attempt to establish a school for young actresses in the middle of the century.

The association between prostitution and the stage was made over and over again. Of course theatres did attract prostitutes into the audience. Behaviour was often rough and riotous, and, in the first half of the century at least, drinking (and eating and smoking) took place unrestrainedly in the pit and the gallery; Mrs Jordan's letters talk of riots, the constables being called in, and the theatre smelling like a taproom by the end of the evening.[6] The atmosphere was one in which prostitutes could expect to find clients. Everybody knew, too, that actresses themselves were popular with gentlemen in search of beautiful companions, though the blame for this can hardly be laid entirely upon them. Fanny Kelly's experience is instructive again: when the Earl of Essex tried to force his attentions on her, she turned him away angrily and reminded him that she was friendly with his wife, and that for her sake only she would continue to tolerate his acquaintance.

Other actresses accepted what was oddly called the protection of their aristocratic admirers, the most famous among them being Dora Jordan, who bore ten children to the Duke of Clarence between 1794 and 1810 (she already had four when they met). Mrs Jordan, who invented her own name and was never married, was the foremost *comédienne* of her day, possibly the best-loved actress ever seen on the English stage, extolled by Hazlitt and Byron among others; but this did not prevent her from coming to a miserable end when the Duke decided he must marry a rich wife, and she grew too old and tired to go on working. Had his love continued and had the laws pertaining to royal marriages been what they are today, we might have had an actress as Queen of England in 1830 and one of her sons on the throne as King in 1837, in place of Queen Victoria.* The idea of this narrow escape naturally inflamed some British subjects, particularly those who held that she was a disgrace and deserved her wretched end.

Mrs Jordan earned a great deal of money; she probably gave the Duke more financial help than he gave her at times during their association.[7] Money, and mercenariness, particularly worried those who made it their business to comment on actresses. A *Memoir of Madame Vestris* published in the late 1830s alleged that actresses habitually made 'a handsome living by seducing the sons of the nobility'.[8] In practice only those skilful enough to get their admirers to the altar seem to have made sure of financial security by this means. Apart from this glittering handful, few achieved more than modest comfort, and many ended in destitution. Fanny Kemble, always a good witness, noted the pathetic gratitude of a seventy-year-old actress in Liverpool who got the part of Nurse to her Juliet and drew her own conclusions; the saying that 'playhouses lead to workhouses' was based in bitter truth. Even the Kemble family, though its members earned huge sums and achieved a social position of some eminence, never managed to match it with financial security. Fanny Kelly, also a star for many seasons, ended her long life penniless; a pension was got for her when she was in her nineties, from Gladstone, just in time to pay her funeral expenses.

---

* In the next generation another royal prince, the second Duke of Cambridge, did actually marry an actress, Louisa Fairbrother, and lived in domestic happiness with her and their sons in Mayfair for the rest of his life; but even though he was not in the direct line, it had to be a morganatic marriage, which meant the children could not succeed to his title.

It was hard, if not impossible, for an actress to present an acceptable financial face to the world. If she was poor, she was considered feckless. If she married a rich man, she was an adventuress. If she bargained with managers, was careful with her money and tried to put some aside, she was accused of avarice. This was said of Miss O'Neill, of Mrs Siddons, Vestris and Jordan. Mrs Jordan suffered the cruellest fate of all: her royal lover, who had fondly watched her appear on stage throughout their twenty years together, made it a condition when he dismissed her that she should lose the care of her daughters should she return to the stage. Soon she was obliged to do so – she needed the money for her other children – and saw her daughters taken away; and so died alone. Of her sons, who were given titles and half absorbed into the aristocracy, the eldest committed suicide; another, Lord Adolphus Fitzclarence, took to hanging about Drury Lane to see his mother's old dressing room and spoke with understandably bitter disrespect of his father when he was on the throne as William IV.

Actresses themselves sometimes worried about the moral aspect of their work, on the grounds that it encouraged personal vanity. Although some – Vestris, who kept her physical charm into her fifties, and Jordan in her happy years – clearly enjoyed exhibiting their talent and beauty, others were troubled by the public display of their bodies, always referred to as their 'persons'. Fanny Kemble said more than once that she found performing profoundly distasteful and believed that the public exhibition of herself did a violence to her womanly dignity; she considered the excitement unwholesome and the personal exhibition odious. Another actress wrote of the consciousness that 'one's person was a target for any who paid to make it one' – the idea of being a target well expressing her sense of vulnerability.[9] Fanny Kelly became a literal target when one of her admirers, thrown into a state of excited indignation by her appearance on stage as a boy in breeches, aimed a pistol shot at her from the auditorium. Fortunately he missed, but he could hardly have conveyed the ambivalence of the admiration accorded to actresses more graphically. Breeches parts were enormously popular with audiences, which did not prevent critics from censuring the actresses who played them for their immodesty in dressing in men's clothes.

Even if she was careful not to appear seductive or mercenary, an actress must expect to be 'despised by decent people': so Mrs Patrick Campbell was told by her aunt in the 1880s.[10] When the 47-year-old painter G. F. Watts proposed to the 17-year-old Ellen Terry in 1864, he explained that his chief motive was that he wanted to remove her from the 'temptations and abominations of the stage' and was prepared to compensate her parents financially for their loss of her earnings; and when he dismissed her from the marriage, he gave her a settlement which would be reduced if she returned to her career.[11] At about the same time the daughter of Samuel Phelps was expelled from her boarding school at the request of a parent who discovered simply that she came from a family of actors: she hadn't begun to be one herself, but no doubt she would soon be a victim of the vanity and 'lax principles' prevailing in theatrical circles. 'Would any one of us wish our daughters to go on the stage?' thundered the editor of *Punch* in the 1880s. 'There can be but one answer to this. "No!"' A well-brought-up girl would react to the stage in one of two ways, either recoiling in disgust at "life behind the scenes" and fleeing, or else succumbing to its corruption "until the fixed lines of the moral boundary have become blurred and faint".'[12] *Punch* grudgingly conceded that women brought up from childhood within the theatre might in some way be immunized against its moral infection, though it is hard to see how this process was meant to come about. In the next decade another journalist returned to the attack. 'It is nearly impossible for a woman to remain pure who adopts the stage as a profession . . . There is no school on earth so bad for the formation of character,' wrote Clement Scott in 1898.[13] Essentially his attitude was not very different from that of the *encyclopédistes* of the 1790s.

The truth is that, to succeed as an actress, you needed to be a woman of exceptional courage, intelligence and self-reliance. You had to be prepared to work yourself to the bone, to ignore sickness, pregnancy and childbirth as well as bereavement and any other personal distress. You had to be tough enough to endure the harsh opinion of the world as well as homelessness and discomfort. You had to know how to be a queen or a model of ladylike composure on stage just after emerging from a dressing room with the rain pouring through the ceiling. Being an actress meant, more than anything, that you were prepared for a life of risk. Freedom – of a kind – and real work that was not domestic work, these set you apart from the general condition of women.

Marriage outside the profession almost always meant giving it up and disappearing into obscurity, even if it was aristocratic obscurity; it seemed a good bargain to many, though some, on being widowed, returned to the stage, and one at least – Miss Paton – ran away from her aristocratic husband, Lord William Lennox, fled to America with an actor and became a working woman again. The actress heroine of Henry James's novel *The Tragic Muse* turns down the well-born diplomat who proposes marriage and opts for a nonentity of a husband who is in the theatre and will serve her and promote her career instead of detaching her from it. The scene in which she asks her diplomat if *he* would give up his career for *her* is, incidentally, a remarkable and brilliant statement of the feminist case. It was written in 1890, and James was clear that an actress was the right mouthpiece for these ideas; perhaps some had come through his friend Fanny Kemble, who found herself penniless, homeless and deprived of her children when she divorced her husband.

Outstanding women appear as actresses throughout the century, sometimes among the most obscure provincial players. Mrs Charlotte Deans, who published her memoirs in 1837, ran away from a prosperous home to marry an actor and spent seventy years tramping the north of England and Scotland as a strolling player, appearing in theatres, trade halls and castles, to which she brought Molière, Shakespeare, Schiller, Otway, Vanbrugh, Centlivre, dramatizations of Walter Scott and even Coleridge's play, *Remorse*. The family walked from town to town, sometimes carrying their children through snowdrifts. When she had borne ten children in these circumstances, her first husband died. She was thirty-five, and quickly remarried; her second husband was another actor, aged twenty-two. They continued to act together; she had seven more children and outlived him too; she was still touring on foot in her sixties and died at the age of ninety in 1859.[14]

Marriage to a younger husband was not unusual among actresses. Lucia Vestris took Charles Mathews as her second husband in

1838, when he was thirty-five and she forty-one. It was said that the marriage was made primarily to enable them to visit America together without causing scandal; and that Vestris made full confession of her other previous lovers to Mathews (causing one fellow actress to exclaim at her remarkable memory). In spite of this it seems to have been a happy marriage, was highly productive professionally, and lasted until her death in 1856. Yet Mathews's biographer, writing in 1879, came close to eliminating Vestris from his account of Mathews's life. The biographer was Charles Dickens junior, and his attitude was after all a common enough Victorian one.

This long preamble is necessary to the story of the Ternans if we are to see them in context and understand something of the world into which Nelly was born, to a mother of thirty-eight who throughout her life had never stopped travelling, in England, Scotland, Ireland and America; who was still better known to her public as Miss Fanny Jarman than Mrs Frances Ternan, though she had already given birth to two children; who was still playing Portia, Cordelia, Desdemona and her usual repertoire of youthful leading roles a few weeks before the birth and was ready to return to the stage again a few weeks later; who had been born into the Tate Wilkinson company, grown up in the Regency theatre, acted as a child with all its great names, and observed its values, rewards and dangers with a clear, intelligent eye.

3

Family Saga
1790–1845

This is how Nelly's grandmother started her stage career and her married life. A Yorkshire girl, she applied to Tate Wilkinson for work when she was twenty-one, calling herself Miss Errington, though her real name was a more down-to-earth Martha Maria Mottershed. Wilkinson took her on partly because there was a gap in the company caused by the sudden death of one of the company's leading actresses, Mrs Georgiana Jarman, in the full bloom of her youth.

The bereaved husband, John Jarman, was the company prompter. He had been with Wilkinson for a decade and is said to have been a lawyer before he took to the stage. His job was a good one, for a prompter did very much more than hold the book. He regularly played parts, understudied for all the men and made casting decisions in the manager's absence; he kept a list of all the lodgings in the towns on the Yorkshire circuit; and he was the person who knew everything about the affairs of the company and to whom everyone turned when they had a problem. Evidently he took the new actress under his wing, and soon she was filling the gap left by Georgiana not only on stage but in private. Within a very short time Martha Maria was pregnant by Jarman. He was less quick to save her honour than he had been to attack her virtue, and the wedding took place, only three months before the birth of the child, by special licence in Doncaster on 15 October 1801.[1] Wilkinson gave the whole company a free day.

They moved straight on to Hull and 'Miss Errington' continued to travel the circuit and to appear on stage until three days before her confinement. On 8 February 1802 she gave birth to a daughter, Frances Eleanor Jarman, in her lodgings above a shop in Elephant and Castle Yard, Hull. Downstairs her husband continued to sell tickets for the night's performance; within eight weeks she was back on stage again. Wilkinson grumbled at how often his ladies were 'in the straw', but he was kind-hearted, tolerant and worldly-wise; and the other women of the company were not going to despise Miss Errington for a circumstance which was common enough, even if Miss De Camp, who was to marry Charles Kemble, and Miss Jackson, who was to marry the comedian Charles Mathews, did not allow themselves the same licence.

Jarman put himself down as twenty-five on his wedding day, but since he'd been married for at least ten years to his first wife, this was probably a slip of the pen. Mrs Jarman continued to act and continued to bear children; a second daughter, Mary Anne, was born and died when Frances was one, and a third, Louisa, followed soon after. Before that – in fact, before she was two – Frances was appearing on stage as the child in Sheridan's drama *Pizarro* and as another child in Monk Lewis's musical pantomime *Raymond and Agnes, or the Bleeding Nun*. She was billed formally as 'Miss Jarman'. Her professional début was evidently more important than her reception into the Church, for it preceded her christening by some months; this took place only in November 1804, at St George's Church in Doncaster. Either her parents had been too busy to remember to arrange it or too much on the move to find time for it; religion seems to have played a very small part in the life of the family.

Other children were born to the couple, but the only ones known to survive were Louisa and Frances, who was her mother's pride. By the time she was five she was playing a whole range of parts. Wilkinson knew his audiences loved to see children on stage and obliged them whenever possible, though his own son John was nine before he started. Even where there were no lines, children could be sent on as pages, or fairies, or part of a crowd; and so they grew up knowing the business from the start, moving from lodging to lodging, with the backstage as home and the company as family. They learnt to dance and sing and devise their own costumes. They absorbed the language of Shakespeare and Sheridan. They worked by night and slept when they could; from the time they could walk, work and play were almost indistinguishable in their lives. They lived apart from the other world of people with settled homes and habits; and very early must have understood that, while they commanded applause and admiration, they were also sometimes reviled. Wilkinson always gave his players their honorary title of 'Their Majesties Servants' on the playbills; he also noted in his memoirs the view of a certain Mr Garwood, a Low Churchman, who declared that no player, *or child of a player*, was entitled to Christian burial, because all were damned eternally.

Wilkinson went to meet his maker's judgement in 1803, before Frances was launched. Soon she was playing the Boy in *The Children in the Wood*, Fleance in *Macbeth*, Mamillius in *The Winter's Tale*, the small Duke of York in *Richard III*. The company continued under young John Wilkinson; and, as before, its most successful members continued to move away to London, where Covent Garden and Drury Lane offered more glittering rewards; but the Jarmans were a fixture. They travelled the same circuit, usually going from York to Leeds, on to Pontefract; back to York, then Wakefield, Doncaster and Hull; with occasional stops at Beverley or forays as far as Sheffield. They did the same plays – Shakespeare, Otway, Sheridan, Mrs Inchbald, sometimes Milton's *Comus* – and then innumerable farces, pantomimes and musical entertainments, whose authors were never named on the playbills. Sometimes there were dancing dogs; sometimes trick effects, like the 'Italian Shadows', in which lights were used to make the characters appear as tall as leaping giants. Moonlight was produced by getting a boy on a ladder to hold a pair of candles behind some gauze. Young actresses recited William Collins's 'Ode on the Passions' as a set piece between plays, performed comic or patriotic monologues, danced the hornpipe or put on military uniform and went through mimic manoeuvres. The company continued to receive visits from the great, among them Mrs Siddons, with whom little Frances acted in Leeds in 1805. In 1810 came Mrs Jordan, whose charm and beauty no other comic actress could equal; with her both Mrs Jarman and her daughter acted on several occasions.

Mrs Jordan wrote her own account of conditions on the Yorkshire circuit at this time.[2] At Leeds she found her dressing room floor so wet that she had to stand on her great coat while she was changing. At Hull the audience cracked nuts and threw the shells at the stage; 'they drink porter and about 10 o'clock actually eat bread and cheese . . . By the time the performance is over, the House and stage smell like a taproom'. The following year, in the same city, there was 'a set of drunken sailors in the boxes, who wanted to come behind the scenes, and there was very nearly a riot . . . Wilkinson behaved very resolutely and well by sending for the *constables* and having them forced out of the House. We could not go on with the play, which I was very glad of, as I got home very soon.'

Drunken sailors were not the worst she had to face. One letter from an unknown correspondent, received while she was in Yorkshire, told her that God had '*allowed* me to make use of magic for a certain time, and that he was only *watching* for a good *opportunity* to send me to the *gulph* of hell'. 'What an idea to entertain of the mercy and justice of a great Being!' remarked this intelligent woman; all the same, hatred and malice like this is disconcerting.

Frances Jarman was nine when she played in Andrew Cherry's *The Soldier's Daughter* with Mrs Jordan as the Widow Cheerly – it was normally her mother's part – at the Theatre Royal, York. In her letters from York that August of 1811 Mrs Jordan commented that the houses were poor, and it seemed that young Wilkinson was on the verge of ruin. She was right. He kept the company going for a couple of seasons more but with increasing difficulty. In January 1812 the whole Jarman family twice appeared in Hull with Mrs Siddons; it was her last season on stage and the last season of the Wilkinson management, which was disbanded in 1813. The actors scattered, picking up what work they could in other travelling groups. Jarman seems to have found nothing, perhaps because he was ill; and by 1814 he had either died or disappeared from the scene, leaving his young widow or wife and children to fend for themselves.

What they felt about his loss is unrecorded; but Mrs Jarman and her daughters made a brave and determined little team. Frances was twelve, Louisa ten. They moved south to Bath, where there was a flourishing resident company. For the mother there were no more leading parts – she was glad to play Nurse to young Macready's Romeo – but there were prospects for the daughters. And in Bath Frances, blonde, fine-featured, graceful and obviously gifted, was nurtured through the awkward years, playing a rather mature Duke of York to Edmund Kean's Richard III in 1815 and giving valiant recitations of the popular poems of the day. At seventeen she graduated to Perdita and Jeanie Deans in one of the innumerable adaptations of Scott, and was found 'highly interesting' by John Genest, the historian of the British stage, who resided in Bath and acted as self-appointed expert on the status and progress of British actors and actresses; he described her as 'somewhat above middle size, slender' and noted her 'flexible and intelligent features'.

The following year she played Juliet to her mother's Nurse, and then a whole range of young Shakespearean parts was open to her – Miranda, Ophelia, Cordelia, Beatrice, Rosalind – together with all the Scott heroines. She got an offer from Covent Garden, but either she was too shy or her mother held out for more money and better parts than they could promise. At twenty her mother took her to Dublin, where she was an immediate success. People spoke of a second Eliza O'Neill, whose beauty had been such that men were supposed to have fainted at the sight of her, and whose prudence was such that she kept her head through it all, made a good marriage and left the stage for ever. But there was no husband in view for Fanny Jarman, and after triumphing at Dublin she embarked on a tour of Ireland, still accompanied by her careful mother.

In Sligo she proved especially popular, playing Juliet, Belvidera and Lady Teazle to an audience bulging with the bored gallants of the neighbourhood, officers and landowners' sons; on at least one occasion they were so rowdy that, as in Hull, the police had to be called out to quiet them. Still, she enjoyed herself, was invited to the houses of the gentry, and made the acquaintance of a good number of local people. Her engagement was for a fortnight, but at its end a deputation arrived to press her to give them another fortnight. The gallery joined its voice – 'Arrah, Miss Jarman! Won't you give us six nights longer?' – and she agreed to stay on. A few nights later, after the performance, a gentleman she had already met several times called at the stage door. His curricle and horses were outside, he announced: would she allow him to escort her to the house of his cousin, a nobleman residing near by, who was most eager to entertain the visiting star?

Flattering as the invitation was, and pressing as it became, Miss Jarman declined and would be neither persuaded nor hustled. The next day her mother made inquiries and found that the supposed host was not in his Sligo house at all but away in England. Soon Sligo buzzed with the true story: that the gentleman had planned to abduct and disgrace Miss Jarman – in short, to have her raped. He was acting for one of his gambling creditors, who offered to cancel the debt if he would deliver the actress into his hands. It suited most men to believe that a virtuous actress was as likely as an honest thief. Mrs Jordan was raped as a girl by her Irish manager, Richard Daly, at the outset of her career; her biographer commented that 'brutal seduction' was a common practice with Irish gentlemen, who considered themselves above the law in this respect, and added, 'Who would have believed in the virtuous resistance of an actress?'[3] What made the affair of Fanny Jarman and the gentleman of Sligo notable was not his attempt but her successful self-preservation. She became a byword for purity.

For the next four years, Fanny Jarman worked steadily as a touring star all over Ireland and England. In 1824 she acted with the rising young tragedian Macready at Dublin; it was the beginning of a long professional collaboration and personal friendship. In the same year her mother retired from the stage, and Fanny became the breadwinner of the family. Her sister attempted to follow in her footsteps, but she never achieved the same success.

Fanny's name was not forgotten at Covent Garden, and early in 1827 another offer came, which her mother now advised her to accept. It was her chance to establish herself as an actress of the first rank. She found herself playing Desdemona to Edmund Kean's Othello and Portia to his Shylock; Ophelia to Charles Kemble's Hamlet and Juliet to his Romeo. She arrived with a high reputation, but London audiences were not as appreciative as Irish or provincial ones, and London critics were sharp-tongued; one who had praised her performances in Bath now wrote, 'She does all correctly – elegantly – well – but there is still something wanting. It is a performance – a picture – not the thing itself . . . we rather deem her an actress of study than of impulse.'[4] It was crushing to be told at this point that she lacked the natural temperament of an actress; she had no alternative but to persist. She worked three winters at Covent Garden and became thoroughly familiar with the London theatre world; actresses who appeared with her were Fanny Kelly, Harriet Smithson, Helen Faucit and Miss Goward, later Mrs Keeley. She appeared at the Lyceum as well as Covent Garden. She quarrelled with Lucia Vestris over a boy's part and was scolded by the critic of the *Morning Chronicle* because her legs were not as pretty as those of her rival.[5] For any actress it was a solid commercial asset to be able to write 'of Covent Garden' after your name; Fanny Jarman earned it, but she did not become a favourite. It must have been a period of bitter disappointment, to have the golden chance and see it slipping away. Her sister Louisa enjoyed even less success; and when it came to Fanny's third Covent Garden season, her mother complained that she was not being offered good enough parts. The management made this their excuse to end her contract.

An Irish critic, taking up the cudgels on her behalf, asked, 'Is it that Miss Jarman's name has never been uttered by the lips of scandal that she has been thought less interesting by the Cockneys? Or is it that she would not condescend to those fantastic tricks and meretricious graces which have always a charm for the gross minds of a metropolitan mob?'[6] But it was not a meretricious actress who displaced her at Covent Garden. At this point Charles Kemble, with many misgivings, decided to put his own daughter Fanny on the Covent Garden stage; she was not allowed to enter the green room, for fear she might be contaminated by the other actresses, and she was deeply reluctant, half wild with terror, she said, as she appeared before the public for the first time. Her success nevertheless was immediate and overwhelming. The irony of the situation only made it worse for poor Fanny Jarman, whose fate was now sealed; and the name of Kemble was received with displeasure in her family from then on.

She had been spending her summers, when the London theatres closed, working in Glasgow and Edinburgh theatres, and now she took her wounded pride north and was received with consoling warmth. The Scottish critics, like the Irish, praised her not only for being a delightful and accomplished actress but for her simple, modest yet lively manners, 'a temper which is the sure sign and constant accompaniment of purity and innocence. We must not lose The Jarman', proclaimed 'Christopher North' in *Blackwood's* magazine.[7] Later he drew a comparison between Fanny Kemble, Fanny Kelly and Fanny Jarman, according superiority in 'grace, elegance and beauty' to Jarman. All three, his article added, 'are as much respected for their virtues in private life, as they are admired for their genius on the stage'.[8]

Fanny Jarman was pure, respected and admired; 'the most inexperienced of her sex may safely follow the guidance of Miss Jarman when they seek to acquire the elegant ease and self-possession of a perfect gentlewoman';[9] but still she had failed the great hurdle of London. In Edinburgh, in the autumn of 1831, she found herself playing the Lady in Milton's *Comus* opposite a short, stout Irish actor with a powerful stage presence, a loud voice and a great love of literature: Shakespeare and Byron were his idols, and he wrote occasional verses and prologues for his own performances. His name was Thomas Ternan and, though he never admitted it, he was forty-one to her twenty-nine.

Ternan was the son of a Dublin grocer and, through his mother Susanna Lawless, the grandson of a brewer. He had fifteen full brothers and sisters, and his father had four more children by a previous wife. The Ternans claimed descent from a landowning family, dispossessed and denied entry into the professions by their Roman Catholic faith. Whether this was so or not, they were now without the land or the faith, and Thomas had to make his own way in the world. He was not inclined to go into the grocery business, and there was no money to spare at home. The obvious path was towards England, and there he went, about the year 1808, when he was eighteen.

He found his first work as an actor in Kent, on the Rochester circuit; his brother William accompanied him, and there he settled, marrying a Rochester girl and becoming a barge owner. The life of an actor pleased Thomas, who was convivial as well as literary. It took him all over England and Scotland, and presently back to Dublin, where his acting was judged 'forcible rather than finished'.[10] Now it led him to his future wife.

Thomas Ternan and Fanny Jarman finished their season in

Scotland, went their separate ways, and then met again the following autumn. Each of them did seasons in Dublin; she appeared in London again, at the Coburg Theatre (later the Old Vic), and he went to Newcastle upon Tyne, where he was enthusiastically received. In 1833 Ternan was playing Othello in Edinburgh when Macready visited the city and gave him a few tips on his performance: 'spoke very kindly to Mr Ternan, last night's Othello, on some bad habits and on his merits,' recorded the tragedian in his diary.[11] Ternan, who was several years older than Macready, may have had mixed feelings about his kindly advice; still, fortified with it, he took himself back to his native Dublin. Clearly he was not pleased when Macready turned up again there in March, and they rehearsed *Werner* together. This time Macready noted, 'I do not like Ternan's mode of behaviour: it is difficult to say who will or will not be an actor, but I do not think this person in his private capacity will ever shed lustre on the theatrical profession. He seems to me opinionated, jealous and of course little-minded.' Macready added that Ternan tried to disconcert him deliberately during the performance, 'but I punished him by playing my best'. Macready was not an easy or a modest man himself, and his remarks probably tell us as much about his temperament as Ternan's; but it's a discouraging estimate of the man's talent and character.

Ternan may well have been edgy and distracted in Dublin. He had begun to woo Miss Jarman but was obliged to pursue her from a distance with letters, poems and valentines. Under the circumstances it was a slow courtship; but he persevered, and in due course he succeeded in touching her heart.[12] In the summer of 1834 he made her a proposal of marriage, and she agreed to become his wife. Perhaps she was weary and lonely; she had been working since she was two and was now thirty-two. Perhaps she was intrigued by his plans, which were ambitious and adventurous, and ready to entertain the idea of an alliance that would be both matrimonial and professional. Perhaps she had fallen in love with his rough charm and persistent wooing. Perhaps her mother advised her to accept his offer. The general opinion – certainly shared by Macready – was that Ternan was the lucky one and had done very well for himself.

They were married on 21 September 1834, in London, and on

the very next day they embarked for the United States. It was a bold sort of honeymoon. The crossing by sailing ship took the best part of a month, and was still one that 'few men, and hardly any women, undertook . . . as a mere matter of pleasure or curiosity'.[13] But the British acting profession had begun to appreciate that there were good theatres, good audiences and good money to be made on the other side of the Atlantic. Macready had already done a tour in 1826 and was to return twice: he may have put the idea in Ternan's head. Fanny Kemble, with her father and her Aunt Dall De Camp, had also set off westwards only the year before with the aim of restoring the family's fortunes, and they were still there.

The Ternans certainly hoped to earn and save more money in the new continent than they could expect to in England. His ebullience allowed him to believe he could appear in America as the leading tragedian he considered himself; and if he could save enough, he might return to Britain to establish himself as the lessee and manager of some important theatre. The plan was a good one; but it was clear from the start that it depended heavily on Mrs Ternan. From their first appearances at the Chestnut Street Theatre in Philadelphia in November she was the draw, delighting the critics with her 'beautiful person, commanding stature, rich and flexible voice'.[14] New York gave them a dustier reception, pronouncing them not up to the Kembles, and taking particularly against Ternan's bald head, which might just pass muster for Leontes but seemed altogether less appropriate when it came to Romeo, Macbeth or Rob Roy. Fortunately his temperament carried him over any disappointment he may have felt at his reception. Within a few months he was writing from Philadelphia to a Dublin friend:

Our success has been brilliant – indeed far more so than our most sanguine and best friends could possibly have anticipated. We played a short engagement at Boston lately, and the receipts of the theatre, for two nights, were much greater than even the Kembles had drawn, within the same period. We cleared there, in that time, upwards of $2,200, say £500 sterling. We are equally fortunate here, and the same in every town we have appeared in. We return to Boston on 11th March, to perform fifteen nights more, and I have no doubt a second engagement will be even more productive than the first. So great was the excitement on the last night we played there (my benefit)* that the boxes were sold by auction, and double prices obtained in almost every instance. This is doing well so far; our next move will be back here again, then to Washington, and from thence to Baltimore.[15]

When this jubilant letter was written, Mrs Ternan was in the early stages of pregnancy. It made no difference to their working schedule. Since she had been trained in a tough school, as the eldest daughter seeing her own mother work through all her pregnancies, it seemed quite natural to her to do the same. In June 1835, when she was seven months' pregnant, the couple took a holiday trip to Niagara Falls.[16] In August they were on a coastal paddle-steamer when a storm blew up in Delaware Bay, during which she gave birth to her first child, a daughter named after her, Frances Eleanor.[17] The first few weeks of little Fanny's life were nearly the last: as the family travelled on to another engagement aboard another coastal boat, it was accidentally rammed, and her cot was thrown into the air. Almost miraculously the tiny baby was preserved between two mattresses. Undaunted they continued their travels south to New Orleans, Natchez and Mobile for the winter; early in 1836 they were in Pittsburgh, and then went north to play in Canada.

The transatlantic venture was a success. It was also taxing, especially for Mrs Ternan, who had to deal tactfully with the fact that audiences preferred her to her husband and to work as well as care for her child. In the winter of 1836 she found herself pregnant again. It was time to return to England. They gave a farewell benefit in Philadelphia and set their faces eastward. Fanny Kemble, at least, was left behind; she had acquired an American husband, for whom she had cheerfully – though as it turned out misguidedly – abandoned the stage. The £3,000 she had earned in the States were all handed over to her father, who returned alone to England. Fanny Jarman, her one-time rival, travelled back

* A special performance whose takings went to a member of the company who chose the play. It was often the most important source of income for a performer.

more cheerfully with her new daughter, now one, an active, inquisitive, precocious child.

They arrived in Britain in the first weeks of 1837. During their two-and-a-half-year absence two notable things had happened. The railway had come to London; and *The Pickwick Papers* had begun to appear, establishing their 25-year-old author as the chief entertainer of the age. And the age itself was about to change its name; in June William IV died, and since all his children were Mrs Jordan's, he was succeeded by his niece, Victoria.

In London Ternan found his American experience did him little good with the theatre managers. They offered him only minor parts. Offended, he refused them and had to watch sulkily while his wife played opposite Charles Kean. In the summer she was obliged to take a short break when their second daughter, a black-eyed, dark-haired child whom they named Maria Susanna, was born on 10 August and baptized at Christ Church, Southwark, a month later. The family was living near by in Upper Ground Street; on the baptismal certificate Ternan described himself as 'gentleman'. It was more than ever obvious that Mrs Ternan was the breadwinner of the couple. Things looked up momentarily in the autumn when Alfred Bunn of Drury Lane relented towards Ternan enough to allow him to try Shylock; and when Mrs Ternan was back playing Desdemona to Kean's Othello, her husband was given Iago. But the critics again pronounced against him. There were no further prospects for him in London.

Professionally marriage had put Frances Jarman into an awkward situation; still she made the best of it, loyally setting off on the road again with her two little ones. Soon she was pregnant for a third time. In November 1838 they were invited to play a winter season in Newcastle upon Tyne, old territory for Ternan, where he might regain his confidence in himself as a great tragedian. The Newcastle audiences had always enjoyed his large gestures, his pauses, his tears and rages. He would be able to play all his favourite parts, Lear, Shylock, Macbeth, to shouted applause, and celebrate after the performance with drinking companions from his bachelor days.

He installed his little family in lodgings in Westgate, high above the river and close to the theatre, which had been rebuilt since his last season there. It was now at least as splendid as any in London. Newcastle was booming on its coal, its docks, its shipbuilding, its iron and engineering works, and the whole of the city centre was in the process of being rebuilt to a magnificent plan, with elegant Neo-classical buildings in golden-yellow sandstone. It boasted an Academy of Arts, a Literary and Philosophical Society and a weekly newspaper, the *Newcastle Chronicle*, which reported cultural events enthusiastically; and there was a strong theatrical tradition.

There had been a Theatre Royal in Newcastle since the 1780s, managed at different times by Macready's father and various Kembles; the old theatre had been pulled down in the spate of civic improvements, and the new one opened in Grey Street, among the fashionable shops, a year before the Ternans' season. It was – and still is – a splendid theatre both outside and in, with a great classical colonnaded portico, marble pilasters and ceiling paintings representing Literature, Drama and Art crowned by Glory and Fortune. A statue of Mrs Siddons was planned for the portico (but never materialized). The stage was deep, with a movable section at the back, many traps and machinery for constructing elaborate perspectives and displaying dioramas, then the rage; £1,000 had been spent on stock scenery. Working here must have seemed at least as challenging and exciting as appearing in a London theatre.

There was a vast gallery, with a separate entrance and staircase; soon after opening, its floor had to be leaded to prevent what was referred to as 'nuisances'; but, coarse and uncouth as the gallery audience might be, it was eager to be entertained. In theory, at any rate, the gentry from the surrounding countryside and the rising merchant families in the city could be relied on to patronize serious productions regularly; in practice the best business came with race weeks and assize weeks, when the gentry and the farmers came to town.

Ternan had his wife billed as 'Late Miss Jarman', in the hope that her old name would be a draw. Her pregnancy, now advanced, did not prevent her from playing a boy's part – Ion in Talfourd's play of that name – or Lady Racket in *Three Weeks after Marriage*, as well as her usual Cordelia, Ophelia, Desdemona and Rosalind. She also led in the musical farces and sang Irish ballads to her own accompaniment on the lute. The public took her to their hearts.

The Ternans were not the only success of that winter season. It was also the occasion of the first performance in Newcastle of 'an entirely original, ironical Burletta of Men and Manners founded on the celebrated Papers by "Boz"' – *Nicholas Nickleby*. The Ternans did not play in it, but they were in the theatre for its first performance, when it preceded *Clari, The Maid of Milan*, in which they both appeared; for it was standard practice to give two or three full plays, starting early in the evening and continuing late into the night, and on this occasion several members of the cast appeared in both *Nickleby* and *Clari*.

The curious thing about this *Nickleby* is that it was adapted from an unfinished work. Dickens was only half-way through his book, with ten or so more instalments to write; but the public appetite for anything even remotely connected with him was so great that it had been put together from the episodes that had already appeared and guesswork. There was nothing Dickens could do about this: he was already the property of the whole nation and was to remain so for the rest of his life.

This seems to have been the first certain encounter of the Ternans with the work of Dickens, whose caricature of a country theatre manager and his family in *Nickleby* came uncannily close to reality. Ternan's resourcefulness and optimism, his partiality for a drink, his often pregnant wife, with a scrapbook to rival that of Miss Snevellicci, his American tour – all have their equivalents in the account of Vincent Crummles; he even had an 'infant phenomenon' in preparation in little Fanny.*

Two days after the *Nickleby* performance the season ended, and the Ternans travelled south again for Christmas, announcing that they were to appear at Drury Lane. This was wishful thinking, however, for they had no such engagement. On the two-day coach journey – the railway had not arrived at Newcastle yet – the idea of returning, but on a different and grander footing, was in their minds. They liked the place; Mrs Ternan may have felt at home, with her childhood memories of touring in the north, and it was evidently more welcoming to the talents of her husband than London. They had their savings from the American tour. Why should not Ternan start a northern circuit of his own centred on

---

* The fact that no theatrical adaptation of that period included the Crummles episode may suggest that its accuracy cut too close for comfort.

THEATRE-ROYAL, NEWCASTLE.

Last Night but Two of Mr & Mrs TERNAN's Engagement

This Evening, TUESDAY, Dec. 18, 1838,

Will be produced (for the first time) an entirely original, ironical Burletta of Men and Manners, in two acts (founded on the celebrated Papers by " Boz,") called

Nicholas Nickleby;

Or, Doings at Do-the-Boys Hall.

Mr Ralph Nickleby, Mr G. TAYLOR.   Nicholas Nickleby, Mr DILLON.   Newman Nogge, Mr CORRIE.
Squeers, Mr WILLIAMS.   John Browdie (a Yorkshireman), Mr R. POWER.
Monsieur Mantalini (a man milliner), Mr FITZJAMES.   Lord Verisopht, M. SIDINI.   Sir Melby Hawk, Mr WINDSOR.
Smike (an orphan), Miss MERCER.   Scaley, Mr BIDDELL.   Tix, Mr EDMONDS.
Pluck, Mr LLOYD.   Colonel Chowser, Mr BROWN.
Mrs Nickleby, Mrs HORBMAN.   Kate Nickleby, Miss RICHARDS, her first appearance here
Madame Mantalini, Miss CARR.   Miss Squeers, Miss MULLENDER.   Miss Price, Mrs R. POWER.
Miss Knagg, Miss M. MULLENDER.   Mrs Squeers, Mrs PENSON.

Act I.—Saracen's Head, Snow Hill, on a Snowy Morning.

THE JOURNEY. Breakfast for five—delightful prospect—long ride and short commons—the Yorkshire Pedagogue—Smike introduction—leave-taking—good bye, mother !—jump up—all right—the Highflyer starts for Yorkshire with the "Hero!"—" Over the hills and far away."—TABLEAU.

MADAME MANTALINI'S, THE FANCY DRESS-MAKER.

First starting in the world-delightful occupation-high wages and short hours—Kate Nickleby's introduction to the man-milliner—a duck of a man.

DO-THE-BOYS HALL, YORKSHIRE. A WINTRY PROSPECT.

Victim of avarice !—the arrival—Nicholas' first acquaintance with the mistress of the house—charming peculiarity of Mrs Squeers, and milliner prospect—at Do-the-boys Hall—the letter "—the unknown.

WORK-ROOM AT MADAME MANTALINI's.—TABLEAU. (See Work.)

Insect building—establishment for young ladies—the first morning—Miss Knagg's phlembotropy—a new person—sportive endearments, and family courtship of Mons. and Madame Mantalini—" Sure such a pair."

SUNDAY PARLOUR, DO-THE-BOYS HALL.

The sideboard—tender proposition of Miss Squeers—" Oh ! 'tis love, 'tis love that rules the camp"—tea, cards, and turn out—two pair of lovers—Yorkshire courtship—jealousy, rage & sudden break-up—leaves us, tête-Nicholas with his arms full—what the devil shall I do with them ?

SCHOOL ROOM IN THE CLASSICAL & COMMERCIAL ACADEMY OF DO-THE-BOYS HALL.

N.B. Youth taken in and done for—interesting course of education—brimstone and treacle—TABLEAUX-bow for puss—throw physic to the dogs—practical course of instructing the Squeernian system, and natural logic—new light—injustice detested !—barbarous usage of the helpless orphan, and manly interference of Nicholas—quarrel, blow, and fight—Dotheboys Hall in an uproar—a breaking-up and classical row.

Act II.—BARN AND ROADSIDE!

The orphan boy and his master—misfortune in the ascendant—fidelity and attachment of Smike—a poor and a feeling heart.

THE SHOW-ROOM AT A FASHIONABLE MILLINER'S

A bomb at the financial department—a firm against a legal spectre—swift execution—Mantalini's small throat & sharp razor—a dim'd smash

NEWMAN NOGGS' GARRET.—Scanty meal and warm welcome—Nogge at home—a lady's letter—indignation and determination.

RALPH NICKLEBY'S COUNTING HOUSE.

Upright generosity—sentiments of honour and benevolent motives—discovery—a prison—what's good for the man, good for the master.

DRAWING ROOM AT RALPH NICKLEBY'S.—TABLEAU.

The money-lender's outlet—cards and pigeons—filed cards—unprotected sheep—detected guest—villany and avarice—and happy turn to the fortunes of NICHOLAS NICKLEBY!!!

A PAS DE DEUX by Mr SIDINI and Mrs R. POWER.

After which, the musical Interlude of

NO!

Frederick, Mr REEVE ; his first appearance here.   Mr George Dunbited, Mr BIDDELL.
Commodore Hurricane, Mr G. TAYLOR.   Scowri (Frederick's man), Mr R. POWER.   Andrew Dunbivoise, Mr WILLIAMS.
Jones, Mr EDMONDS.   Thomas, Mr WINDSOR.   William, Mr BROWN.
Lady Dunbited, Mrs HORBMAN.   Maria, Miss GREY.   Mrs Deborah Dunbited, Mrs PENSON.

A PAS GROTESQUE by Mr R. POWER.

The whole to conclude with the interesting Drama of

CLARI,

THE MAID OF MILAN.

The Duke Vivaldi, Mr FITZJAMES.   Rolamo, Mr TERNAN.   Jocoso, Mr CORRIE.
Claudio, Mr LLOYD.   Nicolo, Mr BIDDELL.   Geronio, Mr WILLIAMS.   Nimpedo, Mr R. POWER.
Pietro, Mr BROWN.   Grullo, Mr WINDSOR.   Page, Miss FITZJAMES.
Clari, ...   Mrs TERNAN.
Fidalma, Mrs HORBMAN.   Vespina, Miss MERCER.   Ninette, Mrs R. POWER.

CHARACTERS IN THE EPISODE.

Nobleman, Mr EDMONDS.   Pelgrino, Mr LYNNE.   Wife, Mrs PENSON.   Leoda, Miss CARR.

On Wednesday, The GAMESTER ; with (for the 2nd time) the new Farce of TOM NODDY'S SECRET.
VIVAT REGINA.

W. & H. Mitchell, Printers, Newcastle.

thriving Newcastle, make his name as an actor-manager with his wife as female lead and, in time, raise his daughters too to theatrical fame? It was a gamble; but if it worked, they could be rich. He was inclined to take a grand and optimistic view of things; and whatever proportion of the family income was earned by his wife, the disposal was entirely his.

So they made their calculations and laid their plans. For the last months of Mrs Ternan's pregnancy they moved to Rochester. William Ternan was prospering at his barge business, and the two families were on friendly terms, so that it seemed a good place for the wanderers to settle as the birth of another child approached; and there the third Ternan daughter was born, on 3 March 1839, in a small house in Maidstone Road. She was taken to be christened at St Nicholas's on the last day of the month; her parents named her Ellen Lawless.

It's a name with a marvellously dramatic ring, as though the child's christening gift were a licence to defy order and convention; though the prosaic truth is that Ellen's second name came from her great-grandfather, the Dublin brewer. Fanny, now three and a half, welcomed the blue-eyed, golden-haired baby from the start, and the bonds between the three little girls were tied fast from the earliest years. Probably none of them had too much parental attention at this point, and they made their own little world together. Their mother was acting at the Lyceum in London in the summer; nobody even remembered to register Ellen's birth until the end of July, when it was done by a nursemaid. Soon afterwards the family set off for the north once more, leaving Rochester, with its castle over the Medway, its cathedral and cloister, ancient courts, picturesque houses and shabby little theatre, for the altogether livelier and more prosperous Newcastle.

Newcastle gave the new actor-manager an enthusiastic welcome. Ternan determined to do things in style. He printed bills to announce his plans, begging 'most respectfully to announce to the Nobility, Gentry, and the Public of Newcastle and its Vicinity' that he was to be sole manager, with a special stage manager and another 'melo-dramatic director', a new wardrobe, a 'full and efficient orchestra' and a large company recruited from all the major theatres in the country.

Among them was the Bullen family from Norwich: Mr Bullen was to be prompter, his wife was an actress, and their daughter took child parts. But the season had hardly got under way when Ternan and Bullen fell out; a performance of *The Winter's Tale* was scheduled in January, with Miss Bullen as Leontes's small son Mamillius. By then the Bullens were packing their bags. The situation was saved by little Fanny. Mrs Ternan had played the part herself as a child and was confident that her daughter could do the same. Ternan, never one to lose a chance of making a splash, told the printers to get out their biggest type and produced bills announcing the 'first appearance on any stage' of Miss Fanny Ternan, 27 January 1840. She went on with perfect aplomb, spoke her lines clearly and was enthusiastically applauded. She was three and a half, and her career as a genuine infant phenomenon was launched.

Nelly's earliest memories must have been connected with her sister's stage career, for Fanny was kept very busy. Her father saw the value of her precocity, and her repertoire was constantly extended. By the time she was five, she danced, sang, recited her own poems, did male impersonations – they included Richard III – spoke in different accents – French, American, Scots – and appeared in sketches in which she played all the parts, holding the stage without support from anyone. With all this she was described as 'unforced, wild and natural'; 'her manner is pleasing, perfectly easy and confident, without any of that awkwardness too often observable in children brought upon the stage'.[18] Her father was enormously proud of his little prodigy; he used to carry her about on his shoulder and invite her to improvise in verse, an accomplishment she added to her repertoire before she was eight.

The picture of a father ambitious for his outstandingly gifted child and also warmly affectionate is an attractive one. In 1840 and 1841 the Ternans looked like a family that has come into good fortune and happiness. Ternan commissioned a bust of his eldest daughter from a local sculptor.[19] The Newcastle audiences appreciated their new actor-manager; in 1840 Ternan also acquired the lease of the Doncaster Theatre and began negotiations for York and Hull. To add to his dignity, he had become a Freemason. The family moved to larger premises in Pilgrim Street. Mrs Ternan kept a devoted following; even the stage-door keeper sang her praises in verse. He laid particular emphasis on the fact that she performed with perfect regularity on alternate nights, perhaps to give herself the other nights at home with the children. The two younger sisters promised to follow in Fanny's footsteps; Maria showed signs of a sharp wit, and Nelly was a little beauty. Fanny found her adorable enough to address some verses to her, invoking her blue eyes and golden hair, and rhapsodizing with more truth than she could know that:

> I love her now – I'll love her then
> I'll love her while I live
> And any thing that she may ask
> To her I'll gladly give.[20]

Not lines of genius, but Fanny was only just seven when she produced them in September 1842; and they were enough to make Maria jealous. Good Fanny obliged by producing a second poem for her, which I will not inflict on the reader.

As stage children, their education was different from that of most girls of the period, less domestic and almost entirely concerned with professional achievement. In many ways this was an advantage, in that they were being educated to do something rather than simply to be something; they had to learn to compete, to strive for perfection, and they were tested in a real arena. Although some of their female contemporaries did receive a good education – Annie Besant, for instance, Barbara Bodichon and Marian Evans – they were very few. As an adult, Fanny wrote a biting account of the sort of girls' school to which parents aspiring to gentility liked to send their daughters, and she was in no doubt that they did more harm than good.[21] She, quite unschooled as far as we can tell, was taught her first letters by her mother from some bone counters that could be scattered on the floor, with simple pictures scratched into them; then, somehow, she was found books. She read whatever she could; she studied the elements of French, and later Italian and German, becoming in due course a notable linguist. She wrote reams of poetry, always clever and correct if never anything more. She learned to sing and dance, again under her mother's tuition, to a high professional standard. The life of the theatre demanded a wide range of practical activities too. Fanny had to busy herself selling tickets for benefit nights, and she had to learn to be part of a team of workers. Actresses had to plan and sew their own costumes. There was undoubtedly an element of drudgery to being a child performer, which could have made her resentful; it was made worth while by fame and applause, if you were as successful as Fanny, and by the satisfaction of contributing to the finances of the family.

Fanny appeared with the visiting stars, Macready, Charles Kean, the tenor John Braham. For a June race week she got up a new solo dance, the Cachucha; she did a Highland Fling during assize week, and as Maria progressed they performed the newly created polka together. At Christmas there was always a pantomime with terrific scenic effects, in which they appeared as sylphs, fairies, climbing boys, ocean nymphs or the Children in the Wood. The whole family must have spent as much time in the theatre as in their lodgings, giving all the children as their earliest memories the backstage world: parents and sisters changing into their costumes, rehearsing their lines, practising their dance routines; the gas lights and the buzz, or roar, or hush of the audience. This was the world in which Nelly first became conscious and in which she had her first lessons in life.

In the winter of 1841 her mother was pregnant again; and in April 1842 she gave birth to a son. He was named Thomas for his father. This should have been a high point of happiness, yet it was not. Ternan was unwell, the wave of euphoria which had led him into ambitious theatrical management beginning to turn to doubt and depression. The finances of the Newcastle theatre were not as good as he had projected, and Doncaster was not doing much better; York and Hull had fallen through, perhaps fortunately under the circumstances. Theatre audiences were poor everywhere, because there was no money about. Trade was bad, workers were laid off; there were Chartist riots in England and there was famine in Ireland. The gap between the masses of the urban poor and their industrial masters – between the gallery and the boxes and stalls – was stretching to a point which decent people found intolerable; this was the decade in which Disraeli published his novel *Sybil, or The Two Nations* and Engels his *The Condition of the*

Working Class in England, whose common theme was the heartlessness of the rich and the unrelieved wretchedness of the poor. Even in hard times people must be amused; but if they were too hard they couldn't afford even that.

The savings Ternan had made in America were melting away fast. In 1842 he realized he could not afford to go on paying the lease on the Newcastle theatre. A group of prominent Newcastle citizens organized a public dinner to express their appreciation and doubtless to cheer him up; it started at five in the evening and was still going strong in the small hours, with toasts, speeches and songs. A little wearily, perhaps, Mrs Ternan returned to the stage as her son reached three months; she was a mature but still touching Desdemona. Then the family packed up and moved to Sheffield.

Now things looked much bleaker for them all. Ternan's big attempt to become a manager had failed, probably taking most of the savings. Mrs Ternan would soon be too old to play the young heroines in which she had always specialized, and her mother was now too old to help her out much with the care of the children. The baby son was delicate and needed attention. Maria was a very competent dancer, and Nelly, aged three, went on stage for the first time in Sheffield on 15 November, in Kotzebue's *The Stranger*; but they were still little more than babies and could not be worked too hard even if there were the audiences to make it financially worth while.

Fanny's talents offered the brightest prospect for the family. Her success was remarkable even for an age with a particular appetite for theatrical children. She combined genuine skill with a pleasant and unforced stage presence. Her performances sprang so clearly from her own intelligence and enthusiasm that nobody thought she was being forced by her parents. (It was a suspicion that occurred in other cases: Fanny Kemble spoke pityingly of a child actress she saw, 'poor bright little thing!'; a generation later the young Henry James assumed that two little prodigies he watched off duty must have been 'pinched and slapped' into their performances.) But Fanny was a natural, and her appearances were so popular that her parents were able to extract very good money from provincial managers even in the bad times; and there were weeks when she was certainly the main support of the family. She was taken, sometimes just with one parent, to Scotland, to Liverpool, to Dublin and round the Irish provinces. She made a tremendous impression in Glasgow, playing six different characters in *The Young Actress*. This was in January 1843. In February her baby brother died.

Many years later, at a charitable banquet for the Theatrical Fund, Dickens made a speech in which he referred to the hardships of actresses' lives and told the story of one who, now married and comfortably off, confided to him how she had lost her baby brother at a time of real poverty:

> A lady who had been upon the stage from her earliest childhood till she was a blooming woman, once said to me when she was happily married; when she was rich, beloved, courted; when she was mistress of a fine house – once said to me at the head of her own table, surrounded by distinguished guests of every degree, 'Oh, but I have never forgotten the hard time when I was on the stage, and when my baby brother died, and when my poor mother and I brought the little baby from Ireland to England, and acted three nights in England, as we had acted three nights in Ireland, with the pretty creature lying upon the only bed in our lodging before we got the money to pay for its funeral.[22]

It's possible that Dickens knew more than one actress who had been a child performer and lost her baby brother, although likely that this is Fanny's recollection of the death of little Thomas Ternan and the experience of her mother and herself, going out to give their bright performances night after night and returning to the cold small body lying in their lodging.

For Ternan, too, much as he loved his daughters, the loss of the only boy was another cruel blow. Already dejected, he sank into an irritable torpor and seemed less in command of his parts, his old swagger and powerful delivery failing. The family set off for another Irish tour only to be faced with a country driven desperate. The potato crop had failed twice; the people were dying in the streets. Those who could crowded into boats to get to America – the America Ternan had described as being without poverty or hunger. Nobody could have made a success of a tour at that moment; the

Ternans had little choice and toiled on. In Dublin, at least, they found themselves among old acquaintances, Vestris, Mathews her husband, and the comedian John Buckstone; then they returned to the north of England, Carlisle and Newcastle again, Doncaster, west to Ludlow.

In September Fanny was given her first London show, at the Strand Theatre; she came on after some Hungarian dancers. By now she had her own scrapbook full of eulogies for her present accomplishments and prophecies of future greatness. The critics were enthusiastic – there was a good review in the *Spectator* – but there was no question of her settling in for a season. She was a prodigy, a spectacle, but not yet an actress in London eyes.

Her father was having second thoughts about leaving Newcastle. He made an offer of £200 for the lease of the Theatre Royal again, but he was turned down in favour of a richer applicant. Fanny remained the family prop. In the summer of 1844 she earned £68 16s. 3d. in a single night in Newcastle, the accountant noting that this was second only to Helen Faucit's payment (Macready expected £50 for one evening at the same period).

For Christmas 1844 the family was again in Newcastle; Maria took over the part of Mamillius in *The Winter's Tale*, danced a polka with Fanny and sang a duet with her in a melodrama, *The Wandering Boys*. Soon after this their father was taken ill. His collapse may have been precipitated by a scene with some drunken brawlers in the theatre; he attempted to deal with them, and they turned on him and gave him a cut cheek and a black eye. But his illness went much deeper than the few cuts and bruises he sustained in this episode. His wife was soon forced to acknowledge that the trouble was nervous as much as physical, and that she could not control, let alone nurse him. He was in a state of severe mental affliction, and there was a fear that he might attempt suicide.

Somehow he was got to London, where, perhaps with his brother's intervention, he was taken to the Insane Asylum at Bethnal Green. It was a grim place, and treatment of those with General Paralysis of the Insane – this was the diagnosis of Ternan's condition – was necessarily dreadful and humiliating. Since there was no cure, restraint was the only course available; some patients were kept chained in the early stages, when they might be violent or suicidal, though as the disease took its course this became unnecessary. In the last stage they became emaciated, incontinent, unable to feed themselves, with contracted limbs and bedsores; and so died, either of a fit, pneumonia, diarrhoea or exhaustion. This was the well-known medical prognosis, and it meant that, to all intents and purposes, the man so afflicted was simply locked up to await death. It is unlikely that his wife knew or inquired the cause of his illness, which we know must have been syphilis.[23] She was now not only deprived of his support but also responsible for the asylum fees, which meant finding two or three pounds a week from the family earnings.

Hard times indeed. Nelly was not quite six. In all likelihood she never saw her father again. The little family of women drew closer together. In January 1845 'Mrs Ternan and her daughters' were billed to appear in Hull.

4

Little Orphans
1845–1855

Nelly was five when her father disappeared from her life; less than two years later he was dead. An insane asylum was not a place to which anyone in the 1840s would take a child to visit even a less severely afflicted patient than Thomas Ternan; nor was madness in your family something that could be mentioned in conversation. Fanny was old enough and quick enough to understand a good deal, but the two younger daughters must have been left with the impression that something mysterious, terrible and shameful had overtaken their father, leaving them semi-orphaned.

The orphan was a common figure in Victorian life and a popular one in literature. The juxtaposition of innocence and vulnerability has always caught the imagination of writers; it exercised a particular fascination for Dickens, who could hardly present a child without depriving it of one or both parents. Orphaned or motherless boys and girls crop up in almost every book; and although both his parents lived into and – in the case of his mother – even beyond ripe maturity, he made both his alter-egos, David Copperfield and Pip, lose their parents at tender ages. In real life he was much concerned with the fate of orphaned girls and zealous in helping them; and in his books he drew admiring portraits of little stalwarts like Charley Neckett in *Bleak House*, left at thirteen in sole charge of her younger siblings, whom she supports by doing washing. He also drew warning portraits, the most famous being *David Copperfield*'s pretty, passive Little Em'ly, whose character is fatally undermined by the desire to become a lady; it is this that allows her to become the victim of an unscrupulous gentleman.

The Ternans, unpretentious and hard-working, were exactly what Dickens would have approved. Their family finances were precarious, their future was uncertain, and they were going to have to work a hard grind to keep body and soul together; but they were active and courageous in setting about it. Like Dickens's Little Nell, they were homeless; on the other hand they had their mother and one another, and were already part of a community that offered some support; and they were used to constant travel and to the rigours of training and learning lines. Their mother was well able to organize their lives so that they remained together; in fact, as soon as Ternan collapsed, she made an arrangement for herself and all the children with an old friend from Dublin and Edinburgh, John Pritchard, now managing the York circuit. They wasted no time. In January they were in Hull, in March in York, in June in Leeds.

Mrs Ternan still commanded leading and juvenile parts; she played opposite Pritchard as Lady Teazle, Lucy of Lammermoor, Mrs Haller in Kotzebue's *The Stranger*, Pauline in Bulwer-Lytton's *The Lady of Lyons*, as well as her usual Shakespearean roles. It was Fanny, though, who was given the best billing, liberally sprinkled with exclamation marks, as 'The Wonderful Dramatic Prodigy!' Fair enough, because the prodigy worked quite as hard and probably harder than her mother, starring in a great variety of different farces and short plays especially chosen to show off her talents as a virtuoso mimic. They had names like *The Young Actress, or the Manager Perplexed* and required her to play characters as diverse as 'a stage-struck Yankee', a French itinerant musician (male), a Scottish lass called Effie Heatherbloom – she danced the Highland Fling – a quaint rustic and an old woman. She danced the polka with Maria and the hornpipe by herself. She played the young Napoleon with Nelly as her Josephine. She recited her own verses, sang songs of her own composition and played Richard III in a special presentation of Shakespeare's final act.

Maria had her glory, too, as General Tom Thumb – an imitation of the real American midget, who was touring England with his wife at the time to great acclaim. Together Nelly and Maria were the Babes in the Wood and the little princes in *Richard III*, and they filled in any other children's parts needed by the company. Neither had Fanny's extraordinary gifts, but both were thoroughly drilled and taught; by the time a part reached Nelly, it had usually been

THEATRE-ROYAL, YORK.
Under the Management of Mr. J. L. PRITCHARD.

FOR THE BENEFIT OF
Miss Maria Ternan
AND
Miss Ellen Ternan.

This present Evening, TUESDAY, May 6th, 1845,

The Entertainments will commence with Mrs. Inchbald's admired Comedy of

Every One has His Fault

Lord Norland, Mr Bruce Norton—Sir Robert Bramble, Mr M. Smythson—Captain Irwin, Mr T. Holmes—Mr Solus, Mr A. E. Reynolds
Mr Harmony, Mr Bower—Mr Placid, Mr G. Smythson—William, Mr Nicholls—Robert, Mr Kimber—Thomas, Mr Louder
Hammond, Mr Updall—John, Mr Weston

Edward . . . . Miss FANNY TERNAN.
Lady Elinor Irwin . . . . . Mrs. TERNAN.
Mrs Placid, Mrs M. Smythson—Miss Spinster, Mrs Horsman—Miss Woobarn, Mrs Thomason

After which, (for the Last Time in York),

MISS FANNY AND MISS MARIA TERNAN
Will Dance the Celebrated Ball Room, "Polka," As Taught by Cellarius.

A Comic Song by Mr. WASS

For the First Time here, Miss FANNY TERNAN will appear in the Fifth Act of

Richard the Third.

King Richard the Third .... Miss Fanny Ternan
Ghost of King Henry the Sixth, Mr Bruce Norton—Ghost of Edward Prince of Wales, Miss Maria Ternan
Ghost of Richard Duke of York, Miss Ellen Ternan—Ghost of Lady Ann, Mrs M. Smythson
Henry Earl of Richmond, Mr M. Smythson—Duke of Norfolk, Mr Bower—Earl of Oxford, Mr French—Lord Stanley, M. E. Reynolds
Sir William Brandon, Mr G. Horsman—Sir Richard Ratcliffe, Mr G. Smythson

A Favourite Pas Seul by Miss Thomason

Miss FANNY TERNAN will take leave of the York Audience in

A FAREWELL ADDRESS,
Written for the occasion.

And the Performances will conclude with the popular Drama of THE

Children in the Wood.

Boy, Miss Maria Ternan—Girl, Miss Ellen Ternan
Sir Rowland (uncle to the Children) Mr Bruce Norton—Lord Alford (their Father) Mr H. Duval
Walter (a Carpenter, in love with Josephine) Mr Hutchings—Apathy (Tutor to the Children) Mr A. E. Reynolds
Gabriel (Servant to Lord Alford) Mr French—Oliver (Servant to Sir Rowland) Mr G. Smythson—Servant, Mr Kimber
First Ruffian, Mr G. Horsman—Second Ruffian, Mr Nicholls—Third Ruffian, Mr Louder
Helen (Mother to the Children) Mrs M. Smythson—Josephine, Miss Bartley—Winnifred (mother to Walter, Mrs Horsman

PROGRAMME OF THE INCIDENTS

Act I. Apartment in the Castle of Sir Rowland—Love's Follies—A peculiar Courtship—Villainy of Sir Rowland—His determination to Assassinate the Children—The Proposal—Nursery in the Castle—The Children and their Protector—Honour and Honesty—The Oath—Cruelty of Sir Rowland—The Visit to the Uncle—Preparations for the Journey—Affectionate Farewell—Arrival at the fatal Wood—Bravery of Walter.

Terrific Combat between Mr. Pritchard and Mr. G. Smythson

Act II. Hall in the Castle—The Letter—An Unexpected Guest—Walter returns—The reported Death of the Children —The Wood—Dreadful Situation of the Children exposed to the Storm—Attack of the Robbers on Lord & Lady Alford—Timely Arrival of Walter—Interior of Winnifred's Cottage—Alarm of Walter—Return of the Children.

Death of the Cruel Uncle and Happy Denouement !

On Wednesday, a New Tragedy, (never acted in any Theatre) entitled "THE SPY OF VENICE," by the Author of "The Jew's Revenge; with "The Spoiled Child," and "Catharine and Petruchio." Mr. Pritchard begs to announce that the Author of "The Spy of Venice" will have an interest in the Receipts of the First Night.

On Thursday, "The Dream at Sea;" with "Raising the Wind," to conclude with "Bi ki, the Bagman;" the Characters by Distinguished Amateurs

Officers of the Garrisons of York, Leeds, & Sheffield.

Mr. PRITCHARD'S Benefit Night is POSTPONED until FRIDAY, the 16th Instant, the Last Night of the Season, on which occasion the OFFICERS will again Perform.

Tickets to be had of the Misses TERNAN, 16, Petergate, and at the Box Office of the Theatre-Royal.

Reeves, Mr. J. L. Pritchard, 1, Union Terrace, Clarence Street, York.   Book and Printing Office played by their mother as a child, by her Aunt Louisa, by Fanny and then by Maria. Shaped and smoothed by family tradition, it was something she could fit into as easily and naturally as a handed-down garment.

Their days and nights were passed in and out of lodgings, the backstages of theatres and the railway carriages that carried them from town to town. Where most of their peers were limited to a close and settled domestic circle, they were expected to be adventurous and resourceful; inevitably they saw and knew far more than other girls. This is how Fanny Kemble described life for two young actresses on a north-country circuit:

> I suppose that a merrier life than that of these lasses, in the midst of their quaint theatrical tasks and homely household duties, was seldom led by . . . girls in any sphere of life. They learned and acted their parts, devised and executed, with small means and great industry, their dresses; made pies and puddings, and patched and darned, in the morning, and by dint of paste and rouge became heroines in the evening; and withal were well conducted, good young things, full of the irrepressible spirits of their age, and turning alike their hard home work, and light stage labour, into fun.[1]

It's a sunny account, and so it sometimes must have been; but when Kemble came to describe her own touring experiences, she found almost nothing but discomfort, distaste and misery to report, and she was notably silent on her own mother's history as a child performer, abandoned by her foreign parents in England to earn her living before she could even speak the language. Merriment there might be, but some loss of innocence too; precocity, toughness and a thick skin were likely to be developed by a stage child.

The ability to negotiate a salary with the manager, to extract a decent wage and a benefit night, were basic skills for all players, which Mrs Ternan naturally exercised on behalf of her daughters; but drumming up business for their benefit nights was something they had to do for themselves. The recommended method was to keep a list of names of likely people in each town you worked in and to call on as many as possible, a procedure satirized by Dickens in *Nickleby* but an essential part of the players' business; the benefit still offered the only hope of making something above the basic wage. In a country company the players might expect to rehearse for four hours in the morning and then be in the theatre for five more in the evening; there were forfeits for being late for rehearsals or failing to comply with an order from the manager. Pay day was usually Saturday, and the children were sent off to church on Sunday, though the adult members of the company were often too tired. If you were sick, you were not paid. All of them had to contrive and stitch their costumes for both on-stage and off, do their hair and copy out their parts; mother and grandmother would help the children if they had time. Lodgings were usually over shops – chemists, tailors, chandlers – and not always clean; beds had to be shared. They might contrive a few meals for themselves, but on the whole they took what the landlady sent up, carried sandwiches and cake on their travels or had the standard cold meat, bread and ale supplied at railway junctions. Over the next few years the Ternan girls got to know the stations of most of the great cities almost as well as the theatres. Where the railway stopped, they went on by coach; in Ireland, at any rate, they noticed that some of the actors still walked.[2]

They had an occasional base in Birmingham, where Mrs Ternan's sister Louisa and her husband were settled. He was a professor of engineering and also a music lover, acting as a music and drama critic in his spare time; and Fanny took singing lessons in Birmingham when she stayed with her aunt and uncle.[3] The Rochester cousins, who were prospering in the barge business, also offered an occasional haven. Grandmother Jarman travelled with them and did what she could, though she was growing old and infirm. Increasingly Fanny took a commanding position, both because of her earnings and her shared care for the education of the two younger girls; Nelly was her pet, on whom she lavished protective love.

In York in the spring of 1845 they reaped a good deal of praise in the local press. They had several benefits and sold their own tickets from their lodgings in Petersgate, in the shadow of the minster. When they were not working, they could enjoy the other shows: The Chimes was one, a goblin story by Charles Dickens, in which an old London father dreams of his daughter. Nelly was six in March; if she dreamed of her missing father, she was kept too busy to repine. Soon her memories must have become faint and confused.

Before the company moved on to Leeds, its ladies were asked to perform with a group of amateur gentlemen. These were the stage-struck officers from several local garrisons, eager to play in a farce and show off their talents as singers and dancers. There was of course, no question of their own wives or sisters joining them on stage; hence the need for actresses. 'One of the most numerous and respectable assemblages which has ever congregated within the walls of the York Theatre' came to see the hybrid show, and the evening was such a success that it was repeated, this time for the benefit of the manager. It may have been the Ternans' first encounter with a custom that was to be fateful to them, that of mixing amateur gentlemen with professional ladies.

They remained touring in the north all summer, and then Mrs Ternan was offered work by Macready, who was preparing a season at the Princess's Theatre in London. It meant being near her husband, even if there was nothing to be done for him; and professionally it was very important, since Macready was by far the most respected actor of the time, and his approval and support were worth a great deal more even than the money he paid. Actresses complained that he became so absorbed in his tragic roles that they emerged black and blue from certain scenes, but none turned down the chance to work with him.

Macready had also got involved with amateurs, albeit reluc-tantly, and found the encounter somewhat bruising. In his case he had been asked to coach a friend intent on performing Jonson's *Every Man in His Humour*. The friend was Dickens who, in a fever of enthusiasm for the enterprise, declared himself 'born to be the Manager of a Theatre'.[4] Macready's loyalty was stretched, and he was more aggrieved still when Dickens's production, which was played to a glittering invited audience at Fanny Kelly's theatre, received a better notice in *The Times* than had ever been given to him.[5] *The Times* believed, rightly, that 'publicity will not be disagree-able to the persons immediately concerned', and its review was reprinted in several other papers. Macready took to his bed for two days.

He was up again to greet Mrs Ternan. The situation required tact. He was planning to put on both *Hamlet* and *Lear* in October, in which she had always played Ophelia and Cordelia; but now, for the first time, he offered her Gertrude and Regan. If she felt offended, she made no sign; at forty-three it may even have come as something of a relief to her. During the winter she accompanied him to Dublin, taking the children, to whom Macready showed a kindly face; he referred to Fanny as 'a very sweet child'. Back in London he continued to give Mrs Ternan work at the Princess's until the spring.

After another summer tour in the north the Ternans returned, this time to the Surrey Theatre in the Blackfriars Road, again with Macready, for the autumn season of 1846. Mrs Ternan found a lodging above a fire-engine manufacturer. It was close to the theatre but had nothing else to commend it, and suggests that their poverty was now biting. The district left an unpleasant impression on Fanny, who later described its rows of dirty little houses, streaked with soot and rain, where tired men sat out on the steps in their shirt-sleeves and swarms of children tumbled about in the street.[6] No one would have chosen lodgings in Blackfriars if they could have afforded something better; but there, on 17 October, when Mrs Ternan herself was playing Lady Macbeth at the theatre, came the news of the death of Thomas Ternan in the Bethnal Green Insane Asylum.

A rumour went about that he ended his life by his own hand. If so, it was not entered on the death certificate, which stated simply 'general paralysis', and he was not denied Christian burial. His body was brought to Christ Church, Blackfriars, for the funeral, attended by his brother William from Rochester and a small cluster of friends. Children were not taken to funerals; they must have spent a cheerless day in their dirty Blackfriars lodging.

Within a few days their mother was, necessarily, on stage again, appearing as Portia. Macready, much affected, wrote in his diary, 'Heard of the death of Mrs Ternan's husband – died in a lunatic asylum in Bethnal Green. How light are our woes when compared with such a weight of affliction! I think I ought to ascertain if I can at all assist or relieve her.'[7] He was as good as his word, inviting her to visit him with her mother and all three children and offering them what help he could in the form of £10. Mrs Ternan insisted that it should be a loan, but Macready, 'unwilling to hamper her with a sense of a *debt*', asked that it should be transferred as a gift to her little girl; presumably this was Fanny.[8]

An obituary notice spoke kindly of the qualities the dead man had 'inherited from his birth and education ... Poor Ternan, peace to his memory! A kinder heart never existed, and he was truly entitled to the character of an Irish gentleman.' His widow, it added, had been 'a prize in the lottery of life'.[9] When news of the death reached Doncaster, the lodge of Freemasons gave a benefit for the family of 'Brother Ternan'.[10] Apart from these small charities, they continued to have only themselves to depend on. Nelly was now seven, Maria nine and Fanny eleven, growing rather big for an infant prodigy.

But for the moment Mrs Ternan must continue. Again they moved, to Dublin first, where Nelly played the child Orestes to the Iphigenia of Helen Faucit and Mamillius in *The Winter's Tale*. Mrs Ternan appeared with Macready. They all acted with Fanny Kemble, back from America with her disastrous marriage behind her, separated from her two daughters and painfully reconstructing her career. They also performed with Vestris and Mathews.

Another long litany of Irish and northern towns unrolled before them. They could not afford to rest for long, and soon sickness attacked the family again; grandmother Jarman fell ill and could no longer tour with them. They took her to Louisa in Birmingham, and there she died of cancer in the summer of 1849. Nelly was ten.

That year Mrs Ternan was in Newcastle once more, playing Juliet to the Romeo of an American friend, Charlotte Cushman. Female Romeos were a commonplace of the nineteenth-century theatre, but none was more appreciated than that of the remarkable Miss Cushman, who was given a tremendous reception in England for her playing of male parts, including Hamlet. She carried off these feats with intense seriousness; and on this occasion the *Newcastle Chronicle* spoke warmly of both ladies, praising Mrs Ternan for her elegance and spirit, and adding that she was highly respected both on and off the stage.

As for her children, Fanny delivered her usual stirring version of Collins's 'Ode on the Passions' and also led in a musical farce called *The Waterman*, in which both her younger sisters sang, acted a pair of quarrelling rustic lovers and were thought exceedingly clever. So they doubtless were; they had been touring with the piece for at least four years, and Nelly, with her blue eyes and golden curls, usually brought the house down. In Wexford her performance – and parentage – had been celebrated in verse:

> Fair child of nature, young and gay.
> Sweet as smiling flowers in May;
> Say, has the germ of genius sprung
> Within thy heart so pure and young . . .
>
> But coming time shall see thee rise,
> The wonder of admiring eyes;
> Sharing still the well-known fame,
> That gilds thy honoured mother's name.[11]

Popular as the children were, Mrs Ternan and Fanny agreed that she could not stretch out her career as a prodigy any longer. Newcastle, where she had started, was the obvious place to announce her departure from the stage, possibly for good or at least 'till she is of more mature age'. Fanny composed her own long farewell to her audience. It ended rousingly:

> For your past kindness, which my thoughts enshrine –
> Your generous patronage of me and mine,
> My fervent gratitude shall through life's length
> Grow with my growth, and strengthen with my strength!
> And trust me, dearest patrons, the fond theme
> Of my day musings, and my nightly dream,
> Shall be that blessings may your wishes crown –
> Blithe be your lives and prosperous your town;
> May the full tide of commerce hither flow –
> Brisk be its trade, and 'Merry the keel row'!
>
> And now farewell – my patrons and my friends
> For here, the drama of my childhood ends,
> Let it but end to recommence again –
> A second part, but of a higher strain.

THEATRE ROYAL,
NEWCASTLE UPON TYNE

FOR THE BENEFIT OF
MRS. TERNAN,
And positively the LAST NIGHT of her Engagement, on which occasion
Miss FANNY TERNAN,
AND HER SISTERS
Misses M. and E. TERNAN
WILL APPEAR.

ON FRIDAY, MARCH 16, 1849,
Will be presented the Fashionable Comedy of THE

JEALOUS WIFE !

Russet...... Mr. H. YOUNGE. Sir Harry...... Mr. SCHARF. Lord Trinket...... Mr. BELTON.
Major Oakley...... Mr. W. H. STEPHENS. Mr. Oakley...... Mr. DAVIS. Charles Oakley...... Mr. H. NICHOLLS.
Paris...... Mr. GODFREY. John...... Mr. SWAN. Thomas...... Mr. DERWENT.

Mrs. Oakley, - - - Mrs. TERNAN.

Lady Freelove,...... Mrs. ALFRED PHILLIPS. Harriet,...... Mrs. SELTON.
Toilet,...... Miss JULIA PERRY. Chambermaid,...... Miss ROBSON.

END OF THE COMEDY, A
FAREWELL ADDRESS
Will be spoken by Miss FANNY TERNAN.

A DANCE, - - BY MISS KATE KIRBY.

After which, Miss FANNY TERNAN will deliver
COLLINS' ODE ON THE PASSIONS !
With the appropriate Music and Tableaux Vivans!
Portraying Fear—Anger—Despair—Hope—Revenge—Jealousy—Melancholy—and Cheerfulness:

THE HIGHLAND FLING - (in full National Costume) - BY MR. CHADWICK,
From the Theatre Royal Leeds, his First Appearance here!

To conclude with the Musical Farce of
THE WATERMAN !

Tom Tug (a Waterman)...... Miss FANNY TERNAN.
Robin (a Gardener)...... Miss E. TERNAN. Wilhelmina...... Miss M. TERNAN.
Mr. Bundle...... Mr. W. H. STEPHENS. Mrs. Bundle...... Mrs. BELL.

SONG...... "I'm o'er Young to Marry yet." ...... Miss M. TERNAN.
SONG...... "And did you never hear of a Jolly Young Waterman," ...... Mr. JAMES TERNAN.
"Then Farewell my Trim-built Wherry," ...... Miss FANNY TERNAN.
SONG...... "Cherries and Plums are never found," Finale...... Fair Helenore...... Mr. J. TERNAN, &c.

Tickets to be had of Mr. Dunn, at the Box Office; Miss Bell, Grey Street; and Mrs. Ternan, 7, Carliol Street.
Mr. E. D. DAVIS, 20, Blackett Street. Stage Manager...... Mr. BELTON.

On Monday Evening will be produced a New Grand Romance, with entirely New Scenery, Dresses, &c. entitled
"CHERRY AND FAIR STAR; or the Children of Cyprus and the Golden Galley."

On FRIDAY EVENING, March 23rd, the Performances will be by Desire and under the especial Patronage of
COL. POLE and the OFFICERS of the Garrison, on which occasion the BAND of the Regiment will attend.

On FRIDAY EVENING, March 30, the Performances will be under the Distinguished Patronage of the Worshipful the MAYOR OF GATESHEAD and Mrs. MAYORESS.

NEWCASTLE UPON TYNE: PRINTED BY M. BENSON, NO. 5, DEAN STREET.

The smiles that early woke the youthful flame,
In after time the actress yet may claim,
And let it soothe this moment's deep regret,
I go to learn – but never to forget.

No wonder the people of Newcastle appreciated Fanny – she could turn a good couplet and not forget the essential matters of commerce and coal barges in the process. They cheered her, and the *Chronicle* printed the whole of her farewell verses.[12]

For the next five years the Ternans continued their regular progression through the provinces and Ireland, with occasional London appearances. At times they disappear from sight altogether, either resting with cousins or working in theatres whose playbills have not survived. Macready's retirement from the stage in 1851 meant the end of a useful association. Fortunately his place was taken by another actor, Samuel Phelps, whose Shakespeare productions gave Mrs Ternan a good deal of employment. Phelps took over Sadler's Wells theatre in the mid-forties when it was in a state of Hogarthian brutishness.* By disciplining the audience mercilessly – he excluded babies, beer, pipe-smoking and food – and embarking on a programme of serious drama, he transformed the theatre within a decade into a respectable and, indeed, highly respected place. His particular enthusiasm was always Shakespeare, and he played almost the entire canon during his years at the Wells. His triumph was such that in the winter of 1854 he took his company, including Mrs Ternan, to Windsor Castle for a royal command performance.[13]

Fanny's farewell to the stage at Newcastle was not as absolute as

---

* This is the description from *Household Words*, 4 October 1851: 'Without, the Theatre, by night, was like the worst part of the worst kind of Fair in the worst kind of town. Within, it was a bear-garden, resounding with foul language, oaths, catcalls, shrieks, yells, blasphemy, obscenity – a truly diabolical clamour. Fights took place anywhere, at any period of the performance ... Sickly children in arms were squeezed out of shape, in all parts of the house. Fish was fried at the entrance doors. Barricades of oyster shells encumbered the pavement. Expectant half-price visitors to the gallery, howled defiant impatience up the stairs, and danced a sort of Carmagnole all round the building.'

she may have hoped. She continued to perform here and there, at Glasgow and Doncaster, and at the Lyceum in London; but her ambition was to become a singer, and she began to give modest song recitals after the plays on her mother's provincial tours as well as a few concerts in Ireland. In the autumn of 1853 she achieved her first London concert, at the Exeter Hall in the Strand, a huge place seating 2,000; but although a kindly reviewer said she was 'destined to be one of our first native singers', the public failed to see her as another Jenny Lind or Adelaide Kemble. According to one of her father's theatrical friends, she had lost the remarkable beauty of her childhood, taken to wearing green spectacles, and acquired the reputation of a bluestocking. 'She lived in a world of her own . . . her selection of songs was the highest of high art, consequently caviare to the general public' declared the old trouper, who probably liked nothing but a sentimental ballad himself.[14] It was hard on Fanny, who laboured so energetically to fulfil her serious ambitions and had to keep falling back on the sort of work she did not want, playing minor theatrical parts at the Lyceum and the Olympic.

Maria moved through the usual girl's repertoire without ever becoming the star solo performer Fanny had been; but she was spirited, professional and popular with managements. She played the leading part of Little Pickle in *The Spoiled Child* at Drury Lane when she was fourteen and graduated to a permanent place with Charles Kean's company at the Princess's a few years later. If Nelly was working during her mid-teens, she made no particular mark; all the same she was being prepared for a stage career. What alternative was there for her? The girls had to be self-supporting; they had no money beyond what they earned, and they knew no way of earning money but the theatre. A young woman who had been on the stage was not likely to find a place as a governess or teacher in a school – respectable work but hard, lonely and, for girls who had been free, intolerably constricting. Their mother would not have allowed them to sink into the near-slavery of becoming a servant, seamstress or milliner. Through all her vicissitudes she seems to have clung to an ideal view of the theatre as a noble and civilizing profession – the theatre of Macready and Phelps – in which her daughters might follow in her footsteps. If in practice they did not find themselves playing Juliet or Lady Teazle, at least in the theatre they were known and among friends; they had a measure of independence and – in the London theatre especially – some degree of contact with the world of ideas and art.

In the spring of 1855 Mrs Ternan, Fanny and Maria were all three working in London, mostly at the Princess's; and now for the first time they acquired something like a permanent home. They rented Park Cottage in Northampton Park: charmingly named, though the park was purely notional. There were brick fields and a cattle market near by; the little house stood on ground squeezed between the Balls Pond Road and the North London Railway, and was neither central nor convenient, being part of the new, spreading northern suburb of Islington and surrounded by what had until lately been fields and market gardens, now transformed into a chaos of rank grass strewn with broken crockery, bricks and builders' rubble, and marked out into 'eligible plots of building ground' with wooden poles: Fanny said they looked like gibbets.[15] Few of the roads were made up, though Park Cottage was at least tacked on to the end of a neat terrace, St Paul's Place.

The stucco face of the cottage looked north, and a twist of four railinged steps led up to the front door. Inside a steep flight of stairs plunged straight down to the basement, but to the left there was a pleasant small sitting room with one window facing north, and to the right a second room to match. Through this second room lay a third with a window to the west; this was all the accommodation above ground level. The basement rooms had only half-lights on to the pavement, again facing north, except for the flagged wash room opening into the tiny yard, where the outdoor privy stood. One basement room was a bedroom, one a kitchen. If you visit the house today, you wonder how four women squeezed in, together with the maid they must have needed.*

You can see what attracted the Ternans, because the little house

---

* Park Cottage still bears the same name, but it has been improved inside and out, with extra windows on the east side. The present owners have made it into a charming house with an attractive garden. The essential structure remains unchanged, however, and the original disposition of the rooms is clear; the remains of the kitchen range and stone flagging for the wash room can be seen.

has a certain awkward elegance, and the ground-level rooms are good, with their pretty fireplaces, wooden shutters to the windows, neat cupboards and unexpected connecting doors. But you can also understand why Dickens, when he saw it later, objected that it was unhealthy; hot summers and cold winters must both have been uncomfortable in such cramped and low-level quarters.[16] Healthy or not, here Nelly seems to have lived from the age of sixteen. She must have slept with her mother, her sisters or a maid, possibly in the basement. She saw Fanny, Maria and Mrs Ternan off to Sadler's Wells or the West End and woke to hear them arrive home in the night; she listened to the gossip of the theatre, and sometimes put on her bonnet and boots to accompany them to work through the crowded streets, to help them dress backstage and watch from the wings as they performed. She dreamed of her own future, as an actress, perhaps as a wife. She read every book she could lay hands on; all her life Nelly was a voracious reader. She wore her first crinoline, for skirts ballooned steadily as she grew up in the 1850s. Unlike Fanny she remained strikingly pretty.

5

Gaslight Fairies
1856–1857

Mrs Ternan's view of the theatre remained resolutely lofty, even when she or her daughters had to perform in productions that fell below the loftiest standards. In the same way she was always, in her own estimation, and in defiance of her origins and the general view of her profession, a lady. She impressed on her daughters that their father had been an Irish gentleman who could claim descent from the dispossessed O'Tiernans, and that they must always remember that they too were ladies. In the harsh circumstances in which they actually lived this cannot always have been easy for them; and the conflicts set up grew worse when they found themselves obliged to take work which was clearly in breach of what a lady would consider doing.

Perhaps this is why Fanny began to cast about for alternatives to the stage. There is some evidence that she and Maria made an attempt to set up a ladies' school during 1856; or at any rate they acquired the use of a house in Rochester Villas, Kentish Town, which they declared a school.[1] The project seems to have been begun in the summer in the manner of Mrs Micawber, with nothing more than a house and an intention, and it flourished no better than Mrs Micawber's. They had no need to doubt their competence as teachers, for the education of girls was taken seriously by almost nobody in the 1850s and was more concerned with putting on a little social polish than with learning; if anything, the Misses Ternan were probably overqualified, since they could themselves offer the singing and dancing lessons usually provided by a visiting master. No doubt they dreamed that, if they could once get started with a few pupils, there would be plenty to occupy Nelly and a home for their mother too; the house was pretty and commodious. Only the pupils failed to appear. Possibly to interested parents these aspirant schoolmistresses looked too young and frivolous to be taken seriously, and the polish they were offering seemed not quite of the kind that was wanted among the solid householders of the district; there may even have been rumours that Miss Ternan and Miss Maria had been seen on the stage of the Lyceum.

With no pupils in prospect, Fanny and Maria could hardly turn down good offers of theatrical work for long, and the school plan was quickly dropped. They all crammed into Park Cottage together, and in the autumn of 1856 Fanny was acting again. Their failure must have cast some gloom over the end of the year; it was made worse by news of the illness of Mrs Ternan's sister Louisa in Birmingham. She was hardly more than fifty, with four children, some younger than Nelly, but she died in December – a death that must have made all three girls more aware than ever of the necessity to earn their own keep and try to give their mother some respite from work.

Fanny was now appearing at the Princess's Theatre under the management of Charles Kean and his wife Ellen. They were good friends and patrons: Mrs Ternan and Maria had been in their lavish *Winter's Tale*, and they followed this up by offering Fanny the part of Oberon in an equally ambitious production of *A Midsummer Night's Dream*. Whether she relished playing a fairy king or not, she took the work gratefully and stayed through the whole of the long run.

The production was remarkable in several ways. Bottom was played by a seventy-year-old comedian, John Pritt Harley, and Puck by another Nelly, the ten-year-old Ellen Terry.[2] She described in her memoirs how, after each show, she was walked home by her father; it was miles to their suburban home through the dark streets, but he wrapped her in his cloak and just managed to keep her awake and on her feet by telling her stories. Few reminiscences give a clearer impression of the tough conditions in which the actors worked and of the stamina required of players of all ages. Old Harley laboured to the end, suffering a stroke while playing Lancelot Gobbo the following year; Ellen Terry, who was with him when it happened, never forgot how frightened she was by his twisted face and helpless gesturing; he died a few days later, penniless. Old men, women and children were all accustomed to rehearsing long hours in the day and then, if necessary walking for an hour or more through the night after the performance. Fanny was no exception to this rule, and though she was a strong and confident twenty-one-year-old, even she can hardly have enjoyed the nightly trek to Park Cottage. But in April 1857 she had company on her homeward walk when Nelly was launched on to her adult career as an actress. She had been offered work at the Haymarket.

Her role was not a very exalted one: it was a breeches part in a burlesque put on by the busy actor-manager Buckstone, who also wrote his own farces.[3] On this occasion he had turned out a piece of spoof classical drama, a genre very popular at the time. It was called *Atalanta*, written in doggerel and full of puns and topical allusions, in which Nelly was to play Hippomenes, the young man who threw the golden apples in front of Atalanta to stop her running so fast. She was required to wear tights, to do some dancing and posturing, and to sing several solos. She also had to deliver long passages of pastiche Shakespeare. If – still less than Fanny's fairy king – it was not what a Ternan daughter aspired to, again it was work, and she was as conscientious about it as Fanny; and *Atalanta*, rubbishy as it was, was a great success. It ran nightly from mid-April to July; Nelly, well trained like her sisters, did not miss a single performance. By the end of the run she must have taken home between £20 and £30 towards the expenses of Park Cottage and could count herself a fully fledged professional.*

Nelly was now eighteen, though, to judge from photographs, she looked younger. She was not a classic beauty – none of the sisters had their mother's looks – but there was something delectable in her puppy fat, her wide blue eyes with their slightly puzzled expression, and her golden curls, beautifully arranged by her mother. Everything about her signalled innocence and vulner-

---

* The Keans paid Ellen Terry 15s. a week for her Puck until one night when her toe was caught in the trap and Mrs Kean promised to double her salary if she would stop screaming and finish her speech. She did stop screaming, and she did have her salary doubled. Mrs Ternan was paid £3 10s. by the Keans at this time, and Maria Ternan, playing a small part, 30s.

ability. In her neat little dresses and ringlets, she could have stepped out of a children's fairy story. On stage in her boy's costume, she gave the men in the audience something many of them relished – a glimpse of the shape of the female body, displayed by a girl who was visibly embarrassed at exhibiting herself in this way. There is a well-known story which stems from this period of Nelly crying because she did not like appearing in tights. She can't, presumably, have cried nightly for three months; but, faced with one of the rougher audiences, it would not be surprising if there were times when she found the whole business hard to bear.

Drunks in the audience were not the only problem. When Fanny came to write of the life of an actress, she had some cutting things to say about the type of man who hung about backstage while they were trying to work – literary men, critics and the odd 'idle, good-humoured fine gentleman' – and no doubt she and her sisters had plenty of practice in fending them off. Nelly, for all her innocent looks, simply cannot have been as unaware as girls reared in a sheltered middle-class home – girls like her contemporaries, Mamey and Katey Dickens, for instance. She must have learnt her own technique of self-preservation, both backstage and while walking through the streets of London after the performance with a fixed determination not to notice, not to think about, not to respond to what she saw.

In the 1850s the sights of the London streets were something a nice young woman simply had to shut her mind to, even if she could not always shut her eyes to the drunkenness, violence and misery, and the prostitution of women and children. Such things, like the rats that swarmed in the scenery yard behind the theatre, were known to be there and frightening, but nothing could be done about them, so it was better to ignore them. The artifice of the stage, with its beautiful scenery, before which Nelly and Fanny were both appearing in male parts, was mirrored by the artificiality of the real world, in which so much happened which could never be mentioned or queried by any one who aspired to be taken for a lady.

A lady might worry about her gloves, which should have no holes showing, or her bonnet, which should be set straight, or her ankles, which should be more or less invisible; indeed, clothes, their neatness and good repair, the messages they sent to other people, were written about, and were a proper topic to take up with other ladies, who might offer useful and practical advice. But nobody talked, or wrote, about the messages sent by tights. And inside the clothes the body itself was as unmentionable as the rats or the night life in the streets of London. In her mind Nelly might determine to be a lady, but the body was a piece of secret machinery, sending out and receiving disquieting and shameful messages. They could be considered only privately; and there was no guidance available on how to decipher and deal with them.

Vanity was another problem. A lady must not be vain, but an actress was obliged to show off bits of herself to dazzle the eyes of the men who paid to come and look at her. Whatever Mrs Ternan said to Nelly, they both knew that she was being dressed in a particular way for a particular purpose. The roar of admiration she sometimes heard now was entirely different from the admiration accorded to her when she was a child actress. That had been jolly, even sometimes tender; this was brutal, voracious, with something contemptuous about it. Seeing a dancer on stage in flesh-coloured tights, wrote Thackeray, offered a thrill rather like the thrill of a public execution; it gives one some sense of the Roman holiday atmosphere that could be generated in the theatre.[4] Daumier's drawings of men watching the stage made a similar point. A strong, blithe actress like Vestris might face such an atmosphere, use it and subdue it; a nervous girl could hardly hope to.

And Nelly had no father and no brothers to take the mystery out of the male sex. Living in a house of women, it was easy for her to divide men into two distinct categories, on the one hand the brutes and ogres, on the other idealized distant figures, her lost father among them. In the audience and in the streets she faced ogres every night, while the ideal replacement for her father had yet to materialize. Still further away was the possibility that he too might turn into a ogre.

At much the same time Nelly faced her audience of ogres, Dickens produced a whimsical account of the little actresses he called 'Gaslight Fairies' in his magazine *Household Words*.[5] He begins by describing the recruitment of girls to dance in pantomimes. His fairies are poor, good-humoured and patient, and they earn their money hard. Their age range is from 'an anxious woman of ten, learned in the prices of victual and fuel,' to a Miss Fairy of twenty-three, very pretty, and 'makes up very pretty' too. Some of the fairies live with their mother, an actress who was once a country manager's wife and played 'the whole round of Shakespearean beauties', often with her children hanging out of a box as she did so.

Dickens's tone is humorous, and his essay is a piece of light-hearted and sentimental entertainment, but it is not just that. He knows what he is talking about when he describes the backstage world. He knows where the theatrical families live and just how they have played Shakespeare in the provinces. He knows how anonymously shabby they appear off-stage, how the 'fairies' have to trudge through the mud in flimsy shoes to get to the theatre, what they are likely to be paid if they land a job – 12s. a week – and how it will have to go into the family housekeeping purse.

He also knows how the eldest Miss Fairy watches over her younger sister, 'who might otherwise come to harm one day, in this hard and dangerous theatrical world'. Throughout the piece Dickens, too, takes a protective tone towards these young women of Drury Lane, Soho, Somers Town and Blackfriars. 'Whatever you may hear to the contrary (and may sometimes have a strange satisfaction in believing), there is no lack of virtue and modesty among the Fairies. All things considered, I doubt if they be much below our own high level.' In the face of a prejudice he finds objectionable he goes on to wish that 'we were not so often pleased to think ill of those who minister to our amusement'. Finally he draws a touching picture of the devotion of one gaslight fairy to her family – the pretty Miss Fairy of twenty-three, with a drunken old out-of-work actor for a father, a sick mother and brothers and sisters all working in the theatre: the young John Kemble Fairy, Miss Rosina and Miss Angelica Fairy aged fourteen and ten, and little Master Edmund, eight.

The fairies of Park Cottage would not have accepted inclusion in Dickens's pretty, vulnerable flock for a moment. They knew themselves to belong to a higher order, even when they appeared in remarkably similar fairy costumes before the same gaslights; even though they sensed how slender the dividing line could be between the higher and lower categories of fairy. Yet what he describes is, in fact, remarkably close to their experience and in more ways than one. Missing from his account, of course, is the gaslight fairy's own point of view. It may well have been less quaint, less gentle and less resigned than he believed, or wanted to believe.

Fanny Ternan's own account of the experience of being an actress was actually published by Dickens, though not until another decade had gone by, and then anonymously.[6] *Mabel's Progess* is not autobiographical in form but heavily disguised as fiction, and Fanny carefully made Mabel's family connection with the stage remote. Her people come from 'the upper half of the middle class' – her grandfather is a clergyman – and it is only through the marriage of her uncle to an actress and his subsequent blindness, which forces him to depend on his wife's professional exertions, that Mabel is put in touch with the theatre at all. Her mother and the young man who loves her are both horrified at the degradation involved in becoming a 'strolling player'. There is talk of the necessity of shunning publicity if you are a woman and of her entering on 'the broad way that leadeth to destruction'.

All this allows Fanny to describe the world she knows and to insist on its virtues and dignity. She is at pains to show the good qualities of theatre people and to mock the prejudice of those who see a career on the stage as nothing but exhibitionism and sin. She gives a vivid account of working in Ireland with a country company and then in a London theatre, with no glossing over the dirty lodgings with black beetles on the brick floors, the shared beds, the inevitable diet of bread, cold meat and beer, the hard slog of learning four new parts in a week while making costumes, and rehearsing all day and acting long hours in the evening; or the squalor and grime of the London streets, and the condescension of the theatre goers, one of whom insults Mabel by referring to her as a 'nice young person'. Mabel has to wear shabby old clothes and threadbare gloves. She has to act in farces and melodramas and a great deal of trash, and try to make it seem not trash; she has to accept that a tightrope act will mean more to most managements than Shakespeare, and that even if she does appear in Shakespeare she will be asked to perform not the text she knows but a very different acting version.

It is a convincing account of learning her trade, which includes an understanding of the characters of her fellow players; there is a nice portrait of the thin, anxious leading lady, who has a husband and three growing children and has seen many hardships but carefully preserves her juvenile ringlets; and there is sympathy for the poverty of the old members of the company, who face a very bleak future. Mabel is kindly welcomed and offered good advice. She is taught not to allow herself the wasteful luxury of real tears on stage but to calculate all her effects: 'Your voice, and your face, and your figure are the tools you have to work with, and you can't carve out your own ideas unless you've first learnt to handle your tools properly.'

Acting gives her, she finds, slightly more freedom and – once she is successful – a better income than teaching in a provincial girls' school had done. She also discovers that, despite condescension and disapproval, 'the frank recognition of her professional position was agreeable to her'. She views acting 'in the matter-of-fact light of an honourable means of employing her faculties to win a subsistence for herself and for those dear to her'. Here is a real stage heroine in the making, the reader feels; and after these fine words, it is disappointing to find Mabel making such rapid progress that she becomes a London star, with a house in Highgate for good measure, only to retire from the stage for ever, marrying for love as she does so. It may be that Fanny thought this was the correct way to end a novel about a young woman; it may also have represented a strictly honest account of the sort of fantasy entertained by the young women at Park Cottage.

PART TWO

6

The Amateur: Dickens in 1857

The real situation at Park Cottage in July 1857 was not cheerful. Mrs Ternan and Maria were both out of work, and *Atalanta* was closing, leaving Nelly also at a loose end. Fanny had a few more weeks at the Princess's, though her heart was hardly in it; her dream of becoming a singer seemed as distant as ever, and nothing more interesting presented itself. Mrs Ternan had to face the fact that she could expect little more than understudying and occasional work now she was fifty-five. None of her daughters showed any sign of equalling her early success. They were well-tutored professionals, but they were not stars; no one had invited any of them to play Juliet. The whole family had one firm engagement in prospect, for two weeks in mid-September in Doncaster, where all the girls had played as children. Until then they had the prospect of being cooped up together in the little house through the discomforts of a hot, unhealthy London summer. News of mutiny and massacre from India was the chief, unwelcome distraction of the season.

Maria at least found a better diversion. She got herself a ticket for the theatrical sensation of the summer. It was a melodrama called *The Frozen Deep*, got up by its author, Wilkie Collins, with his famous fellow writer Charles Dickens. Both men fancied themselves as amateur actors and were giving a few performances at the Gallery of Illustrations in Regent Street. All the cast were Dickens's friends or members of his family, and they included his sisters-in-law and two daughters; the whole thing had begun as a private entertainment, which had now burgeoned. The settings were spectacular, and the story was of a man who triumphs over his own murderous impulses; this part was played by Dickens, who died on stage to a specially written orchestral accompaniment. In the best

71

theatrical tradition he rose again immediately to play the farce that concluded the entertainment. He did it with great relish and much impromptu gagging; and in this he was partnered by his pretty seventeen-year-old daughter Katey.

Maria found the whole experience overwhelming. So did the press. Dickens might be an amateur but not so as to fail to send out invitations to the critics to see his work. The *Saturday Review* said nothing else currently on the stage equalled it, and the *Athenaeum* declared that Dickens's acting 'might open a new era for the stage'. The ladies in the cast were particularly commended: 'Everyone accustomed to professional theatricals must, on this occasion, have felt how novel a charm it was to hear the ladies of a play talk like ladies.'[1] The Queen herself asked to see *The Frozen Deep* and was persuaded to come to the Gallery of Illustrations by Dickens, who said he preferred not to take his ladies to the palace 'in the quality of actresses'.[2] She came accompanied by Prince Leopold of Belgium and Prince Frederick of Prussia, and they all expressed themselves delighted. Dickens, summoned for a private word, refused the Queen not once but twice, on the grounds that he did not want to appear before her in his costume: a further triumph of his will over hers, for which she graciously and, under the circumstances, very sensibly forgave him. When Dickens chose to be unbudgeable, not even a queen could move him.

The Frozen Deep had begun as pure amusement but was now the means of raising money for the family of the playwright Douglas Jerrold, a friend of Dickens who had lately died. The generosity with his time and energy was typical; the chance to hurl himself body and soul into directing and acting meant still more. He needed relief from the loneliness of writing and told friends it gave him a marvellous feeling of liberation from his usual activities, that it was like 'writing a book in company'. So he was well disposed to listen to an invitation to present the production in Manchester in August. Anyone else might have quailed, but he was in a mood to take on the challenge. He agreed to go with his company for two performances to be given in the Free Trade Hall.

At this point he began to worry about the ladies in the cast. Jessie Wills, who played the old Scottish nurse, had already suffered a sprain and could not go on; and, once he had refused to take his ladies to the palace on the grounds of delicacy, he began to think it might be still more indelicate for them to appear in a public performance on the scale of the Manchester one. Would their voices carry in the spaces of the Free Trade Hall, which was vast? The men would manage, but the women's parts, he decided, had best be taken over by professionals. Collins said he knew of some, though he failed to come up with any, and at the beginning of August Dickens wrote to the actress Emmeline Montague, an old friend, inviting her to take over the main female part.

When she declined – she had recently married – Dickens turned to another professional friend for advice, the actor and playwright Alfred Wigan. They had known one another for over twenty years, since the 1830s, when Wigan had played in Dickens's own farce, *The Strange Gentleman*; since then Mrs Wigan had also acted in one of his fund-raising productions in Manchester.[3] Wigan was currently managing the Olympic Theatre. Fanny Ternan had worked there recently; he knew her mother and sisters, too, and felt able to recommend them to Dickens, and Dickens to them. In this way they were brought together early in August.

Mrs Ternan was invited to take over Jessie Wills's part of the Scottish nurse. Maria was to be the heroine, Clara: this was the part Mamey Dickens, who was the same age as Maria, had played. Nelly was to have the small part played by Mrs Dickens's younger sister, Georgina Hogarth. All three were also to be in the farce, Buckstone's *Uncle John*, in which Dickens acted the old man ludicrously in love with a young girl he has educated. Nelly was to take over the girl's part from Katey Dickens, and at this stage Dickens planned to withdraw and hand over his part to a friend.

It was a standard procedure, as we have seen, for professional actresses to be invited to appear with amateur gentlemen, and Mrs Ternan agreed to the proposal readily enough. The chance of working with a man of acknowledged genius, of getting away for a few days and taking her girls for a trip to the north, of being involved with an already successful enterprise and introduced into a circle of people who might further their careers – all these things must have made the offer, coming at this difficult time, something of a godsend.

*

To the Ternan girls, Mr Charles Dickens was, before he was anything else, the old friend of their benefactor Macready, who had acted with their father and behaved kindly at the time of his death. That was a good start. They also knew – as did everyone in the profession – that he had been personally involved with the theatre himself for many years. Alfred Wigan was not the only one to recall *The Strange Gentleman*; old John Pritt Harley also remembered acting alongside Dickens in it one evening twenty years ago. In fact, he had been a close friend, frequently dining at Dickens's house, and even attending the christening of little Katey with her godfather, Macready, in 1840.[4] Although Dickens had not gone on writing for the stage, he had maintained a special relationship with the theatrical world. Not only were some of his closest friends in the theatre, but he was regularly seen in audiences, London and provincial, for everything from Shakespeare to burlesque. He was also a constant and generous supporter of theatrical charities, which kept him in contact with Ben Webster and John Buckstone, both at different times managers of the Haymarket. When Macready's friend, the actor Edward Elston, drowned, leaving six daughters and one son, Dickens devoted himself to raising enough capital to ensure the children an income and made sure they all received professional training.[5] Generosity of this kind did not go unnoticed in the acting community.

All this gave the Ternans reason to look forward to the encounter with their new amateur manager. For his part, although there was nothing new for him about meeting professional actresses, they had the particular charm of being natives of a world to which he was drawn by something stronger than a purely rational appreciation of what it had to offer. There was no time of his life when he was not fascinated by the stage and by the idea of performance. As a tiny boy his parents had stood him with his sister on a table in a Rochester inn to give a song to the company, much like any other infant prodigy; and before he was ten, he was taken to the Theatre Royal in Rochester. He may even have seen Thomas Ternan acting there, perhaps in *Macbeth*, as one of the witches whose male clothes Dickens noticed clearly showing through their ragged costumes. At this same period he wrote his own tragedy, *Misnar,*

The Sultan of India, and joined in amateur theatricals with his Aunt Fanny's family.

Dickens's very first taste of the dramatic monologue had come still earlier, from his mother, who was renowned for her powers of mimicry. Then, when his father was in the Marshalsea Prison, Charles would ask his mother to 'do' Mr Dickens's fellow debtors, each of whom she could hit off to perfection; later, of course, he 'did' them himself. Although as an adult Dickens often said unkind things about her and showed embarrassment at her boisterous spirits, it's noticeable that women with her characteristics pleased him, and that he especially admired female mimics; his sister-in-law Georgina was one, and all the Ternans excelled at mimicry. And he was a superb mimic himself, something he must have first learnt from his mother, and the basis for the dramatic monologues which became a central device in his writing.

London school friends claimed to remember him begging in the streets of Camden Town for the sheer fun of impersonating a real beggar boy, as well as organizing more formal theatricals at Wellington House School. His much loved elder sister Fanny trained as a singer, and the two of them got up at least one of the popular musical plays of the period together in their parents' house: *Clari, The Maid of Milan*. When he began to work as a clerk, his stage fever was such that for several years he went to the theatre almost every night of the week. At twenty he resolved to become a professional actor. It was not a light-hearted decision but carefully thought out and planned. He applied for an audition at Covent Garden, which was granted; he was to be seen by the manager George Bartley and by no less a personage than the actor Charles Kemble.

Dickens prepared for his audition with characteristic intensity. Through his regular theatre-going he had already studied the techniques of many actors and sensed that his own strength would lie in comedy. He decided to concentrate on imitating the comedian Charles Mathews, who had himself learned from Tate Wilkinson and become a phenomenal impersonator and ventriloquist. Mathews's best act was to play a farce in which he took every part, dashing behind a screen to reappear in a few seconds as someone different. Another trick was to take his audiences on conducted 'trips' to Paris or America, describing the scenery and encountering a whole gallery of other travellers on the way; he called these picaresque performances 'monopolylogues'. Dickens copied Mathews's act night after night in front of a mirror. His sister Fanny helped by accompanying him in his songs; but when the day arrived Dickens had a cold in the head which made it impossible for him to perform. The audition was postponed, and before another opportunity arose, he had begun his triumphant career as a writer, using picaresque narratives not entirely unlike those of Mathews. He never ceased to dream of the stage, and the techniques mastered in 1832 were not forgotten; he brought them out twenty-five years later, when he began reading from his own works.[6]

The theatre remained a focus of intense interest. He always relished green room gossip, and for several years he acted as an occasional theatre critic. On the death of the clown Grimaldi in 1836, he undertook to edit his memoirs, an inchoate but fascinating jumble of anecdotes of the London theatres and provincial circuits. While he was working on the memoirs, Fanny seemed to be headed for a career as an opera singer and became engaged to a fellow student, Henry Burnett, with the same ambition. Burnett, however, developed religious scruples that made him turn against the theatre, and Fanny was docile enough to accept his verdict. Dickens remained devoted to her, but he was contemptuous of his brother-in-law and more than once referred to him as an imbecile for his bigotry and prejudice.

Another of Fanny's student friends, John Hullah, collaborated with Dickens on an operetta, *The Village Coquettes*, performed in 1836, the same year that *The Strange Gentleman* was put on. Both had moderate success, but his dramatic writing was so completely eclipsed by *Pickwick* that there was no doubt about his future direction. Ironically, once he had abandoned any idea of writing for the stage himself, his novels were adapted one after another, in countless versions and almost always without permission or profit for him. He would sometimes stumble on one of these adaptations and was observed rolling on the floor of his box in mock agony at what had been made of his work. Yet he bore curiously little malice; his pleasure in the theatre made him view even its gross failings with tolerance. And within less than a decade, busy and successful as he was, he began to get up his own amateur theatricals on a lavish scale.

The Frozen Deep was a continuation of this long run of theatrical ventures, organized up to – and often beyond – the standard of professional productions, Dickens involving himself in every detail of the business, script, casting, carpentry, costumes, programmes, lighting, music, even publicity. He co-opted and marshalled friends, family and professionals with irresistible force; and those who left a record of the experience seem to have found it enjoyable and extraordinarily impressive. In the last months of his life he said that his great dream was to be an actor-manager, with supreme control of a theatre in all its aspects; both the amateur productions and his readings owed something to this dream. Yet his warmth towards the stage did not lead him to sentimentalize it, either in his writing or in life. When he described a theatrical troupe in *Nickleby*, it was done with good humour – they are likeable people – but no glossing over their falsehood and absurdity, or their ineptitude as performers. When his daughter Katey told him she had been offered the opportunity of earning good money as an actress, he warned her off as too sensitive to be able to bear the life: 'Although there are nice people on the stage, there are some who would make your hair stand on end,' he told her.[7]

With a man so versed in the theatre as Dickens, the Ternans might expect to feel at home – to a degree but not entirely. A certain awe was in order, too, because he was a great man, and as famous as any in England. For the past twenty-five years – since before the births of Nelly, Maria or Fanny – he had been the supreme entertainer of the nation. Pickwick, Sam Weller, Mrs Gamp, Oliver Twist, Tiny Tim and Little Nell were all household names, signifying laughter or tears wherever they were invoked, through all classes of society. Even the illiterate knew Dickens through the theatre.

Dickens was to rehearse his new ladies himself. From early August he spent more time in London than at his Kentish country house, Gad's Hill Place, where the children remained with their Aunt Georgina and their mother, who was not well. His London dwelling,

Tavistock House, had been stripped for the summer, making plenty of room in which to work: a very imposing place on the Bedford Estate in Bloomsbury, a few blocks south of Euston Station. The Ternans had been sent their parts to study at home. When they presented themselves for their first rehearsal, they found themselves in a large, light, very clean, dust-sheeted house and face to face with a most businesslike man. It was plain from the start that he knew exactly what he was about professionally.

Dickens was physically rather slight; but his power and energy more than compensated, enabling at least one woman who acted with him to see in him the 'complete beauty of manliness'.[8] He met new acquaintances with a remarkably keen gaze, usually credited to the intensity of a great writer, in fact more attributable to short sight. He did not wear glasses; it was part of his dandy's streak, which appeared in his cravats, his beautifully cut trousers, his white jackets and velvet waistcoats, his looped gold watch-chain. Dickens, like Mrs Ternan, was formed by the Regency and kept some of its traits; he always favoured coloured plumage over the black frock-coated aspect of true Victorian man. And although the long curls of his youth were coarsening and thinning, and a moustache and beard now covered his lip and chin, there was nothing patriarchal about these, rather a hint of the raffish and piratical; he didn't look or seem old. He held himself as straight as a soldier and moved with a dancer's agility; his step was quick, light and precise.

The Ternans saw that everything about him was decisive, orderly, clean-cut, from his personal appearance and domestic arrangements to his manner of conducting a rehearsal. He had a neat little box of notes and gave his instructions absolutely clearly. He was exactly punctual in starting and finishing work, and expected as much of everyone else, which was fortunately how Mrs Ternan had brought up her daughters. At the same time he was full of high spirits and as attentive to the Ternans as though they had been guests rather than workers; and he never failed to arrange refreshments for them whether at Tavistock House or the Gallery of Illustrations, where they were rehearsing for most of the 17th, 18th and 19th August.[9]

By then he had changed his mind about the part of Uncle John and decided he must play it after all, for fear the public would be disappointed. Possibly, too, he found that he enjoyed working with his new pupils more than he had expected. His energy never flagged; he made rehearsals more like a game than work, but a game played with great intensity and absorption. All the Ternans were irresistibly caught up in the flow of his plans and his imagination.

As a novelist he was naturally curious about them, and how they lived, how they managed, a houseful of brave little women alone, unprotected, unguided. Dickens could read as well as anyone the signs of faded bonnets, carefully mended gloves and worn shoes, and he was quickly taken with these girls, as young and fresh and gifted as his own daughters, but fatherless, penniless. He found out at once that they lived in a rubbishy little house in an unwholesome suburb, struggled in and out of the West End, were forced to play parts their respectable mother could not want her daughters to appear in – parts no father could want his daughters to appear in. Yet they were so brave, so ready to laugh and sing, as though nothing frightened them; and how they worked! They had hardly been to school, but they had worked all their lives, had read everything they could lay their hands on, and knew a great deal more than most of the young women Dickens came across. Being actresses, they knew both the things that were written down and the other things that were never written. Or so he supposed. The ambivalence of actresses, the fact that so many of them felt able to break the rules of society without bearing any apparent mark of their guilt – quite the contrary – was precisely what made them so attractive.

Of course he knew many actresses already, had known some for years, like Emmeline Montague, Fanny Kelly, Fanny Stirling and Mary Ann Keeley and her daughters; but he had never been so close to a whole family of them. A whole nest of singing birds. There was a fascination in their blend of knowledge and innocence. In due course he must have gone to inspect Park Cottage, climbed the awkwardly twisted little steps to the narrow door, cast his practised glance through its few small rooms and determined inwardly that they must move to a more convenient house as soon as he could persuade them.[10] He was intrigued by each of them, the dignified, hard-working widowed mother; quick, clever, ambitious Fanny, not at all frightened of him; dark-eyed Maria, who shifted so suddenly into laughter or tears; and the youngest, the child with the head of curls, who could not remember her father – who could have been his own daughter: Ellen.

Only not Ellen. They all called her Nelly. Little Nell: the name of his most famous heroine, the beautiful, doomed child who, like this girl, had travelled across England with show-people. Dickens was instructed to call her Nelly, too. As he asked her history, and she began to tell it, he made a discovery that can't have failed to stir him. Nelly, alone of the sisters, had been born in Rochester; and Rochester was the city where his own imagination had begun to flower. In Rochester he had first seen Shakespeare and panto-mime; had written his own first play; had sung in his childish voice with his own sister Fanny, now dead. Rochester was enshrined as the happy place of his own childhood. He had left it fifteen years before Nelly appeared on the scene, but the coincidence was still extraordinary.

Dickens was forty-five. His career as a writer had been one of brilliant and unbroken success from his early twenties onwards. He was the father of nine living children and the master of two establishments staffed with their full complements of servants. Tavistock House had a drawing room that could take 300 guests. Gad's Hill, a solid old Kentish house standing on a hill above Rochester, had been newly acquired in the fulfilment of a boyhood ambition.

He took his holidays where and when he chose, renting houses at Broadstairs or Boulogne; for months at a time he might install the whole family in France, or Italy, or Switzerland. His earning powers were prodigious, and he knew how to manage his money. He supported his widowed mother in a separate household and was often approached for financial help by his improvident brothers Frederick and Augustus, both of whom were better at getting children than earning money. Proud of his pre-eminence in the family, he was also sometimes grimly amused by the obligations it brought with it.

His fame as a writer went with him wherever he travelled. He had toured America and Canada with his wife and been fêted in

Nelly's mother, Fanny Jarman, as a young actress, splendidly
ringleted. She was the child of strolling players, her stage
career beginning in 1804 when she was two. Her 'beautiful
person, commanding stature, rich and flexible voice' were
acclaimed in England, Ireland, Scotland and America, which
she toured in the 1830s on a working honeymoon.

Nelly's father, Thomas Ternan, born in 1790, was the son of a Dublin grocer; he came to England to make his way as a romantic actor. He had a passion for Byron and wrote verse himself, but he never equalled his wife's success in the theatre. She is shown below acting Gertrude to the great tragedian Macready's Hamlet; Macready admired and befriended her, but he declared that Ternan would never 'shed lustre on the theatrical profession'. The first of the Ternans' three daughters, Fanny, was born during their American tour in 1835; after their return to England and the birth of two more daughters, Maria and Nelly, he became a theatre manager in Newcastle upon Tyne.

It was standard practice for actresses to appear on stage with their own babies. Mrs Ternan herself was carried on as a tiny child, and she did the same with each of her daughters in turn. This is her colleague, the great comic actress Dora Jordan, as she appeared in the popular part of Cora in Sheridan's *Pizarro*; the baby here is one of her many children by the future king, William IV.

The life of a company manager and his family was not always as riotous as suggested by Cruikshank's 1841 drawing of a 'Theatrical Fun-Dinner', but a successful Benefit evening might call for a celebration of this kind. Note the Infant Prodigy standing on the table to the left, with sword and plumed helmet. Fanny Ternan was just such an acclaimed child performer from the age of three, and her younger sisters followed in her footsteps.

(*Left*) Maria, dressed as a fairy.

(*Above right*) Daumier's drawing suggests the view from the stage into the sort of audience that would be attracted to *Atalanta*, a scene from which is shown below; it was a burlesque in which Nelly had her first adult part when she was eighteen, at the Haymarket Theatre in 1857.

"THE TEMPLE OF HYMEN," FROM THE NEW CLASSIC STORY OF "ATALANTA; OR, THE THREE GOLDEN APPLES," AT THE HAYMARKET THEATRE.—(SEE NEXT PAGE.)

The view of the theatre as a flesh market is still more nakedly
expressed outside in the street, as evidenced by this scene after the
show in 1860, where gentlemen and prostitutes are making their
deals in the Haymarket. The cartoon comes from Henry Mayhew's
study of London life. Eminent Victorians like Gladstone and
Dickens were simultaneously horrified and fascinated by the vice of
the streets, and Dickens worked for several years as an enthusiastic
reformer of fallen girls; his intimate knowledge of attempts to
police their activities made him especially indignant when Maria
and Nelly were mistaken for prostitutes by the police.

Nelly in 1858: the earliest known photograph, taken in Florence, where the Italian photographic process, unlike the English, did not darken her blonde hair. Compare her appearance with Dickens's description of Lucie Manette: 'a short, slight pretty figure, a quantity of golden hair, a pair of blue eyes that met his own with an inquiring look, and a forehead with a singular capacity . . . of lifting and knitting itself into an expression that was not quite one of perplexity, or wonder, or alarm'.

As in so many stories of three sisters, one of the
Ternans was wise (Fanny, *right*), one merry (Maria,
left) and the youngest endowed with a fatal beauty, as
well as the gift of being able to transform herself at will.
They loved and supported one another throughout
their lives.

Edinburgh. In France, where English writers are never sure of a welcome, he was acclaimed by the critics; his entire works were in process of translation for a splendid French edition. He was the author, so far, of eleven novels, not to mention the stupendously successful Christmas stories, as well as half-owner and active editor of *Household Words*.

Dickens struck admiration into almost all his contemporaries. Even Thackeray, his rival, acknowledged that he was at the top of the tree; he was 'the great Dickens', 'abominably coarse, vulgar and happy'.[11] He was not born a gentleman, like Thackeray; his grandmother had been a servant in a great house, his father a perpetual embarrassment with his debts and sponging. Dickens had made himself virtually out of nothing. Friends like Lord Jeffrey or Macready noted that his dinners could be over sumptuous, the sign of a parvenu, perhaps, but more simply an aspect of his immense geniality. He was much lionized yet resisted the invitations of the great, preferring his own comfortable circle. Family parties, games and theatricals which included the children were what he enjoyed; he would dance Sir Roger de Coverley till the pianist fell back exhausted. Sometimes his conviviality overboiled, and he might grab at a lady harder than she had reason to expect; on one occasion, on the pier at Broadstairs, a young woman he had whirled into an impromptu dance by the rough sea had her dress soaked through as she struggled. He could tease, he could retreat into a black mood, and he had a temper that came to the boil quickly. But more often he was sweet-natured; the actress Helen Faucit remembered him helping her out discreetly with a whispered clue in a game of charades. He was a kind man, with little malice; justifiably proud of his achievements, boyish in his enthusiasms, always eager to help others.

Dickens loved children; he played with them and gave them absurd nicknames; his wife believed that babies delighted him, and she was right, up to a point; only they had produced more than he wanted. He viewed their frequent arrival with a helpless, humorous resignation, as though they were a visitation from God rather than a consequence of his own actions. When she was expecting their ninth child, their old friend Lord Jeffrey wrote affectionately to Dickens, 'as I would to a younger brother', urging him not to get her pregnant again (though not apparently offering any advice on how to avoid it). Dickens, curious and alert as he was to scientific advances – Catherine had been given chloroform at the birth of Henry in 1849 – does not appear to have investigated the matter of birth control, unless the arrival of yet another son, Edward Bulwer Lytton (Plorn), in 1852 prompted some attempt to do so. At least the last five years had seen no further additions to the nursery.

As a father he was devoted and strict. He took his children on forays to toy shops, taught them games – Dumb Crambo, Twenty Questions, Proverbs – and performed conjuring tricks for them. Christmas was celebrated *chez* Dickens with as much verve as any child could ever wish. He also inspected their rooms daily for tidiness, and confiscated his sons' cricket bats and balls if they allowed their clothes to become too unkempt; his son Alfred remembered all his life the scolding he got for brushing his coat in the wrong place – the dining room. His own cleanliness was almost fetishistic; he took a cold bath or shower every day and had his clothes kept impeccably. Dickens was puzzled by his boys' shortcomings and pleased by any effort to put them right. He went to considerable lengths to cure Frank of a stammer by reading Shakespeare with him every morning. He also taught Henry, the brightest, shorthand. Yet as one son after another failed to measure up to his own strength of character, he grew more irritable with them. The girls were pretty well exempt from criticism, being girls, and only two in number, and Katey certainly intelligent. Charley, the eldest boy, was also bolstered against his father by being put through Eton at the insistence of his godmother, Angela Coutts; he did not do well enough to go to a university, but in 1857, when he was twenty, he was at least keeping afloat at Baring's Bank. Dickens was fond of him; but a grown-up son at home was also a perpetual reminder that time was passing and that his own youth was irretrievable; and behind this thought another nagged, of how his huge family had failed him, of the 'one happiness I have missed in life, and one friend and companion I have never made'.[12]

Even at the height of his enthusiasm for family life, Dickens had absented himself frequently in order to pursue his own interests. For years he had made a habit of going out riding by day and to the theatre by night, with his men friends. They also had a walking club and regularly took dinner out of town, at Greenwich, or Jack Straw's on Hampstead Heath, or at the Star and Garter in Richmond. The friends included John Forster, his chief literary adviser, who shared his enthusiasm for the theatre; Daniel Maclise, the painter; Douglas Jerrold, the playwright; Mark Lemon of *Punch*; and other hard-working journalists, artists and writers, among whom Wilkie Collins was a new favourite from a younger generation. Collins appeared on the scene in 1850. He was a bachelor and regarded himself as a connoisseur where pleasure was concerned; and he seems to have acted as Mephistopheles to Dickens's Faust, organizing sybaritic nights out and accompanying him on trips to Paris for a taste of its sophisticated '*diableries*'.

Dickens was also a solitary walker. He often set off alone at night and sometimes stayed out until morning. In this way he came to know the whole of London: the grimmest parts of the East End, regarded by most as impenetrable alien territory; the docks and the river from Hammersmith to Greenwich; slums various, around Seven Dials, around Somers Town, around the Borough; the Hampstead Road of his boyhood, passing through Euston, Mornington Crescent, Camden and Kentish Towns; and the miles of new suburbs eating up fields, market gardens, farms and the old green lanes to the north and south. He said these walks helped him to plan his next day's writing, which was certainly true, but there was something else at work, too. For all his geniality, Dickens was a man who did not wish to be known and summed up by anyone. He needed a private existence in which he could cease to be either the convivial friend or the well-organized father and become nothing but a watching eye, a listening ear, a dreaming mind.

From the early 1850s he had made what he called a 'gipsey camp' in two rooms above the *Household Words* office at 16 Wellington Street, off the Strand, so that he could be free to remain there overnight when he chose. It was convenient for his nocturnal walks, his bachelor dinners and also his clubs, the Athenaeum and the Garrick; still more so for his frequent visits to the theatres clustered in the area – the Lyceum, the Adelphi, the Olympic, Covent Garden and Drury Lane – as well as the Surrey and the Victoria on the other side of Waterloo Bridge. His letters and other personal writings are sprinkled with references to these theatre-going habits: a note to Madame Celeste, manager of the Adelphi, asking for a box; a complaint to William Farren, manager of the Olympic, about being given a seat in the stalls already occupied when he went in, late and alone, to see the burlesque on a Friday night;[13] a vivid description of a walk through Bow Street, Longacre and Drury Lane on a wet winter evening, when the theatrical suppliers and ticket vendors are closed down, on his way to Hoxton, where the Britannia Theatre under Sam and Sara Lane is putting on pantomimes to huge, appreciative local audiences.[14] Out of this solitude – the single man moving through the oceanic London crowd – he made the world of his books.

If domesticity meant less to Dickens than he liked to suggest, and if he had rather more of the Regency buck in him and less of the Victorian paterfamilias than is usually believed, it must also be remembered that his adult life was lived out during a period of acute hypocrisy in these matters. The domestic virtues were loudly proclaimed, public displays of bad behaviour – such as royal princes consorting with actresses – were no longer tolerated, and while prostitution of every kind flourished, discretion, or hypocrisy, was required from all but the lowest social class. Dickens's response to this hypocrisy was never simple. He liked the idea of the neat little home and the neat little wife and mother, particularly when rounding off his plots; but it was not the only idea he liked. Recently a letter to his friend, the painter Daniel Maclise, has come to light which suggests that even in the early years of his marriage his interest in the sexual underworld may not have been purely that of an observer; he urges Maclise to join him in Broadstairs for a break, promising 'conveniences of *all kinds* at Margate (do you take me?) and I know where they live'.[15] Unless Dickens meant the ponies on the sands, living conveniences could mean one thing only in this context.

Throughout his life he had friends of both sexes who flouted the conventions. Wilkie Collins is the best known, with his two illicit households, but there were plenty more. The divorced Mrs Frances Elliot, whom he advised in her matrimonial problems, was another. He was intimate with the Count d'Orsay and Lady Blessington, whose reputations – whether justly or unjustly – were deeply tarnished. He was on friendly terms with Fanny Kelly, who had an illegitimate daughter living with her, and with Fanny Stirling, separated from her husband and living with another man. Julia Fortescue, who took part in his amateur acting group, had a large family by Lord Gardner, whom she was able to marry only after the death of his wife in 1856. Privately Dickens accepted all this; publicly he kept up a strict front and never felt strong enough to defy the prevailing social codes. When, for instance, he learned (on a bachelor trip to Paris in 1850) that the highly regarded French actress, Mademoiselle Denain, whom he had previously entertained in his home in London, was known to be the mistress of the British ambassador, Lord Normanby (a married man), he immediately wrote to Catherine instructing her to apologize to all the ladies who had been present when she dined at their house.[16]

The same taboos prevailed in his writing. He might protest to Forster, as he did in 1856, of the partial and unnatural portraits he was forced to give in his novels because of the tyranny of 'your morality'; but he made no attempt to break out of the tyranny, and the young men of his later novels are as emasculated as those of the early ones. There's little change in his sweet, silly, plump, fluttering young women either. Paradoxically, the most alluring of his heroines is Estella (in *Great Expectations*, not written until 1861), who is made frigid by her upbringing as part of the plot. All the others are inoculated against sexuality by their creator before their stories begin; they are about as tempting as wax fruit.

This is a commonplace of Dickens criticism. It fits oddly with what is known of his relations with real women. Leaving aside his own family – an insistently pleasure-loving mother, a notably fertile wife, the two idealized sisters-in-law, Mary who died at seventeen and Georgina who made herself into a super-servant – a whole category of other young women he knew and studied to the point of obsession is missing from his work.

Dickens expended an enormous amount of time and energy working with the delinquents – or more properly the victims – of the Victorian sexual system, and he went out of his way to be understanding and helpful to them. The interest began early. As a young man serving on the jury at a coroner's inquest, he helped to get the sentence on an unmarried girl accused of killing her baby lightened.[17] He sent comforts round to the prison during the trial and insisted that medical evidence suggesting the child could have died naturally should be properly attended to; and he appears to have followed up the fate of the girl. He was still concerning himself with this sort of problem in the last years of his life: on his visit to America in 1867 he gave money to a chambermaid in his New York hotel to enable her to leave for the West with her illegitimate child.[18]

Between those two cases there were many more. In 1848 he helped Mrs Gaskell to arrange for a sixteen-year-old girl, who had been 'seduced' at fourteen by a surgeon with the connivance of her dressmaker employer, to be saved (in theory at any rate) by being sent to Australia in the care of a kindly couple. He was able to help her in this way because he was already involved in similar efforts in London. This work for young prostitutes covered many years in the middle of his life, from 1846 to 1857, during which, with the help of Miss Coutts, he established a refuge or Home, Urania Cottage, at Shepherd's Bush, intended to reclaim them and help them to emigrate.* He interviewed and selected many of the girls himself, working with the governors of Bridewell, Pentonville and Tothill Fields prisons, and visiting Ragged Schools for likely candidates. It is obvious that he was fascinated by their appearances, their manners, their histories, and noted down his observations and talks with them with relish. He made frequent visits and involved himself closely in all the details of the organization of Urania Cottage, from the question of the girls' clothing – he favoured bright colours – to whether they should be encouraged to think of marriage after their reformation: he thought they should be, whereas Miss Coutts took the conventional view that they should not.

Many of the girls had already served prison sentences. Some

---

* By a nicely ironic touch, Miss Coutts's enormous fortune came to her through a bequest from a notorious (and exceptionally good-natured) Regency actress, Harriot Mellon, who married her grandfather, the banker Thomas Coutts, in his extreme old age, inherited his entire fortune, went on to marry the Duke of St Albans, and then returned the money to the Coutts family. Miss Coutts, later Baroness Burdett-Coutts, devoted herself to good works, many of them under the guidance of Dickens.

were hardly more than children, sold into prostitution by their families. Some genuinely didn't know their own ages; at least one had concealed the birth of a child, for which she had to stand trial. Many were lousy on admittance; one so covered in sores that she had to be sent to hospital. Some trembled when he spoke to them, but little Sesina, he noted, 'would corrupt a Nunnery in a fortnight'. Emma Lea was violent and defiant, but Mary Anne Church was a smooth liar, all too good at deceiving chaplains, and he was not surprised when she returned to a life of crime. Isabella Gordon caused Dickens great anxiety; when he spoke to her about her misbehaviour, he was not sure whether she looked white from anger or contrition; she was expelled, then pardoned, then expelled again. On one occasion Dickens recorded how he followed a girl who had been expelled up the road towards Notting Hill. It's a curious picture, the great author slouching along secretly behind the anxious, angry little reject. Sometimes he worried that the very men who recommended girls to the refuge were implicated in their fates. If he ever questioned his own motives at all, he left no record of that anxiety.

This sort of practical work, whatever its origins within his psyche, was greatly to his credit, the response of a decent man to a society that worked a cruel double standard. The decency appears in his writing here and there, though in a curious form. Dickens spoke up in his journalism for a kinder attitude to erring women and boldly published Mrs Gaskell's story of a Manchester prostitute, 'Lizzie Leigh', in the first issue of *Household Words*; and in his novels he invited compassion rather than censure for women disgraced for sexual reasons, from Nancy in *Oliver Twist* and the smart girl at the race meeting who buys flowers from Little Nell to Lady Dedlock with her guilty secret in *Bleak House*. But his presentation draws entirely on stereotypes of the Fallen Woman. Nancy shows the self-loathing the good reader required of a prostitute; beyond that, she is null. None of the knowledge Dickens picked up from his encounters with such girls and women was ever allowed to get anywhere near his fiction. It's as though an automatic shutter came down when he approached the subject.

Imagine what he could have done with the story of Caroline Maynard, if he had felt able to tell it. Dickens was involved in trying to help her for eighteen months, between the autumn of 1854 and the summer of 1856. She was an unmarried mother in her early thirties, working as a prostitute. She was also strikingly unlike any of the Fallen Women of his novels. Nothing about her – not her background, not her appearance, not her character – resembles in any way those weeping, breast-beating, clothes-tearing, passionately remorseful sinners. He described her as 'rather small, and young-looking; but pretty, and gentle, and has a very good head'.[19] He found her manner exceedingly natural and decided that 'there can never have been much evil in her, apart from the early circumstances that directed her steps the wrong way'. Consulting Miss Coutts as to how best to help Caroline, he insisted that Urania Cottage would be quite unsuitable for her, as her manner, character and experiences were altogether different from those of the girls installed there. He went on:

It is a very remarkable case. I very much wish you would see her, and judge for yourself of its peculiarity. There is nothing about her from which you could suppose she had come to this. You might see her and her brother a thousand times – you might meet them in the street, every day in the year – and only notice them as brother and sister who were no doubt living together and taking care of one another. I cannot get the picture of her, out of my head.[20]

It was through the brother that Caroline had come to Dickens's attention. Frederick Maynard had been trying to get work as a ticket-seller at the Olympic Theatre to augment his slender income as an architect's draughtsman, but he had no luck, though perhaps it was at the theatre he heard of or saw Dickens and thought of applying to him. Maynard's architectural work brought him only £1 15s. a week, and with this, he told Dickens in a letter, he was trying to support his sister and her child. Dickens agreed to meet him. The young man burst into tears as he told his story.

He was only twenty-three. Caroline, ten years older than her brother, had lived for nearly a decade with a businessman, to whom she had borne a daughter, now two years old. The man was either married already or unwilling to marry her; and although they had lived in a seemingly conventional ménage, when his business failed, he simply abandoned her and disappeared. She had no money and felt she could make no personal application to anyone under the circumstances. Caroline was devoted to her small daughter. According to Frederick, she had gone on the streets and remained a prostitute ever since, as this was the only way of supporting the child.

Dickens's first suggestion was the standard colonial solution he had offered for little Em'ly and Martha in *David Copperfield*, for the inmates of Urania Cottage, and for Mrs Gaskell's Manchester protegée: that Caroline should emigrate to Australia or the Cape. Frederick took this to mean she would have to leave her daughter behind, and he told Dickens that nothing would make her part with the child. Then in November 1854 Caroline wrote directly to Dickens. She was living in South Kensington, at 23 Bute Street, presumably a lodging house. She wrote:

> My Brother has acquainted me with the kind interest you expressed in my unhappy affairs, and of the hopelessness of my securing a situation in England. Altho' as you may imagine I should prefer remaining in this Country, still for my Child's sake I should gratefully accept any honourable opportunity of redeeming my position, even to the breaking of all ties that hold me here – I have no words to thank you for your goodness in listening to my miserable tale, and the hope you have given me of at least one way of escape and which appears to be the only alternative – Should it lie in your power to aid me in this matter you will confer a lasting obligation on me . . .[21]

Dickens called on her in December and found she was indeed prepared to go to South Africa if necessary, with her child, in order to retrieve the past. But the brother and sister were deeply attached to one another and dreaded separation.

Dickens's interest was clear, but Miss Coutts had to deliver her approval and the money to help Caroline. Christmas, with its usual family festivities, intervened, and in January 1855 he had an anxious letter from Caroline, to which he replied reassuringly with a renewed promise that he was indeed trying to do something. In March he asked her to come to Tavistock House with her brother for another talk. An invitation to his home must have been the strongest indication that he regarded her as a socially acceptable person, though one caught in a 'perplexed and complicated' situation – as he explained again to Miss Coutts, who appears to have been reluctant to act – and not a pariah. The gulf between this attitude and the one he adopted in his fiction is striking; evidently Caroline had a dignity and self-possession unknown among the fallen women of literature.

The trial solution he offered her was also less absolute, more daring and more humane than might have been expected. Caroline was to be installed in a house in a district of London where she was not known and could safely take on a new identity. Dickens was confident that this manoeuvre could work – that it was possible to become someone else simply by moving from one part of town to another. (Later he was to demonstrate the trick himself.) The house rented for Caroline would be furnished – you can't help wondering whether Dickens chose the furniture and decorations himself, as he had done for his parents when he moved them – and she would be able to earn a living by letting out furnished lodgings. She would appear as that most respectable figure in Victorian London, a widowed landlady. Dickens had ascertained that 'Mrs Thompson' was a good housekeeper, had received a decent plain education and 'acquired accomplishments' during her years with her protector. There was nothing gaudy or silly about her.

In the midst of dealing with Caroline Maynard's problems, he received a jolt from a very different sort of woman. The girl he had loved as a young man, parted from bitterly and not seen again, Maria Beadnell (now Mrs Winter), wrote to him. He was painfully stirred, and still more painfully disillusioned when he came face to face with her: virtuous and respectable but now charmless. Mrs Winter was firmly excluded from further intimacy and her middle age cruelly immortalized as the fat, giggling Flora Finching in *Little Dorrit*: she made a notable contrast with the culpable Caroline, who remained quiet and charming but could never be written about truthfully.

He kept in touch with Caroline, both by letter and meetings. He took his family to Paris in the autumn of 1855, where they remained until the following spring; but he made constant journeys back to England during these months. Meanwhile Caroline struggled with her new role as landlady with little success. Perhaps the district chosen was unsuitable – we don't know where it was – and there was simply not enough demand for rooms; or she may not have known how to go about it. Possibly she found she disliked being a landlady almost as much as being a prostitute; however respectable it was, it also demanded toughness which may not have come easily to a gentle and anxious young woman.

By May 1856, when Dickens brought his family back to Tavistock House, Caroline had decided she could not make her lodging house work. She and Dickens agreed that she would give notice, sell the furniture and, with the £150 raised from the sale, emigrate to Canada after all. She hoped to find work there as a companion, housekeeper, superintendent of children, or anything which would allow her to be with her daughter. Dickens made a final appeal to Miss Coutts to think of some way of helping her in Canada, and said he himself was trying among the Canada Railway people, though he was doubtful if they would be able to do anything. Once again he insisted on her virtues: 'She writes very well, is a good plain accountant, and generally neat and handy.'[22]

This is his last known reference to Caroline Maynard Thompson or her brother. Two things about the episode are especially striking. One is the sheer amount of time and energy Dickens was prepared to put into this single case during a period when he was writing *Little Dorrit* in monthly instalments, dealing with an emotional upheaval of his own and making frequent cross-Channel trips. Another is the straightforwardness of his approach. Caroline appears in his description as a credible human being, small, neat, pretty, efficient, a good housekeeper, able to keep her own accounts and devoted to her brother as well as her child. In short, she was not a Fallen Woman but just the sort of young woman he admired. She had been driven to prostitution for one clear reason only: because she had trusted a man who failed to make proper provision for her.

Although he would not, or could not, draw a realistic portrait of a Caroline Maynard or a Mary Anne Church, the years of his involvement with these young women also produced novels in which his humour was increasingly subordinated to social analysis and criticism, to a degree that nettled the establishment and also some intellectuals who thought he had no right to diagnose the ills of the nation.* The first of the three, *Bleak House* (1853), put on display an England in which the connecting tissue of society is provided by disease, bad drains, bad housing, bad education, a bad legal system and sexual hypocrisy. The plot is centred on an illegitimate child, and a woman who faces social disgrace should the existence of the child be revealed; in fact, she chooses to die rather than be so disgraced. The child is raised with the burden of her mother's sin on her shoulders, and she is saved partly by the kindness of a whimsical guardian and partly by her own virtues. These virtues are so low key that most readers find her exasperating and the 'happy ending' falsely contrived. *Bleak House* is essentially a tragic story peopled by a cast of comic characters, and from now on this became the hallmark of Dickens's work.

The next book, *Hard Times* (1854), dedicated itself to declaring that imagination, relaxation and entertainment are all essential ingredients of civilized life, even and especially for the poor, including the factory fodder of the midlands and north. The entertainment may take the form of the circus, poetry, the theatre or any other imaginative art; Dickens's message is that if people are not amused, they will become not merely dull and desiccated but brutal and evil. *Hard Times* has another bleak ending: although its heroine draws back from the abyss of adultery, she is left facing a peculiarly grim future, still a young and passionate woman but with no prospect of love or happiness.

Little Dorrit (1857) again cut a cross-section through London society. In part it is a satirical attack on the greed and corruption Dickens observed around him, with the Marshalsea debtors' prison, remembered so well from his childhood, as its central symbol; but it also draws a contrast between the mean and rigid world of the hero's supposed mother, a joyless religious bigot, and the spontaneous and generous world of his real mother, who is a singer, sweet but imprudent, and made to suffer for it. The dichotomy is the same as in *Hard Times*. The real mother, however, is kept entirely out of sight, killed off before the book begins. Dickens does not

---

* For example, J. F. Stephen held Dickens to task, in his review of *Little Dorrit*, for pouring 'contempt on all the institutions of the country'.

accept the challenge of presenting her as a person rather than as a symbol, and her behaviour is tidied up for the purposes of family fiction; she is said to have gone through a form of marriage before becoming a mother, and she dies conveniently soon afterwards, so that she can remain a pure, sweet, simple memory.

There is another female artist in the story who is neither sweet nor simple, and who in a sense avenges the dead singer. This is Fanny Dorrit, who has learnt the lessons of the world so well that she despises her own art, regards her fellow dancers as common, and makes her way into rich society with ruthless skill. Fanny attracts the attention of a well-off young man, rejects his initial dishonourable advances and so brings him to the point of proposing marriage. The young man's mother, Mrs Merdle, alarmed at the thought of this *mésalliance*, visits Fanny with the idea of simultaneously bribing her to give him up and warning her that if she *does* marry him, he will be cut off without a penny. Fanny's view of the young man is that he is 'almost an idiot', and that she has no wish to marry him in any event. She tells Mrs Merdle so and adds that her family is as good as his, only slightly spoiling the effect by accepting gifts of jewellery and dresses. Mrs Merdle voices her scorn of a professional dancer: 'I pointed out . . . the impossibility of the Society in which we moved recognizing the Society in which she moved – though charming, I have no doubt.' Mrs Merdle knows that contempt and social abhorrence are the correct responses to professional theatrical ladies; but so does Fanny.

Dickens makes Fanny Dorrit into something of a monster, so bent on avenging herself against Mrs Merdle that she does later marry her son, dooming herself to a life of riches, vacuity and permanent warfare with her mother-in-law (which may indeed have been the fate of some actresses who married into Society). But there is no suggestion that Fanny's defects of character are part of her professional armour, or that Dickens holds the stage responsible for them. In fact, the one backstage scene in which she is shown with her fellow dancers ('young ladies' or 'darlings', depending on who is addressing them) is written with quite striking warmth; you believe it is drawn from life. Fanny Dorrit is made mercenary not by the theatre but by her experience of poverty and humiliation; and as Dickens's young fictional women go, she is almost believable.

It is Fanny's younger sister, Amy ('Little Dorrit' herself), who is mysteriously immune to the experiences that corrupt Fanny. Amy is a practical girl rather than an artist, and although she has been born and bred inside the Marshalsea Prison, her moral sense is flawless; so much so that she becomes a touchstone for everyone else in the book. Still a child, she supports her family. She is thoroughly familiar with the seedy, seamy side of London yet walks through it unscathed.

Dickens finds it easier to locate this virtue in a little girl than a woman, and he keeps her looking like a child even when she is fully grown: as 'a woman . . . of not less than two and twenty, she might have been passed in the street for little more than half that age,' he writes. It has been suggested that Little Dorrit is also little Dickens, fixed for ever as the good child at the centre of an evil world, which is how he remembered the worst part of his own boyhood. This innocent child is a recurring figure in his novels up to *Little Dorrit*, though after this it appears no more. When Dickens came to write *Great Expectations*, three years after *Little Dorrit*, he had become a different man and drew for the first time a child who is realistically vulnerable and flawed: not innocent but easily corrupted through conceit, ambition, snobbery and sick, obsessive infatuation.

But *Great Expectations* was still in the future. There is something else in *Little Dorrit* that has a bearing on Dickens's state of mind in 1857. The reader senses that Amy has an extra significance for her creator. She is not just the innocent child but also the child bride of middle-aged fantasy, the unlooked-for reprieve, the new start in life for the hero whose own youth lies behind him. When Little Dorrit loses her father, she finds a husband who becomes a second father to her. He is eighteen years older than her and reluctant to believe in her love. And when finally he acknowledges it, Dickens puts it like this: 'He took her in his arms, as if she had been his daughter.'

As though to match his latest fiction, he was now confronted with a real girl who could be seen as the embodiment of two of his themes. Nelly, her sisters and mother were all actresses; they inhabited the world of art and imagination, had the joyous freedom of manners that went with it, and for their pains they were slighted and despised by conventional people. At the same time the theatre was part of the seamy side of London, in which this young, fresh, fair girl, living in poverty, earning her own bread, obliged to walk through the dark, corrupting streets and appear before sometimes ignoble audiences, seemed to preserve a childlike innocence. She was fatherless. She had been born in the same year as his own daughter Katey and was stepping into Katey's part in *Uncle John*. Dickens had an exact memory for his own phrases. 'He took her in his arms, as if she had been his daughter' may have rung alarmingly in his mind when, if only for the purposes of the drama, he did just that.

7

Manchester, Doncaster and Scandal
1857–1858

A bright, penniless girl of eighteen who found herself admired by a rich older man had good reason to be excited. The roles laid down by her society were suddenly reversed: having been always power-less, she now began to be in command. In Nelly's case the man she might command was also brilliant and famous, a charming and entertaining companion, and in a position to transform her life, which in any case held few counter-attractions. The trip to Man-chester may have been the most exciting thing that had yet happened to her.

The whole company of *The Frozen Deep*, with various wives and families – both Mrs Dickens and her sister Georgina were included in the party – took the Manchester train from Euston on the morning of 20 August. They filled several specially reserved car-riages and were all in high spirits, at any rate according to Francesco Berger, the young composer and conductor of the inci-dental music, who was in the carriage next to 'the Manager' himself and was the only person present who left an account of the trip. Dickens's theatrical expeditions were organized on an im-pressive scale; the Ternans must have felt the contrast with their own usual modest arrangements. No question of lodgings over a shop for them this time. Twenty-three rooms had been taken at the Great Western Hotel, with a special private dining and sitting room for the use of the company. Lavish meals had also been ordered in advance for everyone. Dickens's pleasure in planning menus was celebrated; the beef, pies, tarts, cold fowls, jellies, beer and punch ordered for the suppers that would follow the perform-ances make them sound like schoolboy feasts. In fact, the whole affair seems to have had something of the atmosphere of a school outing. When the train was delayed and there were complaints of hunger, Dickens proposed a game of Conundrums. They had to be passed from window to window on sticks and umbrellas; it sounds dangerous, and produced almost hysterical hilarity. Travel put Dickens into good humour; on other railway journeys we hear of him playing Twenty Questions, singing drinking songs and dancing the hornpipe in a moving carriage, a feat that even a much younger man might hesitate to perform. Catherine, who had travelled all round America, Canada and Europe with him, knew what to expect; she was probably thankful if she did not get a poke in the eye from a Conundrum-bearing walking-stick. Her spirits may have been rather damper than those of the rest of the party.

The performances were scheduled for Friday and Saturday. The Ternans knew the city, but they had never before experienced the delights of a large luxury hotel. Manchester – Cottonopolis, they called it – was crowded to bursting point with visitors from all over the world to an enormous summer exhibition of World Masters of Painting.[1] Dickens was eager to fit in an educational visit; whether he took his company along is not known. He developed an attack of neuralgia in his face on arrival, and was busy supervising the staging and lighting effects on which so much of the show's success depended. His own performance offered him the least worry; he knew how easily he could step inside the skin of the suffering, misunderstood and fundamentally noble Richard Wardour.

The Frozen Deep was written by Wilkie Collins, although it was Dickens who had suggested the plot; he participated enthusiastically in revising the text and supervised the painting of the elaborately realistic scenery and the complicated lighting. Unfortunately it carries no trace of his genius in the dialogue, and to modern readers it's almost impossible to see how it made its appeal. Yet it did, hugely, helped perhaps by its theme of absent suffering men and anxiously awaiting women, which found an echo in so many Victorian households in the heyday of the Empire and the year of the Indian mutiny.* Voyages like those of Darwin with the *Beagle*

---

* Dickens had, only a month before, tearfully but resolutely sent off his sixteen-year-old son Walter to serve in India as a cadet, even as the news of the Mutiny was arriving. Walter died there at the age of twenty-two, without seeing either of his parents again.

and Sir John Franklin to the Arctic naturally aroused tremendous interest and excitement; it was, in fact, the Franklin expedition, which had run into trouble and led to allegations of cannibalism, that provided some of the inspiration for *The Frozen Deep*. Waiting, fearing the worst, and wondering about the state of mind of men under stress was an experience familiar in many families, though you can't help hoping that the young ladies who stayed behind were not all as vacuous as those depicted by Collins.

The curtain rises on a group of these young women in an English country house drawing room. They are chaperoned by their old nurse (Mrs Ternan) and have been cooped up together with nothing to do for three years, while their menfolk make an expedition to the Arctic. The hinge of the plot is provided by Clara (Maria Ternan), wasting away because she realizes that her rejected suitor Richard Wardour (Dickens), a man of erratic temper, may find out that another member of the Arctic party is now engaged to her. She fears that Wardour will seek to murder him out of jealousy. Wardour's parting words to her, she tells her friend Lucy (Nelly), were: 'The time may come when I shall forgive *you*, but the man who has robbed me of you shall rue the day when you and he first met.' Nurse Esther talks of her second sight, which warns her of bloody scenes taking place in the 'the land o' ice and snaw'; 'Oh my bairn, my bairn,' she addresses Clara, 'the stain o' that bluid is on *you*!'

The second act takes us into the ice and snaw, where the explorers are stranded. Two men are needed for a dangerous relief expedition. It is no surprise to find Wardour and his rival Aldersley (Wilkie Collins) are the two chosen. In the last act the ladies have travelled to Newfoundland to seek the men. Wardour enters, half dead and apparently deranged; Clara recognizes him and fears he has murdered Aldersley. Instead he staggers off, to reappear carrying his rival, weak but alive. He blesses the reunited lovers and dies of exhaustion as the curtain falls – a man who has triumphed over his evil tendencies, sacrificed himself and become an example to all. Dickens was so pleased with this role that he used it when he came to write his next novel: Sydney Carton is a variant on Wardour.

Real life proved more complicated. The Manchester performances were a triumphant success. According to Collins, Dickens gave new meaning to the phrase 'he electrified the audience'. His fellow players felt the electricity, too. Maria Ternan was overcome on stage. Dickens's accounts of her storm of emotion, which he described more than once, make her palpable as few of his fictional women are. Perhaps this is why he chose to write about himself in the third person – as Wardour, not Charles Dickens – when he described the effect of the girl holding him in her arms, with tears dropping straight into his mouth, in a letter to Miss Coutts:

At night when she came out of the cave and Wardour recognized her, I never saw anything like the distress and agitation of her face – a very good little pale face, with large black eyes; – it had a natural emotion in it (though it was turned away from the audience) which was quite a study of expression. But when she had to kneel over Wardour dying, and be taken leave of, the tears streamed out of her eyes into his mouth, down his beard, all over his rags – down his arms as he held her by the hair. At the same time she sobbed as if she were breaking her heart, and was quite convulsed with grief. It was of no use for the compassionate Wardour to whisper 'My dear child, it will be over in two minutes – there is nothing the matter – don't be so distressed!' She could only sob out 'O! It's so sad, O it's so sad!' and set Mr Lemon (the softest hearted of men) crying too. By the time the curtain fell, we were all crying together, and then her mother and sister used to come and put her in a chair and comfort her, before taking her away to be dressed for the Farce.[2]

The choice of Miss Coutts as confidante was curious, since she disapproved of his theatrical ventures; but Dickens could not help himself. Too much electricity had been generated to contain the intensity of his emotions within the confines of the performance; at least, by naming Maria rather than Nelly, he could present it as an innocent intensity.

The *Manchester Courier* heaped praises on Dickens, commended Mrs Ternan for her clever performance and allowed that the other ladies' parts were 'very well filled'.[3] On the Saturday night there was a triumphant supper after the performance; it continued for the young men of the party into the small hours, long after the ladies and the Manager had retired. The noise brought him back, in dressing-gown and slippers, candlestick in hand; he put his finger to his lips silently and retired again. But he was not as calm as he appeared to the young men; he seems to have been in one of his near-manic states, struck not only with neuralgia but with a violent, as yet imperfectly defined excitement. He was easily persuaded by the Mancunians to put on a third, unscheduled performance on the Monday, brushing aside all the extra oganizational problems and hotel bills involved.

The Monday performance was another triumph, and afterwards he told Maria he was sure she 'had one of the most genuine and feeling hearts in the world; and I don't think I ever saw anything more prettily simple and unaffected'.[4] It wasn't quite what he'd expected from an actress 'born in a country theatre'.[5] He still did not know quite how to place the Ternans.

On Tuesday the whole party returned south, this time without Conundrums. At some point Dickens elicited the information he wanted about the Ternans' next engagement, which was to be in Doncaster in mid-September, the time of the St Leger Day race. He returned to Gad's Hill with this secret knowledge like a talisman. The sight of the Kentish countryside, with steadily falling rain signalling the onset of autumn, threw him into gloom.[6] Further sadness came with the news that Macready's son Henry had died of tuberculosis, the disease that picked off his large family of children one after another; Dickens wrote him a letter of comfort, sending Catherine's love. It was the last such message. A few days later he wrote to Miss Coutts's companion, Mrs William Brown, saying,

> The restlessness which is the penalty of an imaginative life and constitution – we all hold whatever we possess, on the strict tenure that it must and shall be used – so besets me just now, that I feel as if the scaling of all the Mountains in Switzerland, or the doing of any wild thing until I dropped, would be but a slight relief.[7]

This was from Gad's Hill. The next day, a Saturday, he was back in Bloomsbury, confessing to Collins that he wanted to escape from himself: 'my blankness is inconceivable – indescribable – my misery amazing'. 'Shall we talk at Gad's Hill?' he asked, saying he was on his way back there, but would be in town again on Monday. Dickens sometimes claimed he was forced into perpetual travel by

FREE TRADE HALL.

UNDER THE MANAGEMENT OF MR. CHARLES DICKENS.

SUNDAY EVENING, AUG. 24th, 1857,

(At EIGHT O'CLOCK EXACTLY,
when the early attendance is respectfully and particularly requested is solicited),

In memory of the late Mr. Romantic Drama, in Three Acts, by

MR. WILKIE COLLINS,

called

THE FROZEN DEEP.

The whole produced Directly by the FIRST by Mr. FRANCESCO BERGER, who will conduct

New Scenes, Various of Machinery Properties, and Miss WILKIE, of Curiosities room, Fancy Robes, Dresses by Mr. WILSON, of the Strand.

Captain Ebsworth	(of the "Wanderer")	Mr. EDWARD PIGOTT.
Captain Helding		Mr. ALFRED DICKENS.
Lieutenant Crayford		Mr. MARK LEMON.
Frank Aldersley		Mr. WILKIE COLLINS.
Richard Wardour		Mr. CHARLES DICKENS.
Lieutenant Steventon		Mr. YOUNG CHARLES.
John Want	(Ship's Cook)	Mr. AUGUSTUS EGG.
	(One of the "Sea-Mew" people)	Mr. SHIRLEY BROOKS.
	(One of the people of the "Wanderer")	Mr. CHARLES COLLINS.
Officers and Crews of the "Wanderer" and "Wanderer."		
		Mrs. GEORGE VINING.
		Miss ELLEN SABINE.
		Miss ELLEN TERNAN.
		Miss MARIA TERNAN.
		Miss TERNAN.
		Miss MEWTE.

Scenery and Scenic Effects of the Third Act, by Mr. TELBIN.

The other Effects of the First and Third Acts, by Mr. STANFIELD, R.A., assisted by Mr. DANSON.

At the end of the Play, a Quarter of an Hour's Interval for Refreshments.

To conclude with Mr. Buckstone's Farce

UNCLE JOHN.

		Mr. WILKIE COLLINS.
		Mr. LUARD.
		Mr. CHARLES DICKENS.
		Mr. MARK LEMON.
		Mr. YOUNG CHARLES.
		Miss MARIA TERNAN.
		Miss ELLEN TERNAN.
		Miss TERNAN.

Performance will be heightened by the Characters.

THE REPRESENTATION TAKING PLACE, WITH THIS VERY LIBERAL CONCUR...
In consequence of the overflows, to the two
on account of the convenience of a large portion of the
Objectors are arranged as follows:—

Front Seats reserved, 10s. Private Box Seats, Reserved, 5s.
Gallery at the Centre of Hall, 2s. 6d.

REST OF HALL, ONE SHILLING.

Tickets to be had of the London Committee,

MR. CHARLES DICKENS, Chairman.
ARTHUR SMITH, Honorary Secretary.

his work, as though to excuse the craving for movement, change, freedom and anonymity that was met by an empty carriage and a fast-moving steam engine. The truth was he very quickly grasped the possibilities opened up by the new speed and availed himself of them to the utmost. To the end of his life he behaved like a Flying Dutchman of the railways, movement always more necessary to him than repose.

The talk with Collins resulted in their agreeing to go away together, to write a sketch for *Household Words*. So Dickens told Forster. In the same letter he reverted to something he'd seen at the Zoo earlier in the year and been back to watch again – the feeding of live guinea pigs and mice to the snakes. The sight revolted but also fascinated him; perhaps he felt half guinea pig, half snake, and hardly knew which was more painful.

A few days later he and Collins set off on their 'walking tour'. The plan was to write it up humorously as the 'Lazy Tour of Two Idle Apprentices'. They made for Carlisle; but their real destination was Doncaster. For the sake of appearances the two men did a little walking, in the rain. Collins slipped and sprained his ankle. Dickens used the enforced leisure to write to Forster on a theme he had already touched on more than once, saying that 'Poor Catherine and I are not made for each other, and there is no help for it. What is now befalling I have seen steadily coming.'[8] To Catherine he neither wrote nor sent any message.

They found Doncaster bursting at the seams with race-goers; even the railway station had taken on a score of extra porters to deal with them. Dickens had booked rooms at the Angel Hotel in the city centre and also engaged an open carriage and pair for the races. He lost no time in setting off for the Theatre Royal with Wilkie, himself a considerable connoisseur of little actresses, and without a doubt encouraging his friend in his pursuit. Their presence was immediately noted, the *Doncaster Gazette* reporting that

During the performance this evening Mr Charles Dickens and Mr Wilkie Collins entered the Boxes and both gentlemen (especially the former) at once became objects of the most marked attention and conversation. In fact the distinguished author of *The Pickwick Papers* – his greatest work – was evidently the lion of the evening.

On this particular evening no Ternans appeared on stage. Instead there was a performance of his friend Bulwer-Lytton's *Money*, enlivened with young ladies in jockey costume doing a dance in which they put their whips into their mouths and worked imaginary winners up to the float; 'an immense success' noted Dickens drily. He was back in the theatre the following evening, which 'introduced three young ladies who have, in former years, been distinguished as juvenile actresses. We allude to Misses Maria and Ellen Ternan, daughters of the late Mr Ternan, lessee of this theatre, and to Miss Fanny Addison, daughter of the present lessee.' Maria sang to her guitar and played Mrs Major Mortar in a Mark Lemon play; Nelly was in *The Pet of the Petticoats*. The audience was rowdy. When Dickens came to write up the occasion in 'Lazy Tour', he said the town was full of lunatics and drunkards, and singled out one drunken theatre-goer who made remarks about the actresses so offensive that he wanted to fling him into the pit. The offender saved himself from Dickens's indignant assault by falling asleep; Dickens remained brooding as to whether 'that is a wholesome Art, which sets women apart on a high floor before such a thing as this, though as good as its own sisters, or its own mother'.[9] The drunken sot was evidently not fit to look at Nelly and Maria up on the 'high floor'. He may of course have given Dickens himself a passing moment of unease about his own motives in being in that particular audience. If the Ternans were surprised to see him after the show, they could not fail to be pleased and excited to have drawn the great man.

Wednesday was St Leger Day, and Dickens went to the races. He picked three winners, rather to his own surprise. The account he gave in the 'Lazy Tour' describes how one of the apprentices falls into

a dreadful state concerning a pair of little lilac gloves and a little bonnet that he saw there. Mr Idle asserts, that he did afterwards repeat at the Angel, with an appearance of being lunatically seized, some rhapsody to the following effect: 'O little lilac gloves! And O winning little bonnet, making in conjunction with her golden hair quite a Glory in the sunlight round the pretty head, why anything in the world but you and me! Why may not this day's running – of horses, to all the rest: of precious sands of life to me – be prolonged through an everlasting autumn-sunshine, without a sunset! Slave of the Lamp, or Ring, strike me yonder gallant equestrian Clerk of the Course, in the scarlet coat, motionless on the green grass for ages! . . . Arab drums, powerful of old to summon Genii in the desert, sound of yourselves and raise a troop for me in the desert of my heart, which shall so enchant this dusty barouche . . . that I, within it, loving the little lilac gloves, the winning little bonnet, and the dear unknown-wearer with the golden hair, may wait by her side for ever, to see a Great St Leger that shall never be run!'[10]

Perhaps Dickens wrote this with his tongue in his cheek, or perhaps he only hoped his readers would think so; in any case the piece was unsigned and written after he had left Doncaster. But the lilac gloves, golden hair and little bonnet suggest that Nelly was at the St Leger Day race and possibly in the Dickens carriage. In a letter to his assistant Harry Wills,* Dickens confessed that 'the strongest parts of your present correspondent's heart are made up of weaknesses. And he just come to be here at all (if you knew it) along of his Richard Wardour! Guess *that* riddle, Mr Wills!'[11] The mixture of club room jocularity and apology suggests how uncertain Dickens was of his own emotional ground. A few days later, on Sunday 20 September, he wrote again, 'I am going to take the little – riddle – into the country this morning. I think I shall leave here on Tuesday, but I cannot positively say . . . I did intend to return home tomorrow, but have no idea now of doing that . . . So let the riddle and the riddler go their own wild way, and no harm come of it!'[12]

Dickens is telling Wills that he is in pursuit of Nelly, and hopeful enough of success to be postponing his return south. But he had misunderstood the situation. For Nelly, thrilled as she was by his devotion, any idea that he hoped to seduce her must have seemed

---

* William Henry Wills, known as Harry but always addressed by Dickens simply as Wills, started his literary career in the 1830s as a playwright and theatre critic; later he worked on the Edinburgh magazine *Chambers's Journal* (and married Jessie Chambers in 1846). Dickens first met him in the late 1830s, and took him on as his assistant on *Household Words* in 1849. He was two years older than Dickens, who regarded him as solidly reliable and discreet, someone he could confide in and entrust with delicate private business.

at this stage as unlikely as the transformation of Father Christmas into a satyr. The trip into the country in his open carriage took place, and the local newspaper reported the distinguished visitor's viewing of the ruins of Roche Abbey and his walk in its beautiful grounds; whatever else happened – a Dickensian meal, laughter, flattery and flirtation – there can have been nothing very wild about it. Either Nelly's own manner or a warning from her mother made him draw back from his headlong wooing and understand that she and her sisters were not easy game, not the type of little actresses he and Collins and Wills might make admiring jokes about, accompanied by manly winks and encouraging nudges. Yes, they were working girls, and born into an equivocal profession; but they had been brought up by a virtuous mother to be virtuous themselves. The little riddle, even if she gave every sign of being dazzled by Dickens and pleased by his attentions, could not simply be swept off her feet and carried away wherever and whenever he chose. When he understood this, if part of him was disappointed, another part exulted in her innocence. His feelings seem to have become more complex, more painful and more intense.

So he left Doncaster on the Monday after all, and Nelly continued to fulfil her engagements at the theatre.[13] She acted with her mother in a Tom Taylor play, *Victims*, while Maria appeared as Jessica in *The Merchant of Venice*, Fanny as Gertrude in *The Loan of a Lover*. A benefit under the aegis of the Freemasons followed, at which Nelly and Maria starred in a farce called *A Game of Romps*, and Fanny sang 'Lo, Hear the Gentle Lark'. Then Fanny set off alone for a tour of Ireland and Scotland, and the others returned to London and Park Cottage, where Mrs Ternan, who cannot have been unaware of the meaning of Dickens's descent on Doncaster, had to do some hard thinking.

An instructive story of a young actress and her mother was told at exactly this time by a French writer, Edmond About, in his novel *Tolla*.* A young Roman aristocrat is sent on his travels to break an unsuitable attachment and is soon ensnared by a Parisian actress,

* *Tolla* appeared in 1858 and became a European bestseller: Mrs Gaskell had her copy specially bound in vellum, and the schoolboy Henry James read it with

Cornélie. About clearly knows the world he is describing and presents her with some sympathy. She is charming and cheerful, lives with her modest, respectable parents, and has friends who are journalists and painters as well as actors. On-stage she is obliged to show off her good points – there are special opportunities in different scenes for displaying in turn her legs, her hair, her shoulders – but off-stage she is a nice girl who enjoys picnics, family parties and good conversation. Her aristocratic friend calls on her at home and joins in several family occasions; when he makes his admiration plain by sending her presents, her mother explains the facts of life to her. 'I should like to see you married to someone rich enough to provide for you and later, for your parents,' she tells her, 'but I realize this is hoping for a good deal. I don't expect you to remain at home until you are thirty. If you tell me you have fallen in love with a well-to-do man, I shall begin by giving you a sermon on morality, and then visit the man in question to explain all the sacrifices I have made to educate you. Then, *S'il a bon coeur, il me laissera ma fille, ou du moins il me remboursera mes dépenses.*' * Cornélie's mother calls on the man, makes her little speech, and receives 20,000 francs for her daughter, who is in addition installed in an expensive apartment of her own. Her family and friends, far from being upset, are pleased.

The British liked to see Paris as a far more wicked place than London; that was part of its attraction. In practice it is unlikely that it was; it was only the manners and style of vice that differed. I am not suggesting that there was a moment at which Mrs Ternan thought of selling her daughter to Charles Dickens, any more than he thought of buying her, in so many brutal words. She was a good, self-respecting woman, and he had neither the insouciance

---

passionate enthusiasm. Edmond About (1828–85) knew the world he was describing; he was a journalist and playwright as well as a novelist. Two years after *Tolla* his story 'Le Roi des montagnes' was put on in a dramatized version at the Lyceum in October 1860, translated by Tom Taylor as *The Brigand and His Banker*, with Madame Celeste, Mrs Keeley and Maria Ternan in the cast; it ran for only a few performances, though it was 'capitally played' according to Michael Williams in *Some London Theatres* (1883).

* 'If he is a decent person, he will either leave my daughter alone or reimburse me for my expenses in bringing her up.'

nor the limitless funds of a lord. At the same time he had hurried to Doncaster in a state of obvious excitement about her, and she and her girls had to live, and manage as best they could in the circumstances in which they found themselves.

A prudent mother should have warned him off at this point, and warned her daughters against him, in the clearest terms. Yet it's obvious that she didn't. It would have required something like heroism to send away the great and charming Charles Dickens with a flea in his ear, when he beamed attention and flattery on a woman whose life had been as harsh as Frances Ternan's, and when she saw her daughters' faces light up at the sight of his cheerful visits and generous gestures. A strict morality now demanded it. Yet looking back at her own life of impeccable virtue, she may have reflected that it had been ill rewarded. She may have persuaded herself that, with due care and subtlety, they could keep Dickens's friendship on their own terms; or her daughters may have simply declared themselves unwilling to give up the prize fate had sent their way. Whatever agonies of conscience or family disagreements took place at Park Cottage, they were soon all meeting again in the friendliest way.

Dickens, too, found himself uncomfortably trapped in his own morality. He was faced with the example of Wilkie Collins setting up a cheerful ménage with Caroline Graves, the pretty young widow he had literally picked up in the street. Caroline acted as hostess, cook and mistress; she sometimes served dinner, appearing in a delightfully informal negligé, to Collins's men friends, with whom she was on the most naturally friendly terms, though she was never, of course, introduced to their wives. Dickens liked her well enough; but that did not mean Nelly, now established as a chaste, if not entirely discouraging, young lady, could be put into the same category as Caroline. Nelly was not a widow but an untouched girl. If Dickens once touched her, he would become the villain who put her into the category of his own Little Em'ly or Mrs Gaskell's Ruth, girls seduced by gentlemen and doomed never to be good wives and happy mothers.

This was not how he wanted things to be at all. What he wanted was to start life again as a romantic bachelor, in romantic purity. A few weeks after Doncaster he wrote to Lavinia Watson, a married woman friend to whom he could unburden some, at any rate, of his feelings. His letter contains a fantastical account of being in love with a beautiful Princess. It reads like a veiled confession, and the accents of tormented love are genuine and painful. Dickens sounds like a boy:

> I wish an ogre with seven heads . . . had taken the Princess whom I adore – you have no idea how intensely I love her! – to his stronghold on the top of a high series of mountains, and there tied her up by the hair. Nothing would suit me half so well this day, as climbing after her, sword in hand, and either winning her or being killed. – *There's* a state of mind for you, in 1857.[14]

But he was not a boy, and there were no ogres or mountains. He found relief in more prosaic gestures. One was to order the blocking of the door between his dressing room and what had been the marital bedroom at Tavistock House, and now became Catherine's alone. This is the action of a romantic, not a worldly man, who would see no harm in continuing to sleep alongside his wife, however many mistresses he might pursue or take. It was also exquisitely hurtful to Catherine, being done without prior consultation or discreet agreement with her, so that she was humiliated in front of her servants. The cruelty is also romantic, suggesting a man in the grip of a force he can't and doesn't want to control.

Yet Dickens had not become consciously hostile to Catherine, and for some time he continued to acknowledge her affection for him; 'She has a great tenderness for me,' he told his solicitor.[15] He only wanted to banish her from his presence and abolish her from his imagination. And thus driven he began to rewrite the history of their relations from the start, to claim that the marriage had always been unhappy, to insist on the acquiescence of his children and friends in the new version of history, and indeed to enrol his sister-in-law as his chief ally against her own sister. Georgina's letter to Maria Winter is one of the nastier surviving documents from this episode:

> . . . by some constitutional misfortune & incapacity, my sister *always* from their infancy, threw her children upon other people, consequently as they grew up, there was not the usual strong tie between

them and her – in short, for many years, although we have put a good face upon it, we have been very miserable at home.[16]

This is the Georgina observed by Hans Christian Andersen, who had stayed with the Dickenses in the summer of 1857 at Gad's Hill: 'piquante, lively and gifted, but not kind', he called her, and added that he had sometimes seen Catherine come out of her room with tears in her eyes.[17] But Dickens was rapidly becoming blind to anything but his own dreams.

Throughout the autumn Nelly was acting at the Haymarket; and two days after the door blocking, Dickens wrote to Buckstone there, saying how pleased he was that she was working for him, and how much he hoped to hear of her being offered more work:

> I need hardly tell you that my interest in the young lady does not cease with effecting this arrangement [i.e., her engagement], and that I shall always regard your taking of her and remembering her, as an act of personal friendship to me. On the termination of the present engagement, I hope you will tell me, before you tell her, what you see for her, 'coming in the future'.[18]

After another two days he was so restless that he walked from London to Gad's Hill, setting off at two in the morning: again, it is more like the action of a very young man than a middle-aged one. On 23 October he sent a cheque for £50, uncrossed, made out to Buckstone, with whom Nelly was now playing in *Speed the Plough* – a farce by Thomas Morton in which, appropriately enough, the figure of Mrs Grundy was first presented to the public.[19]

She continued playing in farces, sometimes at the Haymarket, sometimes the Lyceum; between mid-October and March 1858 she gave ninety performances. She was at last offered two parts worthy of her family name, as minor Shakespearean heroines: Hero in *Much Ado*, and Celia in *As You Like It*. At this point it must have seemed to her that she was establishing herself well in a London career: a busy, satisfying time, with the extra glitter of her admirer's attentions over it.

In December Dickens reduced his household by sending Henry, eight years old, off to join his brothers at school in Boulogne. For the first time they all stayed at school over the Christmas holidays. So much for the children and the spirit of Christmas present. Only little Plorn, the girls and Charley were still at home, and there were no festivities or theatricals. Dickens and Collins had collaborated on a Christmas story called 'The Perils of Certain English Prisoners', an account of heroism in the face of foreign barbarians, intended as a tribute to the British who had suffered during the Indian mutiny; but it was a lack-lustre piece of narrative. No one has ever seen much merit in it except perhaps Nelly who, long after Dickens's death, used to read aloud from it; which may suggest it had some special significance for her.

At the end of the year Dickens was still writing to friends about the stunning effect of Maria's performance in *The Frozen Deep*. He gave Lavinia Watson the same details about her tears pouring 'all over me like Rain' and the effect on everyone else, tears, nose-blowing, drying of eyes and administering of sherry: 'You would have remembered it for a long, long time,' he finished.[20] On New Year's day 1858 he told Forster that, although he was making improvements at Gad's Hill, 'yet I have no interest in the place'.[21] For his forty-sixth birthday in February, he summoned only Forster and Collins to a dinner at Gravesend. He was busy planning a series of readings from his works intended, for the first time, to make money for himself. For this he needed a manager. He appointed Arthur Smith, who came from the heart of the professional theatrical world; his brother Albert was a popular comedian, married to Mary Keeley, daughter of the Keeleys with whom Nelly was currently acting.

In March she was nineteen; she was alternating between Buckstone's *Shocking Events* and Celia in *As You Like It*. Two days after her birthday Dickens was at the Lyceum to see Maria's benefit performance. Later he wrote to Collins,

> The Doncaster unhappiness remains so strong upon me that I can't write, and (waking!) can't rest, one minute. I have never known a moment's peace or content since the last night of *The Frozen Deep*. I do suppose that there never was a man so seized and rended by one Spirit.[22]

At about this time poor Catherine Dickens is said to have

received a bracelet ordered by her husband for Nelly and wrongly delivered to Tavistock House.[23] Dickens made a habit of giving small presents to those who took part in his theatricals, but one can see why this particular offering might now be cruelly upsetting to his wife. Katey Dickens also reported finding her mother crying in her room because he had ordered her to call on the Ternans – a story that has a ring of truth to Dickens's character as a man who imposed his will and his version of things on everyone around him.[24] Catherine Dickens was too cowed not to obey her husband; it must have been an uncomfortable afternoon for all at Park Cottage, as the ladies did their best to exchange light conversation over the tea cups. If any of the Ternans felt compassion for their visitor, it was not enough to change the course of things.

Another glimpse of the situation comes in a letter of Thackeray's daughter Anny, who knew the Dickens children well, in which she says she has heard that 'Charley met his Father & Miss whatever the actress' name out walking on Hampstead Heath.' And although she adds stoutly, 'But I dont believe a word of the scandal,' this seems a plausible picture, Dickens striding along with a pretty, young and blessedly energetic companion at his side, eagerly listening, eagerly agreeing; and then the embarrassment of the father caught out, face to face with a son old enough to understand the significance of what he was seeing, older indeed than Nelly herself.[25]

A few weeks later, in May, as she was playing Maria in *The School for Scandal*, and Dickens began public readings from his own works in St Martin's Hall in Longacre, he and Catherine separated. She left Tavistock House and never returned there or to Gad's Hill. Her parents and the rest of her own family took her part indignantly, with the exception of Georgina, who remained in charge of both houses. For the sake of appearances Dickens also left Tavistock House for his lodgings in Wellington Street, though he continued to spend time at Gad's Hill. This is likely to be the period at which he wrote a formal letter to his elder children accusing their mother of not having the character to appreciate his platonic attachment to Nelly; and of which Katey Dickens, then also nineteen, said, 'nothing could surpass the misery and unhappiness of our home'.[26] London gossiped, enthralled, and Dickens seemed to most of his friends to have gone half mad.

On 25 May he gave a written statement to Arthur Smith, with an accompanying note giving him permission to show it 'to anyone who wishes to do me right, or to anyone who may have been misled into doing me wrong'. In it he made several remarkable statements. He said that Catherine suffered from a mental disorder; he said she had been asking for a separation for some years; and he went on to discuss the accusations of 'two wicked persons' (he meant her mother and sister Helen) who 'coupled with this separation the name of a young lady for whom I have a great attachment and regard. I will not repeat her name – I honour it too much. Upon my soul and honour, there is not on this earth a more virtuous and spotless creature than this young lady. I know her to be as innocent and pure, and as good as my own dear daughters.'[27] For the moment Smith did nothing with this statement.

On 27 May there is a payment of four guineas 'to N.' in Dickens's Coutts account. On 7 June he published a statement in *The Times* which was repeated on the front page of *Household Words* a few days later; milder than the one he had given to Smith, it still insisted on his entire innocence in the matter of the separation from his wife:

... Some domestic trouble of mine, of long-standing, on which I will make no further remark than that it claims to be respected, as being of a sacredly private nature, has lately been brought to an arrangement, which involves no anger or ill-will of any kind, and the whole origin, progress, and surrounding circumstances of which have been, throughout, within the knowledge of my children. It is amicably composed, and its details have but to be forgotten by those concerned in it.

By some means, arising out of wickedness, or out of folly, or out of inconceivable wild chance, or out of all three, this trouble has been made the occasion of misrepresentations, most grossly false, most monstrous, and most cruel – involving, not only me, but innocent persons dear to my heart, and innocent persons of whom I have no knowledge, if indeed, they have any existence – and so widely spread, that I doubt if one reader in a thousand will peruse these lines, by whom some touch of the breath of these slanders will not have passed, like an unwholesome air ...

I most solemnly declare, then – and this I do, both in my own name and in my wife's name – that all the lately whispered rumours touching the trouble at which I have glanced, are abominably false. And that whosoever repeats one of them after this denial, will lie as wilfully and as foully as it is possible for any false witness to lie, before Heaven and earth.[28]

The public made what it could of this declaration. We have seen that *The New York Times*'s correspondent thought it worth reporting supposed details of the scandal before denying their veracity. Dickens's kind old friend and fellow actor, Mark Lemon, who had wept during *The Frozen Deep*, flatly refused to publish it in *Punch*. At this, Dickens severed the friendship, not only with Lemon but also with the magazine's publishers Bradbury & Evans; they also handled his books, which he now took back to Chapman & Hall.

In June he told Collins that he was living chastely and found it best 'to wear and toss my Storm away'. There was a break in his London readings, and he went off to Boulogne alone at the end of the month, complaining of kidney trouble. In July Nelly joined her company in Manchester for a summer season of six weeks. A few days later Dickens wrote to a cousin of the Ternans in Boston, Richard Spofford:

> Your cousin Fanny has shown me a letter of yours in which reference is made to me. I would not for the world do her or you the wrong of giving you any assurance upon a subject on which your own generous nature is perfectly clear. But what I wish to do is to thank you most heartily for the comfort and strength I have derived from the contemplation of your character as it is expressed in that letter beyond the possibility of mistake, and to convey to you, in a manner as plain and unaffected as your own, my admiration of the noble instinct with which the upright know the upright, all the broad world over. Your cousin well deserves to be its subject. From the first month, I think, of my knowing your cousin Fanny, I have confided in her, have taken great interest in her, and have highly respected her. You may be sure (as I know her mother and sisters are, and as I know, my own two daughters are), that there could not live upon this earth a man more blamelessly and openly her friend than I am, or to whom her honour could be dearer than it is to me.[29]

There are two striking aspects to this letter. The most important is its clear evidence that his relations with the Ternans were now on an unusually intimate footing; intimate enough for Fanny to show him family letters, whether he actually confided – or confided fully – in her or not. The other is the difference in tone between his words to Spofford and his remarks to Wills on the subject of the 'little riddle'; they seem to come from two different people. The whole letter, with its resonant protestations of virtuous intent, sounds like an exercise in allaying suspicion. Dickens had no difficulty in turning out high-sounding phrases when the situation required, and he signally failed to mention to Spofford what his current plans for Mrs Ternan and Fanny were. The fact was he had arranged for them both to leave England for a considerable period.

Once again Dickens appears in a double light: as the disinterested benefactor, eager to fulfil the ambition of a deserving young woman, and as the bearer of dangerous gifts. Fanny's desire to train as a singer with a first-class foreign teacher was to be met by his offer to pay for a year-long trip to Florence to study singing under Pietro Romani. Of course he would not dream of sending her alone. Mrs Ternan should go with her. This would leave Maria and Nelly on their own, without the chaperone still considered essential for all respectable young women. Perhaps Dickens promised to keep an eye on them.

Why did Mrs Ternan agree to the plan? It would have been cruel to deny Fanny her golden opportunity when at last it was offered her. Somehow she was convinced that Maria and Nelly would be able to look after one another during her absence. Or she may simply have decided that she could not afford to think too closely about what was happening. The most important factor throughout must have been the sheer steady willpower of Dickens, who would use every weapon to get his own way, even when he was perhaps not clear what it was exactly he wanted. From Mrs Ternan's point of view he could offer seemingly limitless benefits and favours to all three girls, without which they faced an uncertain and possibly stony path ahead; she withstood him no more easily than anyone else.

In August Dickens was touring the provinces, reading from his own works, while Nelly worked in Manchester. She had the boy's part in a play called *The Honeymoon* and understudied for Lydia Languish in Sheridan's *The Rivals*. But when her chance to play the part came on 20 August, the critic of the *Manchester Guardian* did not think much of her:

> The comedy was completely successful, as far as the hearty enjoyment of the audience was concerned, although Miss E. Ternan being the Lydia there were the strongest reasons for regretting the continued indisposition of Miss Amy Sedgwick.

Understudies are not usually singled out quite as cruelly as this. She may have been no good in the part, of course, but she may have attracted unfavourable attention for another reason. A few days before, on 16 August, the statement Dickens had given to Arthur Smith in May appeared in the *New York Tribune* and was taken up in England, where the press, northern and southern, expressed its disapproval of his behaviour and disbelief of his words.[30] Only a year before he had appeared in Manchester with 'Miss E. Ternan'; there was bound to be gossip. Gossip was unpleasant, but the bad notice was wounding and frightening, and cast a question mark over her future, even if Buckstone promised her work at the Haymarket when they returned to London. Dickens, regretting the statement, claimed that he had not authorized its publication, but he failed to reprimand Smith; in any case the damage was now done.

8

Mornington Crescent
1858–1862

While Nelly finished her not very successful season in Manchester, and Dickens set off from Liverpool to give his highly successful first readings in Ireland, Catherine made a visit to Miss Coutts. She took several of the childen with her, and Miss Coutts was so affected by her candidly expressed grief and evident affection for her little sons that she wrote to Dickens on the subject. His reply shows once again how far he had travelled into fantasy, how easily he deluded himself as well as others when the facts did not suit him. He accused his wife and children of play-acting when they showed love for each other and suggested it would be 'better' for the children if they desisted. He also accused Catherine of having 'struck' at him with her weak hand, backed by her wicked family, on whom he had previously loaded so many benefits. He wanted, he said, only to 'forgive and forget' her.

She was now installed in a small – but pretty – house in Gloucester Crescent, on the north side of Regent's Park. Dickens had agreed to pay her £600 a year for life. It was not going to tax him too hard: in one month, September 1858, he made a profit of £1,000 from his readings alone. The Dickens childen were obedient to their father's wish that they should remain in his care – which meant in effect the care of their Aunt Georgina – except for Charley, who defiantly moved with his mother, compounding his misbehaviour by becoming engaged to the daughter of Dickens's estranged publisher Evans. Father and son now broke off communications altogether for some time.

Nelly returned to London at the end of August, and the new season at the Haymarket opened on 6 September. She kept her place in the company, but was assigned to small and undemanding parts. The stars were Charles Mathews Junior, Buckstone and Amy Sedgwick, and the plays were mostly light comedies and farces, a Labiche translation, a revival of *The Soldier's Daughter*, in which she had played as a child with her mother, and a series of undistinguished modern pieces with titles like *Used Up* and *Grimshaw, Bagshaw and Bradshaw*. In most of them she had to do little more than run on and off stage, help set up the jokes and appear decorative. The few press notices she got were only polite; one critic praised a 'well-conceived performance' as a governess in one of the more serious plays, another described her as 'petite and pretty'. Maria was doing altogether better, playing in burlesques at the Strand Theatre alongside the young Marie Wilton and under the management of Ada Swanborough; they had a successful and hilarious season. *The Maid and the Magpie*, in which Wilton and Maria both played male parts, was a hit – Dickens visited it in October and urged Forster to go too – and the Christmas show was a spoof on *Kenilworth* in which Maria, as the unfortunate Amy Robsart, was the centre of a bit of business in which she was saved from being dispatched through a trap-door by her enormous crinoline; later in the season she switched from female victim to male villain, and appeared as the Earl of Leicester. Maria knew how to assert herself in the company.

At the end of September Mrs Ternan and Fanny left for Italy, armed with letters of introduction from Dickens to Anglo-Florentine acquaintances, among them the elderly novelist Frances Trollope, living there with her son Tom, also a writer and occasional contributor to *Household Words*. Maria and Nelly were now on their own in London. Park Cottage, of which Dickens had disapproved so strongly, was given up. The two newly independent working girls moved into lodgings in Berners Street, just north of Oxford Street. Setting up house alone in the West End was an adventure for them, and certainly more convenient. Nelly now had only to walk through Soho to be at the Haymarket, and Maria had not much further to go to the Strand Theatre. They may have found the lodgings for themselves; but given Dickens's general habits and his frankly expressed interest, it seems likely he took a hand in the matter and perhaps made a tactful contribution to the rent. The Ternans had replaced the Hogarths as worthy objects to be 'loaded with benefits'.

But the plan was not as good as he had imagined. Berners Street had unexpected drawbacks. Coming and going at late hours as their work demanded, the girls became uneasily aware that they were being watched. The men observing them were, in fact, policemen. One evening Maria was stopped and questioned. The questions were insulting and the manner of the questioners no less so. The implication was clear: they were thought to be prostitutes. Whatever sophistication their years in the theatre may have given them, this was a moment of shock and humiliation. No doubt they were frightened too; once stigmatized, a young woman without protection might find that things could quickly become very nasty in London in the 1850s, when the age of consent was twelve and the word of a policeman would carry more weight than any protest by a pretty young unchaperoned actress.

Fortunately for the sisters they did have a protector, and a powerful one. It's possible, of course, that he had brought the trouble on them in the first place, by calling on them at indiscreet times, escorting them home after the theatre or taking them out for late suppers. We don't know; but it would have made his explosion of rage when they told him what had happened all the more terrific. Wills, the trusty and indispensable, was instructed go to Scotland Yard – where Dickens had many contacts – to call off the police, complain of their 'Dangerous and unwarrantable conduct' and ask 'what the Devil the mystery means'. He should also visit 'our two little friends' – whom Wills apparently already knew -- for their account of the trouble, 'between three and five' the following afternoon. Dickens stressed that he must insist to the police on the fact of both sisters being 'in all things most irreproachable in themselves and most respectably connected in all ways', owning their own furniture, etc.[1] No more talk of little riddles now. Wills succeeded in his mission to the Yard, and the annoyance ceased.

Dickens knew a good deal about police surveillance of young girls through his years of work for the Urania Cottage project. This now came abruptly to an end. Miss Coutts's firm support for Catherine and her anxiety to reconcile the separated couple made his partnership with her uneasy, though he could have gone on helping with the organization without being on particularly close terms with Miss Coutts. It looks as though he chose to give up

Urania Cottage for more private reasons. Perhaps he felt the loss of that springy moral confidence that had always characterized his dealings with the girls there. It must have become rather more difficult to look them in the eye when he was involved in something that led him to view the police as enemies and single girls living unchaperoned in a new light. This was not all. For years the visits to Shepherd's Bush and talks with the girls had been important to him: 'a most extraordinary and mysterious study it is, but interesting and touching in the extreme'.[2] Like some other reformers – Gladstone is one – he had a genuine wish to do good by reclaiming lost innocents, but at the same time was indulging a need of his own, a curiosity about another world, and particularly the world of young women who existed on the margins of society. The enjoyment with which he made his visits and talked to the girls was always obvious in his letters; with the advent of other young women to answer this particular need, the pressure to keep up his role at Urania Cottage slackened. Once he abandoned it, it became clear just how much the project had depended on him as its mainspring and driving force. Without him the whole enterprise failed, and in a few years it closed down for good.[3]

The public readings on which Dickens now embarked were hard work in themselves, and meant a great deal of travel and nights in hotel rooms, but he found them enjoyable and even relaxing. The real strain upon him had other causes. A woman who had known him well in earlier years observed him at a reading and noted the change in him: 'The nostril was still sensitive and dilated like that of a war-horse, the whole aspect spoke of power, sensibility, and eager restlessness, but overcast with a shadow which blighted its geniality. The open, frank steadiness of eye was gone. He seemed to have withered and dwindled into a smaller man,' she wrote.[4] He was acutely aware of what the public thought, and to another correspondent who asked him if she should change the picture of him she had in her mind, he wrote back assuring her of the happiness and wholesomeness of his home life; only knaves and fools, he said, were responsible for the other rumours.[5] He could not bear the image of a rake; he also had genuine difficulty in seeing himself in it. He fought off self-knowledge and quarrelled with the friends who wouldn't reassure him that he was in the right in everything he did. Yet he knew his actions were disapproved. He knew he had made his children unhappy. He knew, too, that there was a real danger of spoiling the reputation of the Ternan girls and even perhaps of putting their careers in jeopardy.

There were other serious annoyances to deal with at this time. In October his brother Frederick's wife, Anna, taking advantage of the new divorce laws, sued him on the grounds of adultery with an unknown woman. Frederick contested the case, saying it was condoned, and the name of Dickens was unpleasantly dragged through the courts. Then his youngest brother, Augustus, following what began to look like a family tradition, also deserted his wife and children, and departed for America with another woman, with whom he started a second family. One of his mother's brothers, John Barrow, a writer who had fallen on hard times, died, leaving an illegitimate daughter who put in a claim to the Royal Literary Fund. None of this can have pleased Dickens at a time when he needed to shield himself from gossip. At the Garrick, after quarrelling with Thackeray over a trivial literary matter, he resigned from the club (it was the second time he had done so). Thackeray made a point of befriending Catherine, and the two men did not speak to one another again for years. In addition to these troubles his mother, now senile, was still a charge upon him, yet another woman who had to be maintained in a house of her own.

With all these difficulties and anxieties, Dickens kept up his discreet and persistent attentions to Nelly. The traces are of the faintest, but they are there. Before Christmas 1858 there is another gift of £10 from C. D. to E. T.[6] The idea that Nelly – who had probably never been further than Ireland – might be sent to join her mother and sister for a holiday in Florence some time during the following year began to be considered. Slowly he persuaded her of his constancy and reliability; slowly the family's indebtedness to him built up. Dickens, by nature impetuous, was exercising restraint and patience now. 'We know that the Muses were women, and we know every day of our lives that the Fates are women,' he announced in a speech in December, proposing a toast to the 'softer and better sex' who gave so much 'both in happiness and pain'.[7] The all-male audience gathered to honour him roared with appreciative laughter – after all, Dickens was a humorist – though his remarks may not have been intended entirely humorously.

The year 1859 came in, and in mid-January Dickens exchanged letters with Forster and Wills on the subject of assigning his lease of Tavistock House to another family (it had thirty-seven more years to run). It's clear that he had a specific family in mind, and both men advised him in the strongest terms against the plan, Wills telling him bluntly it would be wrong, Forster that 'such a step would *most decidedly be very damaging indeed*'.[8] No other family is known of in this connection, and the vehemence of Forster and Wills on the subject suggests that Dickens may have been thinking of the Ternans, following their trouble in Berners Street. Certainly within the next few weeks an 84-year lease on a large house just to the north of Tavistock Square, and forming part of the same Bedford Estate, was purchased by – or for – 'Frances and Maria Ternan, spinsters, of 31 Berners Street'. This must have been something of a formality, since Fanny was still in Florence; and in any case the house was 'sold' by them to Nelly a year later, when she reached her majority, in what was obviously a carefully worked-out plan. No. 2 Houghton Place, Ampthill Square, was a tall, handsome, four-storey terraced house with an iron balcony at the front and a garden at the back; it was near Mornington Crescent, then a pleasant, leafy place with many open spaces, close to Regent's Park and no great distance from the centre of town.[9]

There is no proof positive that Dickens was the real purchaser, though Nelly later said he was, and the likelihood of the Ternans suddenly finding themselves rich enough to buy such a large and well-placed house, and choosing to buy it for the youngest daughter through a curious manoeuvre, is too remote for serious consideration.[10] It must surely be seen as a gauge of Dickens's seriousness and a guarantee of her future security, whatever happened; a generous and even delicate gesture, since it gave Nelly her liberty if she chose. It was also a gift no respectable woman would have accepted, and no mother who cherished her daughters' good names would have permitted.

Nelly continued to act, still with Buckstone, but with diminishing commitment. In March she was given another chance of a leading role in *The World and the Stage*, a drama adapted from the French, in which she played a titled lady saved from debt by her sister, who is an actress, and so socially unacceptable. The irony may have amused the cast, but Nelly left the production after a single performance. She made one or two more appearances, but then appears to have departed for her first holiday abroad, joining Fanny in Florence. The photograph of her taken in a Florentine studio – was it done for Dickens? – shows her as a very juvenile twenty, 'petite and pretty', with her hair in ringlets and a slightly puzzled air. If she felt perplexed by the rapidity of events, it was hardly surprising. In eighteen months the situation of the Ternan family had been transformed from poverty and uncertainty to something approaching luxury. They were now householders, Mrs Ternan was no longer working, Fanny was a student, and they were all able to travel abroad.

For Dickens, Nelly may have been the flawless embodiment of his fantasies, so much so that her image had emerged from the Don-caster episode not only undamaged but enhanced. But fantasy does not convey much about the hard centre of truth, the real person inside the image; whether she was a mercenary minx or a doll-like victim, installed in her doll's house in Mornington Crescent. Is it possible to tell what she was really like?

No surviving accounts from this period contain anything more than the bare professional and physical description – a young actress, small, pretty and well developed (a phrase which meant, then as now, that she had noticeable breasts); moderately compe-tent as a performer but not outstanding. She had been admired as a sweet child performer, though without the formidable talents of her sister Fanny; and it's safe to say she enjoyed acting for its own sake, or she would not have returned to it as she did, as an enthusiastic amateur, later in her life. But no friend or observer has ever stepped forward from these early years to speak on her behalf and say, I remember her well, a nice girl; or I hated her, we acted together at the Haymarket; nor does a single scrap of writing in her hand survive from this period.

What we do know is that Dickens's daughter Katey, Nelly's exact contemporary, considered her clever and well able to educate herself. We also know that Katey did not hold her responsible for

Dickens's behaviour, although she said she flattered him, and he was 'ever appreciative of praise': but then all his family also flattered him constantly. Katey may have seen her on stage, for she declared she was not a good actress; however, 'she had brains, which she used to educate herself, to bring her mind more on a level with his own [Dickens's]. Who could blame her . . . He had the world at his feet. She was a young girl of eighteen, elated and proud to be noticed by him.' Clever Katey did not become the friend of this intelligent, elated girl, whereas her mild elder sister Mamey, less acute and much more subject to their father's will, evidently did.

We know that Nelly, like her sisters, was a good mimic and became a fine linguist; that she loved books, and read widely and seriously; and that she had literary aspirations of her own, which later expressed themselves in various ways, including the composition of verse and an attempt at a play. She enjoyed music both light and serious, and had opinions on the subject, unlike Dickens. With him she shared a pleasure in singing and dancing, and a sentimental fondness for dogs; the Ternans always kept pet dogs, large and small, about the house, and sometimes on their laps. She was also physically brave: not learning to ride until she was an adult, she became notably skilful and fearless on horseback.

Nelly had no roots, no one place of childhood memories to which she yearned. Perhaps because of this she was not a settler; again like Dickens, she was always restless and ready to travel or move on. What survived all the moving was her profound attachment to her sisters; they represented home for her as no place ever did.

She was – or she became – acutely sensitive to what people thought of her; always careful of her appearance and prettily dressed, she had the vanity of a woman who knows herself to be attractive. People who made her acquaintance later in life spoke of her as cultured and charming, and of the quickness and wit of the conversation of all three sisters, and their perpetual interest in books, the theatre and politics. Their interests were thoroughly secular, and although Nelly went through a period of religious observation, she was never devout; indeed, there is no sign that religion played more than a formal part in the life of any of the Ternans.

Surprisingly perhaps, given Dickens's much proclaimed love of busy little housekeepers, she was always totally undomesticated; household management and cookery were of no interest to her at all. He described her character as gentle; if this was a true view, she evidently changed once she emerged from his giant shadow. Then she acquired a reputation as a tease, high-spirited and rather imperious; and as she aged, her vitality, and her temper, became more marked. She had a fiery streak, was notably dominant, and is said to have made extraordinary scenes when she did not get her way.

All this may have been held in check as long as she was Dickens's 'dear girl'; time and circumstance do change character, and the force of hers may have developed slowly and been scarcely apparent when he first knew her. But even in his lifetime the little riddle in the lilac bonnet and gloves became, in his own description, a proud and self-reliant woman.[11] How the balance of power was held between him and her (and her family), and how much she made her own decisions and plotted her own course of action, must be mostly guesswork. What is not in doubt is that, although she lacked the ambition of her mother or her sister Fanny, she was, like them, both intelligent and brave. One more characteristic: she loved children. Later she talked of being eager to have a whole nursery full of babies.[12]

During the spring of 1859 Dickens was rearranging his own affairs. He moved his office in Wellington Street a few doors along to No. 26, on the corner of York (now Tavistock) Street, where he could have a larger and more comfortable apartment for himself, with a housekeeper in attendance. It provided a serious bachelor residence, very conveniently placed; from his balcony on the first floor he had a direct view of the Lyceum Theatre opposite.*

During these months his portrait was painted by Frith; it depicted, as he acknowledged ruefully, a man in whom ferocity prevailed over geniality. His behaviour bore out the message of the picture. He fought a lawsuit against Bradbury & Evans, his co-

---

* This corner building is still standing. There is now a shop on the ground floor, and a blue plaque commemorates Dickens's years there.

owners of *Household Words*, bought it, closed it down and reopened it without them under a new name, *All the Year Round*. Even the new novel on which he embarked as a serial in the newly named weekly brought a potential fight with it. *A Tale of Two Cities* took some of its chief inspiration from Carlyle's *French Revolution*, a book that had gone to Dickens's head like strong spirits; but there appears to have been another source for the story in a play by an obscure writer, Watts Phillips, on the theme of a substitution at the guillotine. Dickens had read Phillips's play in 1857 and, presumably, half forgotten it; the luckless author, himself accused of plagiarism, called witnesses to the fact that his was the earlier work and known to Dickens. The potential scandal was quickly suppressed and forgotten, but the incident provides a good example of the efficiency and ruthlessness of Dickens's handling of public relations. He gave Phillips the *coup de grâce* by dramatizing his own novel; it was produced at the Lyceum under his own direction.[13]

There was one further source for *The Tale of Two Cities* which Dickens proclaimed happily enough when he wrote that he had been inspired by his role as Richard Wardour in *The Frozen Deep* in creating the character of the dissolute but self-sacrificing Sydney Carton; and the name of the girl acted by Nelly in the play – Lucy – is given to the girl Carton loves, Lucie. Dickens discussed his work in progress with Nelly; in July, back from Italy, she was reading proofs for him, which he had sent round to Mornington Crescent.[14] She can't have failed to notice that Lucie Manette was physically modelled on herself. Dickens gave her a

> short, slight, pretty figure, a quantity of golden hair, a pair of blue eyes that met his own with an inquiring look, and a forehead with a singular capacity (remembering how young and smooth it was), of lifting and knitting itself into an expression that was not quite one of perplexity, or wonder, or alarm, or merely of a bright fixed attention, though it included all the four expressions.[15]

This distinctive physical appearance makes Lucie's character, or lack of it, all the more disappointing. Far from breaking the mould of his vapid heroines, he makes her almost a blank, a paper princess, an innocent who undergoes a series of ordeals – loss of father, loss of child, loss of husband – with perfect passivity; she is required to be only sweet, simple and enduring, as she is swept along in the wake of great events. As in *The Frozen Deep*, melodrama blots out any possibility of finer considerations. The morally uncertain world of purely private dangers in which Nelly was actually struggling remained as distant from the fiction of her distinguished admirer as the moon.

Dickens complained of his health several times during the summer of 1859. In June he put it down to his bachelor state. Chastity was held to be unhealthy for men, and it was not something he had endured much since his youth.[16] The contrast with Collins, enjoying all the pleasures of a domestic ménage round the corner in Albany Street, must have irked him. In the same month he told his fortunate friend that 'The "cold" is pretty much in the old state. So I have made up my mind to think no more of it, and to go (in a general way) the way of all flesh' – a richly ambiguous statement of dissatisfaction.[17] In June he complained to Wills of feeling 'languid and short of starch'.[18] At the same time he explained to his American publisher that he was financially tempted by an invitation to cross the Atlantic, but that 'several strong reasons would make the journey difficult for me'. To his manager Arthur Smith he had already written of his reluctance 'for a private reason, rendering a long voyage and absence particularly painful to me' and to Forster he now insisted that 'I should be one of the most unhappy of men if I were to go'.[19] These remarks add up to a picture of a man who feels intermittently ill, is suffering from sexual deprivation, and does not want to go away: and the 'private reason' for not wanting to go away was surely to be found in Mornington Crescent.

In August, still not feeling right, Dickens visited Collins at the seaside in Broadstairs, where he was comfortably installed with Caroline and her little daughter. Whether or not he discussed his difficulties with his friend, and whether Collins gave him advice which helped towards resolving them, Nelly made her last appearance on stage as a professional actress on 10 August 1859, still at the Haymarket, as Mrs Gatherwool in Charles Mathews's *Out of Sight, Out of Mind*. She was then firmly removed out of the public's sight. Her adult career, which had lasted for a little more than two years, was over for good, at twenty. Maria took over her sister's part and continued her stage career without a break. In September Fanny was with her mother in Paris. Dickens wrote recommending her to his friend Philoclès Régnier of the Comédie-Française, in the hope that he would help her to find work. She was, he wrote, 'uncommonly clever and accomplished . . . as good and diligent as she is *spirituelle*'.[20] Régnier, however, either could not or chose not to help Fanny, and a cooling in the relations between the two men followed. Dickens's financial involvement was again signalled in his Coutts account, which shows '£50 to Mrs E. F. Ternan at Paris'.[21] In January he paid £50 for 'E. Ternan's Bill'. At this point Maria appeared to be the only member of the family not dependent on him. Then, on 3 March 1860, her twenty-first birthday, Nelly acquired the Ampthill Square house as her own property. Dickens was reported to be living very quietly, while at Thackeray's dinner table the breaking of his marriage was confidently attributed to 'Miss Teman'.[22]

Fanny's Italian training did not make her the *prima donna assoluta* she had hoped to become. Although she was given leading soprano parts, it was either in the Mile End Road, where the Eastern Opera House was grandly named but not grandly attended, or slogging round the northern provinces again; she attracted neither serious critical attention nor popular following. Maria spent some time touring with her and also continued to act at the Lyceum with Mrs Keeley and Madame Celeste; but although she, too, sang well and was a skilful *comédienne*, she failed to progress to leading roles. The life of a perpetually touring singer or actress below the first rank was not something to be contemplated with enthusiasm, and Mrs Ternan may have been thankful that one of her daughters at least had some security – and that they all now had a good home at Ampthill Square. Her relations with Dickens remained entirely cordial.

In May Annie Fields, the wife of Dickens's American publisher, meeting him for the first time at Tavistock House, noted that he was not the cheerful person she had expected but 'rather the man of labor and of sorrowful thought'.[23] One reason seems to have been the impending wedding of his daughter Katey to Wilkie Collins's younger brother Charles. Charles was not another libertine, quite the reverse, a soulful artist, member of the Pre-Raphaelite group, gentle and ineffectual, and suffering from the beginnings of an illness that would soon kill him; he was twelve years older than Katey. The marriage precipitated feelings of remorse at his own behaviour in Dickens, who believed – probably rightly – that his daughter was marrying to get away from an unhappy home and not for love; certainly without passion. Perhaps she felt there was enough passion in the family, and also that her father had found himself a daughter – a whole family of new daughters – with whom she simply did not wish to compete. Her wedding in July at Gad's Hill was attended mostly by Dickens's younger friends – the French actor-manager Charles Fechter and Edmund Yates, also from an acting family; Mr and Mrs Wills, her niece Nina Lehmann with her German husband; the journalist Percy Fitzgerald, whom Dickens hoped Mamey might marry; Mary Boyle, an unmarried cousin of Lavinia Watson, whose devotion to him had begun with amateur acting and survived his marital crisis; and Marguerite Power, niece of Lady Blessington. There were a few local families present also, but the wedding was solemnized without the presence of the bride's mother. When it was over, Dickens allegedly wept and said, 'But for me, Katey would not have left home.'[24]

As Catherine Dickens whiled away empty days in Gloucester Crescent, Nelly settled into her new life less than a mile away. She had gained leisure and freedom, and with them another gift: invisibility. Her sisters' names continued to appear in playbills and newspaper reports, and indeed from time to time in the letters of Dickens, who went on recommending their talents to producers; but not Nelly's, who was suddenly nowhere and nothing. Even in the census for April 1861, although she was listed with the rest of her family (and two servants) at Houghton Place – Mrs Ternan was described as an 'annuitant', Fanny as 'vocalist', Maria as 'actress' – Nelly alone went without any description beyond her age, correctly given as twenty-two.

What was she doing, beyond the process of self-education described by Katey? Francesco Berger recalled, as an old man, that he had spent pleasant evenings at her house, when she and Dickens sang duets together to his accompaniment, and there were card games: something that suggests a certain stability of routine, a relaxed atmosphere, an acceptance both by Mrs Ternan and a circle of trusted friends that Dickens had his place in the household.[25] She continued to read his proofs and he to 'set great store by' her 'intuitive sense and discretion'.[26] Another glimpse: this may have been the period at which Dickens took his real Nelly to see where he had imagined the home of her namesake Little Nell, in the original Curiosity Shop, then still a flourishing enterprise, behind the National Gallery at the corner of Green and Castle streets. He pointed out the bedroom where he had imagined Little Nell sleeping behind a glass partition. It was the sort of outing he would relish; we know of it only because a lady 'personally acquainted with the great novelist', but unwilling to give her name, gave 'positive assurance that it was so' many years later.[27]

Inevitably it is through Dickens that Nelly's story has to be traced during these hidden years; but it is precisely at this point that his own record also grows more obscure. In September 1860, having at last got rid of Tavistock House, he made a great bonfire of all his correspondence; at the same time he asked his friends to destroy his letters to them. Many did as he asked. It was a harder task for a famous man to disappear from view than for a girl; but he had perfected a way of life which allowed him freedom to come and go as he chose, always living in more than one place, and sometimes with three or even four semi-permanent addresses, quite apart from his reading tours and working trips.* It meant that he could be inaccessible and virtually invisible whenever he wished.

Very little social life is recorded, though he still dined respectably at Forster's from time to time and, less respectably, called on Collins, Caroline and 'the Butler', as he chose to call her daughter Harriet. When he was at Wellington Street – for instance during a spell in the winter of 1860 – he went to the theatre almost every night: in September 1860 he was at a first night of Maria's at the

* For example, early in 1861 he had a rented house in Hanover Terrace, Regent's Park, Gad's Hill and his flat in Wellington Street; in 1866 he still had Gad's Hill and Wellington Street, plus a rented house in Somers Place, Hyde Park, and a cottage (probably two cottages) in Slough.

Lyceum, and on Boxing night the same year he was at the Covent Garden pantomime.[28] Some of these were solitary visits; Wills and Collins were occasional companions; and it would be surprising if Nelly had not also sometimes been at his side, a shadowy figure in a box.

In April 1861 Miss Coutts made another attempt to reconcile him with Catherine, with no greater success. In the same month he heard of the widowed Macready's remarriage, at the age of sixty-seven, to one of his daughter's friends, Cecile, a young woman more than thirty years his junior.[29] It must have been hard not to envy him, and hard for Nelly not to reflect on the chances of life. When Dickens visited the Macreadys the following January, he found Cecile delightful. She was just the sort of diminutive and vivacious young woman he appreciated. She was also pregnant; and a few months later she gave Macready a healthy baby son.

Throughout this winter and spring Dickens was writing *Great Expectations*, and in May he went off to Dover to work on it, alone. It is his saddest book, clearly marked with pain and with the acknowledgement that mistakes can be irrevocable, despite the 'happy ending' counselled by his friend Bulwer-Lytton. It is also the most sustainedly beautiful piece of writing he ever produced. Out of anxiety and guilt came a masterpiece cast in an unfamiliar mould, subtle and haunting, and with a new note of self-questioning and self-knowledge. At the centre, instead of an innocent child – a Nell, a David, an Esther, an Amy Dorrit – he put a thoroughly corruptible boy. Pip is snobbish, ambitious and treacherous; he deludes himself about his own and other people's motives, is chastened and punished, and reaches no real fulfilment. Instead of an angelic, fluttering doll – a Dolly, a Dora, an Ada, a Lucie – he is partnered with Estella, who is quick, clever and undomesticated, an icy beauty plucked from the underworld and trained to trust nothing but money and to wreak vengeance against the false male sex.

Edmund Wilson is not the only commentator to suggest that the frigid and mercenary aspects of Estella may have been drawn from Nelly, or to assert that 'we know something about what Dickens thought of her from the heroines in his last books who are derived from her'; and that there is something confessional about Pip's declaration that he loves her 'against reason, against promise, against peace, against hope, against happiness, against all discouragement that could be'.[30] Perhaps we should believe that Nelly kept Dickens dangling while she extracted financial tribute from him; that she exulted in making him suffer and succumbed to his embraces only reluctantly in the end. Mrs Ternan makes an unconvincing Miss Havisham, but that's not the only reason for questioning this version. From what we know of the Ternans, of Nelly herself and the whole situation, it is at least as likely that she was nervous, confused and uncertain as that she was indifferent or frigid. She was, in Katey's words, elated by Dicken's attentions; he had appeared in her life as a benefactor who would give her the chance of bettering herself: a kind, good man. And so he was; only, confusingly, the kind, good Dickens was mixed with the man who wanted to ruin her, as Steerforth ruined Little Em'ly. Dickens had written his own condemnation too often to expect to have it easily forgotten. Inimitable, irresistible, as loving as a boy he might be; all the same, the aspirations of Nelly and the aspirations of Dickens cross like lines on a graph at this point. Where he was eager for release from the conventions and hypocrisies of British middle-class society, she wanted to leave behind the equivocal world of the theatre in which she had been reared and become respectable. It puts Dickens in a painful dilemma; for by the time he realized she was not quite the sort of young woman he had imagined at first – that the dream of sexual bliss promised by a little actress was as delusive as the dream of domestic bliss promised by a wife – it was too late. He was caught. He may well have hesitated to urge her into a step whose dangers he understood, but he still yearned for her. What he had to do was to reassure her that he would never allow her to suffer as he had seen other young women suffer. The one sure protection he could offer was to make her financially secure.

There is no reason to think she was not responsive to his charm, which dazzled so many young women, or grateful for his devotion. Indeed, it's perfectly possible she was in love with him. The duets in the drawing room at Houghton Place, the heads together over proofs, the walks and talks about London and Hampstead Heath, all carry their own suggestion of warmth and intimacy. In the late twentieth century it's easy to forget that people could be deeply in love and still struggle to maintain chaste relations, often for years, for reasons of morality, as well as terror of the consequences. Nelly may have hoped that a solution would appear, and that they would be able to marry; even if divorce, resorted to by his brother, was unthinkable for Dickens himself, Catherine might die, as Kitty Macready had. But no such solution presented itself.

Macready, who once said it was almost impossible for a young woman working in the theatre to remain virtuous, is supposed to have taken 'the Ellen Ternan affair, etc., calmly – as Dickens was not the celibate type'.[31] If so, his attitude suggests that he accepted the licence of the theatrical world readily enough in private, even when it concerned a girl he had known from childhood; he was more concerned that Dickens should not risk public scandal. No doubt he believed that, at the sensitive point where the theatre met the outside world, hypocrisy became not only excusable but absolutely necessary.

After the completion of *Great Expectations* in June 1861, Dickens did not embark on another novel for two and a half years; this is sometimes attributed to his putting his energy into public readings and earning more by these than by writing. However, between January 1862 and April 1866 he did no public readings, except for a few in Paris in the winter of 1863. For a man of fifty the change of pace in his working life is marked enough to point to a major personal upheaval. Collins could take a mistress lightly enough – he could take two, still lightly – but Dickens was cut to a different pattern; besides, he had not found Nelly in the street, like Caroline Graves, or serving at table in a country inn, as Wilkie found Martha, his second. As far as we know Dickens did not introduce Nelly to Wilkie's women, let alone take her along to participate in those unbuttoned evenings *chez* Caroline. Later he wrote that his 'magic circle' consisted of one member only. She was one whose dignity increasingly demanded the protection of isolation and silence.

In June 1862 Dickens sent a plea to Forster, asking him to understand his character over the past five years – the years since he had met Nelly – by referring to his childhood unhappinesses. 'The never to be forgotten misery of that old time, bred a certain shrinking sensitiveness in a certain ill-clad, ill-fed child, that I have found come back in the never to be forgotten misery of this later time.'[32] This is a key confession. Dickens's childhood misery was like a sacred totem, a secret source of power from which he drew, and Forster was one of the very few who knew of it, and who could therefore understand the strength of what was being said now. Those early sufferings were caused by his parents' – and particularly his mother's – failure to cherish him and see his true worth during a time of trial; they were the spur to the enormous act of will that made him great. If he was now again faced with a situation which produced an all-encompassing misery, a 'shrinking sensitiveness', an equivalent cause has to be discovered.

It began partly, no doubt, in the fear of losing the love of his public, which some believe meant more to him always than any woman. Yet the scandal of the separation was now four years behind him, his children were loyal – even Charley became reconciled – and his public had not turned against him; his reputation stood as high as ever. Still he was not delivered from misery. Any displays of capriciousness from Nelly, who had now after all given up any attempt to lead a self-sufficient life, simply do not seem enough to explain his depth of unhappiness. Guilt, on the other hand, does. The unhappiness of the woman he loved, caused by shame or fear, does. Nelly was evidently not someone who could be used lightly and easily, but a proud and sensitive girl. The more he loved her, the more painful must have been the knowledge that his love might be responsible for making her submit to difficulty and disgrace. Further: if she became his mistress, every time he took her in his arms, he would be inflicting on her the fear of becoming pregnant with a child which would shame her, and which could never be openly acknowledged by its father; a child which must carry the worst stigma society could inflict on shoulders as innocent as those of little David, little Pip, little Esther – or little Charles himself. Such a dilemma – such a prospect – might well prompt a misery 'never to be forgotten' in this later time of his life.

One other sighting of Dickens at this time. In the bitter winter of

1861, walking near Gloucester Gate in Regent's Park late one afternoon, as the darkness thickened and the air began to freeze, he passed the lodge and heard the driver of a hansom cab asking for a pole. Provided with one, the man set off, followed by a curious Dickens, for the bridge over the canal, where the park-keeper and a policeman were looking over the parapet:

> Looking over too, I saw, lying on the towing-path with her face turned up towards us, a woman, dead a day or two, and under thirty, as I guessed, poorly dressed in black. The feet were lightly crossed at the ankles, and the dark hair, all pushed back from the face, as though that had been the last action of her desperate hands, streamed over the ground.

As they stood there, a barge came up the canal, steered by a woman; the horse on the towing path got his hoofs into the dead woman's hair, and the tow-rope threatened to catch and twist her head. There was a general cry of horror,

> at which sound the steering woman looked up at us on the bridge, with contempt unutterable, and then looked down at the body with a similar expression – as if it were made in another likeness from herself, had been informed with other passions, had been lost by other chances, had had another nature dragged down to perdition – steered a spurning streak of mud at it, and passed on.[33]

It's the contempt of one woman for another, the way the living woman dissociates herself from the dead victim, as though she could have nothing in common with her, which makes Dickens wince. The canal suicide quite naturally led him to recall that other incident of twenty-five years earlier, when he had served on the jury at a trial of a girl accused either of concealing the birth of her baby – which had died – or of infanticide. He noted that she was a servant, maid-of-all-work to a cruelly virtuous mistress who testified against her, and whose cold wet doorsteps she had scrubbed immediately after giving birth to the child. The Dickens who reports these two cases is sparing with the rhetoric and unsentimental, as though he feels no need to drum up feelings about such bleak but common London tragedies. A young woman, dead or alive; a baby, dead or alive; a policeman, or a court of law; the contempt of the virtuous: all delivered the same message.

9

Vanishing into Space
(*1862–1865*)

Nelly now disappears from view completely, conjured into thin air. For four years she remains invisible. Her name does not figure in any surviving letters. She and her mother are not even at Maria's London wedding in June 1863: a striking absence in a small, mutually devoted family. She has become a perfect blank.

When she reappears in the summer of 1865, she is travelling in a private first-class carriage in a 'tidal train', part of the rapid service between Paris and London. She is beautifully dressed, wearing a gold watch and trinkets, and is sitting next to Dickens and opposite an elderly lady, almost certainly her mother. They are accompanied by luggage, including several hatboxes. She is by now an excellent French speaker; her hair is darker and no longer arranged in curls; she is thinner, more elegant, a little hollow-cheeked. She is coming from abroad; but how long she has been abroad and where exactly remain conjectural.

At a guess, she has been living in France. It is only a guess. This is to be a chapter of guesses and conjectures, and those who don't like them are warned. No one has come up with any proof of her residence in or near Boulogne, or Paris, or anywhere else on the Continent. Arrivals and departures were not recorded by the boat companies or at the Channel ports. She herself never referred to this period of her life but abolished it altogether; though the fact that she chose to go to Paris, where she appears to have had friends, in the aftermath of Dickens's death, could indicate that she had lived there earlier. If she was in England between 1862 and 1865, it leaves unanswered questions about her absence from Maria's wedding and about Dickens's 'perpetual' (his own word) cross-Channel trips during these years. He had already sent one

Ternan sister first to Italy and then to Paris; if Fanny could go, Nelly could follow, though the reasons might be rather different. There is no doubt that he was intensely involved, or in love, with her in 1862, when she disappeared from view, and still so involved in 1865, when she – inadvertently – reappeared; or that, after finishing *Great Expectations* in the summer of 1861, he remained singularly idle and unproductive, giving very few readings or public speeches and writing very little until he started on a new novel in the autumn of 1863. Something was happening during those carefully blotted out years; and it was happening somewhere discreetly distanced from prying eyes.

Dickens knew France and was enchanted by most aspects of the French way of life from his first encounter with it when he was in his thirties; he pronounced Paris 'the most extraordinary place in the World'. He took his wife and children across the Channel many times, enjoyed whole summers at Boulogne, sent his sons to school there, and made jaunts with bachelor friends. He became lyrical in praise of the speed at which the South-Eastern railway could transport him to Paris, comparing it to an Arabian Nights excursion:

> So, I pass to my hotel, enchanted; sup, enchanted; got to bed, enchanted; pushing back this morning (if it really was this morning) into the remoteness of time . . . murmuring, as I wing my idle flight into the land of dreams, 'No hurry, ladies and gentlemen, going to Paris in eleven hours.'[1]

He wrote the language efficiently and spoke it fluently, though some say with a shocking accent. His books were popular there, and he had friends in the Parisian literary and theatrical world; he had noted the domestic arrangements of Victor Hugo, whose mistress of many years' standing was the actress Juliette Drouet. Dickens could be critical of French immorality, dirt and disobligingness, but as the years went by he found less to complain of and more to love.

In the early 1860s he wrote a series of stories about a London lodging-house keeper, Mrs Lirriper, whom he sent off on a trip to Paris and Sens. Mrs Lirriper's delight in French customs and the beauty of its landscape and architecture would do credit to a tourist board copywriter. 'What do you think of this lovely lovely Paris, Gran?' asks her young protégé, and she answers that it's 'like beautiful fireworks being let off in my head'. Paris, she declares, is

> town and country both in one, and carved stone and long streets of high houses and gardens and fountains and statues and trees and gold ... and clean tablecloths spread everywhere for dinner and people sitting out of doors smoking and sipping all day long and little plays being acted in the open air for little people and every shop a complete and elegant room, and everybody seeming to play at everything in this world.

The people are much more 'homely and domestic in their families and far more simple and amiable in their lives than I had ever been led to expect' and much better than the English at taking 'little enjoyments on little means'. Mrs Lirriper is one of Dickens's most purely amiable characters, and there's no doubt that her views are those of her creator.

Privately he sometimes boasted about his frequent trips across the Channel. He told a Swiss friend,

> my being on the Dover line, and my being very fond of France, occasion me to cross the channel perpetually ... away I go by the mail-train, and turn up in Paris or anywhere else that suits my humour, next morning. So I come back as fresh as a daisy.[2]

To another friend he wrote that a visit to France always cured the touch of neuralgia to which he was subject.[3] There was nothing new about his liking for the country itself; what was new was the secretive and apparently solitary nature of many of his trips, and his sometimes disingenuous accounts of them. Nelly's presence, somewhere within reach of Paris or the Channel ports, is the most obvious explanation for all this.

We know he was in France during the second half of June 1862 and again in July. On 7 July he told one friend he had just been in France and was preparing to return.[4] But on the same day he wrote to another,

I am away to France forthwith, for a holiday, and am not likely to be in London for many weeks to come. It is some years since I was last across the channel, and I am going on a little tour of observation that may keep me wandering for some time.[5]

On 1 January 1863 he wrote to Collins to say he would be at Wellington Street for two nights (2 and 3 January, a Friday and Saturday), then 'on the Sunday I vanish into space for a day or two; but I must be in Paris about Thursday the 15th' – giving him another period of invisibility.[6] To one correspondent he wrote at this time that he might be visiting 'a sick friend' and possibly going to Lausanne or Geneva; perhaps he did, but if so he left no other trace of such a visit. To another friend he said he might go to Genoa, but again there is no evidence that he did. In February 1863 he took a break in northern France: 'a little perfectly quiet tour for about ten days', during which he apparently – and uncharacteristically – spent his fifty-first birthday alone, at Arras; he had even dismissed his manservant.[7] In August 1863 he again spoke of 'evaporating for a fortnight'.[8] In June 1864 he gave more conflicting accounts of his destination abroad, telling one friend it was to be Belgium, another that it was Paris; he referred to it as a 'Mysterious Disappearance'.[9] His daughter Mamey mentions in her memoir that he made 'several runs into France' in the later part of 1864, and it was in December of this year that he attributed his cure for neuralgia to just such a trip. Since it was so easy for him to set off either from Gad's Hill or from Wellington Street; since he was served by totally loyal and discreet people in both places, who accepted without question that his comings and goings might be unpredictable and unaccounted for; and since he was blessed with prodigious energy, there is no knowing how many more times he was in France. Things were made even easier for him in 1863, when Charing Cross Station was opened, putting the Channel service within a hundred yards of Wellington Street. Like his contemporary Flaubert, he was very quick to grasp the possibilities offered by rail travel to those who wanted to live a double or secret life; there was a moment in the summer of 1865 when both writers were making clandestine dashes between England and France.[10]

*

Enchanting as France could be to Dickens, there was a period in 1862 and 1863 in which his journeys there were not cheerful ones. The letter to Forster in which he spoke of his 'never to be forgotten misery' coincided with the trip of June 1862. On 20 July he was still talking of a 'load of troubles' in a letter to Collins; a week later he wrote again to Collins, telling him he planned to be at Dover on 4 August, and on 1 September he referred to a visit he had been making 'at a distance'. By 5 September he was planning a series of readings to be given that winter in Paris, which would necessitate a long stay in France; and on the twentieth of the same month he told Collins he had 'rather miserable anxieties which I must impart to you one of these days when I come to you or you come to me. I shall fight out of them, I dare say; being not easily beaten – but they have gathered and gathered.'[11] Forster was reminded again of his 'unsettled fluctuating distress' on 5 October, a week before Dickens crossed the Channel again. Paris was his base now until the end of the year, although, restless and busy as ever, he made two brief trips to London between October and December.

In mid-October he collected his daughter Mamey and Georgina at Boulogne, and escorted them back to Paris, where he took a house in the Faubourg St-Honoré for them. If Nelly was installed somewhere in the Paris region, their tolerant presence would hardly have changed things. They knew her and were entirely trustworthy; Dickens was giving them a treat, and in any case he could do no wrong in their eyes. Georgina had been ill, allegedly with 'heart trouble', and the ten weeks in Paris were meant to be restorative. Her biographer has suggested that her ailments may have had their origin in emotional turmoil caused by a crisis in Dickens's relations with Nelly; a diagnosis that looks the more convincing in the light of Georgina's complete recovery, and the fact that she was never troubled by her heart again in the course of a long life.[12]

Dickens certainly worried about her, though quite openly, just as he worried over the care of his whole tribe of family dependants; but the painful centre of his private misery seems to find expression in some remarks written in Paris in February 1863. He had returned to England for Christmas at Gad's Hill with Georgina and his younger sons, and there seen his first grandchild, Charley's month-old daughter. He then went back to Paris alone to give a few more readings. After seeing a performance of Gounod's opera *Faust*, he was moved to write to Georgina: 'I could hardly bear the thing, it affected me so, and sounded in my ears like a mournful echo of things that lie in my own heart.'[13] To Macready also he wrote a description of the scene in which Marguerite is shown accepting the jewels from Faust:

> After Marguerite has taken the jewels placed in her way in the garden, a weird evening draws on, and the bloom fades from the flowers, and the leaves of the trees droop and lose their fresh green, and mournful shadows overhang her chamber window, which was innocent and gay at first. I couldn't bear it, and gave in completely.[14]

Gounod's *Faust* was a new opera, and its libretto fitted the story to suit the taste of the day. Goethe's metaphysics were removed to make it a simple sex drama centred on a vulnerable girl and an ageing man desperate to recover his youth. Mephistopheles's offers of riches and power do not tempt Faust; what does is the promise that he will rejuvenate him, and so allow him to secure the love of Marguerite. Faust, magically young again, makes her the gift of jewels, which pleases and flatters her. She falls in love with him and willingly becomes his mistress. When she has a baby, he abandons her, and she finds herself ostracized. She goes mad, kills her baby, is imprisoned and dies; but her soul is carried up to heaven, because her sins all derive from Faust's seduction.

It's not too difficult to guess which aspects of the story produced the mournful echo in Dickens's heart. He was fifty, a grandfather, but pursuing a youthful love; a rich, eminent and powerful man in a position to bribe, fascinate and seduce an innocent girl. Whatever he offered her in the way of money and protection, she must lose her reputation in the process. He could not sit through *Faust* without identifying with the guilty lover. The further implications of this guilt are reinforced by his later statement that Nelly had been through some long and lonely ordeal.[15] If Nelly, like Marguerite, bore a child, a likely time for it seems to be 1862 or 1863, and France a likely place.

Nelly was not, of course, abandoned by her Faust–Dickens, any more than she was rejected by her mother. Nor was she going to be driven to madness, suicide, prostitution or even the colonies. If we imagine Mrs Ternan and her daughter installed in some pleasant spot in France, Nelly in the guise of a young married woman, and Dickens making regular visits, the situation, while still anxious and painful, looks a good deal less black than that of a Marguerite or any of the erring women in his novels. All the same there cannot have been much joy in becoming a mother, even in these relatively comfortable and discreet circumstances.

For Dickens, if there was indeed a child, its prospective arrival meant, as well as concealment, provision to be made for its future. He was not an aristocrat, a French poet–playwright or a man indifferent to what anyone thought of him, but one who felt intensely and peculiarly vulnerable to scandal. The likelihood of discovery, of a blight over his good name, must have loomed more threateningly than before; it was one thing to make clandestine visits to a young woman, another altogether to be responsible for a child who could grow up to claim you as its father. Nelly's disappearance from England would help to keep the first part of the secret at least. And if there was indeed a child, the problem of providing for its future was soon solved in the simplest way: 'there was a boy but it died' – or so said Dickens's son Henry.[16]

Inconvenient and upsetting for Dickens, but for Nelly it would have been infinitely worse. To give birth, to cherish for a few months perhaps, and then to lose a baby, is a terrible thing. It becomes more terrible if the child is not to be acknowledged and can be remembered only as a dreamlike guilty secret: first shame, then love, then grief. If Nelly went through this ordeal, rawly painful in itself, it must have raised in her mind the question as to whether there would be more babies for her, and what their circumstances were likely to be; whether she would ever be in a position to take pleasure and pride in children of her own. These were questions to which Dickens would scarcely have been able to offer reassuring answers.

From time to time people have turned up claiming to be children or descendants of Dickens through women other than his wife. The most persistent case is that of a man called Charley Peters, who applied to a charitable foundation in India in 1908, saying his name was Hector Charles Bulwer Lytton Dickens, and that he was the child of Georgina Hogarth by Dickens, born in 1854, and well known to the family, although he had been turned out. For good measure he produced letters of support from several Australian worthies, who were scandalized by the story of Dickens's wickedness and believed that Charley Peters's son, the callously unacknowledged grandchild, should be given assistance. The truth was that Peters had simply changed his name in Australia in 1900. He was not even a clever liar; he did not know, for instance, that his alleged mother, Miss Hogarth, was still alive at the time of his claim. The story was kept from her and easily shown to be false.* But understandably the family was enraged, and Sir Henry Dickens was vigorous in making sure that any such claims were disproved. In one case only he appears to have acted differently. In 1928 he is alleged to have stated that a child *was* born to his father and Ellen Ternan.†

We have seen that there is no hard evidence that Nelly had a child; but there is too much soft evidence to be brushed aside entirely. Gladys Storey, a close friend and confidante of Dickens's daughter Katey (she became Kate Perugini through her second marriage), is the chief source of this evidence.[17] Kate Perugini instructed Gladys Storey to write a book after her death, revealing certain facts she wanted on record. She died in 1929, and Gladys Storey in turn delayed publication until 1939. *Dickens and Daughter*

---

* The story persisted, however, and surfaced again from time to time right up to the 1980s, when it was confidently brought to the present writer in London at the *Sunday Times*: there was no more evidence then than before, just an accumulation of false claims, now covering three generations of 'Dickenses'. Charley Peters's mother was now said to be a servant girl seduced and abandoned by Dickens rather than Georgina Hogarth, which made a more appealing story to modern ears, though there was still not a shred of 'proof'.

† Sir Henry was Harry, born to Catherine and Dickens in 1849, their penultimate child, and the only son to win his father's entire approval. He was clever and hard-working, won a Cambridge scholarship, read law, prospered, became a QC and made a happy marriage; after the death of his eldest brother Charley in 1896 he became the effective head of the family and the defender of his father's reputation.

states categorically that Ellen and Dickens had 'a son, who died in infancy'. Gladys Storey added nothing to her bald statement and gave no definite date or place of birth.

Among her unpublished papers, however, is a note saying that Kate Perugini told her of the existence of a child in February 1923, and that Sir Henry Dickens confirmed the story on 9 September 1928. She gave two versions of her conversation with him, the first reading, 'Sir Henry and I ... talked about Ellen Ternan – that there was a boy but it died.' Gladys Storey added that Sir Henry told her this while Lady Dickens was out of the room. A later note repeats 'Sir Henry and I then spoke about Ellen Ternan the girl Dickens really lived with – Sir H. said there was a boy (as Mrs P. had told me) but he died.' Still not proof, of course, but it should be borne in mind that Kate and Henry were certainly the most intelligent of the Dickens children, and the most likely to have known what was going on; and that they had no reason whatsoever for fabricating a story about their father, whom they loved.

Gladys Storey was regarded as trustworthy by the scrupulous Dickens scholar, the late Madeline House, who had several long talks with her and later wrote:

> I'm convinced Mrs T was with Ellen at the time of the baby's birth. This I have from Gladys Storey, who – with Kate Perugini – read the letters from Dickens to Wills making plans concerning the baby, before destroying them. – It was something of a triumph to get this out of Gladys, who is a jealous guarder of her secrets; but I'm convinced by the way it was said and the way it came up that it was the truth G was telling me.[18]

Gladys Storey also left a copy she had made of a letter from C. E. S. Chambers, great-nephew of Wills's wife, to Walter Dexter of *The Dickensian*. Wills is known to have been in the confidence of Dickens and Nelly; he forwarded their letters, visited them, dined with them, transacted business for them and was regarded as a friend, although there is no trace of a continuing friendship with her after the death of Dickens: so perhaps Wills liked her less than Dickens wanted him to, and was less careful with letters concerning her than he might have been. Chambers refers to a packet of letters in Dickens's hand which he (Chambers) sent to Sir Henry Dickens and which were never seen again. The letters were said to have been written from America during Dickens's second visit, and they contained, according to Chambers, instructions from Dickens to Wills concerning the welfare of 'a certain lady' approaching her confinement. It is believed that the letters were destroyed by Sir Henry, though not until Kate Perugini had also seen them; and it is true that there are gaps in the Dickens–Wills letters from America which suggest they have been culled.

The trouble with this story is that it puts Nelly's pregnancy much later, in 1867–8, and that there are reasons for doubting that she was pregnant then. Of course she may have been pregnant more than once. Purely on the basis of probability, an association of thirteen years between a man who has fathered children regularly on his wife over a period of sixteen years and a healthy young woman who had no difficulty in conceiving children later might be expected to produce children. On the other hand, Dickens may finally have taken the brotherly advice of Lord Jeffrey about avoiding conception.

Stumbling through this morass of conflicting and uncertain evidence, one is tempted to dismiss the whole subject with a 'not proven'. No trace has been found of any birth in English registers, though an illegitimate baby could go unregistered up to 1874 – as Wilkie Collins's first two children by Martha Rudd did – or it could have been registered under a false name.[19] The French were more rigorous about registering births; but if Nelly was in the Paris region no record would remain, because the archives were burnt during the Commune in 1871. I found no trace in the Boulogne area archives, which are clearly kept and distinguish between legitimate and illegitimate births. But again, the birth and death of a baby in England, France, Switzerland, Italy or indeed any other European country could have been registered under a false name or simply lost in archives subject to destruction by the hand of God or man.

What Dickens continued to refer to as 'mysterious disappearances' and 'evaporating for a fortnight' continued, and the unhappiness connected with the *Faust* performance seems to have passed. The unlamented death of his mother in September 1863 saw him in England; in October he started a new novel, *Our Mutual Friend*, which was to keep him occupied for the next two years. A stranger who observed him walking near his office in the summer of 1864 noted his light step, sanguine complexion and jaunty air, the 'spruce frockcoat, buttoned to show his good and still youthful figure' and the 'brand new hat airily cocked on one side'.[20] Again, this seems closer to the Regency dandy than the Victorian patriarch; Dickens is still presenting himself in the costume of the juvenile lead, even if he sports a stick and has deepening lines etched in his face. He was in France in December 1864, for a week or so at the end of March 1865, again at the end of April, yet again in June. From this last trip he returned on 9 June; and this is the occasion on which Nelly makes her re-entrance.

The three travellers were at the front of the Folkestone to Charing Cross train which ran in conjunction with the ferry boats. On this particular day it had left at 2.30; Dickens had his latest instalment of *Our Mutual Friend* in his travelling bag and his usual flask of brandy. The afternoon was brilliantly sunny and hot. He described what happened in a letter to his old friend Thomas Mitton, written four days after the crash:

> Two ladies were my fellow-passengers, an old one and a young one. This is exactly what passed. You may judge it from the precise length of the suspense: Suddenly we were off the rail, and beating the ground as the car of a half-emptied balloon might. The old lady cried out, 'My God', and the young one screamed. I caught hold of them both (the old lady sat opposite and the young one on my left), and said: 'We can't help ourselves, but we can be quiet and composed. Pray don't cry out.' The old lady immediately answered: 'Thank you. Rely upon me. Upon my soul I will be quiet.' The young lady said in a frantic way, 'Let us join hands and die friends.' We were then all tilted down together in a corner of the carriage, and stopped. I said to them thereupon: 'You may be sure nothing worse can happen. Our danger *must* be over. Will you remain here without stirring, while I get out of the window?' They both answered quite collectedly, 'Yes', and I got out without the least notion what had happened . . .[21]

Dickens does not dream of naming his companions even to an intimate old friend, or mentioning the fact that the young lady was injured; but he cannot resist making them into dramatic characters.

The remark of the 'young lady' suggests Nelly was quarrelling with Dickens, or at least not feeling very friendly at this particular moment, but that the danger made her wish to be reconciled, even at the risk of their bodies being found with linked hands, should the crash kill them.

The accident was caused by men working on the railway forgetting to signal back that the track was interrupted over a small bridge at Staplehurst in Kent. The train had simply steamed over the gap, its middle section collapsing into it; some of the coaches then ran out of control down a bank and overturned into boggy ground, crushing and killing passengers in a tangle of iron, wood and mud. Only the front coach, in which Dickens sat with his party, was held firm by its coupling to the tender, though it was tilted at a steep angle.

Dickens was shaken but not injured; Mrs Ternan was also unharmed; Nelly was not so lucky. She was evidently thrown about and jammed into the broken corner of the carriage, badly enough to have her jewellery torn from her in the struggle to extract her; and, like many of the passengers, she seems to have sustained an injury to her upper arm, possibly a fracture.[22]

Dickens, humanely seeking the wounded and dying with his brandy flask in hand – there were engravings of him at this work in the press – was at the same time absolutely intent on covering up the fact that he had not been travelling alone. He made sure the name of his injured companion was given to no one, and he categorically refused to give evidence at the inquest. The accident was widely reported, since ten people died in it and about forty were injured badly enough to require hospital treatment. One report mentions a young woman who refused to give her name, ostensibly for fear of alarming her relatives. It is not at all clear how Nelly was got from the scene of the crash to a hospital or doctor; it must have been a nightmare for all three of them. Whatever treatment she received, she was soon back in Mornington Crescent with her mother and Fanny, where for some weeks she remained an invalid needing special care.

There is a glimpse of Dickens fussing over how to cheer her up in a note written on 25 June to his manservant John Thompson, instructing him to take

Miss Ellen tomorrow morning, a little basket of fresh fruit, a jar of clotted cream from Tuckers, and a chicken, a pair of pigeons, or some nice little bird. Also on Wednesday morning, and on Friday morning, take her some other things of the same sort – making a little variety each day.[23]

His most indiscreet action was to write, three days after the crash, to the station master at Charing Cross about her lost jewellery:

A lady who was in the carriage with me in the terrible accident on Friday, lost, in the struggle of being got out of the carriage, a gold watch-chain with a smaller gold watch-chain attached, a bundle of charms, a gold watch-key, and a gold seal engraved 'Ellen'. I promised the lady to make her loss known at headquarters, in case these trinkets should be found.[24]

It seems rather a lot of gold to be hanging about the person of one young woman, but no doubt it represented the eight years of Christmases and birthdays celebrated by Dickens, who took such things seriously; he sometimes noted down the letters HBD – for Her Birth Day – against small sums laid out at the end of February and did not willingly accept any other engagement for the day itself, 3 March.

From the time of the accident Dickens began calling Nelly 'The Patient' in his letters to Wills. On 12 July and again on 16 August he assured Wills that the Patient was much better, though still not quite right. On 25 July the Patient was 'still much the same'. He went on to say he planned to go away again in September.[25] Although he often claimed the accident had left him with a fear of train travel, there is no evidence of this in any aspect of his arrangements, which continued to rely heavily on the railways; and in September he did indeed return to Paris, with or without a companion, for two weeks. He records another short break – four days of 'rest and recreation' – in November. Between these two holidays it was decided that the Mornington Crescent house should be let and the Patient should move – or be moved – out of London again.

This chapter has tried to make some sense of the known facts of the years between 1861 and 1865, and suggested a simple outline of a narrative to fit them: that Nelly became pregnant by Dickens and that to minimize the possibility of scandal he moved her to France, probably somewhere in the Paris area; that she had her baby there, with her mother in attendance, some time in 1862; that the baby died, probably during the summer of 1863; and that she then stayed on in France or spent most of her time abroad until June 1865, when the Staplehurst accident happened.[26]

Some or all of this may be wrong. She may not have had a baby; she may not have lived in France but only visited it for brief holidays. Staplehurst, however, is incontrovertible, and it put Dickens into a panic. Staplehurst also enforces the point that, whatever the truth was, there had to be an innocent version of Nelly's activities. It was the version used by Dickens when necessary and by her sisters. Whatever Fanny and Maria thought of Nelly's progress – her acquisition of a house, her abandonment of the stage, her transformation into a well-dressed woman who travelled abroad clandestinely – and whatever they thought of their mother's acquiescence in all this, they had this version which they could use to one another, and possibly to themselves.

The version went like this. Dickens was a friend of the family. He was devoted to them all, but Nelly was most like a daughter to him, or perhaps a god-daughter; and she reciprocated his affection with a true, daughterly devotion. She helped him with his work, and he very reasonably wanted to give her an education – travel abroad was educational – so that she could help him still more. Because she was sensitive, he wanted to save her from the harshness of life in the theatre; but he could not be open about his friendship, because the world was too ready to lay blame and see scandal where there was none. His separation from his wife, while it had nothing to do with Nelly, meant he had to be especially careful not to appear publicly as their friend.

It may be hard to credit that Fanny and Maria really believed this, but they needed it to offer to people who asked about their sister and Dickens, among them no doubt cynical colleagues in the theatre. And if Fanny and Maria didn't believe it, they probably tried to, in order to square their own consciences over any suspicion that the house they lived in and the help they received from Dickens was paid for by their younger sister's sexual favours.

The Staplehurst accident brutally threatened Dickens's privacy and brutally brought home to Nelly the humiliations of her position; for whatever physical injuries she received, his fear of exposure and his inability to give her help and comfort openly when she most needed it must have been painful too. It made very clear to Nelly and her sisters that, whether she was guilty or whether she was innocent, she was obliged to live her life somewhere in the gap between what could be said and what really happened. The gap was a wide one in mid-nineteenth-century England, but that did not make it any more comfortable.

10

Fanny and Maria Get Married

(1863–1866)

When Nelly reappeared in June 1865, everything about her family had changed. Maria was married and living in Oxford, and Fanny was working as a teacher from the house in Ampthill Square. The theatre no longer had a place in any of their lives; all their skills and efforts had failed. Even Dickens's faith in them and his efforts to promote their careers had been disappointed.

He believed strongly in his own ability to wrench the world into the shape he wanted, the stage manager of real events and lives as well as imaginary ones. 'I know my plan is a good one – because it is mine!' he wrote to Miss Coutts once, with a proposal for Urania Cottage.[1] It was not a joke: in his dealings with his publishers, in his quarrel with his wife and in-laws, he behaved as a man who never doubts that what he wants is what is right and will surely be brought about. He was not often defeated; in the case of the Ternans and theatre, however, he was. The energy with which he attempted to assist them in their careers is obvious from the few scraps of letters that have survived. After Nelly left the stage and Fanny moved into the operatic world, he continued to write enthusiastically to stage managers on Maria's behalf. In the autumn of 1861 he reminded Ben Webster at the Adelphi of the strong interest he took 'in her and her family'. The following spring, when Charles Fechter (the French actor-manager he had met in Paris in 1859 and encouraged to move to London) took over at the Princess's Theatre, Dickens recommended Maria again to him and his colleague Edmund Yates, asking them to give her work,

> not because I have a great friendship for her and know her to be one
> of the best and bravest of little spirits and most virtuous of girls (for

that would have nothing to do with it), but because I have acted with her, and believe her to have more aptitude in a minute than all the other people of her standing on the stage in a month. A lady besides, and pretty, and of a good figure, and always painstaking and perfect to the letter. Also (but this has never had a chance) a wonderful mimic.[2]

Aside from the slight note of condescension in his insistence on her virtue and gentility, he could hardly have written in more glowing terms of Maria's qualities, personal and professional; but his recommendations led nowhere. Perhaps Maria was not as talented as he believed, or perhaps managers were nervous of her name.

Finding it impossible to work in London, Maria had to pick up what she could in the provinces: small jobs here and there, touring with Fanny in opera; a few weeks in Oxford, a few more in East Anglia. It was a tough business. In January 1862 she fell ill with bronchitis after being required to jump into a tank of water on stage during a performance of Boucicault's *Colleen Bawn*. This was in Rochester, where her Uncle William lived, and where Dickens gave a reading to a rapturous audience in the same week. She recovered and struggled on again.

By now Maria and Fanny knew everything there was to know about the status, working conditions and expectations of professional actresses. It had become increasingly clear that, despite Dickens's faith in them, neither had the capacity to become a great popular actress or singer – an Ellen Terry, a Marie Wilton, a Jenny Lind – and that if they chose to go on with the grind of the provincial tours, the second-rate companies, the small parts and perpetual uncertainty about the next job, they would never earn more than a pittance, wearing their neat black silk dresses into shabbiness and losing the freshness of youth, all in the service of an increasingly precarious future. Even the most successful actresses could fall into the abyss of poverty: Fanny Kelly, who had been at the top of the profession once, rich, famous, beloved by critics and public, was now living in penury with her daughter, supporting herself by taking in lodgers. For lesser talents, the long-term prospects looked grim indeed.

Neither was inclined to wait passively on fate. At midsummer

1862, when the latest opera tour reached Hull and closed there, while Dickens – and probably their mother too – was distracted by other problems, they decided to give up. For all its promise, the clan of Thomas Ternan had not lasted long in the theatre. Fanny turned back to her old idea of teaching. She decided to concentrate on lessons in music and Italian, and hoped to keep up her own singing with occasional concert work. Maria, bolder and younger, turned to what was generally regarded as a more legitimate womanly ambition than the stage. She became the first of the sisters to find a husband.

Her bridegroom, whom she may have met during her last tour, was the son of a prosperous Oxford brewer and town councillor. Rowland Taylor could offer her everything a sensible Victorian bride hoped for: a good steady income, a respectable social position, a comfortable home with servants and a carriage. From being an actress with a failing career, she was to be transported into a world in which she would have no financial cares and no duties beyond the running of her husband's establishment. The marriage took place on 9 June 1863 at St Matthew's, Oakley Square. It was only a step from Nelly's house, from which Maria must have set out for the church; and she was given away by her Rochester uncle, William Lawless Ternan. The absence of her mother and younger sister could plausibly be ascribed to reasons of health.

Rowland Taylor managed one of his father's breweries, and the couple was to settle in Oxford. According to family tradition, Maria was not in love with her husband but married him on the rebound from another, unhappy affair. It did not make a good start for either of them; she had, however, joined a very solid and respectable family. One of her brothers-in-law was a solicitor, another a clergyman preparing to become a schoolmaster; a few years later the Revd John Taylor became the principal of the school in Tunbridge Wells to which Dickens sent his youngest son, Plorn, and Plorn – who was in most respects as unsatisfactory as most of the Dickens sons – was happy in his care.

In spite of this solid beginning Maria failed to turn into a model wife; or perhaps it was the very solidity that proved too much for her. She was known in the family as the merry sister, and with nothing to do but run a house – at first the beautiful old Paradise

House in the centre of Oxford – and please her busy husband, she found things quiet. Soon she was bored. She was not used to being idle, and she had interests and wishes that were not met in the society into which she had entered, which was neither artistic nor intellectual. Oxford University took little note of women and none at all of the wives of brewers. Like all her family she was restless. She had been on the move for too long to settle easily. It looks as though she began to consider quite early how she might escape from the comfortable trap into which she had ventured. Like innumerable Victorian wives and daughters she developed the secret weapon of delicate health. In her case it did not confine her to the sofa, but dictated that she must travel, to the seaside or, better still, abroad, like her sister Nelly. No children appeared to interfere with this programme. Maria acquired a pet dog and dreamed of another life altogether.

Fanny also dreamed of achieving something more than being a north London singing teacher. Her performing career did not prosper. In June 1865 she was approaching her thirtieth birthday, still a trim, neatly turned-out young woman, clever, observant, hardworking, conscientious; and by now clearly destined for spinsterhood. As a governess she was in demand and had just acquired an interesting new pupil in little Beatrice Trollope. Fanny had first known Bice – so she was always called (pronounced in two Italian syllables, bee-chay) – as a five-year-old in Florence. She was the only child of Dickens's friend, the Anglo-Florentine writer Thomas Trollope, and his wife Theodosia, also a writer, who had entertained Fanny in Italy seven years earlier. Theodosia, always delicate, died suddenly in the spring of 1865; and the grieving Thomas, hardly knowing how to cope, either with his loneliness or with his thirteen-year-old daughter, availed himself of the kindness of his brother Anthony, who collected Bice and took her to England to spend the summer with him and her comfortable Aunt Rose.

The Anthony Trollopes lived at Waltham Cross in Essex, then unspoiled country, though easily reached from London; and here it was arranged in May that Miss Ternan should come down on alternate weekends, staying from Saturday until Monday, to give Bice a lesson on each of the three days. For this she was offered £2 per visit in addition to her board and lodging.[3] If Thomas Trollope was surprised at the transformation of the aspiring opera singer into a governess, he made no objection; indeed, singing was something Bice enjoyed. The proposal did not originate with him but with his brother; how Anthony came to know of Miss Ternan we can only guess.

So on alternate Friday afternoons Fanny set off from the Shore-ditch Station with her little bag and travelled out into Essex. She took to her pupil: Bice was beautiful, a tiny, sad, dark-eyed sprite, with an exotic look of her mother, who had both Indian and Jewish forebears; and she was in need of attention and affection, which Fanny was happy to give her. The weekends at the pleasant Georgian house, with its lawns and cedar trees and surrounding fields and woods, where its master hunted vigorously each winter, were probably worth as much to Fanny as the money. Anthony Trollope was reaching the peak of his success as a novelist in 1865; within the last year he had published two of his most popular books, *The Small House at Allington* and *Can You Forgive Her?* – both centred on young women of character, one a study in constancy, the other in inconstancy – and he was also involved in the setting up of a new magazine, the *Fortnightly Review*. This meant there were other interesting visitors at Waltham Cross, publishers and writers summoned to discuss literary and journalistic matters; all grist to Fanny's sharp wits. Another bookish young woman who met Trollope at this time found him detestable, noisy, domineering and as vulgar as Dickens, she wrote;[4] yet if Trollope lacked delicacy, he and his wife were a genuinely kindly couple.

They did not, for instance, treat the governess with condescension. Several of Trollope's heroines were meek-seeming little governesses with surprising inner resources and staunchness of character, who turned out more worthily than their social superiors. Fanny could in any case hold her own in company. She could look like a lady, and knew when to speak and when to be silent; and when she did speak she had something to say, because she read a great deal and was interested in everything around her. She made the very most of her time at Waltham Cross, aware that she could now count two of the giants of contemporary fiction among her friends; and during these months she began to try her hand at writing a story of her own.

Some time in the late summer Thomas Trollope appeared at Waltham Cross and renewed his acquaintance with Fanny. When he returned to Florence in October he took Bice with him, but the governess promised to correspond with her pupil, and was as good as her word. Friendship was now well established between all the Trollopes and Miss Ternan, and when Christmas came she was invited to a ball and kindly told she might bring her younger sister. Fanny's description of the ball, or rather of the matching dresses and flowers worn by herself and Nelly – 'pale green silk covered with tarlatane of the same colour, trimmed with white lace and dewdrops, with scarlet geranium and white heather in her hair' – has something pathetic about it, because it is one of the very few occasions on which we hear of some ordinary girlish enjoyment in the lives of the sisters. For one evening Fanny, so quick-eyed, so industrious, so eagerly pressing forward, and Nelly, with her burden of secrecy, were able to appear almost as simple and untouched as a pair of Barchester girls.

Were some young men assembled for the occasion? The Trollope boys, Harry and Fred, were both under twenty but old enough to dance with the Ternans. Fanny, whose account of the ball was written for Bice, divulged nothing more than the details of their dresses and flowers. We can note in passing that the scarlet geranium in their hair was known to be the favourite flower of Dickens and may not have been altogether easy to come by in midwinter.

Anthony Trollope obviously liked Fanny, and Nelly too. He was not a snob; nor was he a womanizer, but he responded to quick, clever girls. In 1860 he had met in Florence a young American, Kate Fields, twenty-five years his junior, and ever since cherished a passion – open, platonic but intense – for her. It could have made him somewhat sympathetic to Dickens's position with Nelly and inclined him to believe in its innocence. And even if he didn't, he was a tolerant man. *The Belton Estate*, another novel he published in 1865, defends the heroine's decision to remain friends with a woman she likes, after discovering that she has committed adultery and lived with her husband for some years before they were able to marry – a piece of broadmindedness with no parallel in the work of Dickens, incidentally. Trollope's invitation to the ball says something in his favour, and his liking for the sisters says something in theirs.[5]

By this time Houghton Place had been let to a tenant. After October 1865 none of the Ternans ever occupied the house again; the rent, however, provided Nelly with a steady income of £50 to £60 a year almost till the end of her life.[6] Now, for one reason or another, she was to leave London again for the country. Fanny and Mrs Ternan needed other lodgings, which they found still in the Mornington Crescent area, at Lidlington Place, and here Mrs Ternan received a surprising offer.

Early in December Dickens came to her with the news that she was to be invited to take up her theatrical career again, by Charles Fechter, now manager of the Lyceum; although Dickens himself was also deeply involved in the plan to revive a dramatized version of Scott's *The Master of Ravenswood*. Mrs Ternan was wanted to play blind Alice; coupled with this was a revival of Boucicault's *Corsican Brothers*, which had another good part for her. She had last played in it ten years earlier; the idea of acting again was irresistible to her. It meant earning something, and being among old friends and colleagues. Whatever the circumstances of the past few years, they had kept her from the stage; but, after sixty years, the theatre was still in her blood. She was soon busy rehearsing.

Dickens praised her professionalism to Georgina, saying she was word perfect at rehearsals when few of the others, Fechter included, had bothered to learn their lines. He took an active part in the production all through December, having 'an earnest desire to put Scott, for once, upon the stage in his own gallant manner'; and the show opened on 11 January 1866.[7] Fanny reported to her ex-pupil in Florence that all three sisters went to the Lyceum to see their mother perform.

In the same letter she said Maria had been ill. She had gone to St Leonards-on-Sea, Sussex, to recuperate, accompanied by Nelly, each sister taking her own dog. Since railway regulations forbade dogs in the carriage, they smuggled them on to the train hidden in their crinolines. In their lodgings in wintry St Leonards the two sisters were on their own, probably for the first time since Berners Street: a chance to exchange confidences and advice, to consider the condition of marriage and non-marriage, as they tugged their dogs along the sea-front or settled cosily for the long, dark evenings. Maria then set off for Italy; she had decided she must get away from the English winter. Nelly remained in England and was with Dickens for her twenty-seventh birthday. He turned down an invitation to attend the meeting of a charity he supported, telling the organizer that 'an annual engagement which I cannot possibly forego will prevent me attending next Saturday's meeting'; and next Saturday was HBD, 3 March.[8]

Nelly was now settled in Elizabeth Cottage in the High Street of Slough. In 1866 it was a small and sleepy market town, close to the banks of the Thames and set amid fields, with just a central street, a few small shops, modest terraced cottages and a picturesque old church, St Laurence Upton, just restored. Slough had another particular virtue for Dickens and Nelly: it was blessed with exceptional communications. A fast train from Paddington took only eighteen minutes; alternatively you could walk the two pleasant miles across parkland and fields to either Windsor or Datchet and take a different line to Victoria or Waterloo; and Waterloo was only a step across the river from Wellington Street.[9]

If you looked up as you walked across the fields, you saw Windsor Castle floating above, presided over by the widowed Queen, symbol and upholder of the domestic virtues. The Queen did not hear of her best-known writer's visits to Slough, for the simple reason that no Charles Dickens was known of there. Rates were paid on Elizabeth Cottage by a Mr John Tringham, who later became Charles Tringham, and then again 'Turnan'; later Charles Tringham's name appeared again, and for a while Mr Tringham paid rates on two cottages in the High Street. None of the rate books were kept with any great effort at precision, so a certain variation in spelling is not a matter of much moment, but in this case there is a clear pattern. Over the next four years the names 'Turnan', 'Turnham' and 'Tringham' all crop up in rate books; there is a Frances Turnham and a Thomas Turnham (the first name of Nelly's mother and father), but the most persistent is Charles Tringham.

Dickens had since childhood made a habit of using false names whenever it suited him; it's likely he picked out this one from his tobacconist, Mrs Mary Tringham, who kept her shop just round the corner from Wellington Street.[10] The convenience of the pseudonym is obvious: it gave him the same initial as Nelly and was close enough to her name to allow an inattentive clerk to confuse the two. She might be Miss Ternan or Miss Tringham, or Mrs either, as convenience dictated. Whether she laughed about it with 'Mr Tringham', shrugged it off or felt humiliated by the charade, she had little option but to accept it. The disguise was not perfect, and some of the citizens of Slough certainly understood that Mr Tringham was really Dickens, among them a carpenter who did some work for him; but it was a quiet place, and nobody made trouble.[11]

Mrs Ternan was engaged at the Lyceum until June. Maria was in Florence, and now Fanny's life also took a surprising twist. She was invited by Thomas Trollope to go out to Florence as Bice's full-time governess. The fact that Maria was already in Italy was an extra incentive; and without too much hesitation she agreed. London would hardly miss a teacher of singing and Italian; in April she set out to join Bice and the disconsolate widower.

They had left Villino Trollope, where she had last visited them in 1858. It was simply too full of memories of Theodosia for Tom, who made up his mind to move. He acquired, at considerable expense, the Villa Ricorboli, a large house outside the Porto San Niccolo, where there was all the space he needed for his collection of antiquities, curios and books, and all the scope he needed for his architectural and gardening ambitions, which were grandiose. Fanny arrived to find everything in disorder. Most of the house was open to the air, there were planks laid everywhere, and the builders were living on the premises. They were just beginning work on a tower intended to house the library; meanwhile Trollope's enormous collection of books lay scattered everywhere. She took all this in her stride. She was a good organizer, her Italian was excellent, she was happy to be abroad again, she was a kindly and conscientious governess, and she impressed the Anglo-Florentines with her 'almost masculine' cleverness. Still more important, Tom Trollope, who had suffered under the regime of an earlier French governess, found her congenial. So did his friend, the poet Alfred Austin, who was also installed at the Villa Ricorboli; in the evenings the whole party would climb down the steep hill to an empty villa below and sing *stornelli* – Tuscan folk songs – joined no doubt by Maria, as they sat on stone steps or a marble bench. The fire flies appeared and the crickets chirped.[12] It was a blessed change from Mornington Crescent, from touring with second-rate opera companies, and from giving lessons by the hour.

Tom Trollope was a big, bearish man; strikingly ugly, as were most of the male Trollopes, but sociable and good-hearted. Like his mother, who spent the last years of her life with him, he was a prodigious worker, turning out huge amounts of journalism as well as novels and works of history in an unending stream: he averaged more than a volume a year over fifty years. He had a special, almost unvarying routine, and wrote standing upright at a lectern from eight until two every day, sustained by cigars and glasses of milk. He was devoted to his daughter but awkward and short-tempered; he did not expect his activities to be interrupted and was quite at sea in handling her needs; above all he was accustomed to a strong presiding female presence, and now, gratefully, he had found one again. Within three months, in the heat of the Florentine July, the governess and the widower had exchanged lovers' vows.

Whether Fanny was in love with the 56-year-old Trollope or not, she got on with him well enough to see that this was a sensible solution to her problems as well as his. Books, history, music, languages, travel, were passions with both of them. She was thirty-one; the age gap was only a little less than that between Dickens and Nelly. Of course there was no other comparisons to be drawn between their cases; Fanny was to be a bride and take a distinguished name.

Her engagement coincided with something which she regarded as of almost equal importance: the serialization of her first novel, *Aunt Margaret's Trouble*, in Dickens's *All the Year Round*. A pathetic story of a girl whose lover is stolen from her by her beautiful and evil-natured younger sister, and who nobly forgives the wrong, it is told simply and is not altogether without charm, though on the sentimental side. Dickens was 'absolutely enchanted' with the story and 'enthusiastically invited his friends to read and admire it as much as he did', wrote Percy Fitzgerald later. He added, 'It was written by, I believe, Mrs Trollope, *née* Ternan, then living in Italy. I am not certain as to this, but I am as to the rapturous way in which Boz praised it. The authoress was presently given a commission for a long and serious novel called, I think, *Mabel's Progress*.'[13] Dickens himself sent a copy of *Aunt Margaret's Trouble* to Frederick Chapman of Chapman & Hall, who published it in book form. Both in the magazine and in hard covers it appeared anonymously, and the discreet dedication was to 'E.L.T.'

In August Fanny received a payment of £75, from Dickens's private account rather than through the usual channels of the magazine. In this way the name of Ternan was kept out of the office book-keeping. It made no odds to Fanny. She could now feel she was not going penniless into her marriage, and that she might join her future husband honourably in his profession. The news of the coming wedding appears to have delighted everyone, with the rather natural exception of Bice, who may well have felt she was losing her father and her governess in one stroke, and faced the less than enchanting prospect of being sent to boarding school in England not much more than a year after the death of her mother.

In Slough, meanwhile, Nelly ruled over Elizabeth Cottage, Mariana-like awaiting the visits of her Mr Tringham. In the spring of 1866 he was on a reading tour, though, like all his tours, it was organized to allow frequent returns to London – and from London to Slough. His visits must inevitably have provided the dramatic focus of otherwise empty weeks; his eager arrival, anxious to find out how she was, bearing news, excitement, little presents, the latest number of *All the Year Round*, brought her the breath of the world from which she was sequestered as well as the proof of her power.

More mundanely, he may have brought her housekeeping money; at Gad's Hill this was handed over to Georgina with the most exact regularity. If he had something to write during the day, he is likely to have settled down to read what he had written to her in the evening; and if she was sulky, he probably tried to tease her out of it, as he had teased his wife before their marriage, urging her not to be 'coss'. As a young man he had called Catherine darling Tatie, dearest Pig, Wig, Mouse, Titmouse and old lady. No doubt

Dickens, aged forty-seven, as painted by Frith, who said he had the look of a man 'who had reached the topmost rung of a very high ladder and was perfectly aware of his position'. At this time he owned both Gad's Hill in Kent and, in Bloomsbury, Tavistock House (*above*).

'The Manager': Dickens, lying on the grass, with his acting group in 1857. Among the ladies are his daughters and sisters-in-law, among the men his son Charley, Wilkie Collins, Augustus Egg and Francesco Berger.

A modern view of the modest front of Park Cottage in Islington, very little altered since the Ternans lived there in the 1850s and Dickens judged it 'unwholesome'.

The scene outside the Free Trade Hall, Manchester, where Dickens and the Ternans played together in *The Frozen Deep* in August 1857.

'There is not on this earth a more virtuous and spotless creature
than this young lady,' wrote Dickens in the spring of 1858. On the
other hand, 'I do suppose that there never was a man so seized
and rended by one Spirit,' he also wrote of his longings. The Spirit
was embodied by Nelly, here seen in an English photograph of the
period when she was trying to establish herself as an actress, and
he was doing everything he could to promote the careers of all
three Ternan sisters.

Catherine Dickens, sad but dignified in her rejection by her husband, who insisted that even their youngest children stay with him.

Her sister Georgina Hogarth, who eagerly stepped into her place, becoming Dickens's housekeeper and apologist.

Katey, the brightest of Dickens's children, who resembled, understood and criticized him.

Maria Ternan: 'A very good little pale face, with large black eyes,' wrote Dickens.

'Near Covent Garden this afternoon I met Charles Dickens . . . clad in spruce frockcoat, buttoned to show his good and still youthful figure; and with brand-new hat airily cocked on one side, and stick poised in his hand' – Arthur Munby, 10 May 1864

A painting of the popular subject of the Fallen Woman by
Dickens's friend Augustus Egg. Note the advertisements for
excursions to Paris and the show at the Haymarket.

A print showing Dickens ministering to a woman
passenger after the accident to the train in which
he was returning from France with Nelly and her
mother in June 1865.

The Villa Ricorboli outside Florence, where Fanny Ternan was first governess and then the wife of Thomas Trollope, and where Nelly was a frequent guest.

The main street of Slough, where Nelly was installed in a cottage in 1866, much visited by the mysterious 'Charles Tringham'.

(*Above*) Dickens giving his Sikes and Nancy reading to a rapt audience during the 'farewell readings' of 1869 and 1870. Nelly was sometimes present on these occasions; Dickens's American friend Annie Fields noted in her diary for June 1869 how he told her husband 'that when he was ill in his reading only Nelly observed that he staggered and his eye failed, only she dared tell him'.

(*Left*) A copy of this photograph of Dickens in his last year, cut to fit a small oval frame, was among the few family trinkets and pictures left after the estate of Nelly's daughter had been disposed of.

he produced a similar range of lover's endearments for Nelly; and perhaps his phrase 'neuralgia flying about' is a reference to her bouts of ill humour.

It's unlikely that it was all ease and pleasure for the man of fifty-four and the girl of twenty-seven. Long after his death she said she loathed the memory of his attentions; it's not possible to know whether she found them loathsome at the time. There was always the fear of pregnancy. There was also the matter of how she saw herself mirrored in his eyes. In a society which divided women into the good and the bad, even the most cherished mistress could only be bad; it was her very badness that made her desirable to the man. Good women, it was widely agreed, were not sexually enthusiastic; coldness could thus become an assertion of virtue, a demand to be loved for something other, and better, than sex. If Nelly wished to see herself elevated into a platonic muse, and Dickens longed for the release of her embraces, it was a recipe for some miserable days and nights for them both.

Yet whatever she felt about her position, her life was now bound to his in a permanent arrangement from which she could scarcely escape – for where was she to go, and what was she to do but wait on him? And he could be the most delightful of companions; there were things they enjoyed together unequivocally. In good weather she sometimes rode with him; or they walked to Datchet or Windsor through the meadows of Upton cum Chalvey, or by way of the playing fields of Eton. We know he took this route, because there is a letter to his new manager, George Dolby, in August 1866, headed 'Eton' and written 'on a pause in a walk, while waiting for a train': and we know Nelly sometimes went with him, because he noted the fact in his diary of 1867.[14] Sometimes she even took the train with him as far as town, and occasionally they dined together in a restaurant in Regent Street or went to the theatre, though these were rare treats.

Whether from the effects of Staplehurst, the bearing and loss of a child, or the sheer anxieties and uncertainties of her life, she was now, like Maria, 'delicate'. All domestic tasks being out of the question, she took on a local girl, Jane Wheeler, as her maid; it was the start of a lifelong relationship, for Jane took a great liking to her mistress, and remained on affectionate and protective terms with her for the next fifty years.[15]

What else did Nelly do with her days? She had her music; and her mother was often with her, bringing her St Bernard, Tell, to keep company with Nelly's dog, named Lady Clara Vere de Vere after Tennyson's blue-blooded heroine. It's a relief to find her spirits were good enough for a mild joke of this kind, and no surprise to find her drawing on Tennyson; the commonplace book she kept later shows that she appreciated the poetry of the laureate. Other poets she enjoyed were Thomas Hood, John Greenleaf Whittier, the popular American author of 'The Barefoot Boy', and the Romantics – at any rate Keats, Shelley and Wordsworth – as well as, inevitably in an acting family, Shakespeare. Reading was perhaps her chief, most consoling occupation. Her circle and family connections must have kept her supplied with novels, and she can scarcely have avoided the bestseller of the decade, Mrs Henry Wood's melodramatic *East Lynne*, with its adulterous but penitent heroine who practises an extraordinary deception upon her husband and children, faking her own death in a railway accident and returning, disguised, as a governess. She read her way through a good number of the historians, essayists, sociologists and biographers of the time, Carlyle, Buckle, Macaulay, Matthew Arnold, Froude, T. H. Huxley, Lecky, Crabb Robinson and Lockhart. She seems to have managed some Schiller and Goethe in German, and among French writers was acquainted with Victor Hugo, de Musset, Béranger, Beaumarchais, Rousseau and Michelet; and with George Sand, whose work Dickens was said to dislike, though not apparently with Balzac, whom he enjoyed. One must be careful not to overestimate the significance of an extract in a commonplace book, but the list suggests at the least a determined assault on culture which none of Dickens's heroines can be remotely imagined undertaking; nor was Dickens himself renowned for his cultural range or breadth of reading.

In late October she went with her mother to Paris to attend Fanny's wedding. A few days before this Dickens's accounts show a payment into something described as the 'N trust', followed up by other small sums over the next three months, when they apparently ceased: another glimpse into his byzantine procedures.[16] Dickens was not of the wedding party, but Maria travelled from Florence with the bridal couple, and her husband came from England to join them. Mr and Mrs Anthony Trollope also came with their son Henry; Bice was left in Italy with friends. A delay to the train from Florence meant the ceremony was postponed for two days, during which Nelly did some shopping, or at least bought a blue collar with a silver bell for Lady Clara. Then, on 29 October at the British Embassy, Fanny became Mrs Trollope – Frances E. as opposed to her late mother-in-law Frances – and the new couple departed immediately for a long, rambling honeymoon through south-western France. Fanny, determined to be a good stepmother, sent off volleys of letters to Bice, laden with affectionate messages from herself and Papa – who sometimes contributed a short scrawl – and with educational descriptions of scenery, architecture and local costumes, backed by sketches. Although they were dutifully preserved by Bice, they did not prevent her from feeling that she had been pushed out of the nest, and from bitterly resenting the fact.[17] But Fanny had at last found a life to her taste: and she was already half-way through a second novel for *All the Year Round*, this time a long one.

Maria had taken to life in Italy and became interested in painting; but she had to make up her mind to return to Oxford with her prosperous, uninteresting but indubitably patient husband. Nelly was back in Slough by 1 November, and she reported on the wedding to Dickens. He wrote to Tom Trollope:

> I should have written immediately to congratulate you on your then approaching marriage, and to assure you of my most cordial and affectionate interest in all that nearly concerns you, but that I thought it best to wait until I should have seen Nelly and her mother on their return, and should have known from them how best to address you.[18]

The easy reference to Nelly suggests that Trollope understood the existence of close ties between her and Dickens; linking her with her mother makes it a family matter, and leaves Trollope free to interpret the ties as he chooses. Dickens's letter went on:

> No friend that you have can be more truly attached to you than I am. I congratulate you with all my heart, and believe that your

Friday Second November, 1866

My Dope,

... have had the letter in it ...
... to be so on your then
... marriage, and to avoid so as ...
... appreciate ...
... there you, as that ...
... had to wait until I should ...
... Sally, and be active on their
... and should look them from
... ... to ... you ...

... I do ... have care ...
... I am, ... this all my
heart, and believe that your marriage
will stand high upon the list of
happy ones. As to your wife's winning
a high reputation out of your honel — if
you care for that — it is not much, as
an addition to the delights of love and
peace and a suitable companion for life — I

marriage will stand high upon the list of happy ones. As to your wife's winning a high reputation out of your house – if you care for that – it is not much, as an addition to the delights of love and peace and a suitable companion for life – I have not the least doubt of her power to make herself famous.

I little thought what an important master of the ceremonies I was, when I first presented the late Fanny Ternan to you. Bear me in your mind ever as the unconscious instrument of your having given your best affections to a worthy object, and I shall be the best paid master of the ceremonies since Nash drove his coach and six through the streets of Bath.[19]

It's a fine letter of congratulation, though its invocation of 'love and peace and a suitable companion for life' raises the ghost of his own sad marital history. As to Fanny, the tribute is to her intellectual power and strength of purpose; no mention now of her being a sympathetic confidante, as he had called her once. There is a hint that he finds Fanny formidable.

Meanwhile he was preparing to serialize her second book, *Mabel's Progress*. It was to be put out anonymously, like *Aunt Margaret's Trouble*, which had already led to some speculation. Even to so close a friend as Collins, who angled to know the name of the author, Dickens refused to divulge it.[20] The reason for this defensiveness was presumably to be found in Slough. Collins, who had known the beginning of the secret of 'E.L.T.', could not be trusted at all now.

Fanny's attitude to the relations between Dickens and her sister appears to have changed upon her marriage, and within a year the change led to a quarrel. Dickens maintained friendly relations with Tom Trollope and continued to publish Fanny's work, while at the same time hinting bitterly in private at her ingratitude and at the necessity of keeping quiet to her on the subject of Nelly's recent history.[21] Something had made Fanny hostile to him. The situation was awkward for her. There was nothing to be ashamed of in the fact that he had helped her and now paid her for her work; but for anyone to connect this with his relations with Nelly would be intolerable. Another thing that must have concerned her was the thought of any breath of scandal affecting her stepdaughter. Nelly's name was often mentioned by Fanny in her letters, and at some point she was introduced to Bice; the introduction would be regarded as deplorable if Nelly's position were known to be compromised.

Fanny may have reasoned that as long as nothing spoilt the image of her sister as an unremarkable well-to-do young lady who travelled about with her mother and her sister, and lived a quiet life, not too much damage was done. Fanny had not been an actress for so many years for nothing. Appearances become the truth. Anything unfortunate that might have taken place during the past nine years could simply be effaced. It was essential, however, that no more unfortunate events should occur. This may have led Fanny, from the time of her marriage, to encourage Nelly towards detaching herself from Dickens's close companionship or changing the nature of their tie. If so, Dickens, not unnaturally, would have viewed her attitude with furious resentment.

I I

The Year of the Diary
(1867)

Nelly was kept hidden by an expert, but even Dickens could not prevent accidents like Staplehurst or the loss of his diary; and it's because of this that we have, for one only of the twelve hidden years, a document which gives a clear picture of the pattern of their lives. The year is 1867, and the information is contained in a very small memorandum book which he used as a pocket diary from 1 January to 7 November, when he set off for America and stopped making notes. The diary escaped destruction, the annual fate of Dickens's pocket books, only because it was lost or stolen, and someone thought it worth preserving. It went missing at the end of December 1867, when he was in New York; he reported its disappearance to Georgina in a letter, and though he was jocular about it, he was obviously slightly worried, too, saying the loss was one '"which", as Mr Pepys would add, "do trouble me mightily"'.[1] In fact, the daily entries were written in forms so abbreviated that they would have conveyed very little to the casual glance. A typical sequence of three days looks like this:

at SL: To off: from Slo at 2.20. Dine Forster. Back aft.
at SL:
To off at 10.20 at SL

Yet he was right to be perturbed, because the diary is pervaded by the one person he wished to keep out of sight. Here is 'N' – her illness and recovery, the possibility of her joining him in America, her presence in Slough, her visits to the theatre, her walks with him, their joint search for a house and move to Peckham. Once a few notations are understood, it offers a key to the private existence he guarded so carefully.[2]

The diary surfaced in a New York auction-room sale in 1922, billed as coming from an unnamed private collector. The catalogue description suggested that its importance lay in the fact that it covered the period in which Dickens was preparing his American reading tour. It was bought by the brothers Berg with other Dickensiana, and then lay unremarked in their collection until the curator drew attention to its importance in 1943. Since then scholars have been squeezing it like a tiny sponge for every drop of information it can yield.[3] It is a very small booklet – 10 × 5½ centimetres – printed with meteorological and other information, bound in faded red leather and written in a cramped but mostly legible hand; some of the ink has weathered to brown, some is blue.

What it reveals with perfect clarity is a man intent on a split life; a man almost demented in his determined pursuit of it, despite the exhaustion and illness we know of from his letters and the reports of friends. It shows how he used the growing railway system as an essential component of that split life, putting up with as much pressure and discomfort as any commercial traveller in pursuance of his elaborate system of divided days and weeks, hurrying between Gad's Hill and Wellington Street, between Wellington Street and Slough; how Paddington, Waterloo, Windsor, Slough and Datchet stations were almost as familiar to him as his office and his home. He would go straight back to Slough from giving a reading in Bath before setting off to give another in Birmingham, and fit in four secret days there between readings in Cheltenham and his departure for Ireland. On at least two occasions he sent notes to Georgina making excuses about not coming to Gad's Hill, putting it down to pressure of work or ill health, when in fact he was planning to spend the time with Nelly.[4] He would leave a dinner at Forster's decorous establishment to take the late-evening train back to Slough. He would travel from Gad's Hill to London with his married son Charley and then straight on by another train to see Nelly. Whenever possible he fitted in two or three days, sometimes mid-week, sometimes at weekends, usually making it appear as if he were at his office. During the ten months covered by the diary, he spent one third of his time with, or near, Nelly; one third at Gad's Hill; and one third serving his other love, the public. His perfect punctuality and grasp of timetables stood him in brilliant stead, and when he wrote to a friend that 'I am here, there, everywhere, nowhere', it was almost the literal truth.[5] Small wonder that he paid the price in sleeplessness, faintness, piles and, as he described it himself, 'soreness of the whole body'.

Other men close to Dickens seem to have managed their double lives with less stress. Collins acquired a second mistress in 1867, established her in London round the corner from his first establishment, and began a family with her; when Caroline objected and made a defiant marriage to someone else, he took it calmly and equally calmly welcomed her back into residence later, continuing to maintain his second growing family; both women were given simultaneous seaside holidays in adjacent resorts. The artist George Cruikshank also kept two households and two families round the corner from one another near Mornington Crescent, and fathered ten children on his second 'wife', Edith Archibold. William Frith, the popular painter who did Dickens's portrait in 1859, had a similar arrangement: his two establishments were also only ten minutes' walk apart, in the Paddington area, and portraits of both women appear in his famous painting of Paddington, *The Railway Station*. His marriage produced twelve children and lasted thirty-five years; his mistress Mary Alford bore him another seven children, and when his wife died he married her. There was something cosy and domestic about these arrangements; the women involved were not *femmes fatales* or *cocottes* – concepts for which the English were obliged to turn to the French – but comfortable, everyday creatures who were grateful enough to have steady men to support them and their children, and modest about their own position and claims. A man, even if he was not a husband, was after all still the best available source of income for a woman.

The difficulty for Dickens was not only that he felt more vulnerable to discovery and comment, as one whose fame was pre-eminent and tied to a virtuous image which he had ferociously defended at the time of the separation from Catherine; he had also uttered assertions about Nelly, both to his family and to the world, which made the position more difficult than it might otherwise have been. The further problem was that he had picked the wrong sort of woman to be his second 'wife'. She was neither a modest girl of the people nor a grateful widow. If she had given up her professional ambitions, she still had social ones, and she was backed by an intelligent, aspiring and watchful family. Her mother's tolerance of the situation with Dickens must have helped her, in practical ways and by keeping up reasonably correct appearances; but when her two elder sisters both made good marriages, they brought a circle of in-laws who were almost bound to meet her sooner or later, as indeed the Anthony Trollopes already had in 1866. Nelly was becoming more difficult to hide or perhaps more reluctant to remain hidden and accept the many drawbacks of her position.

If Nelly went to Gad's Hill, as both she and Dickens's daughter later claimed, there is no indication of the fact in the 1867 diary. She may have been there with her mother, presented as a family friend, for large-scale entertainments such as cricket matches; and yet this doesn't seem to square with the clandestine nature of his visits to her. Forster knew her, and Georgina and Mamey, too, and Dickens regarded them as trustworthy friends where she was concerned, but that does not mean they engaged in social activities together, and again there is no sign of this in 1867. She may have visited Maria in Oxford; made brief trips to the seaside with her or her mother; or seen her cousins in Rochester, not so far from Gad's Hill. Mrs Ternan may have kept on Fanny's lodgings in Mornington Crescent as a London base; if so, there is again no sign that Dickens saw any of the Ternans there at this time.

The pattern of her life was that she was available when Dickens wanted her; in general she stayed put, awaited visits, and occupied herself as best she could when he was away working or living his official life at Gad's Hill. There Georgina presided, there he saw his children and received guests. Collins, who had become part of the family when Katey married his brother Charles, saw Dickens at Gad's Hill as much as at the office. So did George Dolby, the big, bluff manager who succeeded Arthur Smith, although Dolby did also dine with Dickens and Nelly in town.[6] Wills is the only member of Dickens's circle known to have gone to Slough with him. For Nelly, dinner with Wills or Dolby, both in Dickens's employ, middle-aged, married men, neither of whom would have dreamed of introducing their wives to her, may not have been the greatest treat imaginable.

She was twenty-eight in the year of the diary; her mother was sixty-five, Dickens fifty-five. By now she must have begun to ask herself if her youth was to pass entirely while she lived this curious half-life with an elderly mother and an ageing gentleman friend, cut off from her own generation, unable to meet other young men and women or pursue ordinary social activities, unable to think of marriage. The elation she had felt during the early stages of his love for her was bound to flatten as the years passed; to be singled out by a great man became less wonderful if it had to be shrouded in mystery. Whatever benefits he had given her – the opportunity to travel, financial freedom, the leisure for study – were liable to turn sour when it became obvious they were leading nowhere. However cultivated she might become, there was not much to do with her cultivation if she was destined for a life of nervous isolation.

The details tell the story. In a letter to a friend Dickens said he was going to Buckinghamshire from Sunday, 16 December, to Tuesday, 18 December (1866), very possibly to celebrate an early Christmas with Nelly (Slough was then in Bucks.).[7] The season of domestic goodwill and festivity must have posed a problem to all good Victorian family men with more than one family to take care of, particularly when there were two lots of children to receive the demonstrations of paternal love. Dickens was at least spared this difficulty. Catherine must accept the absence of her children; Nelly had none, but she must also accept that Gad's Hill had the first claim on him and make her own arrangements accordingly, which probably meant staying quietly in Slough with her mother and the pets for company. At Gad's Hill Dickens acted the squire, organizing sports for the local villagers on Boxing Day; 2,000 people turned up to enjoy them. There were also house guests, including Katey and her husband, and doubtless games, dancing, plum pudding and general merriment. It's possible Nelly saw Dickens again on Thursday, 3 January, when he slipped up to town for the day on the plea of office work and went to the Lyceum in the evening. Then he was back at Gad's Hill until all his guests departed on Monday, 7 January, on which day he immediately set off for Slough, where he remained until Wednesday, 9 January, and probably returned again on Thursday.

After another weekend of guests at Gad's Hill, he was in Slough again on Monday, 14 January, looking in at the office on the way. On 17 January he departed for Liverpool, spent ten days giving public readings in the north and was back in Slough on Monday, 28 January, where he remained for two nights. On 30 January he was at the office, dined with Georgina and went on to visit Fechter, who was of course well known to the Ternans; and after another London reading departed on 1 February for a further tour of the north, from which he returned south three times, and three times spent nights in Slough.

This is very much the pattern throughout the diary. The longest periods of his absence from Nelly were occasioned by his reading tours. He appears to have taken no real holidays; in marked contrast to his activities in the early sixties, there was not a single excursion to France. Nelly welcomed him back from the north of England for a long weekend from 8 to 11 March, then saw him off to Ireland, from which he returned straight to her for another four days and nights, from 23 to 27 March.

During this time there is a diary entry 'Houses' and two days later 'Meet for houses at 12 1/2. To Peck^m: To SL:' – the first indication that he and Nelly were considering moving on, this time to the southern suburbs of London. He was back in Slough on 27 March, and again on 30 and 31 March after reading in Cambridge and Norwich. During the whole month he was not at Gad's Hill at all; the correspondent to whom he said he was spending only one night in London was being told the literal truth, for Slough is not London. And this may have been one of the reasons for moving, for the journey must have become particularly wearing in the winter months. Another could have been the difficulty and inconvenience of using two cottages, prudent as it may have seemed in a small place like Slough. In February there were public readings of the works of Charles Dickens in a hall in the High Street, which may have caused Mr Tringham to worry about being recognized.[8]

Peckham was carefully chosen. It was wholly unlike the Peckham of the twentieth century, being still a pleasant, open rural area: 'There is not in the immediate neighbourhood of London a more agreeable country then Peckham Rye, Nunhead and adjacent localities.'[9] But what must have made it irresistible to Dickens was that it had just acquired a rail link with Waterloo; a fine new station appeared at Peckham Rye in 1865. Since Gad's Hill was also on the London, Chatham and Dover line, Peckham became at a stroke easily accessible both from Dickens's office and his country house.

The move could not, however, be made immediately. The month of April is the most enigmatic in the diary, with its entry '(N. ill latter part of this month)' across the bottom of the page, and its mysteriously prominent word 'Arrival' on Saturday, 13 April, followed by another large, square-bracketed word 'Loss' a week later. During this week (marked at the side 'Holiday') Dickens was at Slough on the nights of 13 and 14 April, at Gad's Hill for the next three, then at Wellington Street on 18 April; and on 19 April he took Wills with him to Slough, leaving again on the next day, which is the one marked 'Loss'.[10]

When I researched Nelly's life story in the late 1980s and wrote about this episode – the words 'Arrival' and 'Loss'; the bringing of Wills, who is known to have been Dickens's confidant and practical helper in all matters concerning Nelly; and the indication that she was ill at this time – all these did seem to raise the possibility of a second pregnancy in 1867. On the other hand, Gladys Storey, questioned by a Dickens scholar, had categorically stated that 'no child was born in 1867'.[11] And Felix Aylmer, who deciphered the place names in the diary in a brilliant piece of detective work, and who believed in the birth of a child, had spoiled his case by elaborating it into a tale of false names and adoption, which was swiftly disproved.[12]

The possibility still seemed to me worth considering then, and remained so until my friend Graham Storey, one of the editors of the Pilgrim edition of *The Letters of Charles Dickens*, gave me a piece of new information that knocked it out conclusively. Dr Storey received a hitherto unknown manuscript letter by Dickens dated Saturday 20 April 1867, which made it clear that the 'Loss' had nothing to do with Nelly's indisposition. The letter reported the loss of a travelling bag Dickens had with him on the train from Slough to Paddington that day, and left in a hansom cab taken from Paddington to his office in Wellington Street. He addressed his letter to the Station Master at Paddington, and it described his bag as 'A small black bag or Tourist's Knapsack – containing one book and a bundle of MS.'[13] One of the manuscripts was probably an instalment of Frances Trollope's novel *Mabel's Progress*. Dickens was serializing this in his magazine *All the Year*

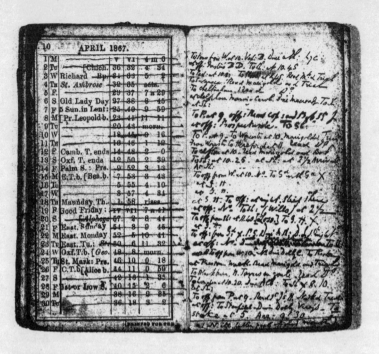

		V	VI	4 m 0
1	M			
2	Tu	[Chich.	36	32	4 54
3	W	Richard Bp.	34	33	5 2
4	Th	St. Ambrose	32	35	sêts.
5	F		29	37	7 m 29
6	S	Old Lady Day	27	38	8 45
7	F	5 Sun. in Lent	25	40	9 59
8	M	Pr. Leopold b.	23	41	11 11
9	Tu		20	43	morn.
10	W		18	45	0 16
11	Th		16	46	1 0
12	F	Camb. T. ends	14	48	2 0
13	S	Oxf. T. ends	12	50	2 39
14	F	Palm S.; Prs.	9	52	3 13
15	M	C.T. b. [Ben. b.	7	53	3 43
16	Tu		5	55	4 10
17	W		3	57	4 34
18	Th	Maunday Th.	1	58	rises
19	F	Good Friday;	57	1	7 m 4
20	S	[Alphege	57	2	8 14
21	F	East. Sunday	54	4	9 46
22	M	East. Monday	52	5	10 41
23	Tu	East. Tu.; Shr.	50	6	11 32
24	W	Oxf. T. b. [Geo.	48	8	morn.
25	Tu	St. Mark; Prs.	46	10	0 18
26	F	C.T. b. [Alice b.	44	11	0 59
27	S		42	13	1 35
28	F	1st or Low S.	40	15	2 6
29	M		38	16	2 35
30	Tu		36	18	3 2

				slow:	
1	M	11 m 15	slow:		
2	Tu	0 a 12	3' 44"		
3	W	F 2	3 20		
4	Th	1 49	3 9		
5	F	2 58	2 51		
6	S	3 10	2 34		
7	F	3 52	2 16		
8	M	4 37	1 59		
9	Tu	5 25	1 42		
10	W	6 18	1 26		
11	Th	7 20	1 9		
12	F	8 29	0 53		
13	S	9 43	0 38		
14	F	10 53	0 22		
15	M	11 51	0 7		
16	Tu	morn.	fast.		
17	W	0 39	0 23		
18	Th	1 21	0 37		
19	F	1 59	0 50		
20	S	2 38	1 4		
21	F	3 16	1 17		
22	M	3 54	1 29		
23	Tu	4 32	1 41		
24	W	5 12	1 53		
25	Th	5 56	2 4		
26	F	6 42	2 14		
27	S	7 29	2 24		
28	F	8 25	2 34		
29	M	9 28	2 43		
30	Tu	10 34	2 51		

LUNATIONS.

New Moon, 4th, 10 aft.
First Quar. 11th, 3 aft.
Full Moon, 18th, 11 aft.
Last Quar. 26th, 9 mo.

PLANETS.

First Day.

	Rise.	Set.
☿	5m 10	5 a 40
♀	4m 23	2 a 25
♂	10m 24	8m 17
♃	4m 26	2 a 18
♄	10m 9	7m 20

Thirteenth Day.

	Rise.	Set.
☿	4m 38	4 a 30
♀	4m 6	2 a 54
♂	10m 5	2m 41
♃	3m 44	1 a 44
♄	9 a 19	6m 30

Twenty-fifth Day.

	Rise.	Set.
☿	4m 15	4 a 27
♀	3m 47	3 a 25
♂	9m 49	2m 7
♃	3m 1	1 a 9
♄	8 a 27	5m 51

1	W	St. Phil.&Jas.	IV VII	3m 29
2	Tu	Pr. Arthur b.	33 21	3 53
3	F	Inv. of Cross	31 23	4 25
4	S		29 24	sets m
5	F	28.aft.Easter	27 26	8 a 55
6	M	Jn. Ev. a P.	25 28	10
7	Tu	[Lat.	24 29	11 7
8	W		22 31	11 59
9	Th		20 33	morn
10	F		18 34	0 40
11	S		17 36	1 18
12	F	9 S. aft. Easter	15 37	1 49
13	M	Old May Day	14 39	2 15
14	Tu	East. T. ends	10 40	2 39
15	W		11 42	3 5
16	Th		9 43	3 30
17	F		8 45	3 57
18	S		6 46	rises
19	F	4 S. aft. East.	5 47	9a 31
20	M	(Dunston	4 49	9 58
21	Tu		2 50	10 15
22	W		1 52	10 48
23	Th		0 53	11 25
24	F	Qu. Vict. b.	118 54	morn
25	S	Pra. Helena b.	58 56	0 8
26	F	Rog. Sunday	56 57	0 32
27	M	D. Cumb. b.	55 59	1 5
28	Tu	V.Hs. T.T.b.	51 59	1 30
29	W	K.Ch.H.rest.	53 VIII	1 56
30	Th	Asc. H.Thurs.	50 2	2 28
31			59 3	3 53

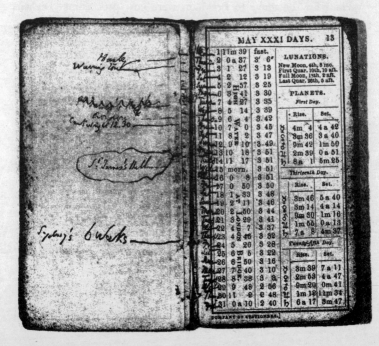

MAY XXXI DAYS.   13

1	1m 39	fast.
2	0a 37	3' 6"
3	1 27	3 13
4	2 12	3 19
5	3 57	3 25
6	3 41	3 30
7	4 27	3 35
8	5 14	3 39
9	6 4	3 42
10	7 0	3 45
11	8 2	3 47
12	9 10	3 49
13	10 18	3 51
14	11 17	3 51
15	morn.	3 51
16	0 8	3 51
17	0 50	3 50
18	1 33	3 48
19	2 11	3 46
20	2 50	3 44
21	3 27	3 41
22	4 7	3 37
23	4 43	3 32
24	5 26	3 28
25	6 5	3 22
26	6 50	3 16
27	7 40	3 10
28	8 38	3 4
29	9 43	2 56
30	11 2	2 48
31	0a 10	2 40

LUNATIONS.
New Moon, 4h, 3 mc.
First Quar. 10th, 10 aft.
Full Moon, 18th, 2 aft.
Last Quar. 26th, 5 aft.

PLANETS.
First Day.

	Rise.	Set.
	4m 4	4 a 42
	3m 36	3 a 40
	9m 42	1m 50
	2m 39	0 a 51
	8a 1	5m 25

Thirteenth Day.

	Rise.	Set.
	3m 46	5 a 40
	3m 14	4 a 14
	9m 30	1m 16
	1m 55	0 a 13
	7a 8	4m 37

Twenty-fifth Day.

	Rise.	Set.
	3m 39	7 a 11
	2m 53	4 a 47
	9m 20	0m 41
	1m 12	1m 34
	6a 17	3m 47

Round. It went out anonymously, and he guarded Frances's anonymity so carefully that she was not paid like other contributors, and no one else on the magazine knew who the author was.

So in this respect there was a connection with Nelly. And in fact Fanny herself arrived in England at the end of May, without her husband, who was left to follow later. By then Nelly was on her feet again: Dickens noted twice 'N. walks'. She had even been to the theatre with him. On 8 May the entry is 'Lyc: (N there too)' and the following day 'N and M' (Nelly and either her mother or, possibly, Maria) dined with him at Verrey's Restaurant, and he returned to Slough in the evening; this was the occasion on which he told Georgina he could not get to Gad's Hill until Monday, 13 May, because of pressure of work. With Nelly convalescent, Georgina fussing on the one hand and Fanny undoubtedly anxious about Nelly's illness and curious about her preparing to move from Slough to Peckham, things were difficult for Dickens. Someone made sure that his and Fanny's visits to Slough did not coincide.[14] If they met at Wellington Street to discuss her *Mabel's Progress*, appearing weekly in *All the Year Round* throughout the summer, neither recorded the fact. Fanny's letters to Bice conveyed Nelly's love and her mother's, but gave no address or indication of where they were living.

Plans for the move to Peckham were now proceeding. Dickens was also mulling over a renewed proposal that he should go to America for a reading tour in November. If he went, he wanted to take Nelly with him. On 6 June, when he was at Slough, he wrote to Wills, on paper headed with the monogram 'E.T.', about the proposed American trip: 'The Patient, I ack. to be the gigantic difficulty. But you know I don't like to give in before a difficulty, if it can be beaten.'[15] This reluctance to give in before the difficulty of having her at his side in America grew no less as the weeks went by; and it can only be presumed that she was herself keen to make the journey. She had all her family's love of travel and must often have heard her mother speak of her own transatlantic trip.

While Dickens was revolving this plan, he expressed his hostility towards Fanny in a letter to a friend who had evidently asked some probing questions about his relations with the Ternan family. The friend was Frances Elliot, a Scottish heiress with literary aspirations, divorced under Scottish law from her first husband and now married to her second, the Dean of Bristol; she was known to both Anthony and Tom Trollope, and was on surprisingly close terms with Dickens, who later advised her about her second bout of marital problems. This is what he wrote to her:

> The 'magic circle' consists of but one member. I don't in the least care for Mrs T.T. except that her share in the story is (as far as I am concerned) a remembrance impossible to swallow. Therefore, and for the magic sake, I scrupulously try to do her justice, and not to see her – out of my path – with a jaundiced vision . . .
>
> I feel your affectionate letter truly and deeply, but it would be inexpressibly painful to N to think that you knew her history. She has no suspicion that your assertion of your friend against the opposite powers ever brought you to the knowledge of it. She would not believe that you could see her with my eyes, or know her with my mind. Such a presentation is impossible. It would distress her for the rest of her life. I thank you none the less, but it is quite out of the question. If she could bear that, she could not have the pride and self-reliance which (mingled with the gentlest nature) has borne her alone, through so much.
>
> . . . Of course you will be very strictly on your guard, if you see Tom Trollope, or his wife, or both – to make no reference to me which either can piece into anything. She is infinitely sharper than the serpent's Tooth. Mind that.[16]

This is a reasonably, though not entirely, plain communication. To begin with, Dickens is declining absolutely to introduce Nelly to Mrs Elliot, on the grounds that Nelly would not wish it; Mrs Elliot has heard of Nelly through a friend who argued with the 'opposite powers', presumably the supporters of Catherine Dickens. His insistence that Nelly is the only member of his 'magic circle' is important; so are his remarks about Fanny, of whom he has had such a high opinion. Now, rather like the Hogarths, she has proved unworthy of all the benefits he has loaded on her; he finds her ungrateful and is, or pretends to be, nervous of her and what she and her husband might find out.

But the chief purpose of the letter was to stop Mrs Elliot talking.

Dickens did not break off his relations with Tom Trollope, who arrived in London at this point, and whom he immediately invited to a bachelor dinner; perhaps among men he felt better able to remain in control of what was said and what left silent. He also continued with the serialization of Fanny's novel. Fanny sent a Dickens autograph to Bice. She was at Waltham Cross with the Anthony Trollopes in June and visited the Elliots with Tom in August. Dean Elliot acted as a steward at a farewell dinner given for Dickens before his departure to America in November, with Anthony Trollope as another.

Only 'N' was in purdah. Whether Fanny approved her sister's move to Peckham we don't know; it was not mentioned in her letters. On 21 June Dickens wrote in his pocket book, 'To temporary P. 1st Day' and on 22 June, 'at P. Long wait for N at house'. A few days later he was at P. again, working on a story, and on 26 June the name of the street in which the permanent house they had taken appears, 'Linden'. Linden Grove, where a single row of large and handsome newly built villas stood, was across the fields to the south-east of the cluster of houses at Peckham Rye and close to Nunhead Cemetery, one of the great landscaped burial places established in the 1840s. All around was the Surrey countryside, still supporting farms, with streams, cornfields and grassland; where the houses were going up, it was to meet the needs of a new, floating, anonymous population. Nunhead itself, no more than a hamlet of a few hundred souls in 1840, expanded over the next half century to over 10,000 inhabitants. It was a place in which Nelly could be set up without risk of attracting attention, yet in considerable style. The house they had chosen was called Windsor Lodge; it had an imposing porch, gardens front and back with trees and lawns, and a view over the fields and up the slopes of Telegraph Hill.[17] Dickens took a lease as he had done at Slough, and under the same name of Charles Tringham. The rates were paid by the usual assortment of Turnhams and Tringhams; in January 1868, when both Dickens and Nelly were abroad, the entry showed 'Thomas Turnham' altered to 'Thomas Tringham'; perhaps it was the good Wills who paid and found himself confused.[18]

At the beginning of August Dickens was suffering from his foot, which was painful enough to give him wretched nights and make him retreat to Wellington Street to endure them in solitude, though he returned to Peckham and then travelled to town with 'N & M' on 12 August. He was well enough for two cricket matches at Gad's Hill, with visits to Peckham in between; but in September his foot was worse again. Now, as the American trip seemed more likely – Dolby had been sent across the Atlantic to sound things out – and Fanny had gone off to Germany with Tom, Dickens spent more nights at Peckham. On 29 September he wrote, 'Decide to go' in his diary and sent off a telegram to that effect to his American publisher.

Just over a week later Fanny announced to Bice from Germany that she was expecting Nelly and her mother to come out to Florence at the end of October. Nelly must have communicated with her sister as soon as she heard Dickens's decision. From 21 to 25 October he slept at Peckham and went in to the office each day; there was a farewell dinner at Verrey's with N on 25 October, inscribed in large letters and boxed in by thick lines to indicate its importance. Then they parted, for Dickens had to go through much business, including a huge public farewell dinner on 2 November at which it would not, it seemed, be possible for her to join the hundred ladies watching the diners from a gallery. Instead she was on her way to Florence, where she arrived with her mother at the Villa Ricorboli in the evening of 30 October. She had with her secret instructions from Dickens about returning to England and following him to America in December.

Still hoping that these instructions would be implemented, he embarked for Boston from Liverpool on 9 November. Wills was the appointed go-between. The arrangement was that Dickens would send him a coded telegram if everything looked propitious, which Wills would forward to Nelly in Florence. Wills was also to tell Forster and Gad's Hill of any arrangements he made. Nelly was to expect the telegram, whose code she understood, on either Saturday, 23 November, or Saturday, 30 November, with the further expectation that she would be back in London by 10 December, ready to embark for America on 11 December. Dickens wrote the code in his pocket book, after the last diary entry, which was for 7 November; it read:

> In any case. Tel:
> Tel: all well means
>> *You come*
> Tel: Safe and well means
>> *You don't come.*

At the side was written 'expect it (thro' Wills) – on Sat 23 or Sat 30th'. Beneath this are the words:

> To Wills who sends the Tel
> on c/o Villa Trollope
> fuori la porta
>> S. Niccolo   Florence.

Below this again are the words:

> 10 December If   R   N in London
> 11   If   R   N in Liverpool.

With Wills he left a note that read:

NELLY   If she needs any help will come to you, or if she changes her address, you will immediately let me know if she changes. Until then it will be Villa Trollope, a Ricorboli, Firenze, Italy [he wrote this out again in capitals]. On the day after my arrival out I will send you a short Telegram at the office. Please copy its exact words, (as they will have a special meaning for her), and post them to her as above by the very next post after receiving my telegram. And also let Gad's Hill know – and let Forster know – what the telegram is.

In a further note Dickens wrote that Forster 'knows Nelly as you do, and will do anything for her if you want anything done'.

On 19 November Dickens arrived in Boston; he appears to have believed that Nelly was planning to leave Florence, because he wrote to Wills on 21 November, saying,

After this present mail, I shall address Nelly's letters to your care, for I do not quite know where she will be. But she will write to you, and instruct you where to forward them. In any interval between your receipt of one or more, and my Dear Girl's so writing to you, keep them by you.[19]

But in Florence there seemed to be no thought of the Dear Girl leaving. Whether she would have done had the summons come from Dickens, we don't know; but on Friday, 22 November, Dickens sent the telegram indicating that there was no possibility of her joining him – 'Safe and well expect good letter full of hope'.

From now on Dickens enclosed letters for Nelly with every one to Wills, adding little notes which often included some words of love and longing: 'my spirits flutter woefully towards a certain place at which you dined one day not long before I left, with the present writer and a third (most drearily missed) person' (on 10 December); 'I would give £3,000 down (and think it cheap) if you could forward *me*, for four and twenty hours only, instead of the letter' (on Christmas Eve); 'Another letter for my Darling, enclosed' (on 30 December). Nowhere does his feeling for her appear so nakedly as in these scraps to Wills from America. There is a gap in the letters – it is thought some were destroyed by Sir Henry Dickens when they came into his possession – and then they resume in 1868 with the same yearning additions.

Dickens's darling, though deprived of her American trip, was, at any rate, well settled in Florence. Sharp-eyed, gossipy Isa Blagden called to take a look. 'Mrs Taylor and Ellen Ternan are pleasant and rather pretty, but Fanny is the flower of them,' she reported firmly to Bice in her next letter. Florence was experiencing its coldest winter for many seasons, and Fanny said Ricorboli was almost like a hospital; her mother was not well and Maria had joined them, fleeing on the plea of rheumatism from Oxford and the long-suffering Taylor, who shipped out a cask of bitter beer after her, perhaps intended as a reminder of his forlorn state.

The Ternans seem to have enjoyed being together and got on well with Tom. Mrs Ternan's old friend Charlotte Cushman, the American actress now settled in Rome, invited her to bring Nelly and Maria for the Christmas festivities; but they turned her down, preferring to remain where they were. Perhaps they were justifiably nervous of wandering armies: Garibaldi had just been defeated in his march on the Holy City. Fanny helped to run a committee for his cause, and Nelly busied herself sewing shirts for the wounded. Then, in the new year of 1868, Fanny, Tom and Maria did set off together for a jaunt to Naples and an ascent of Vesuvius, but 'Mamma and Ellen were not strong enough to bear the journey'. They stayed behind with the builders, who had still not completed their labours. Nelly continued to receive frequent letters from her lover. He was suffering from catarrh so bad he thought it might damage his lungs permanently, a badly swollen foot and homesickness; he was also under the impression that she had returned to England, for on 21 February he wrote to Wills, 'You will have seen too (I hope) my dear Patient, and will have achieved in so doing what I would joyfully give a Thousand Guineas to achieve myself at this present moment!'[20]

Dickens was wrong in thinking Wills had seen her. She neither showed any sign of moving nor apparently kept him informed of her plans. When the Vesuvius party returned and the building work was finally finished, they celebrated Mrs Ternan's birthday with their first meal in the new dining room on 10 February, and then lingered on at Ricorboli, past Nelly's twenty-ninth birthday in March and through most of April, to enjoy the Italian spring.

In America Dickens spent two days in mid-March at Niagara and had a small box, addressed to himself, dispatched to Wellington Street with instructions to Wills that it must be kept unopened in his bedroom for his return: intended, perhaps, as a late birthday present for N. He was not unhappy all the time, but he allowed himself to be fussed over by his Boston publisher, James Fields, and his pretty and enthusiastic young wife, Annie. Among other notes in her diary, she wrote down what the housekeeper of his New York hotel told her: that Dickens, in the goodness of his heart, had paid for one of the chambermaids to go to California with her illegitimate child. On the day of his own departure for England he sent off a last letter to Nelly via Wills and was greeted in passing by Anthony Trollope, just arriving in America. It was 17 April, and the crossing was expected to take about two weeks; and on 24 April the Patient and her mother left Florence for London.

12

'This life is half made up of partings'
1868–1870

Nelly had remained in Florence throughout February, March and most of April 1868 with the books, the gardens and the music of Villa Ricorboli to entertain her, and her assembled family to give her good advice. Only on 25 April Fanny noted that 'we are alone as Mamma and Nelly went away yesterday'.[1] Their journey was timed so they would reach England a few days before Dickens. On 1 May he and Dolby came ashore in Liverpool, dined and slept at the Adelphi Hotel, and next morning travelled to Euston; they parted on the platform at three in the afternoon. Dolby's account is carefully vague, describing their farewell at the railway station so as to give the impression that Dickens was on his way to Gad's Hill. In fact, he did not make his appearance there until a week later. Two local papers reported his return and enthusiastic welcome on Saturday, 9 May. For the missing week he had simply ceased to be Charles Dickens and become, presumably, Mr Tringham of Windsor Lodge, Peckham. It was a bold bit of deception, but he had the nerve, the practice and the strength of will of a man determined to have what he wanted.

In Boston Annie Fields imagined this reunion as 'the most painfully and joyfully intense of his whole life' and full of 'the intense joy of his beloved'; she wrote in her diary that it was 'too much to face, even in one's imagination and too sacred'.[2] Mrs Fields was an intense person herself, with a highly developed sense of the drama of Dickens's life; but her remarks can only be based on what he had said to her or her husband. There is no doubt of his joy at the prospect of being reunited with Nelly. The American tour had done what he meant it to do – made a very large sum of money, some of it quite possibly intended for her – but at the cost of both physical exhaustion and emotional suffering for him. He returned to England visibly aged, his hair thinner and more grizzled, his face scored and cragged; yet he was still able to summon up bursts of boyish spirits and charm, to cast aside his age and laugh 'like a man in the full vigour of his life', to display 'a vitality ... and a certain manliness of demeanour which made those who looked upon him believe that nothing that he had yet done had acted injuriously upon the machine of his body'.[3] He was still able to dance tirelessly through an evening, 'light and lithe as a boy of twenty' when the mood was on him.[4] Whether May in Peckham was as pleasant as April on a Florentine hillside, and whether Nelly viewed the reunion with the same joy as her lover or felt it more as the resumption of a burden, they seem to have fallen into their old routine easily enough. The lion was still a lion, and he was still at her feet; and whatever misunderstandings had arisen between them about her movements during their long separation were explained. No doubt there were teasing and laughter, traveller's tales and presents: perhaps the contents of the mysterious box from Niagara. His first letters from English soil, written after his return to Gad's Hill, are buoyant and good-humoured, which suggests that his stolen week in Peckham did not fail his expectations.

Almost immediately he was off again, this time to Paris, to attend a Fechter production, *L'abîme*, a version of Collins's play *No Thoroughfare*. He wrote to Collins to tell him of the trip, and to Macready, boasting of his revived 'health and spirits'. At the same time Nelly and her mother visited Bice at her school in Brighton on 31 May; conveniently on their way if either or both intended to cross the Channel also and join Dickens in France. Although mother and daughter continued to be together a good deal, Mrs Ternan was by no means always at Windsor Lodge; she was to be found at other addresses in Mornington Crescent and later in Pimlico, leaving Nelly to run her own house and order her own life as she chose.[5]

Still Dickens kept up his unflagging pace. At Wellington Street there was a crisis. Wills had suffered a hunting accident; he was obliged to give up work completely for a time, and although he returned to the office occasionally, things were never the same.

Later in the year Charley Dickens, following the tradition of so many of the family, became bankrupt; his father decided to solve the two problems by taking Charley into the *All the Year Round* office where, under the parental eye, he did surprisingly well. Better still another son, Henry, won a place at a university, the only Dickens child to do so; he started his law studies at Trinity Hall, Cambridge, in the autumn. Both these adult sons, like their sisters, must have known something of Nelly's place in their father's life.

Gad's Hill was now entirely free of boys, for in September Edward (Plorn) was packed off to Australia to join his brother Alfred. Catherine Dickens was not consulted on the fate of her youngest any more than that of the others, and Dickens displayed the same blend of callousness and sentimentality as when his other boys were banished; the bewildered and tearful 16-year-old was given a letter at parting in which his father told him he loved him and was sorry to part with him, 'but this life is half made up of partings, and these pains must be borne'.[6] Georgina presented the nephew to whom she had been appointed a second mother with a farewell present of a box of cigars. Even when all the circumstances of Victorian family life and economics are taken into account, it seems a harsh way of treating a not very bright boy. Dickens's obsession with ridding himself of his sons is a recurring reminder both of his ruthlessness and of the complete domination he exercised over Georgina; indeed, one of its effects was that her service ceased to be the general care of the family and became entirely personal to him. She remained fond of the boys and concerned for them but does not appear to have missed them. In her way she was quite as tough as her brother-in-law emotionally, and physically much tougher; she outlived all her nephews except Henry and, as we shall see, controlled the image of their father with a quasi-religious zeal and tenacity.

By the time of Plorn's departure Dickens was planning another large-scale British reading tour. It was to take up the whole of the winter and spring, from October 1868 until May 1869. Dolby was to be his manager again, and they would cover Scotland, Ireland and all the great northern manufacturing towns, as well as East

Anglia, the south-west and the south coast; and just as when he went to the States, Nelly determined not to sit alone at Windsor Lodge throughout his absences. The house was still kept up, but her mother took lodgings on the south coast, at Worthing, for the first six months of 1869, to enjoy the sea air, that sovereign Victorian treatment for delicate constitutions. Maria and her husband joined them for a while, and from there Nelly travelled to town whenever she was needed; for Dickens's tour was planned to bring him back to London several times a month.

In January Dickens took Georgina to Ireland, and in February he was in Scotland; but both Dickens and Nelly were in London for her thirtieth birthday. He wrote to Wills from Edinburgh to fix the celebratory dinner: 'I shall hope to see you at the office on Tuesday. If not, I will write to you from thence, giving you the "fixture" for next day' – which was 3 March. Then he was off again, to Wolverhampton, Manchester and Hull. There, on the day of his reading (10 March), he went into Dixon's, the city's leading silk mercer, in Whitefriargate, and made a purchase which so impressed the young assistant who served him that he never forgot it. He asked for six pairs of ladies' silk stockings. The assistant, Edward Simpson Long, did not at first recognize his customer; but, as he was selecting the stockings, Dickens asked him what he liked to do in his spare time, and when Long said he enjoyed reading Shakespeare and Dickens, and showed his familiarity with the novels, he was presented with a single ticket for that evening's reading: at which point the young draper realized who his customer was.[7]

Dickens was in York the next day and back in London within the week. Later in the same month he attended a Fechter production of *No Thoroughfare* at the Adelphi, and the following day conducted a characteristic 'great burning of papers' in the office at Wellington Street. On another occasion he ran into Anthony Trollope at the Athenaeum and wrote to Tom that he was 'a perfect cordial to me, whenever and wherever I see him, as the heartiest and best of fellows'.[8]

He had already agreed to a request from a group of professional actors and actresses to give them some special readings in the mornings, the only time they were free to attend. The success of his performance had been enhanced by the addition of the famous Sikes murder scene from *Oliver Twist*, which he had tested on an invited audience that included his actress friends Mrs Keeley and Madame Celeste. Everyone in the profession admired it – Macready too was full of praise – but it sent Dickens's blood pressure soaring each time he read it. Charley advised him against doing it but without giving a reason, because he knew he must not tell his father he feared for his health. It was a subject on which Dickens would not be advised. But Charley was right: in April, at Preston, Dickens suffered symptoms of giddiness combined with a deadness on the left side of his body which alarmed him enough to make him send for his London doctor, Frank Beard. The tour was abandoned under Beard's orders; almost certainly Dickens had suffered a mild stroke. A few weeks later he told Fields, who was making a European trip with Annie, 'that when he was ill in his reading only Nelly observed that he staggered and his eye failed, only she dared tell him'.[9] Small, casual references of this kind are the strongest indication of her perpetual presence in the background of his life; her range and influence extended considerably further than Windsor Lodge.

She never came face to face with the Fieldses, however, during their five-month stay in England in the summer of 1869; evidently Dickens took the view that the proprieties made it impossible for him to introduce her to them. The Fieldses themselves are unlikely to have objected – quite the contrary – but they were not given the choice. During the same months Tom and Fanny Trollope were entertaining George Eliot and George Henry Lewes at the Villa Ricorboli, and though they felt obliged to explain that 'all was not strictly normal' in the marital status of the two eminent writers before introducing them to the resident US minister and his wife, they brushed aside the irregularity. But then George Eliot and Lewes were open about their relations and had deliberately rejected a legal and moral system they considered unjust and absurd; whereas Dickens had accepted that he must live by it, outwardly at any rate, and could not now take risks either with his own reputation or with Nelly's and her family's.

Yet his feelings were ambivalent. The hints he dropped, the confidences he gave, the wish he had cherished to take her to

America, all point to a desire that her part in his life should, even if only in some quarters and in some degree, be acknowledged. Macready, however easily he may have accepted the situation in private, was said to have worried about Dickens's lack of discretion, fearing it might lead to a public scandal.[10] Now, with the warning of his stroke, he prepared a new will in which he set Nelly's name down defiantly before all the other beneficiaries. 'Miss Ellen Lawless Ternan, late of Houghton Place, Ampthill Square' appears as his first legatee.

The will has puzzled everyone. The first question is why a man who was apparently at pains to keep his relations with a woman concealed from public knowledge should leave a posthumous sign-post pointing at her. One answer could be that it was an act of defiance against the Podsnaps of his world, the society that had made it impossible for him either to write truthfully of certain things in his books or to live truthfully in his life. He would not have to explain or defend the act himself, but it would at least put on public record for ever something that had been of prime importance to him. Neither of the two executors, Forster and Georgina, were likely to be pleased with this gesture, though both could be trusted to carry out his wishes. And Nelly herself: did he consult her before he wrote her in to the will, and did she decide that the glory of being named first in the will of Britain's greatest novelist was worth any possible scandal? To both questions the likely answer is yes. Nelly, too, was ambivalent. For thirteen years she had played a central part in his life. Some acknowledgement was owing to her pride. It's clear that the will, as a document, was important to her; a *printed* copy was found among the few papers remaining in the household of her family nearly a hundred years later.

Dickens and Nelly may both have believed that the very small-ness of the sum bequeathed to her would shield her from scandal. His daughter Mamey received the same amount; Nelly could explain it as a little nest-egg for a 'god-daughter' from a family friend – which is indeed exactly how she did explain it. The other puzzle from our point of view is precisely its inadequacy: £1,000 from an estate of nearly £100,000. A thousand pounds was certainly not going to go very far. Invested, it would not bring even enough to live on, and it was not a twentieth of the sum required for her to maintain the habits to which she was by now accustomed: a large house, trips to the Continent and prolonged seaside holidays. Catherine Dickens was guaranteed an annual income of £600 a year from his estate in addition to her house; in less than two years she could spend the whole amount of Nelly's legacy. It is inconceivable that Dickens should leave a woman he had loved and taken responsibility for over a period of many years – a woman no longer young what's more, and with a question mark over her reputation – in a penurious situation, when he made such fair financial arrangements for his estranged wife. The only reasonable assumption is that he had made other, proper provision for Nelly through trusts or insurance policies which, added to the rent from the house in Ampthill Square, gave her the income she needed. There is evidence that this indeed is what he did.[11] It is possible that some of the cash he brought from America was used in this way; Wilkie Collins took out insurance policies for his two daughters when he was in America in 1873 and continued to have the premiums paid in Boston after his return.

Dickens was rich – very rich for a writer – but not so rich that he could leave his dependants in luxury. The income from his copyrights was to be divided among his children. His daughter Mamey, in addition to her £1,000, received an annuity of £300 a year which would cease on her marriage; married daughters must be supported by their husbands. Georgina, who could not now hope to marry, received by far the biggest legacy, £8,000, and we know that she had already been given some capital sums during Dickens's lifetime. It was enough to enable her to live comfortably, though even she was obliged in old age to sell off her mementoes and papers to collectors, and was in real difficulties by the time of her death. Did Dickens expect Nelly to marry? At thirty-one it was not very likely; but the will naturally had nothing to say on the subject, and her legacy was outright.

More money matters: in June 1868 the first of a series of payments to a 'Miss Thomas' appears in Dickens's Coutts account. Thereafter,

sums varying between £7 12s. 6d. and £350, and practically never for the same amount, were paid, always on different days of the month, sometimes there being one payment a month, sometimes as many as three. In the year June 1868 to June 1869, Miss Thomas was paid £565. In the year June 1869 to June 1870 £332 2s. 0d.[12]

It is not unreasonable to suppose that these may have been connected with the Peckham household. At the same period Wilkie Collins was paying a more modest £20 a month to his mistress Martha Rudd, installed in Bolsover Street under the name of Mrs Dawson, who bore her first child to him in the summer of 1869.[13] Collins was at great pains to make proper financial provision for the women and children who depended on him, and there is no reason to think Dickens had a lesser sense of responsibility: his care for a whole range of sisters-in-law and assorted children of his brothers bears witness to this. As to the accusation that Nelly was mercenary because she accepted money from Dickens: it can hardly be taken seriously by anyone who considers what her position was, how many years they spent together, and the possibilities open to her after his death.

Nelly's involvement with Dickens lasted from 1857 until his death in 1870. During those thirteen years she changed from a girl – poor but petted by her family, healthy and pretty, with a good if not brilliant prospect of a professional career and, doubtless, a husband – into a woman approaching middle age, in delicate health, solitary and inured to dependence on a man who could give her neither an honourable position nor even steady companionship. Her experience of life was considerable but mostly rather grim. She lived the classic role of the Fallen Woman, held in particular public contempt by the Victorians, but she was not a Nana, not at all a successful *demi-mondaine* in the French style, enjoying sophisticated pleasures and milking her lover for luxuries while she deceived him. Instead, for much of the time she endured the drearier aspects of both domesticity and daughterhood, an outcast of the outer suburbs. Yet in one respect she managed an extraordinary feat. In contemporary English fiction the victims of seduction habitually begged their families to consider them as dead; Nelly, with the complicity and help of her mother and her sisters, kept alive an innocent personality in one section of society and a quite separate one with Dickens.

This is the more of an achievement if, as seems likely, she gave birth to a child, and saw her child die. Death relieved her of the further problems they would have brought, but it was not surprising that her health deteriorated; grief, shame, anxiety, and the injuries she received at Staplehurst all seem likely to have played their part in this. The love of the great man, which must have seemed to promise so much when she was twenty, had become both destructive and a barrier cutting her off from any future of her own by this time. Her sisters were married, their past as actresses put behind them. Nelly, too, had acquired the manners and habits of a lady, but she was still officially in the care of her mother and unable to marry or move in any but the narrowest social circle. Whether she loved Dickens in simplicity of heart or whether her love was partly or mostly dependence on a kind, generous uncle or father-figure, whether she enjoyed his embraces or endured them as the unfortunate aspect of life with a kindly uncle, he had also become a millstone around her neck. Of this he was almost certainly aware.[14] He could not marry her unless Catherine died, which she showed no sign of doing. There was no solution or release in prospect; on dark days she must have seen a long succession of years in Peckham stretching ahead, in which she was always ready for Mr Tringham, arriving in a hired carriage from the station, with his work, his cigars, his exact plans which allowed so much to her, so much to his public, so much to Gad's Hill, Georgina and his official social world. When he departed in another hackney for the station, she was left with alternative fears of loneliness or pregnancy; and when not at Peckham she would be in Worthing, or Oxford, or even Florence, but always as poor, dear, delicate little spinster Nelly.

Dickens remained a good patron to Fanny in Florence, whatever their private quarrel. In August 1869 a new story by her began to be serialized. It was called *Veronica* and was altogether bolder in its theme than anything she had produced before. Fanny made Veronica, a beautiful young orphan, elope to Italy with a man easily old enough to be her father, whom she has met and found fascinating during his convalescence from a hunting accident. The ageing seducer is not only married but – it transpires – married to Veronica's aunt, thereby piling incest on adultery; and the whole story reads as though Fanny were determinedly supplying every sort of sensational effect she could think of; and just possibly indulging in a little malicious teasing of Nelly's ageing lover. Unfortunately *Veronica* is a blunt rather than a sharp instrument. If Dickens read it, he may have allowed his feeling for Nelly's family to overcome his judgement, or he may have convinced himself that it catered to a coarsening modern taste.

He was, in any case, engrossed in planning a new novel of his own, the first since *Our Mutual Friend*. *Edwin Drood* was to be a murder story built around a man who leads a double life, half as a virtuous choirmaster, half as a drug-taker and criminal. It is set in the city of Dickens's childhood and Nelly's birth, Rochester, which he names Cloisterham for the purposes of his story. The descriptions of its ancient streets and cathedral are powerful, dark and vivid; it is hard not to read an elegiac note into them. Most of the characters, however, are Dickensian automata. They are well turned out, but they are turned out on pre-established patterns: the baby-sweet girl, the comic schoolmistress, the self-important conservative citizen, the sprightly young naval man, even the bad boy. The most striking feature of *Drood* – it's been pointed out by most critics – is the link between the villain Jasper's dual personality and Dickens's own experience as one who used different identities in different sections of his life.

The theme of a double identity was not new; but whereas in *Our Mutual Friend* he made John Harmon play a false part with benevolent intentions and effect, Jasper is wholly malign. Where Harmon wins the love of Bella through his trick, Jasper is only terrifying to the girl he loves and pursues. He subdues her will only through his hypnotic powers. Although fiction is not autobiography, it is tempting to read into this Dickens's darkening view of himself, to relate it to his struggle against worsening health, and to connect it with his obsessive performances of the Sikes murder from *Oliver Twist*. If he sometimes thought ahead to his own death, he also perhaps acknowledged that he had been the agent of destruction in the lives of more than one woman and more than one of his own children too.

This is as far as speculation can reasonably go. There is no key that will make the characters in the novel into equivalents of real people. Commentators eager to identify Nelly with the women in Dickens's writing point out that Rosa is small and blonde, as Nelly had been in 1857, and that Dickens changed the name of another character from Olympia Heyridge (or Heyfort) in his notes to Helena Landless, which resembles Ellen Lawless: the first coincidence tells us nothing at all, the second little more than that he took pleasure in incorporating echoes of Nelly's striking name into his work. No doubt it was a private amusement for them both.

As the winter of 1869 drew on, Dickens became absorbed in his writing. In November he wrote to Tom Trollope, saying he had started on the book, responding humorously to his suggestion that he might take a walking trip across the Alps, and mentioning that he'd seen Fanny in connection with a financial arrangement, though he sent her no greeting.[15] In January he was doing a few London readings again and wrote to Wills, sending Nelly's greetings: 'The patient was in attendance and missed you. I was charged with all manner of good and kind remembrance.'[16] A month later he wrote to Wills again about their annual celebration of her birthday. This year she would be thirty-one: 'You know that you are expected at a certain small dinner of four, next Thursday, the 3rd March, at Blanchard's in Regent Street at 6 sharp? Don't you?'[17] It is the last letter he wrote to Wills.

He had only three more months to live. Even they were packed with events to the end. He was received by the Queen and is said to have turned down the honour she offered him. He gave a tearful final reading in which he mispronounced his words; his own Pickwick became 'Pickswick' and 'Pickwicks'. He continued to attend the theatre with obvious relish. He rented a large house in Hyde Park Place, for Mamey's sake he said, and organized a reception there, rather in the style of the old days at Tavistock House, with Joachim and professional singers to entertain the guests. He breakfasted with Gladstone. He spoke at charitable dinners and addressed the Academy at the end of April, praising the literary and scientific achievements of women, 'who even in their present oppressed condition can attain to quite as great distinction as men'.[18] He helped direct some private theatricals with his daughters and London neighbours and the painter Millais. He had the sorrow of hearing of the death of his and Catherine's old friend, the artist Maclise, and a few weeks later that of Mark Lemon, who had acted with him and Nelly at Manchester. Dickens was now white-haired and stooping, obliged to wear elastic stockings and bandages against the pain in his swollen foot, and suffering from disturbances of vision; he took laudanum to get a good night's sleep.

Nelly cannot have seen all this without a sense of what was to come; and yet he could still summon his energies and plan for the future. He told a young woman writer sent to him for advice by Bulwer-Lytton that he thought of going to live abroad in Germany – he specified Thuringia – for two years, in order to study the language thoroughly, accompanied by his daughter; perhaps this was a tactful version of the actual plan, since neither Mamey nor Katey seems to have heard of any such idea.[19] To another intimate friend, Charles Kent, with whom he was in the habit of taking long walks in the southern suburbs of London, he made his confidence now about his most cherished dream of having the management and sole control of a great theatre: the lifelong fascination had never left him.[20] He also wrote vehemently to his son Henry, deploring the 'narrow-minded fanatics, who decry the theatre and defame its artists'.[21]

And he continued to lead his double life and lay false trails; at the beginning of May he told a correspondent that he was 'in attendance on a sick friend, at some distance', without of course further explanation; it was an excuse he had used before.[22] He declined many invitations on the justifiable grounds of his health, yet continued to divide his time between his many different addresses, writing to Georgina from Wellington Street in the old way. On 27 May he wrote to Fechter also from the office, while telling other friends he was in Kent. His last visit to Nelly in Peckham was probably made between Tuesday, 31 May, and Thursday, 2 June; on the Wednesday he had his usual lunch with Dolby near the office. Dolby found him in low spirits, even tearful. There is some conflicting testimony for the next night, which Charley Dickens says his father spent at Wellington Street, while others say he was involved in the amateur theatricals at a neighbour's house in Hyde Park Place. But there is no doubt that he was at Gad's Hill with Georgina and Mamey on the Friday evening.

On the Saturday Katey joined them, and on the Sunday evening she had a long talk with her father in which he warned her off the theatrical career she had in mind. He then told her he felt his strength ebbing and doubted he would finish *Drood*, adding that he wished he had been a better father and a better man.[23] On the Monday she left; he worked all morning and then walked into Rochester to post his letters. He wrote to Charles Kent on Wednesday, 8 June, saying, 'I hope I may be ready for you at 3 o'clock.'[24] He also told Georgina he would be going to the office as usual the next day, but in the evening he began to look ill over dinner. Suddenly he rose to his feet, saying he wished to go to London at once. Then he collapsed on the floor, muttering; he lost consciousness and never regained it or spoke again. The coachman and gardener came and lifted him on to a stiff, narrow sofa. Later Georgina had a bed brought into the dining room, hoping he might be moved into it if he improved, but it was a useless gesture.

Doctors were sent for, and came. Charley, Katey and Mamey arrived. Harry was in Cambridge – he did not reach Gad's Hill until the following evening – and all the other sons were out of reach. The following morning, when Dickens should have been in London, Nelly was sent for, while Katey went to tell her mother what had happened. Two separate accounts state that Nelly was present when Dickens died, at ten past six on the evening of Thursday, 9 June.[25]

She left, presumably, that night or the next morning, either for Windsor Lodge or for her mother's rooms in Pimlico, while the whole nation began its lamentations and tributes. Dickens had expressed a desire to be buried in the simplest manner in Rochester, in a small graveyard under the castle wall, but his wish was not respected. There was a strong sentiment in the government, the press and at Westminster Abbey itself that Poets' Corner was the only fitting place for so great a national figure. Neither the executors nor the family were prepared to oppose this view. The Queen, at Balmoral, sent a telegram to Mrs Dickens in Gloucester Crescent, which perhaps consoled her for being excluded from the burial at the Abbey on 14 June. There appears to have been no invitation for Nelly either, although Collins, Forster, Beard and Frederic Ouvry, Dickens's solicitor, joined the small family group. By chance a clergyman with business at the Abbey noticed the little procession and inquired about it; his name was William Benham, and he had a particular interest in Dickens which was to produce some unexpected results later.[26] Outside, the public was already massing in its thousands to pay its respects.

PART THREE

13

Another Life Begins
(1870–1876)

Nelly was now, for the first time in her life, free. She had an income of her own. She owed nothing to anyone, financially or emotionally. She no longer had to fear pregnancy. She no longer needed her mother as a shield against scandal; and indeed, as soon as she could, she set off for Paris accompanied only by her maid, Jane from Slough, like a well-to-do young widow who goes abroad to recover herself. She was no longer a girl; on the other hand she still looked remarkably young, and who was to inquire how old she was? An age could be chosen as well as a name; by deciding to be a much younger woman than she was, she could simply abolish the inconvenient years. A society which prized youth and innocence so highly in its women might excusably be given what it wanted. Nelly had not learnt deception from a master for nothing.

As for her past: with any luck, it was sufficiently mysterious to be effaced. Who would want to tell on her? Not the wistful lady in Gloucester Crescent. Not any of Dickens's devoted associates, Wills or Dolby; not Collins, who had his own secrets to juggle with. Not the Dickens family, all subject to the will of the master, or Forster, intent on giving the world an image of his friend which, if not sanctified, was at least most scrupulously sanitized.

With money Nelly could travel and live as she pleased. If there were circles in which her name might raise an eyebrow, she should be able to avoid them. The care with which she had kept her two separate identities was now going to prove its value. Even the possible evil effects of being named in the will were lessened by a misprint in *The Times* when it was announced on 22 July: her name was given as 'Miss Fernan'. The mistake was repeated in *The New York Times*; just possibly it was not a misprint but a misdirection from the executors. A small slip, particularly when it involved the first letter of a name, was an easy but effective device under the circumstances. If Dickens's intention had been to make a posthumous affirmation of his love for Nelly, something or someone saw to it that the affirmation was bungled.

While the nation mourned and sang Dickens's praises through the hot June days that followed his death, Nelly packed up Windsor Lodge. The Bishop of Manchester proclaimed that Dickens was a teacher sent from God; the *Doncaster Chronicle* announced that he had helped to raise the moral standard of the whole human race; the chaplain of the House of Commons spoke of 'a purity and healthiness in his writings which were a natural consequence of his character'; and Dean Stanley declared that his grave would be a sacred spot and read out selected portions of his will from the pulpit in Westminster Abbey. Charles Tringham's rates, due in July, were paid for the last time through a ghostly surrogate, but by the end of June the house in Linden Grove was empty, and Nelly had left Peckham for good. She was with Maria and her husband at The Lawn; before the end of the month Fanny also arrived in Oxford from Florence, and Mrs Ternan made up the family party.

How frankly did they discuss Nelly's situation? It's impossible to know. Appearances had to be kept up, as always; the death of a famous friend of the family was to be mourned, decorously. Fanny wrote to Bice, telling her that Nelly had received 'most affectionate' letters from 'the girls' – she meant Mamey and Katey Dickens – expressing the hope that they might meet when they should all be in London. She herself had 'a few lines from young Charles Dickens': which was to be expected, since she was a contributor to the magazine, and he intended to keep it going. You can't help wondering how interested Bice, then a rebellious sixteen-year-old, can have been in this sort of thing; but Fanny continued resolutely with a description of how she and her sisters and mother visited Westminster Abbey to pay their respects: 'We went when in London to see Charles Dickens's grave. He is buried in Westminster Abbey. The tomb-stone was strewn with flowers scattered there by different visitors. I was greatly affected, and so were we all.'[1] She doesn't say where they stayed in London, but does tell Bice that Georgina Hogarth called on them. Later Georgina sent remembrances of Dickens to both Trollopes ('a little medal for Papa, and a paper-weight for me') and also to Maria and her husband. Fanny did love dropping names, but Georgina's gesture indicates a genuine sense of intimacy between the two families at this moment. To Nelly she gave a pen with which Dickens had been writing on the last day of his life: this Fanny did not mention to Bice.

Georgina had spent the first days after his death going through his private papers. She wrote to Ouvry, his solicitor, explaining that she had examined all the locked places at Wellington Street and was sending what she found 'relative to the Trusts &c'. Dolby, she added, had another drawerful of papers. There were known trusts for various dependants of Dickens, such as the widow and children of his brother Alfred, and possibly unknown trusts, too, and it is likely that some arrangements and instructions concerning Nelly passed through Georgina's hands.[2] One receipt in the cheque book used by Ouvry for payment of legacies on the estate may be relevant, simply because it is one of the few left unattributed on the stub: it is dated 16 July 1871 and entered simply 'Trust £500'.[3]

On 20 August Forster wrote to Ouvry to say he had been trying to see him at the Athenaeum but without success:

> Now however I wish you on Monday next, if convenient, to give me the means of paying Miss T—'s legacy. She is lodging in Craven St for a few days before going abroad. Tell me when you send the cheque – what form of acknowledgement must be had from her. Perhaps indeed you will, with the cheque, enclose such a form for her to sign.[4]

Forster wrote to Ouvry twice more on this matter, on 24 August when he said he had appointed to see 'Miss T' on Friday and to pay her the legacy, and again on 26 August when he announced that he was to see 'Miss T— today'. This was not the end of his dealings with her. On 11 November there was another letter to Ouvry in which he wrote, 'I *assume* that you have all the needful consent to payment of the Provident sums – and will therefore write to E.T. accordingly.'[5] None of this is very clear, but then it was not intended to be. At a rough calculation Nelly would have

Steyne Hotel – Worthing – Sussex.
11th Nov. 1870
Palace-Gate House.
Kensington. W.

My dear Ouvry –

As to the Stereotypes (a very important property in themselves merely) the purchasers would probably be entitled to claim them – but as to copyright in articles not yet collected I am by no means so clear. Poor D— was contemplating a volume before his death, and I hardly think he would have required Cotts to pay for their half-share before Cotter it half with his Stereotypes

——— Insofar as we shall have

F. Ouvry Eq.

opportunity to discuss these & kindred questions to gather before any pledge is given –

What you say as to money papers I quite agree in – & shall be greatly obliged by your taking an opinion as to our exact powers under the will.

Enclosed is a memorandum that reached me last night. You will judge whether any shew merit of this we are responsible for – or whether

Charles Dickens would not be the person applied to –

I have not been, & am not, very well – but it is a great comfort, my dear Ouvry, to have an advisor who takes such thoughts over our concerns as you do –

You must stick to Chapman. It is the only way of getting out of the muddle we are in –

Ever yours affec.

John Forster

I assume that you have all needful consent to prevent getting the Boundits Series – and will therefore write to E. T. accordingly

11th Novr 1870
John Forster Eq.

something like £60 a year from the house in Houghton Place, and another £30 income from her £1,000 bequest, if it was invested in something safe. In addition to this there were the unknown 'Provident sums'. It is also possible that she had received something from Dickens when he returned from America, and other gifts of stocks or bonds such as he made to Georgina during his lifetime. From one source and another, Forster's 'Miss T—' found herself with enough to live as comfortably as Dickens must have wished; and which none but the mean and cruel could begrudge her.

From Craven Street she set off for Paris. As bad luck had it, August 1870 was the worst possible time for such a trip. France, goaded by Bismarck, had declared war on Prussia in July; throughout August the Prussians humiliated the French in a series of battles, and at the beginning of September the French emperor capitulated at Sedan. Nelly and Jane just managed to get out of Paris on 19 September before the Germans encircled the city and began their long winter siege, which starved the Parisians into submission in January and was followed by the revolutionary uprising of the Commune. But if she could not be in France, Nelly was still determined not to remain in England. She set off again immediately, by sea, for Italy. Equally momentous though less dangerous events were taking place there; Rome had fallen to the Italians in September, and in October it was proclaimed the capital of the new kingdom in place of Florence. The transfer affected Tom and Fanny, since his work as a journalist would force them to move to Rome; though for the moment they stayed put. Nelly, after another difficult journey – she was detained at Genoa for two weeks under quarantine regulations – arrived to join in what Tom described as a very gay winter at the Villa Ricorboli, with many musical evenings and expeditions into the Tuscan countryside.

No doubt Nelly wanted sunshine, distraction, movement from one place to another. She had lost the dominant force in her life, her second father and protector; and although she had a will of her own, she was accustomed to pitting it against a still stronger one, whose disappearance was bound to be painful. She had to find her balance again. She also had, in effect, to reinvent herself. The process might be easier to start off abroad: so much she had grasped. In Paris she had already achieved one thing useful to someone who sets out to reconstruct herself: the making of a new friend, Mrs Rosalind Brown, a young English widow also travelling abroad to recover from the death of her husband. The two had taken to one another immediately, and Mrs Brown told Nelly she had inherited a house in Bina Gardens, Kensington, and proposed to let rooms once she returned to England; Nelly would be a most welcome 'paying guest' whenever she needed accommodation in London. Nelly was naturally cautious in her account of herself, but she did let drop that there was a Secret in her life. She also conveyed that she had suffered an injury to her arm in an accident; this was not properly healed and was responsible for the extreme delicacy of her health.

Delicate health took people abroad for the better climate, but there were other good reasons for travelling. Society on the Continent could be notably more relaxed about single women with unknown antecedents, who might or might not choose to describe themselves as widows. There are several such in the early stories of Henry James, who made his first visit to Italy in 1873 and was profoundly struck by the freedom of Continental manners, particularly those of women in their relations with men; it became and remained a favourite theme. In one story ('Eugene Pickering') he shows an innocent youth captivated by a clever, pretty German widow considerably older than himself; she has a witty tongue, a decisive way and a girlish appearance, with cascading golden curls, muslin dresses adorned with blue ribbons and a good display of jewellery. In addition she is a writer, something of a feminist and has acted in her own play, *Cleopatra*. James had not met women like this in America or England, but on the Continent, and in Rome especially, he came across many such clever and charming, good companions, and with enough money to keep afloat; only, to the vigilant eye, they carried questions marks over their pretty heads.

Such in her way was Nelly, who gravitated so naturally towards Italy in the 1870s. She was made welcome, although even there she was not entirely safe from gossip. Isa Blagden – dear Isa, who seemed such a friend to the Trollopes – was soon writing from Florence to Robert Browning in London, explaining to him just why Dickens had paid Fanny Trollope so well for her novels.

Browning confessed that 'the relationship between Mrs T. and "Miss T." never crossed my mind: I must have heard it – very likely from yourself – but it took no hold of me.'[6] And even as far away as Boston tongues were also wagging; Annie Fields noted in her diary that her husband had confided in Longfellow, 'as was quite right, about E.L.T.'[7] When even these two august poets had Nelly's story pressed on them, it suggests that lesser folk found it fascinating enough to discuss a good deal.

Nelly remained abroad throughout the winter of 1870. In April 1871 the census shows that neither she nor either of her sisters was at The Lawn, only Mrs Ternan and her hospitable son-in-law. But in the summer Nelly and Maria were both back; in fact, in Eights Weeks they attended a party given in Queen's College together. Their host was a second-year undergraduate, Mr Robinson. George Wharton Robinson was reading history, but his interests were not predominantly intellectual; he was destined for the Church, and rowing was his passion. He was the only son of a Liverpool gentleman who had died young; his widowed mother had sent him to Cheltenham School and settled herself with a troop of daughters in the Lake District, where the Ternans had a married cousin, the daughter of their Aunt Louisa. Hence the introduction to Maria.

The party in Queen's was extremely jolly. Mrs Taylor sang the *Marseillaise* to loud applause, and Miss Ternan teased all the big young rowing men in turn. She was so pleased with the occasion that she wrote some verses about it. They ended with a tribute to the host:

> Ten o'clock! now must all say Goodbye!
> As the ladies get into their fly,
> > They say to each other
> > 'What a charming young brother
> Is Robinson, gallant and spry!'

The light-hearted lines do catch something of the merriment of the Oxford summer evening party, and even of the instant appeal of George, hardly more than an outsize boy, with glossy dark hair and an uncomplicated physical presence. Nelly and George were instantly taken with one another, and although he was apparently already engaged to another young lady called Jessie, he was soon going for walks and rides with his new friend, and listening to her advice as well as her teasing. Within a few weeks he was no longer engaged to Jessie.

Both George and Nelly kept commonplace books, and both wrote verses; George's schoolboy training in turning out Latin hexameters had given him considerable facility. Some acrostics he produced indicate that Nelly gave him to understand she had suffered two tragic bereavements in recent years, in each case of men friends – possibly even prospective husbands. Frank Carter and George Herries are the names that appear; both seem to have been pure inventions.[8] The function of these imaginary dead admirers is somewhat obscure; presumably they provided Nelly with a story for her recent past and served to explain why she always wore black. Later she told a woman friend that it made people think better of you; Dickens, who loved young women to be brightly dressed, would not have approved. George knew that Dickens had been a friend of the family, but whatever else Nelly told him, she kept her age strictly to herself; as it happened, the twelve years she needed to abolish from her life also coincided with the gap between her birth and George's.

The black clothes did not prevent her from being high spirited. George was teased to the limit about his rowing and the poor performance of the Queen's boat. 'George is so silly,' she told Rosalind Brown in London.[9] In July he wrote a poem in her praise in his book. It was called 'A True Friend', and part of it reads as follows:

> Oh – could I but express
>   The debt of gratitude I owe!
>   But words of mine can never show
> My sense of your true-heartedness.
>
> Ne'er has it been before my lot
>   To meet with one so truly kind,
>   So winning, womanly, refined,
> A heart so pure and free from blot.
>
> My privilege to call you friend
>   The purest happiness imparts;
>   I cherish in my heart of hearts
> Your friendship; may it never end!

How well in fancy I recall
> Those rides and those but too-short walks,
> Those heart-arresting heart-felt talks
Which did my mind and heart enthrall.

My heart with joy was then replete:
> But oh! that time of bliss is past!
> Our 'summer term' sped all too fast –
Oh Time, speed swiftly till we meet.[10]

Poor George: whatever he might say about friendship, these sound like the accents of true love. Nelly, however, had no intention of sitting tamely in Oxford to enjoy the flattery of a boy. By the autumn she was back in Italy, first in Florence with the Trollopes and then in Rome. In December Annie Fields in Boston, still grieving for Dickens and with her ear fine-tuned for any word that bore on him, heard 'quite accidentally' that 'N.T.' was in Rome 'with Mrs Tilton'. Mrs Tilton was the wife of an American painter, John Rollin Tilton who specialized in Claude-like sunsets and ruins. If Nelly was staying with them, it meant she was living in their apartment in the Palazzo Barberini – described by Anny Thackeray at the same time as 'a great deal grander than Windsor Castle' – and spending her time with a highly entertaining and cultivated cosmopolitan group. Henry James knew the Tiltons well, described John Tilton as a 'very queer genius', partly modelled a character in *Roderick Hudson* on him and allowed him to attempt a portrait. Mrs Tilton, whom he preferred to her husband, was the 'poor ill-wedded, soured, yet withal clever, Mrs Tilton'. If the Tiltons were not the best advertisement for marriage, they were interesting people; and winter in Rome was almost unmixed delight. You could ride out for hours into the sunny, empty Campagna or fill your days visiting museums, antiquities and churches, where gorgeous rituals were enacted by cardinals and congregations endowed with a natural sense of the theatrical. You could attend concerts in the evening and visit the Colosseum by moonlight. There were salons; there were picnics, parties and dinners at which Americans, English, French, Italians and Germans mingled freely. Nelly's commonplace book filled itself with excerpts from writers in all these languages, and she met a great many people; but she did not form any serious ties. To some, perhaps, she had the allure of a latter-day Claire Clairmont, another repository of the secrets and letters of a dead genius; but Nelly, like Claire, was proof against inquirers at this stage.[11]

She was casting about for something to do. As long as Dickens had lived, she had to a degree been involved in reading his work and discussing it with him. She was eager to be part of the literary world again. So far all she had managed was the publication of some of her verses in an Oxford paper, which hardly counted; but in Italy she met through the Trollopes the poet and novelist Alfred Austin, then in his thirties, who had given up his profession as a lawyer to write, though so far with very little critical success. His own view of his contemporaries was striking in that he dismissed Tennyson, Browning, Arnold, Morris and Clough with equal disdain; he knew he had a better grasp of prosody and would surpass them all. This self-conceit was supported by an adoring wife. The Trollopes were also devoted friends of the couple. Like Tom Trollope, Austin sometimes worked for the *Standard*; he was in Rome in 1870 to report on the Vatican Council, as he had been brought up as a Roman Catholic, and frequently took his holidays in Italy.

There he evidently met Nelly and was sufficiently impressed by her to entrust her with a negotiation with a publisher in England in the winter of 1872. The whole episode is odd. There is no obvious reason why he should not have submitted his new poem, a long narrative work called *Madonna's Child*, in the usual way. He preferred, however, or was persuaded, to use Nelly as an intermediary with Messrs Smith & Elder. George Smith was one of Britain's most eminent publishers; he had been the friend as well as the publisher of Ruskin, Charlotte Brontë, Mrs Gaskell and Thackeray, whose daughter's work he also published. Currently he was Fanny's publisher. He had also been acquainted with Dickens.

Nelly's first note to Smith, written from The Lawn in December 1872, was a formal one; it simply stated that she was offering him a poem 'of exceptional excellence and interest' by a gentleman not at present in England, who wished it to be published anonymously. To this Smith replied politely, saying he would be happy to read the poem. Her second letter announced that she was sending the manuscript. He now apparently made an offer for the poem; she thanked him for his prompt reply and said she had written to the author. She followed this up immediately with another letter to say that the author now thought it right that Smith should be told his name, '*confidentially*'.

This performance elicited a crusty answer from Smith. He knew Austin's work and had previously turned some of it down. He now changed his mind about the proffered poem and stiffly advised Miss Ternan not to treat other publishers as she had him: 'it would be advisable for you to mention the name of the Author or at least that he was a well-known writer who wished to publish a work anonymously, in the first instance'.

Nelly brooded on this rebuke for several days, and then sent a spirited answer:

> . . . Notwithstanding the polite tenor of your note, I cannot conceal from myself that by it you intend to reproach me with not having treated you quite fairly. Now I feel so strongly that the reproach is altogether unjust, that I must ask you dispassionately, to consider the following facts.
>
> An anonymous Poem was submitted to you for publication, and you, influenced solely by what you conceive to be its merit, express yourself happy to publish it. But lest possibly its being by Mr Austin might affect your decision, his name as the author was then confidentially communicated to you. You reply by returning Mr Austin's MS. He is perfectly satisfied; and that being so, I cannot see who can feel aggrieved. All this seems to me so plain and simple, that I cannot but think you will feel disposed on reconsideration to own that you have been treated with perfect straightforwardness.
>
> I ought to add that before receiving your last letter, Mr Austin had communicated to me his intention of publishing *Madonna's Child* under his own name. You are therefore absolved from all secrecy in the matter.

I remain

Dear Sir

Yours faithfully

Nelly Ternan.

Smith wrote a final letter expressing the view that her behaviour was inconsiderate and thoughtless, and that he felt aggrieved at the waste of his time – on the whole a justifiable complaint. Austin and Nelly's byzantine procedure towards a publisher whom Austin already knew well personally has an air of trickery. Smith was the more annoyed, no doubt, in that the trick had worked to the degree that he had been prepared to publish the anonymous poem and been made to look foolish.

Madonna's Child is not a good poem; it is religiose and relies on quaint evocations of the Italian landscape for its better passages. Today Austin's talent seems minimal, and his later appointment as poet laureate absurd, so it was unfortunate that Nelly's attempt to become a literary agent before the career was invented should have been on his behalf. But she displayed some of the necessary spirit, as is shown in her final letter to Smith:

> I am exceedingly sorry if I have wasted time that I know to be very valuable to you; but as I had no reasonable grounds for supposing that a poem you would otherwise be glad to publish, you would be unwilling to publish if written by Mr Alfred Austin – whether issued by him anonymously or not – I still think that for that waste of time, however much I may regret it, I am in no degree responsible.
>
> It was because you are – as you say – personally acquainted with Mr Austin, that it was thought due to you, after you had accepted the poem, that you should be confidentially informed of his being the author. Had you not been personally acquainted with him, this course would have been considered altogether unnecessary. And I am sure you are too well acquainted with those relations between publishers and authors, which have become historical, not to allow that such an opinion and such conduct would have been in strict harmony with precedents whose propriety no one has ever questioned.
>
> Much regretting that you should have had so much trouble in the matter, and still more, if possible, that any difference of view should have arisen between us in connection with it.
>
> I remain
> Dear Sir
> Yours faithfully
> Nelly Ternan.

One thing is clear from this exchange: she had a fluent pen and an ability to make a case and justify herself in clear and even elegant prose. Subsequently Austin's poem was published by Blackwood's, under his name; whether Nelly had anything to do with it is not known. The fact that Smith – who initiated *The Dictionary of National Biography* a few years later – kept the correspondence so carefully in a special bundle suggests that he knew a letter signed with the name of Nelly Ternan was something to be preserved.[12]

She had not proved an effective negotiator, but she had at least been trying to do something. Delightful as it may have been to travel, to stay with the families of American artists in Rome, to flirt with handsome undergraduates, to fill her notebooks with her own verses and excerpts from great writers, it did not fill her life. That remained a problem.

The problem made Nelly ill, or contributed to her illness. A few weeks before her exchange of letters with George Smith, Fanny had arrived at The Lawn and found her mother and sisters all 'pretty well', but then Nelly had 'an attack' in November. Her illness drove her to take rooms at the seaside again, this time Eastbourne, where the Austins were currently settled; she was accompanied as usual by one of her little dogs, Clara having now given way to Dolly. Fanny joined her, leaving Mrs Ternan to the consolations of her son-in-law and her pet parrot. Whatever mortification Nelly felt at Smith's rough handling, Fanny consoled her, and the two sisters returned to Oxford for Christmas. Nelly's present from her mother was the whole set of volumes of Carlyle's *Frederick the Great*: a gift which dispels any doubt about her capacity to tackle difficult and weighty books.[13]

Things were then very quiet. In February Fanny returned to Rome, where Tom now had a job with the London *Standard*; the Villa Ricorboli had finally been sold, at a substantial loss, and they were settled in a modest apartment in the via Rasella. Nelly continued to be ill and was told she must leave Oxford again; in March she departed, this time for Brighton, to lodge in an expensive boarding house run by a Frenchwoman. It was a miserable year. Maria and her husband were on bad terms, perhaps because Maria, too, felt the need to do something more than reign over her domestic empire or drive out in her carriage. There was still no sign of any children for her or Fanny. Mrs Ternan, now in her seventies, was suffering from bronchial trouble, which the Oxford climate did nothing to alleviate.

In the summer George Robinson took his degree in history. He got a third; still intent on becoming a clergyman, he accepted a curacy at St Anne's, Soho, and settled in London.

In October Mrs Ternan died of bronchitis. Fanny and Maria were both with her; whether or not Nelly was there is unclear. The death was registered by Jane, Nelly's maid from Slough, now in service at The Lawn; obliged to specify the profession of the dead woman's husband – she was not expected to have a profession of her own – Jane said it was 'unknown', which would not have pleased the actor-manager. Quite possibly Jane did not know, although she must have been aware of Mrs Ternan's stage career in its last phase; equally it may have been a matter of quietly effacing the less reputable aspects of the past, a typical piece of mid-Victorian bowdlerization in which maid and mistresses colluded discreetly.

Frances Ternan, *née* Jarman on the Yorkshire circuit at the beginning of the century, had lived a more adventurous life than most women of her generation, worked harder and risked more; but the highest prizes had not come to her. As a young actress she had seemed on the point of triumphant success, only to find she could not quite carry it off and would have to settle for the hard labour of the second rank. As a wife she was beloved but tragically unfortunate. A devoted and conscientious mother, she saw the carefully nurtured skills of her daughters fail to carry them where their ambitions aspired. For twelve years she had done her best to help her youngest through difficulties and dangers, and by 1873 she must have become resigned to seeing her as a lonely, dissatisfied semi-invalid.

As long as she lived, she acted as a stabilizing influence on her daughters. Her death precipitated change. Within a few months Maria fled from The Lawn, never to return. She went first to the north of England, then abroad, joining Fanny and Tom in Baden the next summer. Her marriage had lasted ten years. Her husband appears to have been fond of her and given her both a luxurious establishment and all the freedom she could wish for, without succeeding in making her content. In the privacy of the family she complained of unspecified bad behaviour, but the real problem was surely that Maria, overflowing with spirits and energy, was bored by Oxford as well as dissatisfied with Taylor. She felt in herself the stirrings of a New Woman, and without waiting for Ibsen and William Archer to show her the way, she fled from her doll's house, full of ambitious plans for independence.[14]

Maria's action left Nelly without a home in England; she now became a frequent paying guest at Bina Gardens with Rosalind Brown and more of an invalid than ever. 'I am sorry to say that I have not good news of Nelly,' wrote Fanny to Bice in May 1874; 'She does not regain strength or appetite at all. I long to have her near me that I may nurse her and look after her myself. But that may not yet be.' In June, in answer to Bice's polite inquiry, she replied, 'You ask how Nelly is. She has been very ill again, but is now better, and is in the country for rest and fresh air. Her physician orders complete repose. She is not to walk, nor even to stand, beyond the moments or two that may be necessary in cleansing herself.' And a few weeks later, 'Of Nelly my latest accounts are not quite so good. Her recovery is very tedious, and she suffers a great deal.'[15] A grisly picture of Victorian medicine is conjured up here, when a young woman in her thirties who – it later transpires – has nothing fundamentally wrong with her is ordered to immobilize herself to the extent of not even standing up; whereas you can't help thinking that violent activity may have been exactly what Nelly, like Maria, was craving.

Something about her condition did, however, need medical – or rather surgical – intervention. In the autumn of 1874 when, after an interval, George Robinson reappears in her commonplace book, he has taken to Latin verse. His poem makes it clear that she is about to be operated on (or 'tortured' or 'crucified', as he puts it):

> *Ah, mea dulcedo, quum nunc torquenda pararis,*
> *Praesenti in duro tempore fide mihi;*
> *Et quum vox surgit vehemens ad labra doloris,*
> *Da tua blanditiis labra serenda meis;*

Et mihi, quum tandem cruciatu fessa quiescas,
Tunc spatium in lepido pectore cede tuo. *

This is passionate, even earthy stuff, and it obviously made an impression on Nelly, perhaps the more so for being couched in the decent obscurity of a learned language. The separations George had endured over the past few years had only intensified his ardour and determination. When Rosalind Brown, who was herself now engaged to a Mr Wickham, tried to suggest that Nelly might not make him happy, he answered, 'I would rather be unhappy with Nelly than happy without her.' Irresistible words, if they were repeated to her. She reciprocated with her own love poem, which ended with the lines, 'It would fill a big volume to tell ye/All the blessings breathed forth for her boy by his – "Nelly".' All the same, once the operation was over she set off for Italy again; in the spring of 1875 she was in Perugia with the Trollopes for her thirty-sixth birthday. While she was away, George took his MA; he had already been ordained as a deacon. After her return to Bina Gardens the young clergyman became a constant caller; and before the end of the year Nelly agreed to become his wife: a step she might well have hesitated to take during the lifetime of her mother, who might have expected her to mourn Dickens for the rest of her days, and who would have found the disparity of age between her and George unseemly.

They were married on 31 January 1876 at St Mary Abbot's Church in Kensington. Nelly set off from Rosalind Brown's house in Bina Gardens supported by Maria, who acted as one witness, the other being Mr Haymen of Rochester. The view of George's mother is not known. In any case her son was old enough to do as he pleased. Neither bride nor groom gave an age in the register. They were photographed in their finery – George, seated, sporting a moustache and sideburns, Nelly leaning on him in her elaborate white dress, swathed in the sort of bridal veiling that suggests an expensively wrapped present – before setting off abroad for their

---

* Ah, my sweet, now when you are being prepared for torment, in time of stress, trust in me, by your side; and when the cry of pain comes loudly to your lips, give your sweet lips to my caresses. And for me, when at last you grow quiet, exhausted by pain, grant me room upon your charming bosom.

wedding trip. She had already persuaded him to give up his career in the Church. None of the Ternans had ever shown much sign of religious faith, and the prospect of becoming a clergyman's wife, obliged to do good works in her husband's parish and move in narrow ecclesiastical circles, is not likely to have appealed to her. Her idea was that they should acquire a boy's school in a southern seaside town and run it together, something that would give them both scope for many congenial activities. Whether he had misgivings or not, to this, too, George agreed.

George had none of the business sense needed to run a private school, whereas a quiet and undemanding country parish might have suited him very well; but he was a good, conventional young man, healthy and eager for love, and he had been in pursuit of his bride for five years. He was ready to accept whatever terms Nelly chose to make if only he could achieve his goal.

So began 1876, with a new life and a new name. The last of the Ternan girls disappeared from view, and henceforth Nelly was indeed someone quite different: Mrs George Wharton Robinson. George was especially keen on the 'Wharton', which represented, he claimed, a connection with an ancient and aristocratic family.

As though to mark the demise of 'MissT—', John Forster died in February; he had in his lifetime burnt a mass of letters to and from Dickens, and now his executors destroyed a great many more. At the same time Georgina and Mamey were beginning to think of gathering and publishing an edition of their own selection of his letters. Nelly had remained friendly with them both – one of her recent poems was an elegy for Mamey's beloved dog Bouncer – and Georgina was evidently pleased by her marriage, in this instance putting aside her usual disapproval of unions between younger men and older women.[16] Both Dolby and Wills were leading very quiet lives, and neither had as yet published any account of their work and friendship with Dickens. Still a tiny thread of gossip persisted. Wills's niece, Nina Lehmann, received a letter from a friend mocking the Trollope men for insisting that 'it was only friendship between Dickens and Miss Turnan –!'[17]

But the object of her sarcasm had vanished, since there were no more Miss Turnans, Temans or Ternans to be so maligned. Mrs

Thomas Adolphus Trollope was busy working on another three-decker novel for Charley Dickens's *All the Year Round*; for the first time it was to bear her name rather than being published anonymously. *A Charming Fellow* was a tale of provincial snobbery and an unsuitable match between a young man and an older woman; again, it's hard not to suspect Fanny of picking elements of her plots to tease her own family circle, though she turns the story safely into the realms of melodrama, jealousy and murder, crude but energetic stuff, and certainly readable. As for Mrs Rowland Taylor: she had become a mature student. At forty she was busy learning to paint at the recently established Slade School of Fine Art in Bloomsbury.[18] And the third sister, Mrs George Wharton Robinson, was just returning from her honeymoon in Italy, cared for by her good and adoring young clergyman husband; she was still delicate but remarkably improved in health and spirits.

14

The Schoolmaster's Wife and the Foreign Correspondent: Margate, Rome, Africa

The Revd George Wharton Robinson and his wife arrived in Margate in January 1877: a model Victorian couple, he a muscular Christian gentleman with a classical education and an Oxford degree, she delicate, charming and a perfect lady. They had spent the months since returning from their Continental honeymoon in a careful search of the Kentish coastal towns for a private boarding school which would provide him with a good investment for his capital and a teaching career; and of all the places they had seen, flourishing Margate seemed to offer the best opportunity.

It was a healthy, lively, popular town. Margate had been the first of the Kentish resorts – the bathing machine, invented there, gave it an initial boost – and now it rejoiced in an annual regatta, a pier and a newly constructed jetty. France was only hours away, London was easily reached by boat or five-shilling day trip on the railway. When Nelly and George came to consider Margate, it had become as appealing to settlers as to trippers and was visibly growing before their eyes. Street after street of houses was extended along the cliffs to east and west; solid churches and chapels were also going up to serve the new population. They went to look at Margate High School, another new building, close to the centre of town and to the sea, and with five acres of grounds. It took boys from the ages of seven to seventeen, some from local families but mostly boarders from London or further afield; it had made a very promising start, and the headmaster saw every chance of expanding. He was pleased to find a prospective partner with capital, an Oxford degree and a delightful, intelligent wife to join him in the enterprise. George and Nelly decided they liked the place; it was soon settled that he should become co-proprietor.

A new house was prepared in the school grounds for the Wharton Robinsons. Meanwhile they took temporary lodgings just off the sea-front and busied themselves choosing furniture and supervising the decorations. They named their future dwelling Wharton House; there was no doubt that it had more of a ring to it than Robinson. Writing paper was ordered, elaborately monogrammed and with a motto reading *Virtus pretiosor Auro* in blue and red. George looked over his Latin in preparation for his new career and began to investigate the possibilities of getting a rowing club organized. On their honeymoon he had grown a long, curly beard; with the addition of his black Oxford gown, he made a very striking figure.

As did his bride. Mrs Wharton Robinson appeared in Margate as a young wife just emerged from a delicate girlhood mostly spent seeking health in seaside resorts and foreign climates. She had lost her parents sadly young but been fortunate in having a much older sister, Mrs Thomas Adolphus Trollope, to act as a second mother to her. Mrs Trollope and her husband, part of a distinguished family and interesting social circle, kept a tender eye on her from Italy, where, in recent years, she had spent so much time under their protective wing. Her background was a cultivated and prosperous one, and her whole family had enjoyed literary and artistic connections and friendships. Mrs Wharton Robinson, always quietly dressed, usually in black, beautifully spoken, well read, straight-backed on her horse, fluent in foreign languages and a good musician, was altogether more impressive than the usual wife of a Margate schoolmaster; and she knew it.

Nelly determined to take an active part in the running of the school. She was in her element with children and gave the little boys spelling classes; and the warm interest she took in her husband's pupils extended further, to the inmates of a nearby boys' orphanage whom she also took under her wing. From the start she was notable for the amount of charitable work she undertook, particularly to relieve orphans and working mothers, for whom she helped establish a crèche. Her other passion was the organization of plays and concerts, often intended to raise money for her charities. She converted school rooms into charming little theatres and had all the boys performing farces and pantomimes at the end of every term. It was as though the spring of theatrical passion within her, blocked for so long, had suddenly unstopped itself.

As it happened, Margate was a town with a strong theatrical tradition. It had its own Theatre Royal, which doubled as an opera house, and put on everything from *Romeo and Juliet* to Wilkie Collins's *The New Magdalen*, from Charles Mathews Junior in *My Awful Dad* to *Alive or Dead?*, a dramatic version of *Edwin Drood* with a surprise courtroom denouement. The theatre was rebuilt in the booming 1870s; whether Nelly knew it or not, it was full of associations with her past, for her father had performed in the old building, and Dickens had been a frequent visitor during his Broadstairs summers in the 1840s. There were also several concert rooms, where Miss Marian May or Miss Dot Rudge of Drury Lane might give 'Frolicsome Flora' or 'Nelly's Laughing Eyes', or even dance a genuine Sailor's Hornpipe, just as the little Ternan girls had done in their previous existence.

Now, of course, Nelly was entirely an amateur. For her first Christmas she had the schoolboys perform in a farce called *A Thumping Legacy*, followed by a dance. In the second year there was another play, *Poor Pillicoddy* (in which Fanny had played at the Olympic in 1855); there was a concert afterwards, and again a dance. On this occasion 200 guests were invited, and many remained until five in the morning. This was the Christmas of 1878. It was a miraculous time for Nelly, who danced quite undaunted by the fact that she was now in an advanced state of pregnancy. She had never been so well and happy. When her friend Rosalind expressed alarm at the prospect of their dear delicate Nelly undergoing the ordeal of childbirth, she replied calmly and joyously that she hoped to have a whole nursery full of children. In Margate only she knew that she was approaching forty, not an easy age to have a first child: and only she knew if it was a first child or the providential replacement for what had been lost in another life more than decade earlier.

For the birth she chose to go to London, and there Geoffrey Wharton Robinson was born in a private nursing home in Dorset Square. There was no undue strain on her health. He was a healthy baby and became a very pretty little boy, with his mother's crop of blond childhood curls. She must have felt an immense private sense of triumph that, after all the years of unhappiness and uncertainty, she had at last produced this marvel. Neither of her sisters had achieved motherhood, or now would. Whether George inspired passionate love in her or simply gratitude, or something fluctuating between the two, she blessed him for giving her this extraordinary fulfilment, a second chance in life to blot out the shadowy shames and miseries of the past.

So confident was Nelly of her new persona that she (or George, under instruction from her) gave her age in the 1881 census as twenty-eight. It was a reduction of fourteen years on the truth and made her two years younger than her husband, crowning the picture she now presented to the world. By her boldness – the boldness she had observed in Dickens and learnt from him – she had achieved the ambition of the right-minded Victorian girl. She was married to a well-educated and industrious gentleman, and together they were leading lives of quiet usefulness. She busied herself with charitable work, but at the same time they were a merry, happy couple, not neglectful of the realms of art and imagination. They were blessed with a strong and healthy child; and Nelly could be confident that there were not going to be too many more children. Photographs of Nelly with her husband and son in front of Wharton House show a pretty, happy young wife and mother. The Nelly of 1881 bore almost no relation to the Nelly of ten or twenty years earlier; in Margate she achieved what can almost be called an apotheosis.

Now everything was bright, pleasant and secure. She could lavish love on her child and dream of his happy future. Money was not a worry to her; she had a cook and parlour-maid as well as the school servants to make her life easy. She had her own pony cart; and the sight of pretty Mrs Wharton Robinson bowling along the cliff tops and through the Kentish lanes, reins in hand, was a familiar one to the local people. George did start his rowing club; Nelly was much in demand at ladies' tea parties; they were both well liked in the community. Indeed, they were model citizens. When George was appointed Registrar of the Church Institute, Nelly organized a three-day Fancy Bazaar to raise money for it,

with the town band and an elephant hired from Sanger's Zoologi-
cal Gardens on the sea-front. After George was made a magistrate,
she got up a concert in aid of the Working Men's Reading Room,
recited a sketch of her own composition in aid of the fire brigade,
and became Honorary Secretary of the crèche.

There was also time for holidays. In the summer of 1880 she and
George went to Switzerland to join Fanny and Tom, who had just
attended Bice's wedding to a young English politician in Paris. In
August 1882 Geoffrey was taken to Boulogne for a beach holiday,
and the following winter, after he had been ill, Nelly took him to
Rome, where both Fanny and Maria were now settled, Maria with
her own studio. The three sisters indulged themselves by dressing
the child as a clown and entering him for a children's carnival
contest, in which he took a prize; he delighted them by announcing
that he would like to be a clown when he grew up, adding
precociously, 'but I may not have talent enough', in which case he
would settle for being an artist, like Aunt Maria. Back in Margate
Nelly continued to play acting games with him; it was after all the
form of education she knew best. The charm that had subjugated
grown men was irresistible to a small boy. Geoffrey worshipped his
mother.

She was pregnant again, and again it deterred her neither from
travelling nor from joining in the gaieties of Margate. In June 1883
she and George attended a fancy dress ball at Cliftonville Hall with
a large party of friends, he as Fra Diavolo, she as Anne Boleyn;
there was dancing till three. In October she presented Geoffrey
with a sister, Gladys Frances; once more she chose to go to London
for the birth. The good fortune and happiness of the little family
was complete.

The summer term often brought visits from Fanny, Tom or
Maria; they were all roped in, either to sing at concerts or present
prizes on sports' days. Anthony Trollope also came, his grandson
Frank being a pupil at the school for a time. Other figures from the
past put in appearances: Miss Georgina Hogarth spent a week's
holiday in Margate in the summer of 1877, and two years later she,
too, handed out prizes.[1] These ceremonies were important for the
prestige of the High School; for Nelly they were also quite obviously

fun. She loved being at the centre of all the activity, the party atmosphere, games, speeches, songs, tableaux vivants and plays. They were enthusiastically reported in the press, though there may have been some who thought she took the High School too far in this particular direction.

Its stated aim was to prepare boys for the universities and the army. George and Nelly sometimes laughed at the parents of their pupils: she described an interview with an asphalt manufacturer to whom they pointed out a picture of Anthony Trollope hanging in the study. The manufacturer asked whether this was 'Trollope the builder' and lost interest altogether when it was explained that he was not a builder, merely a novelist. Yet the sons of the asphalt manufacturers were no less welcome or necessary to the continued prosperity of the school.[2] At least in part it was in business precisely to turn the sons of manufacturers into something approximating to young gentlemen, a service much in demand in the prosperous late-Victorian period. There was a lot of competition, and the local papers were full of advertisements for other schools with similar aims. Some were offering to keep pupils through the holidays as well as the term. After a few years the High School was obliged to do the same; its finances turned out to be less secure than George and Nelly had assumed.

At the end of 1881 the original proprietor decided to leave. He sold his share to George, who became sole owner and headmaster. The Wharton Robinsons moved into the school building and celebrated their elevation by giving a show of tableaux vivants representing Collins's 'Ode on the Passions'. This was another revival from the days of the Ternan girls' performances; and on this occasion Geoffrey appeared as the infant Bacchus, wearing a tiger skin and crowned with vine leaves, in which he had his picture taken. There are many photographs of him from the Margate days, in a variety of costumes that include a velvet aesthete's suit and cap, and the Highland tartan and sporran in which he gave a scene from *Macbeth* at the age of six. He was a natural poser and a smiling, graceful child.

Georgina Hogarth's evident approval of Nelly's marriage is not difficult to understand. During this period she and Mamey were engaged in producing their edition of Dickens's letters, the third volume of which appeared in 1882 and was hailed as the equivalent of a new biography of the great man. It was also a virtual canonization; the editors cut out anything they thought might reflect ill on the 'beloved memory', omitting any mention even of the breakdown of Dickens's marriage. Catherine was no longer there to remind anyone. She had died in November 1879; her daughter Katey, who supported her during the last months of her illness, said she talked a great deal of her grievances, but told Katey nothing she had not already heard from her father. Wills, too, who could have told so much about Dickens and Nelly had he cared to, died in 1880. With the Dickens family so intent on preserving an unflawed version of the great man, Nelly's presentation of herself suited them as well as it suited her. Nelly made no secret of the fact that Dickens had been a friend of the family; she simply made the necessary adjustment to suggest that she had been little more than a child at the time of his death. It was the version she had given her husband, and it was now passed on to their children.

While Nelly rode the crest of her happy domesticity, Maria pursued her opposite course with great courage and persistence. Although she continued to call herself 'Mrs Rowland Taylor', she had become a totally emancipated woman, and nothing more seems to have been said about her husband. After the Slade she went to Italy, where she worked for and achieved an Artistic-National Diploma; Rome cast its spell over her, and she decided to make it her home. She worked as an artist and also became a journalist, getting her first chance from Tom Trollope, who asked her to fill in for him with the London *Standard* during his summer absences in England, Germany, Hungary and Switzerland – for the Trollopes continued to be great travellers.

Maria made a success of her journalism; she was quick and witty, worked hard at making contacts and knew how to pick up information. She settled in her studio in the via della Mercede and later acquired a small house outside the city, set among olive groves by the sea, where she gave English afternoon parties, with tea and biscuits, in the shade of a lime tree. The presence of her sister and brother-in-law was naturally a help to her at first, but Rome was a city in which there was a well-established tradition of resident single foreign women. Maria remembered her mother's friend, the American actress Charlotte Cushman, who had settled for some years in the sixties; and there had been a whole colony of American women artists before that, who had made it their business to impress on the Romans that 'a Yankee girl can do anything she pleases, walk alone, ride her horse alone, and laugh at their rules'.[3] Where a Yankee girl could go, an Englishwoman might venture to follow, and soon Maria was proving her spirit by being rowed round the Amalfi coast, alone, by some surprised fishermen.[4] She travelled all over the country. An easel and palette were good companions, and with her quick ear she became bilingual; the fishermen asked her if she came from Venice, and no doubt the Venetians assumed she came from Naples. When Italy seemed too tame, she took a two-month trip to Egypt, learning a little Arabic before she set off in her usual independent fashion; this was in the winter of 1880, for Tom Trollope noted her safe return to Europe in May 1881. She was off again to Africa before another year was out.

If she sometimes appeared eccentric, she avoided offending Italian susceptibilities and became very popular in Rome. When the time came for her to leave after twenty years' residence, there were many tributes to her cultivated and civilized character – 'colta e gentile signora Taylor' – as well as her skills. The tributes appear in an album presented to her by the press corps of Rome, of which she made herself a respected member, living proof, as one wrote, that women could hold their own professionally in the nineteenth century: 'una splendida prova che l'avanzarsi del femminismo e' quanto di meglio puo desiderare questa fine di' secolo XIX'.[5] The London Standard thought so highly of her that the bosses in Shoe Lane asked her to take over Tom's job permanently when he was retired in 1886; she kept it for another twelve years, until she was sixty-one.

Thus Maria, the merry and gentle sister, emerges as the most unorthodox, both by leaving her husband and by becoming a successful career woman as a foreign correspondent. Sadly, little survives of her; but there is one short book from which her personality emerges distinctly. It appeared in Rome in 1889 and was

called *Some Old Letters from North Africa*; it describes her trip to
Tunisia in 1881. The title is not so promising, but in the very first
pages Maria springs to life, adventurous, inquisitive, brave and
witty. She introduces herself as she leaps into an open mail-boat
from her steamer off the Barbary coast, for a twenty-minute run
ashore among the bags of letters and newspapers – twenty minutes
which leave her drenched in salt water, but ready to observe that
the port of Goletta resembles nowhere so much as Sheerness on the
Thames estuary, with its blocks of bare little one-storey houses, its
hillocky wastes of sand and rubbish, its drawbridge over the canal
and its cafés and drinking shops full of sailors. Only the turbans
and dark faces mark the difference, and soon the flocks of flamingoes
sighted from the English-made train carrying her on into Tunis.

The timing of her trip was odd enough to raise the possibility
that it may have been something other than simple tourism, perhaps
more in the nature of some mild spying at the behest of either the
English or the Italians. Tunisia, at that time independent and on
friendly terms with Italy, was about to be invaded and annexed by
the French; Maria was received by the ruling bey and later made
an expedition to the Algerian border, where the French were
preparing to advance. She seems to have made friends among
several different groups. In Tunis she visited families of the Jewish
community. Then she travelled inland with an English Gibraltarian
called Levy. She used Italian interpreters when necessary, for her
Arabic was not advanced; and she was accompanied by a French
railway contractor when she crossed into Algiers.

This last was a fairly hair-raising experience. She had expressed
a wish to travel into lion country, and the nearest was in the
mountains on the border; the railway line did not go the whole
way, and the later part of the journey was made largely on foot,
with much scrambling through thorny scrub and up and down
steep river banks. At one point she had to be carried across the
River Medjerda on the shoulder of a 'small, meagre Arab'
summoned up out of nowhere by her guide; the alternative was to
jump from one pier of a ruined Roman bridge to the next. All this
while she was wearing a riding habit with skirt and 'trowsers',
boots, hat and veil, and the temperature was in the eighties at
least. When they finally found horses, there was no side-saddle for

her, and she had to manage by 'getting my knee round the front part of the Arab saddle'. There were no lions to be seen, but presently they saw a moving line of white in the distance: it was a large group of tribesmen advancing at full gallop in their white burnouses. By now she was very tired indeed, her head and neck on fire from sunburn despite her veil; at this point her guide led the horses down a rocky slope so steep that she had to lie flat on her back on the horse not to fall off. 'Are you afraid now?' he asked her. 'Not yet,' she answered very quietly, although she was. *'Ah! une vraie anglaise,'* he laughed.

Discreet as she was about politics, she was clearly sympathetic to the Italians, of whom a large workforce existed in Tunisia. She reported that the French contractor was building his railway line almost entirely with Sicilian labourers, who were very good at pulling Roman ruins to bits – they were used as the basis of the new construction – and she also felt quite at ease with the local Arabs. Maria commented on the niceness of all the Italians settled in Tunisia, their respect for the rights of others and willingness to live and let live. Unlike other Europeans, she wrote, 'they do not treat their fellow creatures of a different race and colour as if necessarily abjectly inferior to themselves'.

She also noted that the Tunisians did not believe the French would invade them, because it was contrary to the 'law of Nations'; whereas she feared that the French desire for an African empire to match the English one in India would drive them on; and she was right. The French invaded just after her visit to the border, and by the summer of 1883 they controlled the whole country.

Some Old Letters from North Africa gives a clear picture of a woman of curiosity and courage who would never let a good opportunity pass. At an age when many of her female contemporaries in England had settled permanently on the sofa, she kept the enthusiasm of a girl, always bobbing up insistently when a journey was suggested and sticking to her resolve through all discomforts and danger. She thought nothing of setting off for several days into the unknown with only a handbag for luggage. She rose cheerfully at three in the morning to the roar of a camel caravan. She got herself taken into the sacred city of Kairouan, where no Christian woman – and scarcely a white man – had ever been, and where there was a real risk of being stoned by an indignant populace.

If her mind ever strayed back to The Lawn, with its flower gardens and croquet, its gardeners, coachman and paddock with her quiet horse prepared for a gentle outing, she obviously had no regrets. The contrasts of her life were even greater than those of Nelly's, her course quite as unpredictable; and it afforded her at least equal satisfaction.

15

Nelly Tells

In Margate Nelly gave charitable readings and recitations from *A Christmas Carol*, *Nicholas Nickleby*, *David Copperfield* ('Our Housekeeping') and *Bleak House* with the special authority of one whose family had boasted a friendship with the author. On her birthday in 1882 she received from Mamey a 'Charles Dickens Birthday Book', affectionately inscribed; and it is said that the infant Geoffrey played on the sands of Boulogne with the children of Henry Dickens, at the instance of Georgina, in 1882.[1]

Any correspondence between Georgina and Nelly has disappeared, making it impossible to know the precise nature of the bond between them, but, however affectionate, it can hardly have been an entirely straightforward friendship. It seems likely that Georgina was keeping something of a watchful eye on Nelly, hoping for a measure of control over any letters she possessed or revelations she might, at some point, be tempted to make. For this very reason Georgina must have welcomed the changes in Nelly's life; the advent of George, and then the children, made it almost unthinkable that she would ever be tempted to show (or sell) her letters or tell her true story.

Yet Nelly did talk. Not very loudly, not very dangerously, not enough to alert Georgina yet; but just enough to produce trouble later. She was a risk taker; everything about her life up to this point makes this clear, and it looks as though something in her rebelled against the rigidly imposed secrecy covering her relations with Dickens, just as it had in Dickens when he came to write his will. She threw out hints about a secret to Rosalind Brown; she muttered darkly about visits to Gad's Hill, and she could not resist mentioning that she had been in the Staplehurst railway accident

228

to at least one friend in Margate, a Mrs Pyne Galton, who sometimes accompanied her singing at concerts. Mrs Pyne Galton gained the impression that Nelly had been Dickens's god-daughter, and in that capacity had been with him on the train that crashed; the story made enough of an impression for her to pass it on to her own daughter.*

Nelly's chief confidant, however, became – very properly, one might think – her local parish priest, the Vicar of St John's, the Revd William Benham. Benham was in his mid-forties when she met him, a jolly, kindly, dynamic man with literary tastes and a fluent pen, who had risen by his own talents from a humble background – a man, in fact, made in very much the same mould as Dickens and, as it happened, of the same age as Dickens when she first met him. In other ways he did not resemble Dickens; one of Benham's particular fortes was said to be 'stimulating character', which seems to have meant a capacity to work with sinners, bracing and restoring them to Christian virtue. He was a disciple of F. D. Maurice and had taken over from Maurice as Professor of History at Queen's College, Harley Street, and taught there for several years before being appointed to Margate; evidently he was at ease with young women and took an interest in advanced causes such as higher education for their sex. His literary work included editing the poems of Cowper, articles for the *Church Times* and lectures on Dickens, to whose work he was particularly devoted. He is the Benham who glimpsed the family group at Westminster Abbey in June 1870, and who would undoubtedly have been highly curious about Nelly's friendship with his idol.

At the time of the Wharton Robinsons' arrival in Margate, Benham was established as the chief pillar of the community. He was chairman of the School Board. It was he who summoned an architect to restore the ancient structure of the parish church. He was a constant organizer of charity concerts; some of his busy evenings were passed in lecturing on Church history, others in throwing delightful supper parties at the Elephant Hotel for his

---

* It finally appeared in print in 1928, only to be strenuously denied by Sir Henry Dickens in the pages of *The Dickensian*, although it was of course true, except for the god-daughter element; and it can only have come from Nelly herself.

church choir. He arranged special services of song so successful that they sound like the Victorian equivalent of pop concerts; there were occasions when 2,000 people tried to cram themselves into St John's, built to hold only half that number, already an impressive size for a congregation.

Benham was zealous and intelligent and, since he had done so well himself, a firm believer in the possibilities of self-improvement. His sermons had attracted the favourable attention of one Archbishop of Canterbury, and he became an intimate of the next, Archbishop Tait, who made him one of the regular preachers at Canterbury; Tait also appointed him to St John's, Margate, where he had been for five years when George and Nelly made their appearance. He was bound to notice and take an interest in the arrival of a young schoolmaster and his wife; very soon we find Benham presenting the prizes at the High School Sports' Day, encouraging Mrs Wharton Robinson to use her talents in the service of various Margate charities, and appearing alongside her on many platforms.

If he ever had reason to think she had once been a professional actress, he undoubtedly took the view that all gifts were welcome to God when used in his service; he was sympathetic to a movement within the Church to establish links between it and the theatre. In the autumn of 1879 he invited a fellow clergyman to give a sermon on this subject; he spoke in favour of theatrical performances and expressed his disapproval of the isolated position into which actors and actresses were forced by society.[2]

Holding the interests and views he did, it is not too surprising that Benham should have become Nelly's confidant. She must sometimes have longed for someone to talk to; few people like their past to be entirely and permanently obliterated, and besides there was pride that Dickens had chosen and become dependent on her, as well as remorse that she had been put into a dishonourable situation. Benham was not narrow-minded but sympathetic, the warmth of his sympathy doubtless increased by his curiosity in this case. As a Christian he believed in the benefits to a sinner of owning up to sin and repenting, restoring herself inwardly as well as outwardly to the community of the good; at the same time he must sometimes have hugged himself with the knowledge of the secret entrusted to him, as he sat on the platforms of Margate raising money by giving 'penny readings' from the works of the great Charles Dickens, with Nelly beside him.

We know she confided in him – although we don't know exactly when – because some years later he passed on some of her confidences to a fellow Dickens enthusiast who was planning a new biography: not good behaviour in the clergyman, though some will think it excusable in the enthusiast. She told him, it seems, that she had been Dickens's mistress; that he had set her up in the Ampthill Square house; that he had visited her two or three times a week; that she had come to feel remorse about her relations with him during his lifetime, and that her remorse had made them both miserable; and that she now 'loathed the very thought of this intimacy'. Doubt has been cast on whether Nelly really said all this from the time her remarks were made public, which was not until the 1930s, right up to the present; but it is hard to imagine why two perfectly respectable men should choose to concoct such a story, which was later supported by independent corroboratory evidence. Beyond the basic assertion of her relations with Dickens, the most interesting aspect here concerns her remorse during his lifetime, which does contribute something to the impression of restless dissatisfaction conveyed during his last years. As to the loathing: we may think it would be more to her credit to say she remembered Dickens with affection and pleasure, but we are not Victorians, and it would have been surprising if a woman in her position, speaking to a clergyman, had uttered any other sentiment than the one he attributed to her. Her expression of loathing of her past must have seemed the only way she had of restoring herself to virtue and decency. Poor Nelly, she was not to know that fashions in sin change as much as other fashions.

Whatever her contrition, it did not prevent her from continuing to recite and perform the works of Dickens. Shortly before Christmas 1885 her activities as an amateur actress reached their climax when she appeared on the stage of the Theatre Royal, playing in the farce *The Obstinate Family*, in a 'comedietta' called *Orange Blossoms*, and finally impersonating Mrs Jarley, the kindly owner of a waxworks display who gave employment to Little Nell and her grandfather in *The Old Curiosity Shop*. The waxworks on this occasion were played by children, one of whom naturally was Geoffrey. Nelly made a witty speech in which, referring to the current elections, she begged her audience to be conservative in preserving their charitable institutions and liberal when it came to their donations. She was again raising money for her favourite charity, the Margate crèche.

This was almost the end of the busy, happy time. In March 1886 George took the chair at another charitable reading called 'An Evening with Charles Dickens'. Almost immediately afterwards this hitherto active and energetic man of thirty-six suffered a breakdown of an unspecified kind. He was told he must rest. Why the breakdown should have necessitated leaving the healthy climate of Margate for London is a mystery, unless it was connected with an impending financial collapse. At all events, the school was sold; Nelly gave two 'farewell readings', eliciting a final burst of praise for 'the lady artiste' in the press; George gave up his magistracy, other appointments and activities, and prepared to take his family away. Whether he had other worries or griefs is not on record.

The sale of the school was financially disastrous, and things became suddenly much bleaker for the Wharton Robinsons. They alighted in very modest lodgings in Artesian Road, Bayswater, living on the first floor while Nelly's friend Rosalind Wickham, widowed for the second time, and now with a baby daughter the same age as Gladys, had the ground floor. The two stricken families took their meals together. For Geoffrey there were no more drives along the cliff tops with his mother and no more trips to Rome. His father was sick and bad tempered; he expected him to work at his Latin, even during the school holidays, and beat him when he failed to prepare his work to the standard he required. His mother took the child's side and protected him from George's anger. Geoffrey began to dislike his father, who seemed little disposed to look favourably on any plan to become either a clown or an artist.

It was not a good time to be facing an uncertain future in London. In July 1887 the Queen celebrated her jubilee, but in November there was a near-riot in Trafalgar Square when the police attacked a meeting led by socialists; the misery of the poorest class was obvious, and even the respectable poor, the workers swarming to their daily labour in dark clothes and false collars, were not an inspiring spectacle to anyone who felt his grip on his social and professional standing might be slipping, as George must have done in his Bayswater lodging house. This was the grim, filthy-aired London described in the pages of George Gissing, Mark Rutherford and the *Autobiography* of H. G. Wells. In the lodging house run by Wells's aunt in the 1880s an old clergyman lived with his wife on the top floor, earning a precarious income as a 'supply' vicar, and dying penniless and unmourned: 'I had never dreamt that a clergyman could end so shabbily, or that the Establishment could discard its poor priests so heartlessly,' wrote Wells. The first-floor lodgers must sometimes have been haunted by the spectres of the top floor; not only George, fearful of the future, but also Nelly, who could remember the ache of real poverty.

From Artesian Road the Wharton Robinsons moved to Sutherland Avenue, and there in Maida Vale they sank into obscurity. Occasionally they moved from one address to another, though never very far. They made various attempts to set up some sort of coaching establishment or school; they faced a dwindling income and, in George's case, an ever-increasing sense of failure and incapacity. He did not consider returning to Church work; in 1888 he took his name out of *Crockford's Clerical Directory*. Fanny Trollope did what she could to help her brother-in-law. In 1890 she was seeking testimonials for a proposed new school, and a few years later she asked advice on his chances of getting a School Inspectorate; evidently they were not good enough.

Whether or not Nelly ever felt at all responsible for their difficulties, she was not defeated by them. She was always prepared to turn to and give lessons in French, deportment, elocution or whatever was required. She had her children to absorb her attention. Gladys's earliest memories resembled those of her brother: she was taught to recite and made to perform at tea parties. Nelly still had a small income; and she still owned the house in Ampthill Square. If George was a disappointment to her once the charm and promise of young manhood had gone and he revealed himself as impractical and ineffectual, she was quite prepared to take over the decision-making in the family. Those who knew the Wharton Robinsons were clear that she was the dominant force, and that

'George made an absolute doormat of himself to Ellen'.[3] If he ever asked himself whether he really knew his wife, or whether she had acted entirely straightforwardly in her dealings with him, he did not dare to make an issue of his doubts. In any case what could he do? There were the children to be considered, and their future lives; and they grew and flourished, innocent of the past.

During 1887 Tom Trollope published the first two volumes of his memoirs, which he called *What I Remember*: an unpretentious title that suits the book, which is a rambling excursion through different topics and times, put together with more charm than method. The second volume contained a chapter on Dickens. It is a warm tribute to Trollope's old friend, going back to their first meeting when the young novelist had called on him in Florence with his wife, and impressed him as singularly youthful in appearance, dandified, pretty-boy-looking, with a 'slight flavour of the whipper-snapper'. The change that came over him in middle age was so striking, said Trollope, that he could have passed him in the street without recognizing him; but they remained friends, and he saw a good deal of him in his last years, laying stress on his continued personal appeal and greatness of heart:

> As I knew him afterwards, and to the end of his days, he was a strikingly manly man, not only in appearance but in bearing . . . Of the general charm of his manner I despair of giving any idea to those who have not seen or known him. This was a charm by no means dependent on his genius. He might have been the great writer he was and yet not have warmed the social atmosphere wherever he appeared with that summer glow which seemed to attend him . . . He was a *hearty* man, a large-hearted man that is to say. He was perhaps the largest-hearted man I ever knew. I think he made a nearer approach to obeying the divine precept, 'Love thy neighbour as thyself,' than one man in a hundred thousand. His benevolence, his active, energizing desire for good to all God's creatures . . . were unceasing and busy in his heart ever and always.[4]

Trollope had sought Georgina Hogarth's permission to quote from Dickens's letters; he carefully cut out a reference to Nelly. It must have been curious for her to read her brother-in-law's account of the man she had known so much better than he had, and to be unable to make any comment. Privately she may have asked herself if Dickens's much acclaimed greatness and goodness meant she must be responsible for his bad, unmentionable side.

In the final volume of Trollope's memoirs, which appeared a year later, he introduced Fanny, handling the subject cautiously. He gave her maiden name and mentioned that they had met during her first visit to Florence in 1868, when she had been a music student and hospitably entertained by his first wife and mother; but no other members of her family were named beyond passing references to an anonymous, occasionally visiting sister-in-law, an amalgam of Nelly and Maria. And although Trollope wrote proudly of Fanny's literary success, he said nothing at all of her unusual – and indeed extraordinary – past. It was not only Nelly who had to excise a large chunk of her life; all three Ternan sisters effaced their working childhoods and theatrical background, bowing to a prejudice they were not strong enough to oppose. In the written record they were to exist only within certain particular limits.

Tom Trollope's praise of Dickens brought a protest from one woman writer who objected that it offended against the truth, that Dickens had been flagrantly immoral in his behaviour, and that she herself had observed him travelling on the Boulogne boat (and strutting about the deck 'with an air of a man bristling with self-importance') with a lady who was neither his wife nor his sister-in-law.[5] This was the first of a trickle of references to his relations with Nelly that marked the 1890s, and which caused anxiety to both her and Georgina. In 1893 a moderately well-known biographer called Thomas Wright announced his intention of writing a new life of Dickens and made a public request for letters; George Augustus Sala, who had known Dickens well during the later years, objected to Wright's proposal in a newspaper article that contrived to arouse rather than extinguish curiosity, by giving as his grounds that there were 'circumstances connected with the later years of the illustrious novelist which should not and must not be revealed for fifty years to come at the very least'.[6] At the same time Georgina Hogarth wrote to Wright asking him to desist from his plan.

For the time being he did desist, though he continued to look for material; and he had begun to discuss Dickens with Benham, now a canon of the church, living in London, and still friendly with Nelly. In this same year according to Wright, a collector of Dickensiana, W. R. Hughes, was offered letters from the novelist to Ellen Ternan; Hughes claimed, a shade improbably, that he advised the vendor to burn them, on the grounds that they could not have been acquired honestly.[7] If this story is true and the letters were stolen, the theft must have put Nelly into a terrifyingly awkward situation; she could hardly raise a hue and cry for her property, however much she feared the thought of their being made public.

She could at least count on the powerful support of the Dickens family. Georgina succeeded in banning publication of Dickens's letters to Maria Beadnell (in England, though not in America) a few years later, and, as we know, Henry Dickens destroyed letters that came into his possession through Wills's heirs. Only Kate Perugini was not so dedicated to suppressing evidence. She told Bernard Shaw in 1897 that she believed there were letters of her father's 'in which the real man is revealed, minus his Sunday clothes and all shams, and with his heart and soul burning like jewels in a dark place! I say there *may* be such letters and they may be one day given to the world'; she had been assured the letters were all burnt, she went on, but did not believe it.[8] They never surfaced, however. Perhaps Hughes was telling the truth; conceivably Nelly burnt them herself. Had they tended to establish the innocence of her friendship with Dickens, she had every interest in preserving them for eventual publication and the vindication of her good name. They were also worth a great deal of money. In 1900 a copy of *The Frozen Deep* with Dickens's annotations was sold for £300 at Sotheby's.

According to Wright, Benham made his revelations about what Nelly had told him in 1897: it was explosive stuff for Wright, who nevertheless handled it with great discretion for many years. It's unlikely that she knew about Benham's betrayal; but she was certainly aware of the remarks of Mrs Lynn Linton in her memoirs, published posthumously in 1899, in which she referred to Dickens's secret history, his mad, passionate love and the way in which he was deceived, tricked and betrayed by one he never suspected or found out.[9] Mrs Lynn Linton named no names, remained entirely vague, and even insisted that it was best that the whole truth should *not* now be written. She wielded a sharp pen, and she may have been romancing; but she had known Dickens well enough and been a close friend of Wills, and she claimed to have heard more than she saw. Dickens himself was 'straight', she declared, and suffered from 'one cleverer, more astute, less straight than himself, who sailed round him and deceived him from start to finish'. We know that Dickens was far from straight, and that Nelly – it's hard to see who else she can have meant – was caught in a web of deceit spun in the first instance by him. All the same, vague as they are, Mrs Lynn Linton's are the most damaging remarks in the whole bundle of late Victorian gossip on this particular subject, because they are the only ones that contain the accusation of trickery by Nelly.

Thus the post-Margate years brought increasing troubles and anxieties on the Wharton Robinsons. Their compensation was always Geoffrey and Gladys. Enough money was found to send both of them off to boarding school, where they received rigorously conventional upbringings; and it was settled that Geoffrey should aim at a career as an army officer. Fanny and Tom were also devoted to the children; at the end of the eighties they settled in England, in a cottage on the Devon cliffs at Budleigh Salterton, where they frequently entertained Nelly and her family. Tom had been through his own tragedy when Bice died in childbirth a year after her marriage, in 1881; his grief was intense, but his robust nature never allowed him to repine for long, and it was mostly Fanny who kept the contact with Bice's widower.

She continued to turn out novels; here and there was a gleam of genuine observation or a hint of authentic feeling, but they were spoilt by melodramatic plotting and pasteboard villains. None are good enough to be worth reviving; perhaps she wrote too fast to establish an individual voice and escape the fictional conventions of her day. She never equalled *Mabel's Progress*, which was also the book in which she drew most on her own experience.[10] The most interesting features of the last books are those that throw a glancing light on her family. *Among Aliens* (published in 1890) is set in Rome, the story of two expatriate English sisters earning their livings, the capable elder as an artist, the sweet and innocent younger as a governess; she is dismissed when the profligate son of her princely employers pays her attentions to which she unwisely responds. She finds her character blackened everywhere. 'Social laws must be obeyed by those who wish to profit by their protection,' her elder sister is admonished; ruefully she reflects that 'a sister, even the fondest, has small chance against a lover, when they are weighed by a girl of eighteen in all the enchantment of a first romance of the heart'. Little blue-eyed Lucy is broken by love and scandal, fades away and dies. The better part of the book is the description of the daily lives of the working sisters, and the awkwardness of being dependent on the patronage of the rich and capricious, subjects well understood by the author and her sister Maria, its dedicatee. The worse part becomes the sort of melodrama to which Fanny so often resorted, in this case given over to the Italian characters, who run through the whole gamut of seduction, suicide, vows of vengeance and sensational murders.

Madame Leroux (also published in 1890) carries the melodrama into English life and has another sweet innocent Lucy as its heroine. She is an orphan who finds herself obliged to earn her bread by teaching in a London girls' school. The headmistress, a woman of uncertain age but great fascination, is 'Madame Leroux'. We soon learn she is not to be trusted; her name is a false one, she has 'remarkable histrionic ability' which allows her to ape the accents of the aristocracy successfully, and she goes secretly to the theatre in the evening, where she entertains foreign men in her private box. When Lucy is taken along for a treat, she naturally escapes in horror from this depraved scene. Madame Leroux drinks cognac from a travelling flask when she is alone and doses herself with chloral. She is financially calculating and, after the fiasco of the theatre visit, treats Lucy coldly and unkindly. Yet Madame Leroux is observed with some sympathy by her author. The story reveals that she has not always been so cold. In fact, 'there had been a time, in her youth, when passion had carried her, as on a strong tide, beyond the limits of selfish prudence'. She had borne a child to a young man, refusing to marry him on the grounds of their poverty, and then given the child away. Lucy is, of course, her daughter; but before she can discover the truth, Madame Leroux, now facing financial ruin, kills herself with an overdose of chloral. Lucy learns the whole history and refuses to condemn her: 'Poor mother! . . . She was so young . . . No wonder she was frightened! And how lonely!' The use of the theatre to signal Madame Leroux's bad character shows Fanny truckling to convention; her endorsement of Lucy's forgiveness of her bad mother is more interesting. Both Fanny's sisters had made themselves vulnerable to social censure by their behaviour in the past, in Maria's case the abandonment of her husband, in Nelly's the association with Dickens; the question of understanding and forgiveness, both by private individuals and society, must have raised itself in all their minds. Cautiously as her comments or themes must be applied to them, there does occasionally seem to be a thread of connection in her work.

Tom made himself a garden in the Florentine style on the English cliffs, and he and Fanny entertained in some style. Although some of the neighbours suspected that clever Mrs Trollope found Devon society rather slow after Rome, she and Tom were both notable conversationalists, he with his fund of reminiscences, she also 'truly delightful . . . She was really intellectual, very bright and amusing and excellent company'.[11] When her sister Mrs Wharton Robinson appeared, she was also judged a very charming woman by the local families, and very pretty too; and she was much admired for the verse speaking with which she entertained the guests at Cliff Corner.[12]

Then in 1892 Tom died, suddenly and in his sleep, in the middle of a pleasure jaunt to Bristol with Fanny; he was eighty-two, had kept his wits and energy, and continued to visit Rome till the last year of his life. For twenty-six years, despite the difference in age, he and Fanny had made a congenial couple, and she had won the warm approval of all his family and friends. She grieved sincerely, but, like Tom himself at Bice's death, she was too robust and practical to give way to grief. She turned to her sisters for support; Nelly came on the first train to be with her, and, as soon as the news reached Rome, Maria arranged for some Italian mosaics to be made and sent for Tom's grave. Fanny sorted out her financial situation, quickly sold up the house in Budleigh Salterton and took another in Berkshire. She was awarded a civil list pension of £50 a year, and she had the money earned from her books and set aside over the years, which meant she was not too badly off; she kept two servants and was still able to travel on the Continent. But there were no more novels from her pen; either she had lost heart or her publishers had lost interest.

Instead, always willing to try something new, she turned biographer. Tom's papers, which she had inherited, included many letters and diaries belonging to his mother, the original Frances Trollope; and with these she set to work to write her life. The story was a good and inspiring one, and had some parallels with her own mother's; both women had travelled, worked, married, borne children and become the breadwinners for their families, though Mrs Trollope's career was the more striking and had brought her great fame and success. Born in 1780, she had been a very sprightly girl, learning and delighting in organizing amateur theatricals, among them Molière's *Les Femmes savantes*; she had made friends with Lafayette on a visit to France and travelled to America to join a utopian community a few years before Mrs Ternan's transatlantic trip; and she had begun her career as a writer after she was fifty. Fanny told her story very well, with a touch of Victorian sententiousness; it can still be read with enjoyment. She quoted from her letters and diaries, and diligently sought personal impressions and anecdotes, including the one of old Samuel Rogers addressing her disconcertingly at a breakfast party with the words, 'They told me Mrs Trollope was to be here. She has written a great deal of rubbish, hasn't she?' Fanny the younger disagreed with Rogers and claimed 'intrinsic merit' for her mother-in-law's books, but what she most admired about her was undoubtedly her persistence as a worker, which she passed on to Anthony and Tom. The two volumes were dedicated to Tom when they appeared in 1895; it was Fanny's last published book.

Nelly had been summoned to assist with the project, and her help is duly acknowledged at the front. The bonds between the two sisters were growing closer than ever as Fanny reached sixty and Nelly (officially at least) her mid-forties.

Nelly found her life in London dull and disappointing, and when George was advised by a doctor that he should give up any further

Mrs Ternan with her three daughters in the early 1870s, at the home of Maria and her husband, the son of a rich Oxford brewer. The Lawn was at 89 Banbury Road, Oxford (now part of St Hugh's), and it boasted a croquet lawn, paddock, flower and vegetable gardens, a vinery and stables for the carriage horses; Nelly was a 'first-rate horsewoman'. The pet parrot belongs to Mrs Ternan; Fanny is on the left, Maria is standing and Nelly is holding her little dog in her lap.

Fanny and her husband, Thomas Adolphus Trollope, brother of
Anthony, friend of Dickens, and her senior by twenty-five years.

Maria, preparing to leave her
Oxford doll's house and become
a New Woman.

Maria's talent as an artist
appears in this drawing of her
mother.

Nelly in the mid-1860s.

Nelly in the 1870s.

A drawing of Nelly done in Italy.

Nelly in fancy dress or acting
costume, late 1870s.

Nelly and the Revd George Wharton
Robinson after their wedding in 1876.

Nelly with flowers in her hair.

Nelly with her schoolmaster husband
after settling in Margate.

The lively young matron, Mrs George Wharton Robinson, with
husband and son Geoffrey: she was active in charitable works and
helped to organize a round of fêtes, readings and dramatic
performances with the school's pupils, culminating in an
appearance at the Theatre Royal, Margate.

On the steps of the High School: Geoffrey now has a sister, Gladys.

A Roman cartoon showing Maria as a working journalist.

Geoffrey attired as Bacchus for a performance of Collins's 'Ode to the Passions'. . .

. . . and as a clown, during a visit to Rome in carnival time.

The Revd Benham, who extracted some of Nelly's story from her.

Georgina in old age, guardian of Dickens's reputation.

Geoffrey as a young army officer, conventional and correct to the last detail.

The old ladies: Nelly (*left*) and Fanny in Southsea, where all three
sisters settled together in their last years, and where they are
buried. They were living here when Dickens's Birthplace Museum
was set up in 1904; but Nelly never visited it and went to her
grave in 1914 with her secret apparently safe from her children.

attempts at brain work, she was glad to move to the country. Geoffrey was now at a crammer's in Oxford; they were going to need money to put him through Sandhurst and establish him in a regiment. So, with whatever they could muster, they acquired a half share in a market garden at Calcot, near Reading.

They seem to have convinced themselves that the place was a small country estate which would run itself; and it was certainly very pretty, surrounded by fields and farms, and with the river near by. It gave them their own fruit, including grapes from a giant vine; it also gave work to a large staff of gardeners. Next to the main house, The Filberts, was a smaller one, The Bungalow; Fanny was invited to live there, and when Maria retired from Rome in the summer of 1898, she came to join her. They seem to have been livelier companions for Nelly than her husband, who, with no experience either of gardening or of managing men, now found himself in charge of the gardeners and their work.

In the summer of 1900 the three sisters were all at Calcot when a young visitor came who kept a vivid memory of their force of character and the range and liveliness of their conversation.[13] This was Helen Wickham, the daughter of Nelly's widowed friend Rosalind. She found Aunt Fanny enormously impressive; everything she did was done with panache, and she brimmed with vitality. Beside her, Aunt Maria seemed gentler, though Helen considered her the most eccentric of the sisters; 'funny Aunt Maria', Gladys called her. Possibly she had not adopted the respect for conventional behaviour and opinions increasingly shown by her sisters. Fanny and Nelly had both turned into true-blue conservatives, full of the horrors of socialism and radical ideas. They supported Lord Salisbury with great fervour and were some of the few to be delighted when he appointed their old friend Alfred Austin poet laureate in 1896.

To Helen, one of the most striking aspects of life at The Filberts was Nelly's total lack of interest in the domestic arrangements. What she enjoyed was sitting talking with her sisters, about politics, books, music and the theatre; and when the talk ran out they organized anyone who happened to be there into playing intellectual parlour games. Helen remembered Nelly saying that Fanny had been a lovely girl, and Maria had been handsome, but she herself had never made any claim to prettiness, with 'a complexion like a copper saucepan and a figure like an oak tree': mock modesty, perhaps, but the turn of phrase is arresting enough to make you believe in Nelly's power to amuse and hold her own in conversation.

Helen was critical of her hostess's moods, her tyranny over husband and daughter – she read all Gladys's letters till she was in her twenties – her bouts of furious temper and 'nerve storms'; but she loved and admired her nevertheless, and considered her a woman of exceptional charm, gifted, cultured and generous. Her own mother had warned her 'not to bother Aunt Nelly about Dickens. She doesn't wish to remember those days – it makes her so sad.' Helen was obedient to her instructions, and indeed there was no sign of anything to do with Dickens about the house, nor was his name ever mentioned in general conversation. Not a single one of his books was in evidence, and when Aunt Nelly read aloud to Helen and Gladys, it was usually from her sister's novels; never from Thackeray, whom she was known to detest, and certainly never from Dickens.

Yet there was a day when Nelly privately showed Helen a picture of Gad's Hill and murmured the information that she had been there 'many times'. She also told Helen on more than one occasion that she was going out to visit Miss Hogarth, without volunteering any further explanation or making any reference to the visits when she returned. The impression is again of a woman painfully divided, as though she needed to hold on to some thread, to keep alive some connection with her lost self, yet at the same time to banish the past altogether from her current life with George and ensure that their children would never uncover it.

Her pride in Geoffrey increased from year to year. He grew tall; he did well in his preparation for the army; and in 1898 he was commissioned as a second lieutenant. He was given a colonial posting and went straight off to Malta with an infantry regiment, the Lancashire Fusiliers. It was the best they could afford, with no pretensions to smartness, but money still had to be found. In those days young men did not beome officers in the expectation of earning a living; they were paid a purely nominal amount and relied on private income to settle their mess bills and pay a servant, keep a polo pony, and have their many elaborate uniforms made. In Geoffrey's case this income had to come from parents already hard pressed themselves. It may explain why in 1901 Nelly decided to sell the house in Ampthill Square. Half its garden had been eaten away when extra railway lines were laid into Euston, but it was still a valuable property. Fanny protested furiously, but Nelly would not, or could not, take her sister's advice in this instance; and the lease on the house she had owned since 1860 was sold. Whatever its origins and her penitence, she must have blessed heaven for the gift which now went to help her son.

16

Southsea

In November 1903 the neat Georgian terrace house in which Dickens had been born in Mile End Terrace, Portsea, was purchased to be made into the Dickens Birthplace Museum; and the following July there was a gathering of dignitaries for the ceremonial opening. The rooms were furnished with appropriate-seeming furniture and relics in glass cases, a pen stand, a piece of the great man's hair, a letter in his hand; on the walls were hung prints of the best-known characters from his books and a copy of the Maclise portrait, showing the handsome young author, clean-shaven and with long curls. Dickens himself had been unable to locate the house when he gave a reading in Southsea in 1866: not too surprisingly, considering he had been carried out of it when he was only five months old, after his father had run into financial trouble of the kind which dogged him ever afterwards. Still, it was the authentic place, and in its honour the nearest public house changed its name to the Oliver Twist; and a few years later free teas were provided for 1,000 Portsmouth children to celebrate the centenary of the local author's birth.

It was a decade of burgeoning enthusiasm for Dickens. The year 1902 had seen the foundation of the Dickens Fellowship, a philanthropic society dedicated to promoting his social aims and also concerned to preserve Dickensiana. The Fellowship organized convivial dinners, as did another group of devotees, the Boz Club, at which solid-looking gentlemen and ladies gathered in formal clothes to toast the glorious memory. In 1905 *The Dickensian*, a magazine entirely devoted to the man and his works, was founded. Dickens was a public idol and a national institution. His books were not only loved, they were declared to be ennobling. He stood for the individual against the system, for merriment against gloom and, on the whole, for the poor against the rich; for generous indignation against everything mean, joyless, cruel, corrupt and hypocritical in British life. Several adjectives were derived from his name: Dickensy, Dickenesque, Dickensish, Dickensian. Shops and streets were named after him, complete editions of his works were regularly issued and dramatized versions of the novels and stories continued to be played in theatres up and down the land. There were Dickens dictionaries and a concordance. No writer since Shakespeare had conquered the public so absolutely. Its view of Dickens was firmly established in the form expressed by his daughter Katey in her private dissenting cry to Bernard Shaw: 'If you could make the public understand that my father was not a joyous, jocose gentleman walking about the world with a plum pudding and a bowl of punch, you would greatly oblige me.'[1] But this is how the public obstinately saw Dickens, as a Father Christmas figure, master of pathos and laughter, and celebrant of cheery and innocent domesticity.

While the Dickens Birthplace Museum was being set up in Portsea, Frances Trollope and Maria Taylor were living only a mile from it, in Victoria Grove, Southsea. Whereas Portsea is the part of the city of Portsmouth that grew up in the eighteenth century between the old town and the naval dockyards, Southsea was developed during the nineteenth century as a resort, with an esplanade, theatre and rows of modest streets named for the royal family and the novels of Walter Scott – the sort of seaside place in which elderly people settled as their lives petered out respectably. Fanny felt comfortable there, and after a while Nelly and George followed her and established themselves a few streets away, in Waverley Road. None of the sisters offered mementoes to the museum or, as far as we know, visited it. All three had accepted that there was a taboo over their memories and indeed over their lives; and it seems that nobody wanted to realize that there were three old ladies who could have talked for hours about their professional association and their long friendship with Dickens. The gap between what the Dickens people wanted to believe in, the tender-hearted icon of the Victorian age, and the actual man who had intervened so forcibly in the lives of three young working women was too wide to be bridged. If anyone did try to talk to the Southsea ladies, they were no doubt repulsed; Mrs Trollope and Mrs Wharton Robinson had come to accept long since the impossibility of their version. Their self-suppression, their fear of the damage they might cause themselves and others if they spoke or wrote of their experiences and knowledge, is one of the saddest parts of the whole story.

Maria, the merry, original and outspoken, might have felt differently, though she would not have done anything to distress her sisters; but in 1903 she was mortally ill. She died the following year, cared for by Fanny to the end. The trio of the sisters was broken; Fanny had her placed in a double grave in which she announced her intention of joining her in due course. Maria's husband was still alive, but there had been no contact between them for years; and she left what she had – a tiny sum of money, a few of her paintings and drawings – to her elder sister.

When the Calcot market garden finally failed, and the last of George and Nelly's investments disappeared, they, too, after a brief spell in Hanwell, were drawn to Southsea to be near Fanny. They were now painfully poor and kept afloat mainly by Nelly taking in French boarders who wanted to learn English. George and Gladys did what teaching they could find; Fanny also had her daily pupils, mostly young officers who needed to pass examinations in French, Italian and German. The pride of the whole family was Geoffrey, away on the business of the Empire and now a major. It was he who sustained their image of themselves as people of a certain standing and made all their hard work and scrimping worth while. After Malta he had been stationed in Ireland; later he was in China and then Nigeria. He had the family gift for languages; he set off for West Africa with a Hausa grammar, and when he was on leave he studied Russian with Fanny, who had decided to learn it herself, partly to help him, partly for the sheer fun of it. Soon she was reading Russian fluently enough to take the literary journal *Novoe vremya* for her own enjoyment, and her 'belovedest of nephews' sailed easily through his army examinations in three languages, French, German and Russian.

While he was in Nigeria, things got no easier in Southsea. In 1907 Nelly was operated on for cancer of the breast; she was nearly seventy but now so used to her false age, which had settled at ten years below the truth, that it seemed quite natural to think of herself as a much younger woman, and she made a good recovery. George, deeply distressed by her illness, fell ill himself. The couple moved down the social scale still further and were living in a tiny terrace house in a dismal street, next to a pub, when he died, aged sixty: the lowest point in Nelly's fortunes since her childhood.

Still she went on working, as a teacher in a small girls' school. Soon after George's death, Gladys was married, from Fanny's house, to a Cardiff solicitor; Fanny didn't think much of him, but he solved the problem of Gladys's future. Only when Geoffrey announced that he also wanted to marry, he had to be told that it was out of the question. He had met a Miss Thackeray, the daughter of an army family. The name did not please his mother, though the connection was too remote to signify anything (there were scores of distant Thackerays); in any case Geoffrey could not propose to a girl when he was still dependent on his family. There simply was not the money.

Now the ties between the two sisters, so strongly formed in their first years of life, were drawn tight again. Fanny took Nelly into her own house. Frail and poor as they were – even Fanny was reduced to asking for genteel 'loans' from kindly Trollope connections – the two indomitable old ladies began to amuse one another and enjoy themselves again. Their thoughts went back to their early days, and they embarked on a final fling by settling down to write for the theatre together. Several comedies in Fanny's hand and one fragmentary plan for a play in Nelly's survive among the family papers. Some take their inspiration – distantly, it must be admitted – from Oscar Wilde and involve upper-class marital misunderstandings and clashes between foreign adventuresses and innocent English ladies. One is set in a Swiss boarding house, one among English rustics. As works of literature they are not exciting, but they are competently thought out and bear witness to the continuous energy and willpower of the Ternans: how many people attempt to become playwrights in their seventies? Nelly, in her spiky hand, started on a comedy built around theatre people: an elderly amateur writer has a wife half his age, and two young men, a manager and an actor are prepared to put on the amateur's

Dramatis Personae.

Mr. Addiscombe. (anxious to bring out a play) aetat. 50
Mr. Graham. Manager of a Theatre. aetat. 30.
Mr. Belton. an actor. aetat. 25.
Mrs. Addiscombe. aetat. 25.
Miss Castle her sister. aetat. 20.

Mrs. A. and Miss Castle in a drawing-room.

They talk of Mr. A's anxiety to get his play acted, and how his great desire to help him. Then Mrs. A. goes on to say that Mrs Belton has given her hope that Graham the manager might be induced to come to their house to hear the play read. She jestingly tells her sister that she suspects that such a piece of good fortune would be due to her beaux yeux; — that Belton seems to insinuate that the manager had been so struck by her when introduced to her at Mrs — party the other evening, that he had found him shortly afterwards rather suspiciously willing, when he found out who she was, to reconsider his previous excuses as to want of time.

Miss C. says something indicating that

effort in order to make advances to the young wife. The cast list and the plot give out a clear, unrepentent signal that Nelly's imagination was still steeped in the theatre.[2]

In her late seventies Fanny continued to make rounds of visits and take a lively interest in politics, with Lloyd George as her particular villain and all radical ideas under suspicion. Early in 1911 she and Nelly joined the Anti-Suffrage League and attended an anti-suffrage lecture given in Southsea by Dickens's granddaughter Mary, known as Mekitty. Georgina Hogarth was also up in arms against 'idiotic suffragettes'; she had long maintained that, with all the education women were now getting, they had only their own personal disabilities to blame if they failed to get on. 'Every kind of Employment which is *women's* work, and not man's, I am too thankful they should have – and the education to be the companions and even the instructors of men, but I don't see what other "*Rights*" they have a claim to, that they have not got – or nearly all.'[3] Kate Perugini, as usual, put a different emphasis on the subject and went out of her way to declare that her father 'had the strongest possible sympathy with women writers, women painters, and indeed, with all women who work in order to gain a livelihood for themselves and those dependent upon their exertions'.[4]

The exertions of the Southsea ladies could not continue for much longer. Fanny, approaching her seventy-eighth birthday, grew thin and weak, and developed a persistent cough. In June 1913 she was bedridden. Like Nelly, she had cancer; and all through that hot summer she was nursed by Nelly who, in spite of her anxiety and devotion, in spite of her own illness, never lost her gaiety or her wish to be in the swim of events. She wrote to Geoffrey:

> Of course all Portsmouth and Southsea had been *en fête* since the arrival of the French ships. Equally of course I have seen nothing of the gay doings. I did meet a group of French sailors in Victoria Road yesterday. I said, '*Vive la France Vive la Marine française Vive M. Poincaré.*' '*Merci Madame merci!*' & with many bows and smiles they went on.[5]

The letter continues with a comment on Kipling and another on the French press: literature and foreign affairs were not to be neglected. When Nelly could manage no longer, a nurse was called in. Fanny's last weeks are chronicled by her sister in clear and touching letters:

> The end was very sudden and unexpected. It was in the morning about nine o'clock. Nurse had given her some coffee and turned away from the bed to get something else when looking round she saw dear Fanny with her head thrown back on the pillow – insensible! Geoffrey rushed to Telephone for the Doctor but the sweet spirit had passed away before he could come. Of course I was with her and held the dear delicate little hand in mine to the last but she was quite unconscious . . . My one comfort is that she *wished to go*. She told me so many times. Forgive me if I have written incoherently or have said too much. These things cannot be written with a quiet hand or dry eyes.[6]

She died in September and was buried in the same grave as Maria, with no inscription but her name; Nelly gave her age as seventy-five, subtracting a modest three years. She called her 'the most loving sister, the most loyal friend, the wisest counsellor, the brightest most uplifting companion that woman ever had' and added that Fanny had loved her children as though they had been her own.[7] Fanny's house was rented, and her pension died with her, but what she had to leave – a very small sum of money, her books and some boxes of family letters – went to Nelly.

Geoffrey now resigned his commission. His mother had only a few months to live. They went to London together and took a small house in Guion Road, Fulham, with Jane, her good old maid, to care for them; and there, alert to the end, and jokingly apologizing for the time it took her, she died on 25 April. Her son was with her and registered her death, giving her age as sixty-five. He then took her body to Southsea, had her buried in his father's grave, and arranged for the inscription 'Ellen Wharton Robinson, His Loving Wife'.

Nelly died a little richer than her sisters. After her will was sworn at £1,200, an extra, secret fund of another £1,200 turned up, and it had to be resworn. She left her books, pictures, and photographs and one or two other personal trifles to her daughter and everything else to Geoffrey; in this way the papers of all three sisters came to him. Presently they would lead him to reappraise his mother and the whole history of his family; but for the moment there were more pressing matters. Three months after the death of his mother the long peace of Europe ended. As soon as war was declared against Germany, Geoffrey returned to the army. Within weeks he was fighting in Flanders. His mother and aunts became as distant as everything that had once made the normal world; they were sealed into a safe, immeasurably remote past.

17

Geoffrey

Geoffrey's war was grim and long. He was wounded at Mons in 1914, recovered enough to serve two years in charge of a detention barracks in Scotland, and returned to the Somme in 1916. In 1917 he was sent home sick, and in January 1918 he became part of the Dunsterforce, a secret expedition sent out to Persia to keep an eye on the Turkish presence there, and also on the Bolsheviks in Azerbaijan, for fear their ideas would spread in the direction of India; it was Geoffrey's Russian, learnt from Aunt Fanny in 1907, that earned him this posting. He remained for two years, mostly at the Persian port of Enzeli on the Caspian, locked in by a boiling mass of fierce and miserable people: disbanded Russian soldiers and Austrian prisoners released by the Russians; Jangali bandits backed by the Germans; Kurds, Cossacks, Gilanis, Turkomans, Tartars, Armenians and Georgians. There was typhus and cholera, in the mountains there was famine, in the towns cases of cannibalism. Geoffrey was besieged in Baku by the Turks and helped evacuate the wounded by boat back to Enzeli; and he was still there, in charge of the refugee camp, more than a year after the end of the war in Europe.[1]

Finally, in January 1920, he resigned his post and returned to England; in the laconic words of the army records, he 'reverted to unemployment'. He had lived through horrors. Now he was forty, a tall, fair, shy ex-major with very little in the world beyond a good command of several languages and a few boxes of books and old letters left to him by his mother. On this rather slender basis he married his Eva Thackeray at last and set up as a second-hand book dealer, also handling manuscripts and autographs. He found a cottage in the old centre of Slough – possibly because of faithful

Jane, who had returned to her sisters there – and named it the Bluebird Book Shop. He bought himself a typewriter and began to go through the boxes of papers and books left by his mother and his aunts.

Either he found things which he did not understand or, more likely, other manuscript dealers approached him with requests to buy his mother's papers. He became aware of statements which did not tally with his own knowledge and memory of her. They upset him. Geoffrey had adored his mother; he had been brought up within the conventions of the correct middle classes and lived all his adult life among fellow officers who set a fixed dividing line between ladies and women, virtue and vice. He had no idea even, at this point, that his mother and aunts had ever worked as professional actresses.[2]

Once alerted to the possibility that his version of his mother's life was not entirely correct, he embarked on a course of painful re-evaluation of the past. It was easy enough to find facts that undermined it. In the boxes were cuttings relating to Fanny's career as a child performer and to his mother's, hers at an impossible date. An obituary notice of his grandfather Ternan's death also failed to tally. Once he began to doubt and search, more evidence came out of books: her name on a reprinted playbill announced her professional, adult appearance in Manchester in the 1857 production of *The Frozen Deep*.[3] No doubt Geoffrey made other inquiries and discoveries. The shock of finding out that she had quite another past, quite another persona, must have been considerable. That she was not sixty-five when she died, as she had told him and as he had informed the authorities, but seventy-five. Had his father ever known or suspected her true age? Not that she had looked old; but how had his parents discussed their lives together without this huge discrepancy slipping out? She must have watched herself, determined not to give anything away, and she must have relied on her sisters not to betray her. Geoffrey began to realize that all the family had been keeping secrets. Why?

For a time it seemed that there was no one he could turn to for the truth. His younger sister knew nothing, and all his mother's generation was dead; but he could not let the thing rest. Some time in 1921 or early 1922 he wrote to Sir Henry Dickens and asked for an appointment. As Gladys Storey put it in her notes, 'the son came to H.F.D. the only surviving son of CD & asked if it was true that his mother was the mistress of CD & HFD had to admit it.'[4]

Geoffrey found his talk with Sir Henry so upsetting that he went home and destroyed virtually every memento of the mother he had loved. For the rest of his life he would not have any book by Dickens in the house; he would even switch off the radio if the name were mentioned. He steadfastly refused to answer questions about his mother or about the family papers he had inherited from her, and he told his sister not to discuss their mother with anyone.

Of course he could not stop curiosity. His sister did not entirely comply with his orders. After the death of Eva – the marriage was not a happy one – he found a warm-hearted second wife who devoted herself to him; not unnaturally, she expressed a sympathetic interest in his mother's history, but even when she pressed him in his old age, he would not talk about her. He kept his study locked, showed no one his papers, and destroyed most of them without letting anyone see them; in this way the Trollope family letters which had gone to Fanny most unfortunately also disappeared.

His silence suggests two things: that he was deeply hurt and upset by Sir Henry's story, and that he accepted it was true. He made no attempt to disprove or deny it when it became public in the 1930s. Why did he react so strongly? Dickens had, after all, died before Geoffrey's mother had even met his father. If she had transgressed, it was long ago and had long been expiated. For Geoffrey, though, it was not so simple a matter. It was bad enough, no doubt, that Dickens's huge fame made him almost inescapable, but much worse that what he had learnt changed his picture of his mother in almost every particular. Her social origins, her upbringing and education, her relations with her own family, the circumstances of her marriage to his father, the significance of other friendships, her amusements, interests and skills – they all took on a different aspect, even to the way she had played with him when he was a child. Everything she had said appeared to him in a new light; and, still worse, everything she had not said. To him and his sister, to their father, it now seemed she had offered a picture of herself that was in almost every essential false. Even on her deathbed she had lied to him.

The young mother Geoffrey remembered had been only a few weeks short of forty when he was born. Her passionate love for him was very possibly not the love of a woman for her first-born but the love of a woman who had lost her first-born and was being offered, at the last moment, another chance. If she was Dickens's victim, her husband and children were her victims, and all her deceptions had been supported by her elder sisters. Geoffrey had loved his aunts, who lavished affection and attention on him, and mourned them, too, when they died. He now saw that the three sisters had formed a magic circle, close and mutually supportive, which at times and over certain matters excluded everyone else.

Gladys Storey told Bernard Shaw that 'poor Miss Ternan' had lived nearly all her married life 'in perpetual fear of her association with Dickens being revealed to her children'.[5] She had at least died in time, and in peace. After his conversation with Sir Henry, Geoffrey had to endure a great deal in his self-imposed silence. In 1928 the daughter of one of his mother's Margate friends published reminiscences in which she referred to her as Dickens's god-daughter, and said she was involved in the Staplehurst crash: Sir Henry's denial of both statements was given in *The Dickensian*, but before it appeared there was worse.[6]

Still in 1928 a writer called C. E. Bechhofer Roberts published a fictional version of Dickens's life up to the separation from Catherine. Roberts claimed that he was forced to fictionalize because of pressure from the Dickens family; whatever the reason, the results were lamentable. Ellen Ternan was described as 'a dismal little person' with a voice that failed to carry across the stage; Dickens's friend Mark Lemon was made to comment, 'I've seldom seen a more voluptuous figure'; and Catherine, ordered by Dickens to invite Nelly to her house, objected and uttered the dramatic parting words as she left him, 'Go to your actress.' Roberts was immediately taken to task by T. P. O'Connor in his magazine, *T.P.'s Weekly*. O'Connor was a friend of the Dickens family and, after consulting with Lady Dickens, he wrote as follows: 'Of course Dickens sinned, and very few men of genius have not sinned in some way. Unhappy at home, he sought relief abroad. The story of Ellen Terman [*sic*] may one day be told.'[7]

No further attempt to tell it was made until after the death of Dickens's last surviving child. Kate Perugini died in 1929, and Sir Henry in December 1933; in 1934 the *Daily Express* printed an article by the now elderly Thomas Wright – he was in his mid-seventies – stating that Miss Ellen Ternan had been the mistress of Dickens. There was uproar and scandal in the press at this attack on the novelist; but the story was taken up by Hugh Kingsmill in the same year in his biography, *The Sentimental Journey: A Life of Charles Dickens*. Kingsmill said Miss Ternan became 'the object of the sensuality with which he [Dickens] tried to drug the unhappiness of his later years'; being an actress, he suggested, she 'knew how to make her resentment against poverty appealing to Dickens, and her resentment against Dickens harrowing to Canon Benham'.[8] Kingsmill's book was quickly followed in 1935 by Thomas Wright's long-postponed *Life of Charles Dickens*, with his account of what Canon Benham had told him. The book was not well written, and Wright failed to back his assertions in a scholarly fashion (it must be said that few biographers did in the 1930s). He was attacked with venomous fury by those who saw themselves as defenders of Dickens's reputation, and they accused him of having fabricated the whole story. He died shortly afterwards, leaving an autobiography which revealed evidence from the Peckham rate books about Windsor Lodge and Charles Tringham. One ardent Dickensian, J. W. T. Ley, was prompted to seek out Nelly's children in order to refute what Wright had written. Gladys was co-operative, but her evidence was vague and inaccurate, if anything tending to confirm Wright's story; at the same time she put pressure on researchers to insist on her mother's 'innocence'.[9] Geoffrey was entirely uncommunicative.

Gladys Storey's *Dickens and Daughter*, based on information given by Kate Perugini, appeared in 1939.[10] The Dickensians did not feel able to dismiss the reported words of Dickens's daughter as they had Wright's book; and Una Pope-Hennessy drew on it for her 1945 biography of Dickens, which again named Ellen Ternan and held her responsible for the breakdown of his marriage. Pope-Hennessy mentioned Georgina's friendship with Nelly; she also suggested that the relationship with Dickens had been largely happy for both of them, seeing that it had lasted until his death;

like Perugini and Storey, she was less inclined to find fault with Nelly than male biographers. Meanwhile the Nonesuch Edition of Dickens's letters contained several references to the Ternans, clearly establishing the family's intimacy with him.[11]

The next characterization of Nelly was the very hostile one of Edmund Wilson, already described in Chapter 1; it was followed by Edgar Johnson's magisterial conclusion that she had failed Dickens's need. Her son endured all this in silence. He kept the same silence when Ada Nisbet published her *Dickens and Ellen Ternan* in 1952, bringing new evidence from her reading of Dickens letters held in California; in these were passages that had been inked out and restored through infra-red light. Felix Aylmer's *Dickens Incognito* attempted to take the story further; just before it appeared in 1959 Geoffrey died, and it was, perhaps fortunately, to his widow that Aylmer had to make his retraction. Geoffrey had suffered increasingly from nervous afflictions as he grew older, and it's hard not to think that his life had been effectively poisoned, with whatever happy memories left of his childhood rendered bitter by scandal.

Such papers as were left in his study were sold to American university collections; there was not a scrap in them that could link his mother with Dickens. His sister, now widowed, had entered into correspondence with various Dickens scholars. She was keen to establish her mother's blamelessness, saying that if she had sinned with Dickens, it must have been through love; and she seems to have enjoyed the excitement of being asked for letters and information; but she possessed almost nothing that could throw light on the subject.[12] She sank into senility in her last years and died in 1973, childless like her brother.

There is one other surprising aspect to Geoffrey that deserves to be noticed. For a brief period in the 1930s he attempted to become a professional actor. He took a pseudonym, 'Terence Clibburn', and appeared in a few small parts in a few small productions at the Grafton Theatre in the Tottenham Court Road: they were modern plays with unpromising titles, *What the Doctor Thought* and *Sharper than the Sword*, and they have not survived. It was fifty years since his appearance as a clown in a Roman carnival, young Macduff or one of Mrs Jarley's waxworks at the Theatre Royal, Margate, so it's hardly surprising that he did not rise to stardom now, or even to better parts or more ambitious productions. He retreated to the countryside again, this time Hampshire, where Eva died; but the alternative personality of Terence Clibburn evidently appealed to him. His second wife never called her husband Geoffrey. He told her he preferred to be known by his stage name of Terence, and for a while after the marriage he devoted considerable time and energy to organizing plays and pageants in the village hall. He gave that up, too, as he became more reclusive, but he made some notes on the stage career of his Ternan grandfather and kept his membership of the British Drama League, always under the name of Terence Clibburn, till the end of his life.

It looks as though he would have relished becoming an actor – a clown rather than a soldier – if only he had been brought up to it; and that he would have been proud of the careers of his mother, aunts, grandparents and great-grandparents, had he known about them at the right time. But his life was knocked into the wrong shape early on, and after that nothing could set it quite right. Of all the participants in the story of Nelly and Dickens, Geoffrey appears to have been the most cruelly damaged.

18

Myths and Morals

Geoffrey became a casualty of his mother's history because he had so faithfully absorbed and accepted the view of women generally put about in his youth and wholly subscribed to – as far as he could tell – in his family. It was also a view deeply embedded in the works of Dickens, who, as we have seen, had difficulty with a whole range of female characters. It is one of the things that makes the loss of his letters to Nelly so deplorable. It would be good to have them for the hidden history of years of his life and for the revelation of a missing facet of his character, but most of all for the light they could throw on this particular failure of his art: how much it owes to ignorance, how much to deliberate omission and suppression.

Dickens himself would not have welcomed our curiosity. He would have been happier to have every letter he ever wrote dealt with as Nelly – or whoever may have acquired his letters to her – dealt with the bundles of twelve years' intimate correspondence; likewise every volume of the Pilgrim Edition. He was wrong by any standards. Kate Perugini, when she ensured that the letters he wrote to her mother should be preserved, helped to set the record of their marriage straight and prevented history from being re-written entirely, as he attempted to have it done, abetted by Georgina. The rewriting of history is a central theme in this whole story, since Nelly, too, almost succeeded in her attempt, also abetted by Georgina and with the support of her sisters. Likewise many Dickensians, from Forster on, have been determined to maintain the version of Dickens they regard as acceptable, even – as in Forster's case – when they know it to be untrue.

The problem arises in people's shifting view of morality: what constitutes innocence or guilt, what makes a man or woman good or bad, who is to blame when someone is shocked, or outraged, or exposed. Marian Evans's (fairly) frank adultery began to be over-looked even in the nineteenth century; some of her friends even called her 'Madonna'; but in a recent biography of her contemporary Emily Davies it was again held against her. Within the last few years Wilkie Collins's illegitimate descendants have decided to become proud of their great-grandfather; it took three generations. Dickens's treatment of his wife was for years glossed over and excused, his version accepted blandly (and blindly) by the most eminent critics and biographers; today even his warmest admirers find it hard to summon excuses for it. Shifting the blame on to Nelly was one shrewd move. Yet Nelly can't really take the blame for his outrageous behaviour towards Catherine. Should we blame her for allowing Dickens to provide for her? For giving up her career? For telling Benham, or for saying she regretted the whole thing? Was Benham worse than Nelly, and Wright worse than Benham? What about Forster and Georgina? Opinions will continue to differ. Geoffrey and Gladys could have taken the view that their mother was to be congratulated on her long association with Dickens instead of accepting that she should be branded as wicked and shameful. It's possible indeed that Gladys did take a less strict line than her brother, though she hadn't the wit to do or say much of interest on the subject. Nobody has yet come forward claiming to be descended from Nelly, but who knows whether one may not yet appear: perhaps even the grandchild of an orphan from the Margate boys' orphanage?

There are Dickens scholars and biographers who still reject the idea that Nelly was his mistress. They rest their case on the lack of written proof, and they tend to buttress it by suggesting that both Thomas Wright and Gladys Storey were liars, he spurred on by prurience, she by self-importance; and that they must have invented or misunderstood what Benham, Kate Perugini and Sir Henry Dickens (each quite independently) told them. Wright and Storey were, of course, the wrong sort of people, and it's easy to make them appear foolish. They were not scholars, they put off publishing until they were old, and they failed to produce conclusive docu-mentation. But if they were both lying or exaggerating – if they were both simply foolish scandalmongers, as they have been called – a great many questions are left hanging in the air. How could Wright have invented a story that fitted so neatly with facts discovered only after his death, such as the evidence of Dickens's 1867 diary and his letters to Wills and others; the discrepancy between his arrival in England and his return to Gad's Hill in the spring of 1868; the discovery of a Tringham in Slough as well as Peckham; and Dickens's further secret financial provision for Nelly in addition to that made in his will? If Gladys Storey was as silly and unreliable as some allege, how should we view Bernard Shaw's support of her account, or the statement of T.P. O'Connor that Dickens 'sinned' with 'Ellen Terman', or Geoffrey's distress and failure to defend his mother's reputation? Above all, what are we to make of Nelly's own silence and the destruction of the letters Dickens wrote to her?

Now that it is no longer possible to dispute the fact that Dickens, at any rate, behaved as though Nelly were his mistress, the argument has shifted to other ground. Miss Katharine M. Longley, who spent years researching the subject, is in the strongest position to make the case against. She believes that Dickens wanted to give the impression to Wills that there was a sexual element to his relations with Nelly out of masculine pride. She has suggested that the Ternans may have had other sources of income which enabled them to buy a house and alter their way of life, though no evidence of this has come to light. She also attributes the many meetings between Dickens and Nelly to her giving him elocution lessons to help him with his readings. Miss Longley doesn't doubt that he was obsessed with her, and that they were on terms of warm friendship, but thinks it out of the question that she would have succumbed to his advances.[1]

Human behaviour does not always run to a formula, and Dickens was an extraordinary man in many respects; but to me there is an element of strain about the attempts to maintain that his relations with Nelly were not those of lover and mistress. Granted that we do not know for certain, and are driven back to personal response and interpretation, I simply say that, in the light of everything I have read, it seems most likely to me that it was so.

*

One implication of this book has been that it was no accident that Dickens fell in love with an actress, since the stage and performance were from his earliest days the other life, the other love, the other ambition; and one object has been to stress just how closely the bonds between his world and Nelly's were established long before they met. It has also concerned itself with her and her family's ambivalence about the status of actresses. All the evidence suggests that there really were two sets of standards that came into conflict where the theatrical world met the world outside. Women in the theatre could, as we have seen, live less like Victorian and more like modern women; they could be managers and arrange their own salaries and finances; they often initiated separation and divorce; they bore and reared children outside marriage and lived openly with men other than their husbands; marriage between older women and younger men was not uncommon. (All these were found outside the theatre, too, but they were strikingly concentrated within it.) There are many indications that Dickens was well aware of this freedom; part of him enjoyed the idea, while part of him found it too much to handle. He chose the youngest and weakest of the Ternan sisters, and removed her from her profession; and he fell out with the eldest and strongest.

Whitwell Elwin, the friend of both Dickens and Forster – he was also Forster's executor and probably responsible for destroying some of the Dickens papers – wrote that 'vulgarity belonged to the class from which Dickens sprung and was deeply ingrained in him. He never got rid of it. He could not even relish the company of gentlemen. His chosen associates, the people with whom he hobnobbed, were nearly all of the type he describes in his books.'[2] This is perhaps to us not quite the put-down the Revd Elwin intended; and no doubt it helped to give him and Nelly the makings of a good couple, since if he was never quite a gentleman, she was never quite a lady, though both had the true Victorian passion for claiming that they were. Both were reared in traditions of hard work and hard play; both had a large capacity for merriment; both knew how to stand on their dignity; and both were subject to bursts of temper and bouts of melancholy and remorse. As Chesterton said, Dickens's behaviour sometimes resembled that of a child who has been kept up enjoying himself at a party too late and is on the edge of tears of excitement and exhaustion: 'His literary life was a triumphal procession; he died drunken with glory. And behind all ... the thing we really see is the flushed face of a little boy singing music-hall songs to a circle of aunts and uncles.'[3] A perfect circle joined the small boy singing in the Rochester pub and the man who spoke at death's door of his ambition to be manager of a great theatre; and within that circle also lay the history of his relations with the Ternans.

Mrs Ternan saw herself standing for virtue and gentility within the theatre, but she too found herself accepting its more usual standards when she failed to forbid Dickens the company of her daughters in 1858, an action which would have protected them and ended at once any possible speculation or scandal. After that, Dickens being as famous as he was, Nelly was embarked on a path which necessitated either concealment or disgrace outside the theatre. Again outside the theatre, it became difficult for her to see herself as anything but culpable; and with her removal from the theatre she lost much of the context and support which might have helped her.

If you read Kate Perugini's account of the life of a young middle-class Victorian woman, with its hours of enforced idleness in which the only distractions were embroidery, letter writing, long walks, reading and possibly good works, you can see that her father may not have known what to do with Nelly once he had got hold of her.[4] Kate threw herself into work with great determination, became a proficient painter and always spoke up for working women. Leaving the stage made Nelly into neither a good house-keeper nor a busy mother, and left her protector with a problem. He could only love her, worry about her, keep her hidden, show her his writing, and arrange little treats and holidays, which were not enough to satisfy someone brought up to be busy and gregarious and always on the move.

He didn't know what to do with her artistically either. *Pace* Edmund Wilson, the most striking thing about Nelly and Dickens's fiction is her absence from it. There have been many attempts to incorporate her into his late heroines, as Adelina Fareway in *George Silverman's Explanation*, as cruel Estella in *Great Expectations*, as capricious but fundamentally cosy Bella Wilfer in *Our Mutual Friend*, and even as the passionate, enigmatic Helena Landless in *Edwin Drood*: none stands up to examination. Bella may be the best candidate, because she represents the interchangeability of daughter and mistress, always powerfully seductive to Dickens. She makes us think of him dancing through the whole evening with Kate in the last year of his life, and of Kate's interest in becoming an actress; she reminds us that Kate and Nelly were born in the same year and were in some respects conscious rivals for Dickens's affection and attention. Some of Nelly's charm no doubt lay in her daughterliness, and Bella is at her most erotic with her father; yet nothing about Bella's background, and nothing about the development of her character from mercenary girl to good little wife who wants nothing better than to sit poring over her copy of *The Complete British Family Housewife*, answers to Nelly.

Nelly's only convincing appearance is the physical one, as Lucie, in *A Tale of Two Cities*, such an undeniable likeness to the girl in the Florentine photograph that, once you have seen it, the nothingness of Lucie's character becomes all the more maddening. But Dickens was never a portraitist, as his most perceptive critics have pointed out; he was a mythologizer. Chesterton claimed that he had to make a character humorous before he could make it human, and John Carey made a similar point, saying that when too much feeling got in the way of his comic invention, Dickens ceased to write well.[5] Perhaps there was always too much raw feeling surrounding Nelly for him to begin the process of mythologizing her. Mrs Nickleby – partly drawn from his mother – and Flora Finching – partly drawn from his first love Maria Beadnell, later Mrs Winter – are wildly alive, because he has made them into mythical, surreal figures; so, rather surprisingly, is Dora – again based on Maria Beadnell – precisely because he has moved her so far beyond credibility. She has the body of an adult woman with the mental age of a three-year-old, and there is not the remotest chance that she will ever learn to control a servant or supervise the cooking of a meal. Enough comic energy has gone into Dora to immortalize her; whereas Agnes, cased in stained-glass radiance and unassailable gentility, is never anything but a perfect blank, like Lucie. Lizzie Hexam has no real character either, any more

than Little Em'ly, Ada Clare, Florence Dombey, Rosa Bud or any
of the young ladies Dickens piously preserves from his own magical
distorting glass.

From time to time you notice him in his letters at work on his
own womenfolk, converting them into figures of comedy a little
larger and stranger than life: his mother is a beneficiary of this
treatment, when in her senility he describes her wanting to be 'got
up in sables like a female Hamlet' or, at the sight of him, plucking
up her spirit and asking for 'a pound'.[6] His wife is also quickly
promoted from 'dearest Kate' to Mouse and then to Pig; then she is
the butt of affectionate enough teasing on the subject of her
clumsiness and her pregnancies; by the last stages of the marriage
she too has taken off into myth. She is 'excruciatingly jealous, and
has obtained positive proof of my being on the most intimate terms
with, at least fifteen thousand women of various conditions of life.'[7]
Not only this: she is now so dangerous to Dickens that she has to be
locked out of his bedroom. Her family, too, has become a family of
monsters, and presently she is transmuted into a madwoman and
accused of cunningly putting on a performance of loving her
children in Miss Coutts's drawing room.

By contrast the few surviving references to the Ternans in his
letters are nearly all couched in tones of respect, deep feeling or
anguish. What could he do with that great stereotype, the Fallen
Woman, with a bad girl who was bad through his fault and also
beloved? The nearest he comes to a touch of mythologizing humour
is in his nickname for Nelly, the Patient; there may be a joke
intended in the phrase 'neuralgia flying about' (i.e., perhaps quarrels or fights with Nelly). He could be working towards something
in an account he gave of the Staplehurst accident in which he said
his carriage had contained two 'unknown women' who became
'wholly engrossed by some missing bonnet boxes' (while other
passengers were dead and dying around them): there is the germ of
a comic transformation here at least.[8] But it is a meagre offering.
What one would relish would be a late Dickensian farce, a second
Strange Gentleman or *Is She His Wife?* in which all the secret addresses,
the train journeys, the false names, the private boxes at the theatre,
the code messages in the notebook, would be built up into a
glorious explosion of comic embarrassment: with Dickens himself

appearing as an amalgam of Pecksniff and Quilp, and with Little Nell in an entirely new role.

Nelly Ternan went through some times almost as bad as Little Nell's, when her father was in the lunatic asylum and she travelled the length and breadth of the country with her sad mother and her sisters, all obliged to work for their bread. Just as it was no accident that Dickens fell in love with an actress, so it was no accident that the fatherless child responded to a lover who could also play the father and offer her the pleasures she had missed as a girl, as well as a way out of what was sometimes demeaning and depressing work. She had the sensibility to suffer from the obvious drawbacks of her profession but, in 1857, no obvious means of doing so until an escape route was offered by the man who must have seemed all-powerful, all-wise and as celebrated as her real father's literary idol, Lord Byron.

Everything else in Nelly's life flowed from her decision to accept what Dickens offered. Once her mother had allowed the first step, she was, at any rate, kinder and more sensible than the classic Victorian parent. This shielded Nelly to a degree; her sisters helped to provide more protective cover. Still, over the years there was anxiety, guilt and pain, enough to make her ill. There was also a good deal of merriment and pleasure: birthday dinners and music, rides, walks and theatre visits, happy excursions to Greenwich, or Paris, or Boulogne, even if the great American trip had to be abandoned. Nelly can't have failed to enjoy her power and position with a man of Dickens's charm and standing; indeed, it is probably one of the things she missed and was casting about to retrieve in her dealings with Alfred Austin and George Smith. The girl who had seemed to fit the only womanly pattern Dickens found desirable – small, pretty, passive – grew, changed and developed into a more formidable creature than he can have expected.

The most extraordinary aspect of Nelly must be her phoenix-like renewal from the ashes of one life to become an entirely new person. By the 1880s she looks like a heroine culled from the pages of Thomas Hardy, a writer who was her contemporary and understood secretiveness about origins and early experiences as well as she did: two thoroughgoing children of their time. Her story, with its vulnerability, secrets and guilt, its spirited attempt to reject guilt, its settling into south-coast respectability, with a schoolmaster husband and a son destined for the most conventionally glorious career in the imperial army, would have appealed to him greatly; it would have made a curious plot for a novel, full of improbabilities, awkwardly moving between pathos, comedy and passion.

But the plotting of Nelly's life was her own personal achievement. Unlike her valiant and productive sisters, who acted, sang, painted and turned out journalism and a great many books between them, she did almost nothing except struggle for her survival, using the weapons she had been taught to use and doing her best to bend circumstances to her will. From one point of view the result may be seen as a classic Awful Warning, with retribution laid posthumously on the son she loved. From another she appears as the obstinate representative of all the erring women who must have kicked against the fate decreed for them in Victorian England. A few were able to surmount it by sheer brilliance and audacity: Ellen Terry was one. Nelly Ternan never had that strength; her resort, when she was rendered invisible by a consensus of the respectable, was to turn herself into someone quite different.

Invisible Nelly has had to be tracked across many old maps and through many heaps of playbills, letters, album and address books, miscellaneous papers, wills and photographs. She has taken me to her birthplace, Rochester, passing Gad's Hill on the way; to Newcastle with its magnificent theatre where her father was manager, and to York and Hull where all the family played. I have pursued her between Slough and Windsor, past Upton Church and into the fields where you can still walk the way she and Dickens must have gone, though the path is now cut by the motorway and a farmer may object to your passing; and through Nunhead and Peckham, where almost nothing would be recognizable to her, the quince and the sumac tree under which Mr Tringham sat gone with the house, and Telegraph Hill entirely built over.

In Boulogne and its suburb of Condette, I was warmly welcomed by French Dickensians delighted to believe Nelly must have put in an appearance at the simple one-storey house Dickens rented from Monsieur Beaucourt, whose very gravestone bears a reference to his famous tenant. In Rome, I saw her in my mind's eye, flitting up the steps of the Barberini Palace with Mrs Tilton and leading her small son in his clown's costume through the carnival crowds.

Ampthill Square and the streets between Mornington Crescent and Regent's Park have suffered much the same fate as Nunhead: tower blocks, factories, railway lines, the disappearance of old houses, gardens and green spaces. Park Cottage, on the other hand, is more delightful now than it can have been when she slept in its unwholesome basement room and gave poor Catherine Dickens a cup of tea in the drawing room. Margate has changed for the worse since the cheerful young Wharton Robinsons lived there; the school was bombed, although the church Benham restored and some of the halls in which he gave penny readings with her can still be seen; and the theatre where she appeared as Mrs Jarley has been reopened. In Southsea Fanny and Nelly's houses are in good order; so in its own way is the old Highland Road Cemetery where the three sisters are buried, fittingly close together after their wandering lives. It is a rough grassy expanse near the sea, surrounded by low houses and crossed by irregular paths, with a few trees, a small grey chapel and here and there a stone angel standing above the stones. Some of the graves go back to the early years of the nineteenth century; most are falling into more or less picturesque decay, and you are likely to need the help of a friendly gravedigger in finding a particular grave. The names of Frances Eleanor Trollope and Maria Susanna Taylor are faint but still legible on their shared headstone, with no dates and no eulogies, just a stone edging around the narrow plot. Two rows to the south Nelly lies with her husband.

In the hot summer of 1989 the graves were mere oblongs of powdery dust; the cross that once surmounted Nelly's had broken off and vanished, and the only greenery was a single encroaching arm of bramble, like an admonishment. Quite soon, by the look of it, the grave was likely to disappear altogether. It seemed a good moment to start putting something on paper which might restore Nelly to visibility.

A Postscript:
The Death of Dickens

Three months after this book was first published in the hardback edition, I received a letter from a Mr J. C. Leeson who had read it with particular interest because of a story that had been passed down in his family, originating with his highly respectable great-grandfather, a Nonconformist minister ('a man of gentle spirit, and deeply spiritual life', according to a study of Congregationalism). He sent me a copy of a letter written by his late father, D. C. Leeson, in 1959, which reads as follows:

> My grandfather, the Revd J. Chetwode Postans, who became pastor of Linden Grove Congregational Church in 1872, was subsequently told by the caretaker that Charles Dickens did not die at Gad's Hill, as was generally supposed, but at another house 'in compromising circumstances'.
>
> My father told me that the old man had emphatically repeated this allegation to him many years later, but had refused to divulge any details as to where the death occurred. He did, however, admit that he, personally, had been involved in the secret removal of the body to Gad's Hill in order to avoid scandal.
>
> At this time nothing was known of Dickens's association with the neighbourhood of Peckham, and the story appeared fantastic in view of John Forster's circumstantial account of the events preceding the novelist's death. The revelation that Ellen Ternan was living at Windsor Lodge – almost opposite the church – at the time of Dickens's death makes it less easy to dismiss the allegation. Some research into this incident might be rewarding.[1]

Linden Grove Congregational Church, Peckham, as it appeared in 1870,
surrounded by fields.

In a second letter, to Felix Aylmer, D. C. Leeson had written:

Although my maternal grandfather moved to Peckham only two
years after the death of Dickens, I am certain that he had no
knowledge of the latter's association with Ellen Ternan or with
Windsor Lodge. If he had heard rumours of this I do not think that
he would have tolerated any of Dickens's works in his house, but I
still possess some volumes that he gave to his young son. They were
not broad-minded times, and a Nonconformist pastor was likely to
be less tolerant than most!

This seems to indicate that the secret of the liaison was well kept,
even in the neighbourhood in which it had flourished.

When my father told me that the old caretaker of Linden Grove
Church had maintained that Dickens had not died at Gad's Hill but
in compromising circumstances, neither of us had heard of the
novelist's association with Windsor Lodge. I think that he, like
myself, thought that if there was anything in this strange allegation
it probably referred to the possible death of Dickens whilst visiting
an opium den in search of local colour for *Edwin Drood*. We neither

272

of us endowed it with any local significance, and the suggestion that the informant had been involved in the removal of the body seemed very fantastic.

Mr Leeson saw, as soon as he looked at the standard biographies, that the caretaker was obviously wrong in maintaining that he had helped transport the dead body of Dickens: there were too many witnesses to his actual death at Gad's Hill. On the other hand, Dickens might have been unconscious, since we know he was unconscious for twenty-four hours preceding his death, and so conveyed to Gad's Hill.

Biographers are on their guard against receiving strange stories that turn out to be spurious, but this one seemed at least worth looking into. Mr J. C. Leeson agreed at once to my suggestion that we should consult a leading Dickens scholar for his opinion before proceeding any further. I sent all his material off to Professor Philip Collins of Leicester, who has an unrivalled knowledge of Dickens and biographical material relating to him. Mr Leeson agreed that if Professor Collins thought the matter not worth pursuing, we would abandon it. In fact he responded with interest and encouraged us to do more research; although it seemed 'too good to be true', he wrote,

> I can't see any fatal flaw in the Leeson family story if one assumes, as you do and I would agree, that, if such embarrassing circumstances had occurred, Georgina would have been willing and able to create (and Forster would accept) a suitable cover story.

Collins pointed out that the weak link seemed to be the servants at Linden Grove and Gad's Hill, and the driver of the carriage; but the story could certainly not be immediately ruled out. He thought it worth publishing in the hope that it might stir some other memories of family stories; such reminiscences had surfaced in 1968 in New Zealand, for instance, to confirm that, as Felix Aylmer had argued, Dickens had a hide-out in Slough.

I now worked through every piece of evidence I could find relating to Dickens's final days. He was last seen conscious by his daughters Katey and Mamey on the morning of Monday, 6 June, when they departed for London, not expecting to see him again until the following weekend (see p. 195). Until now it has been generally accepted that after his daughters' departure he was alone with his sister-in-law Georgina Hogarth until the arrival of the local doctor, Stephen Steele, at about six thirty on the evening of Wednesday, 8 June. One of the maids testified in 1888 that he ordered breakfast to be served early that week, at seven thirty, because he had so much to do; she left to be married on the morning of 8th June.[2] According to Georgina, Dickens worked as usual on Monday morning in his chalet, which was situated in the 'Wilderness', a piece of land reached through a tunnel under the road; it was here that Katey kissed him goodbye before she left. Later he walked into Rochester to post letters. On Tuesday he worked in the morning, and he and Georgina took the carriage into Cobham Park in the afternoon, Dickens alighting and walking back alone; in the evening they sat in the conservatory, admiring some newly installed Chinese lanterns. On Wednesday he seemed unwell; despite this, he broke his normal habit of working in the morning only and returned to the chalet after lunch, coming back to the house at about five to write letters before dinner. When he came to the dinner table at six, Georgina was so worried by his appearance that she suggested sending for a doctor; he refused, muttered some half coherent words about going to London, and then, when she tried to take his arm and suggested he should go and lie down, he said, 'On the ground,' and collapsed heavily on his left side on the dining-room floor. He did not speak again, and he did not regain consciousness.

After Dickens's collapse, Georgina says she had a couch fetched and Dickens lifted on to it, then sent a servant on horseback to fetch Dr Steele – who knew and liked Dickens – and to deliver telegrams summoning his daughters and his London physician and good friend, Frank Beard. The servant was, according to an account given over sixty years later in *The Dickensian* magazine, Isaac Armatage, who was reported as saying he was present in the dining room; he also spoke of riding for Steele on the pony Newman Noggs, but his memory must have grown dim, because Noggs had been put down in 1869, the year before Dickens died.[3] According to Steele's testimony, he arrived at Gad's Hill about six thirty and found Dickens lying on the floor of the dining room, to the right of the door.[4] He says he sent a servant for a couch, and, once Dickens had been lifted on to it, he began treatment, cutting away some of his clothes and applying clysters (enemas) and other unavailing remedies. He was precise in his memory, and remained in sole charge, with Georgina, for five and a half hours; Katey and Mamey arrived with Dr Beard only around midnight, when Steele went home, leaving them to keep vigil and apply hot bricks to the patient's feet.

In the morning Charley, the eldest son, came. Steele also returned. It was suggested by Beard that another London specialist, Dr Russell Reynolds, should be summoned. The family grasped at this straw, but when he came all three doctors agreed there was no hope. The pupil of Dickens's right eye was much dilated, that of the left contracted, his breathing stertorous and his limbs flaccid. He had suffered a large haemorrhage in the brain – what was called an apoplexy – and could not live for long.

Dickens's old friend, Miss Mary Boyle, also summoned by telegram from Georgina, arrived in a fly from Gravesend Station with her maid – they had travelled from London, having been at a wedding earlier – and waited unnoticed on the porch of the silent house. At last Charley came out and saw her, and took her in to the library, where Georgina came and embraced her, but she departed again without seeing the dying man, feeling out of place.[5] At some point Nelly also arrived, summoned by Georgina; though this is not, of course, mentioned in any official account.[6] Dickens's son Henry did not yet arrive from Cambridge, nor his one remaining sibling, Letitia Austin; both were too late to see him alive.

A little after five o'clock some convulsion occurred in the frame of the dying man; then nothing more until, at about ten past six, a tear ran down one cheek. Soon after this his breathing stopped. Georgina, Katey, Mamey, Charley, Dr Beard and (probably) Nelly were present. There was no post-mortem. The news flashed round the world, the nation and the Queen mourned. An account of the death appeared in *The Times* on Saturday, 11 June, preceded by a eulogy of Dickens's work and character ('eminently truthful, trustworthy and self-denying'); it read as follows:

During the whole of Wednesday Mr Dickens had manifested signs of illness, saying that he felt dull, and that the work on which he was engaged was burdensome to him. He came to the dinner-table at six o'clock and his sister-in-law, Miss Hogarth, observed that his eyes were full of tears. She did not like to mention this to him, but watched him anxiously, until, alarmed by the expression of his face, she proposed sending for medical assistance. He said 'No' but said it with imperfect articulation. The next moment he complained of toothache, put his hand to the side of his head, and desired that the window might be shut. It was shut immediately, and Miss Hogarth went to him, and took his arm, intending to lead him from the room. After one or two steps he suddenly fell heavily on his left side, and remained unconscious and speechless until his death, which came at ten minutes past six on Thursday, just twenty-four hours after the attack. As soon as he fell a telegram was dispatched to his old friend and constant medical attendant, Mr Frank Carr Beard of Welbeck Street, who went to Gad's Hill immediately, but found the condition of his patient to be past hope. Mr Steele, of Strood, was already in attendance; and Dr Russell Reynolds went down on Thursday, Mr Beard himself remaining until the last.

On Monday, 13 June, *The Times* called for burial in Westminster Abbey. It had clearly already been agreed to, and followed quietly, with the barest ceremony, on 14 June. Afterwards the public came in its thousands, bearing flowers, for several days; and on the following Sunday both Jowett and Dean Stanley preached sermons on the dead man to packed congregations.

No one has ever doubted Georgina's account, which is both circumstantial and moving. It was the basis for the version in *The Times*, for Forster's biography (he was away in Cornwall and not summoned until Dickens was dead) and necessarily for all subsequent accounts. The slight discrepancies in the different versions, which occur only in the earlier part, up to the arrival of Steele, have never seemed worth troubling over – indeed, they don't appear to have been noticed. Could Georgina have lied? I think she could. Can she be regarded as trustworthy in any conflict between truth and the reputation of Dickens? The answer to this is that she cannot. Georgina concocted a cruel and untrue letter about her sister Catherine Dickens at the time of the separation.

Georgina cut and destroyed letters that might in any way be thought to dim the lustre of Dickens's reputation. Her edition of his letters omitted any mention even of the separation from his wife. She made herself the dragon guardian of the shrine. The friendly relations she maintained with Nelly Ternan throughout her life may have rested on genuine fondness, but also, as I have suggested, to keep an eye on her and any letters from Dickens she might have in her possession. A further reason for collusion between the two women now seemed possible.

I decided to test the plausibility of the Leeson family story – could it be true? – by attempting to construct an alternative account of Dickens's last day of consciousness, Wednesday, 8 June. What follows here is therefore largely, though not wholly, conjectural. He rises, early, for his seven thirty breakfast. He writes some letters, including one to his friend Charles Kent, saying he expects to see him in London on the following day, another to his son Henry in Cambridge, enclosing a cheque. He tells Georgina he is going to town later in the day, and will be away until Friday. She knows his ways well enough to make no inquiries; officially it is assumed that he will be based at his bachelor flat in Wellington Street, over the office of his magazine *All the Year Round*. He works for an hour in the chalet on *Drood*. Then he walks, or is driven, the mile and a half to Higham Station and takes a London train, alighting at New Cross, where he hails a cab. He arrives at Windsor Lodge, Linden Grove, in the late morning, and sits for a while with Nelly in the garden under the sumac tree, reading to her and talking. They have not seen one another for a week, probably since 2 June. Perhaps he gives her the Windsor Lodge housekeeping allowance. They go in for lunch. Some time between one and two he is taken ill. He collapses, muttering as he does so about toothache and how he must go to London, and answering her anxious suggestion that he should lie down with the words 'on the ground'.

Now Nelly, near panic but determined to remain in command of the situation, sends one of her two servants to their usual jobmaster: a jobmaster is a man who hires out horses, carriages and cabs, and we know Dickens was in the habit of employing one in the Peckham area. In any case there are plenty of jobmasters who will hire out horse-drawn vehicles around the King's Arms on Peckham Rye, ten minutes away.[7] Nelly needs a closed carriage, with two horses.[8] She also dispatches a telegram to Georgina – the post office is also on the Rye – warning her to expect her arrival within the next four hours, with Dickens seriously unwell. The carriage arrives. There is almost no one about in this half-built street of detached houses facing on to a cornfield and open country, with just a church opposite and the entrance to Nunhead Cemetery up the road; but the caretaker from the church appears, or is sent for. He is a handy man, and is asked to give his assistance in a terrible situation by a distressed young woman. He does help her and the driver to get the inert Dickens into the carriage. Nelly swears the caretaker to secrecy. Her reputation depends on it, and he is a kindly man; and indeed he keeps his vow, for although he names Dickens later, he never divulges her name or address.[9] She has plenty of money for the driver who, like most drivers, has seen everything, and can draw his own conclusions as to whether the elderly man he has helped to haul in to the carriage is drunk, dead or in a fit. She joins her unconscious lover in the carriage, and pulls down the blinds.

Nelly has the spirit and resolve to organize this. All the same, the thought of that journey – the unconscious man, the terrified, watchful woman, the carriage, coachman and horses steadily moving along roads so familiar to Dickens – is a solemn and terrible one. Once they are on their way the danger is much less, and the route itself is not difficult. It is less than twenty-four miles, and should take about three hours. They are quickly in Hatcham and then New Cross; then it is the good Roman road, Watling Street, almost the whole way. The roads in 1870 are strikingly empty, their traffic taken by the railway. They go straight across Blackheath and Shooters Hill, and along through the empty Kentish countryside, passing through a few sleepy villages – Welling, Bexleyheath, Crayford – on the hot June afternoon. Nelly holds Dickens as best she can, the carriage jolting and rushing onwards. This is the very route Dickens gave David Copperfield when he left London to walk to his Aunt Betsey in Dover; and the same, in reverse, he made Pip walk after Estella rejected his love.

They have done twenty miles, and now they must turn off the

main road at Shorne Wood and go uphill for the last lap, the cool, concealing woods in full leaf about them. At Gad's Hill Georgina is waiting in the porch, but in any case the dogs will not bark at Nelly. It is easy for Georgina to make sure she is alone. They have been back at Gad's for less than a week, and the few servants are in their separate quarters away from the main house; even the cook, preparing dinner, is confined to the basement, from which all the food comes up in a dumb waiter (Dickens's manager Dolby particularly commented on the fact that you never met a servant at Gad's Hill except waiting at table).[10] But now, in the bright light of six o'clock on a June evening, the two women, assisted only by the coachman, have to get Dickens into the house. There are five steps up to the front door, and then the hall, with first the drawing room and then the dining room on the left. They take him to the dining room with some thought that it is the most appropriate place for him to be at dinner time; and in fact Georgina has told the servants to prepare dinner for the master. But once in the room there is no question of getting him on to a chair; they can do no better than lay him on the floor.

Nelly, after a few whispered words with Georgina – she tells her what he said, how he fell to the floor at Windsor Lodge – returns to the carriage and begins the slow journey back to Peckham. Her part is over, and Georgina is fully capable now of organizing everything else. Isaac Armatage, a simple lad of sixteen, is summoned and sent off with the telegrams and a note for the doctor. Once this has been done, and Georgina's story given to the family and the world, to *The Times* and to Forster, it is not likely to be questioned, or contradicted by servants. They are about to receive legacies of £19 19s. from the dead man, and a suit of mourning clothes each. Armatage also receives a great many presents and is kept in the family service, taken as a houseboy and 'ecstatic' at the prospect of donning livery in his new situation; and Georgina arranges a special legacy for the garden boy George Woolley, another possible witness.[11]

There are undoubtedly a lot of awkwardnesses and rough edges to this version, enough to make it seem indeed much too good to be true. On further consideration, Professor Collins wrote,

I remain quite unable to account for a respectable and doubtless veracious man's having told such a plausible (as we now know) tale so early, which was at odds with the Georgie/Forster account. I remain puzzled, but less inclined to disbelieve Forster.

One of the points of my version, however, is that it makes Georgina the only one in the know (apart from Nelly, who never said anything beyond telling her daughter she was present at the death of Dickens): Forster did not need to be involved in any deception.

Going once more through everything I had mustered, I found a further piece of evidence. On 8 June ('only the day before his death'), Dickens had gone into the Falstaff Inn, which stands opposite his house, and cashed a cheque with the landlord, Mr Trood. The cheque was for the very large sum of £22, but Trood was quite accustomed to acting as banker for his distinguished neighbour, who must have gone off with the cash in his pocket.[12] The other thing I noticed was a letter from Georgina. Georgina wrote to Dickens's solicitor Frederic Ouvry almost daily in the aftermath of the death, as she busied herself going through Dickens's papers in her capacity as executor. She was obliged to draw on Ouvry for any money she required, for instance to have the mourning suits made for the servants, but also simply to keep the household going. She explained in one meticulous letter that money was needed for the housekeeping, since at the time of Dickens's death there was only £1 15s. 9d. in the housekeeping purse and £6 6s. 3d. in the pocket of his coat.[13]

Now if Dickens cashed a cheque for £22 with Mr Trood at the Falstaff Inn, some time on 8 June, and spent the whole day working in his chalet, seeing no one but Georgina and going nowhere all day until he collapsed at six in the evening, then what happened to the £16-odd difference between the money he took with him from the inn and the £6 6s. 3d. found in his pocket when he died?

Sixteen pounds was a lot of money in 1870, when an average weekly wage for a man was less than £1, for a woman 11s., when a cab fare was 1s. a mile; when you could rent a very comfortable London house for £50 a year; when a young lawyer could get married on an annual income of £250.[14] Could some of the £22 have been for Nelly? And could it then, after all, by one of the ironies of fate, have paid for the undoubtedly expensive carriage that carried Dickens home on his last journey along the Dover Road?

NOTES

1. Mr D. C. Leeson's letter was sent to the editor of the *Sunday Times* on 23 November 1959. The *Sunday Times* did nothing to follow it up beyond passing it to Felix Aylmer, then embroiled in controversy over his book *Dickens Incognito*, extracts of which had appeared in the paper. Aylmer was interested, but he failed to investigate the story beyond making inquiries about undertakers in Peckham, doubtless because he had suffered such a setback over the mistakes in his book. Mr Leeson's letters were passed to the Dickens House Museum on the death of Sir Felix in 1979.

The Revd Postans remained at Linden Grove Church until 1901, when his health failed, and he died in 1905. His daughter Mary was married to G. H. Leeson, a lay preacher and City merchant, educated at the City of London School, in the church in 1887, with her father and her brother, also a Congregational minister, officiating. Leeson's business career was chequered, but his devotion to the Church culminated in his becoming an established minister in his old age, in 1929. He died in 1943, leaving a huge collection of books, according to his grandson J. C. Leeson, who provided this information.

2. W. R. Hughes, *A Week's Tramp in Dickens-Land* (1891), pp. 369–70. Hughes was an indefatigable collector of Dickensiana who collected testimony from many people, but he appears never to have approached Nelly Ternan or her sisters, or Dickens's two valets John Thompson and Scott, whose first name is unknown, though he was observed 'fallen on evil days' and living in an 'incommodious attic' in Shaftesbury Avenue with his aged wife, in 1895, by a curate at St Anne's, Soho, who later became Canon Freeman and divulged this information at the age of ninety-three to *The Dickensian* (1949), p. 110. Hughes died in 1899.

3. The pony was named for the character in *Nicholas Nickleby*. The story about Armatage comes from p. 234 of *The Dickensian* for 1931, and was given when Sir Frederick Macmillan purchased some relics in Armat-

age's possession. He had apparently been given Dickens's travelling mirror, a case of razors, a toddy glass and ladle, a cup and saucer, a cheque [sic], an ivory paper knife and a chain purse and silk handkerchief by Georgina and Henry Dickens. He was very reluctant to part with them, and died soon after doing so, at the age of seventy-seven, on 27 February 1931; he was buried in the churchyard of St Mary's, Higham, so was obviously a local boy. I am indebted to Mr Alan Watts, President of the Dickens Fellowship, for pointing out that Noggs was put down more than a year before Dickens's death: see Arthur A. Adrian, *Georgina Hogarth and the Dickens Circle* (1957), p. 122, where we read of Georgina being advised to have 'poor little Noggs . . . humanely and promptly killed' in the spring of 1869.

4. Stephen Steele, MRCS, LSA, of Bridge House, Esplanade, Strood, was then in his early sixties; he had trained at Guy's and St Thomas's hospitals. He was categoric that he found Dickens on the floor, so much so that when the Dickens scholar William Hughes visited Gad's Hill in 1888, he was shown by the current owners the exact spot where Steele, who was still alive and also spoke to Hughes, had found Dickens, and the other spot on which the sofa was placed, on the other side of the door. See W. R. Hughes, *A Week's Tramp in Dickens-Land*, pp. 173–4, 243–4.

5. See *Mary Boyle: Her Book* (1901), p. 242.

6. See note 25 to Chapter 12.

7. Among the Thomas Wright papers at Dickens House Museum there is a letter dated 22 November 1935 from a Linden Grove resident, Guy Buckeridge, claiming that his family used the same jobmaster as Dickens; he was said to be called Cox, to work from the King's Arms area, and to have stated that he often drove Dickens, fetching him from and to Linden Grove. I have not been able to trace a Cox.

8. For information about the speed and availability of hired horse carriages I am indebted to C. J. Nicholson and to Francesca Riccini of the Science Museum.

9. The Leeson family were particularly struck by this point.

10. George Dolby, *Charles Dickens as I Knew Him* (1885), p. 49.

11. For Woolley's legacy, and for Armatage's ecstatic response to the prospect of wearing livery, see Arthur A. Adrian, *Georgina Hogarth and the Dickens Circle*, pp. 156–8. Armatage, who went on to become a waiter at Shoolbred's, continued to take Georgina Hogarth an annual bouquet or pot plant until her death, according to the entry in *The Dickensian* already mentioned in Note 3.

12. W. R. Hughes, *A Week's Tramp in Dickens-Land*, p. 207.

13. See Arthur A. Adrian, *Georgina Hogarth and the Dickens Circle*, p. 151 and note; the letter is dated only 'Thursday', which suggests it was written on 16 June.

14. This is the sum Traddles marries on in *David Copperfield*, installing his bride and her *five* unmarried sisters in his chambers; see Chapter 59.

Notes

1 'N'

1. The incident occurs in his story, 'Lovel the Widower', which appeared in the *Cornhill* magazine in 1860.
2. See William Makepeace Thackeray, 'The Ravenswing' (1843).
3. Gordon N. Ray (editor), *The Letters and Private Papers of William Makepeace Thackeray* (1945–6), Vol. IV, p. 86.
4. *The New York Times*, 8 June 1858.
5. Edmund Wilson, *The Wound and the Bow* (revised edition, 1952), pp. 64–5.
6. Edmund Wilson's Foreword to Ada Nisbet, *Dickens and Ellen Ternan* (1952), p. xii.
7. Edgar Johnson, *Charles Dickens: His Tragedy and Triumph* (1953), Vol. II, pp. 992, 1007 and 1104.
8. Reported by Gladys Storey, *Dickens and Daughter* (1939), p. 100.
9. Edmund Wilson's Foreword to Ada Nisbet, *Dickens and Ellen Ternan*, pp. xi–xii.

2 'AGREEABLE AND BEAUTIFUL TALENTS'

Information for this chapter comes from playbills studied chiefly in the Minster Library, York, and the Newcastle upon Tyne Public Library; from the *DNB*; and from many theatrical memoirs and biographies. They include A. Aspinall's *Mrs Jordan and Her Family* (1951), John Bernard's *Retrospections of the Stage* (1830), James Boaden's *Life of Mrs Jordan* (1831), Alan S. Downer's *The Eminent Tragedian: William Charles Macready* (1966), Basil Francis's *Fanny Kelly of Drury Lane* (1950), L. E. Holman's *Lamb's Barbara S.* (also about Fanny Kelly; 1935), Frances Kemble's *Record of a*

Girlhood (1878), Anne Mathews's *Memoirs of Charles Mathews* (1838–9) and Tate Wilkinson's *Memoirs* (1790).

1. As late as 1881 Walter Donaldson's *Fifty Years of Green-room Gossip* still recommended the stage as 'the only position where woman is perfectly independent of man, and where, by her talent and conduct, she obtains the favour of the public.'

2. See Alan S. Downer, *The Eminent Tragedian: William Charles Macready* (1966), p. 151.

3. See William J. Carlton, 'Dickens as Dramatic Critic', *The Dickensian* (1960). An unsigned article in the *Morning Chronicle* in November 1835 is convincingly attributed to Dickens by Carlton, along with a good many other theatre reviews in which he praises Lucia Vestris, Mrs Keeley, Charles Mathews Junior and a John Buckstone farce.

4. See Alan S. Downer, *The Eminent Tragedian: William Charles Macready*, pp. 42 and 82.

5. From the diary of Margaretta Grey (1853) quoted in Josephine Butler, *Memoir of John Grey of Dilston* (1869), p. 326n. (My source here is McGregor's *Divorce in England*, 1957.)

6. Mrs Jordan's letters are quoted in A. Aspinall, *Mrs Jordan and Her Family* (1951).

7. See Philip Ziegler, *King William IV* (1971), p. 80.

8. 'Arthur Griffinhoofe', John Duncombe's edition of the *Memoirs of the Life, Public and Private Adventures of Madame Vestris* (n.d. but British Library suggests 1839).

9. This was the American actress Mary Anderson in her memoirs *A Few Memories* (1896).

10. This warning was given to Mrs Patrick Campbell by her Aunt Kate in 1889, quoted in Michael Sanderson, *From Irving to Olivier* (1984), p. 8.

11. G. F. Watts to Lady Constance Leslie, quoted in Joy Melville, *Ellen and Edie* (1987), p. 26, from letter in the Watts Gallery, Compton, Surrey.

12. F. C. Burnand in 1884, quoted in Michael Sanderson, *From Irving to Olivier*, p. 32.

13. Quoted in Michael Sanderson, *From Irving to Olivier*, p. 11.

14. See Frances Marshall (editor), *A Travelling Actress in the North and Scotland* (1984), which reprints the *Memoirs of Mrs Charlotte Deans 1768–1859*, published in Wigton in 1837: an extraordinarily interesting memoir and an outstanding piece of editing.

3 FAMILY SAGA

1. Information about the marriage of John Jarman and Martha Maria Mottershed from Miss K. M. Longley, who obtained it from parish register transcripts in the Borthwick Institute, York. Other information from my own study of playbills in Minster Library, York, and from Tate Wilkinson's *The Wandering Patentee; or, A History of the Yorkshire Theatres from 1770 to the Present Time* (York, 1795).

2. All the quotations given here come from Mrs Jordan's letters to her lover, the Duke of Clarence, as quoted in A. Aspinall, *Mrs Jordan and Her Family*.

3. See James Boaden, *Life of Mrs Jordan* (1831), Vol. I, p. 360.

4. Oxberry's *New Series of Dramatic Biography* (1827), p. 171.

5. Charles E. Pearce, *Madame Vestris and Her Times* (n.d.), p. 148.

6. Cutting in the Ternan family scrapbook, Morris L. Parrish Collection of Victorian Novelists, Princeton University Library.

7. From the *Noctes Ambrosianae* by 'Christopher North' (i.e., John Wilson) published in *Blackwood's* magazine and in book form in 1855, Vol. II, p. 392. I am indebted for this reference and the next to Miss K. M. Longley.

8. ibid., Vol. III, p. 361.

9. Cutting from the Ternan family scrapbook, Princeton.

10. *History of the Theatre Royal, Dublin* (Dublin, 1870), p. 89.

11. 3 April 1833, William Charles Macready, *Diaries 1833–1851* (1912), Vol. I, p. 111.

12. Some of his letters and poems were carefully preserved by her. They are now held at Princeton.

13. Frances Ann Kemble, *Record of a Girlhood* (1878), Vol. III, p. 230. She gives a detailed, vivid and highly entertaining account of her first transatlantic crossing.

14. From the Ternan family scrapbook, Princeton.

15. Thomas Ternan to unnamed Dublin friend, letter dated '26th February Philadelphia', Princeton.

16. A certificate stating that 'Mr and Mrs Lawless Ternan' made the visit and went behind the falls on 18 June 1835 and a leaf plucked from a nearby tree were preserved in the family; Princeton.

17. Frances Ternan the younger gave her place of birth as Philadelphia on her marriage certificate.

18. All these tributes come from cuttings in the Ternan family scrapbook, Princeton.

19. The sculptor was R. G. Davies, a well-known Newcastle artist; unfortunately the bust has disappeared.

20. From the Ternan family scrapbook, Princeton.

21. In her novel *Mabel's Progress*.

22. The speech was made on 14 February 1866, when Dickens spoke for the Dramatic, Equestrian and Musical Sick Fund Association on its tenth anniversary, with the actress Fanny Stirling beside him. See K. J. Fielding (editor), *The Speeches of Charles Dickens* (1988).

23. General Paralysis of the Insane (paresis) was then known as a disease of middle life and the male sex, especially 'vigorous, energetic, successful men, who have lived full, active, busy lives in cities; who are married; who have indulged freely in eating and drinking, and in sexuality; and in whom an hereditary disposition to insanity is absent' (C. A. Mercier, *A Text-Book of Insanity*, 1902). At the time of Ternan's illness the cause was 'thought to be' syphilis in 80 per cent of the cases; by the twentieth century it was known to be in all cases. No doubt Ternan contracted the disease during his bachelor days and was unaware of the fact.

4 LITTLE ORPHANS

1. Frances Ann Kemble, *Record of a Girlhood*, Vol. I, p. 31.

2. See the account by Fanny in her novel *Mabel's Progress*.

3. Information from Miss K. M. Longley, derived from a letter by Tom Trollope to his nephew Harry, May 1889, Rare Book and Special Collections Library, University of Illinois at Urbana-Champaign.

4. Dickens to Madame de la Rue, 27 September 1845, Madeline House, Kathleen Tillotson and Graham Storey (editors), the Pilgrim Edition of *The Letters of Charles Dickens* (1965), Vol. IV, p. 389.

5. See Pilgrim Edition, *The Letters of Charles Dickens*, Vol. IV, p. 390n, for an account of Macready's somewhat natural resentment.

6. Fanny's description of the Blackfriars area comes in her novel *Mabel's Progress*.

7. 19 October 1846, William Charles Macready, *Diaries 1833–1851*, Vol. II, p. 347.

8. ibid.

9. From the Ternan family scrapbook, Princeton.

10. ibid.

11. ibid.
12. *Newcastle Chronicle*, 23 March 1849.
13. According to Malcolm Morley in *The Dickensian* (1958).
14. Fred Belton, *Random Recollections of an Old Actor* (1880), p. 74.
15. The description is taken from Fanny Trollope's account of the house in Barnsbury in *Mabel's Progress*.
16. Dickens's word is 'unwholesome': see his letter to Wills, 25 October 1858, quoted in Ada Nisbet, *Dickens and Ellen Ternan*, p. 49.

5 GASLIGHT FAIRIES

1. The deeds of the house, 28 Rochester Road, Camden Road Villas, were kindly shown me by the present owners. They indicate that the house was quite new and was owned by 'William Hayman', almost certainly the brother of Mrs William Ternan in Rochester. Haymen was a thriving businessman with a wide range of interests who became mayor of Rochester. The Haymens and the Ternans were on very friendly terms, and it seems likely that he allowed a house in his possession to be used by Fanny and Maria for their intended school, no doubt with the proviso that they would pay rent once it prospered.
2. Harley had been a friend of Dickens since the 1830s; there is a picture of him playing Pickwick in the Berg Collection, New York Public Library; and see Pilgrim Edition, *The Letters of Charles Dickens*, Vol. III, p. 598.
3. Buckstone was also well known to Dickens over a period of many years; see Pilgrim Edition, *The Letters of Charles Dickens, passim*.
4. I am indebted for this Thackeray reference to John Carey's *Thackeray: Prodigal Genius* (1977), p. 104.
5. It was actually a couple of years earlier: see *Household Words* (1855).
6. *Mabel's Progress* appeared in weekly instalments in *All the Year Round* from April to November 1867 and was first published in book form by Chapman & Hall in the same year.

6 THE AMATEUR: DICKENS IN 1857

1. *Saturday Review*, 1 August 1857.

2. The phrase is given by Arthur A. Adrian in *Georgina Hogarth and the Dickens Circle* (1957), p. 37.

3. For Wigan's playing in *The Strange Gentleman* see the *DNB*. For Mrs Wigan's participation in Dickens's 1847 production, see Pilgrim Edition, *The Letters of Charles Dickens*, Vol. V, pp. 126n and 133.

4. On 29 September 1836 Dickens played in his own *The Strange Gentleman* with John Pritt Harley, according to Theodore Taylor writing in 1870; see T. E. Pemberton, *Dickens and the Stage* (1888), etc. See also Dickens's diary note for 7 February 1839, which records Harley's presence at his birthday party, Pilgrim Edition, *The Letters of Charles Dickens*, Vol. I, p. 640; his letter to Harley, inviting him to christening, 17 August 1840, Pilgrim Edition, Vol. II, p. 117; and Dickens's letter inviting Harley to dinner, 3 April 1841, Pilgrim Edition, Vol. II, p. 250, etc.

5. Elston died in 1843, three years before Thomas Ternan; the help given by Dickens to the orphans enabled one to train as a teacher, one as a singer, one as a wood engraver; the boy became an actor in due course.

6. Paul Schlicke's *Dickens and Popular Entertainment* (1985) contains a fine account of Charles Mathews and Dickens's use of his techniques.

7. Gladys Storey, *Dickens and Daughter*, p. 133.

8. Mary Cowden Clarke in a letter to Frederic Kitton, 13 December 1886, which appeared in *Dickens by Pen and Pencil* (1890), p. 171, quoted by Philip Collins in his invaluable *Dickens Interviews and Recollections* (1981), Vol. I, p. 96.

9. Information about Dickens's way of organizing rehearsals comes from various accounts, among them those of Francesco Berger and Mary Cowden Clarke.

10. This can be deduced from his later insistence on their leaving, explained in a letter to Wills, 25 October 1858, quoted in Ada Nisbet, *Dickens and Ellen Ternan*, p. 49, from a letter in the Huntington Library.

11. Thackeray to his mother, 7 January 1848, and to Mrs Brookfield, 24 July 1849, quoted in Philip Collins, *Dickens Interviews and Recollections*, Vol. I, p. 68.

12. John Forster, *Life of Charles Dickens*, Vol. III, p. 160.

13. 26 August 1851 and 24 October 1851, Pilgrim Edition, *The Letters of Charles Dickens*, Vol. VI, pp. 472 and 528.

14. 'Two Views of a Cheap Theatre', *All the Year Round* (1860), reprinted as No. 4 in *The Uncommercial Traveller*.

15. Dickens to Daniel Maclise, probably 16 August 1841, letter shown at Sotheby's prior to a sale in July 1987.

16. Dickens to Catherine, 28 June 1850, Pilgrim Edition, *The Letters of Charles Dickens*, Vol. VI, pp. 119–20.

17. Dickens described the episode in 1861 in 'Some Recollections of Mortality', *All the Year Round*, placing it twenty-five years earlier, when he was twenty-three, before his marriage; it is reprinted as No. 19 in *The Uncommercial Traveller*.

18. See George Curry, *Charles Dickens and Annie Fields* (1988), p. 25.

19. Dickens to Miss Coutts, 11 December 1854, Edgar Johnson (editor) *Letters from Charles Dickens to Angela Burdett-Coutts 1841–1865* (1953), p. 280.

20. ibid.

21. ibid., 16 November 1854, p. 279.

22. ibid., 20 May 1856, p. 317.

7 MANCHESTER, DONCASTER AND SCANDAL

1. Mrs Gaskell's letters contain complaints about the exhaustion induced by a constant flow of house visitors wanting to see the exhibition. Despite her friendship with Dickens there is no mention of his visit to Manchester or of *The Frozen Deep*.

2. Dickens to Miss Coutts, 5 September 1857, Edgar Johnson (editor), *Letters from Charles Dickens to Angela Burdett-Coutts 1841–1865*, p. 347.

3. *Manchester Courier*, 22 August 1857. I am indebted to Miss K. M. Longley for this reference.

4. Dickens to Miss Coutts, 5 September 1857, Edgar Johnson (editor), *Letters from Charles Dickens to Angela Burdett-Coutts 1841–1865*, p. 347.

5. ibid.

6. See his letter to Hans Christian Andersen, 2 September 1857: 'The corn-fields that were golden when you were here, are ploughed up, brown; the hops are being picked; the leaves on the trees are just beginning to turn; and the rain is falling as I write – very sadly – very steadily.' Elias Bredsdorff, *Hans Andersen and Charles Dickens: A Friendship and Its Dissolution* (Copenhagen, 1956).

7. Dickens to Mrs William Brown, 28 August 1857, Edgar Johnson (editor), *Letters from Charles Dickens to Angela Burdett-Coutts 1841–1865*, p. 346.

8. Dickens to Forster, quoted by him in *Life of Charles Dickens*, Vol. III, p. 162.

9. Chapter 5, 'Lazy Tour', *Household Words* (1857). As Miss K. M. Longley has pointed out, Forster stated that this chapter was the work of Collins; in fact, it is clearly by Dickens.

10. ibid.

11. Quoted in Ada Nisbet, *Dickens and Ellen Ternan*, p. 57, from letter in Huntington Library, punctuation corrected by editors of Pilgrim Edition.

12. ibid.

13. According to the *Doncaster Chronicle*, 25 September 1857, he left on the Monday; information from Miss K. M. Longley.

14. 7 December 1857, letter printed in *The Dickensian* (1942).

15. Dickens to Frederic Ouvry, 26 May 1858, letter held by Messrs Farrer.

16. 31 May 1858, quoted in Adrian A. Arthur, *Georgina Hogarth and the Dickens Circle*, p. 57, from letter in Huntington Library.

17. Elias Bredsdorff, *Hans Andersen and Charles Dickens: A Friendship and Its Dissolution*, quoted in Michael Slater, *Dickens and Women* (1983), p. 137.

18. Unpublished letter, 13 October 1857, quoted in Michael Slater, *Dickens and Women*, p. 207.

19. The cheque to Buckstone is among letters currently being edited for the Pilgrim Edition; I am indebted to Graham Storey for allowing me to see these.

20. Dickens to Lavinia Watson, 7 December 1857, in *The Dickensian* (1942).

21. January 1858, Nonesuch Edition, *The Letters of Charles Dickens*, Vol. II, p. 888.

22. 21 March 1858, Nonesuch Edition, *The Letters of Charles Dickens*, Vol. III, p. 14.

23. The story was told by several people and appears in an unpublished paper of 1935 by J. W. T. Ley, held at Dickens House. Ley says it was first told 'about thirty years ago in a book of reminiscences by the daughter of one of Dickens's friends . . . who knew the household quite well'. Thomas Wright told the same story without giving a source, and Mrs Thomas Whiffen's *Keeping off the Shelf* (New York, 1928) also gave the story, referring to Nelly as Dickens's god-daughter.

24. Gladys Storey, *Dickens and Daughter*, pp. 96 and 133–4.

25. Undated letter from Anny Thackeray to Amy Crowe, Gordon N. Ray

(editor), *The Letters and Private Papers of William Makepeace Thackeray*, p. 478n.

26. For Dickens's alleged letter to his elder children, see letter, probably 30 August 1858, from Catherine Dickens's aunt Helen Thomson to her friend, Mrs Stark, the text of which is given by K. J. Fielding in *Études anglaises* (1955); Fielding argues convincingly for the authenticity of the letter, which was at one time said to be a forgery. For Katey's recollection, see Gladys Storey, *Dickens and Daughter*, pp. 93f.

27. The so-called 'violated letter' is printed in the Nonesuch Edition, *The Letters of Charles Dickens*, Vol. III, pp. 21–3, and also in Michael Slater, *Dickens and Women*, pp. 373–5.

28. These are paragraphs 5, 6 and 8 from the front page of *Household Words* for Saturday, 12 June 1858, headed 'Personal' and signed 'Charles Dickens'.

29. 15 July 1858, quoted in Ada Nisbet, *Dickens and Ellen Ternan*, pp. 51–2, from letter in Pierpont Morgan Library.

30. The *Liverpool Mercury* was one paper which accused Dickens of 'unmanly selfishness and heartlessness'; see Edgar Johnson, *Charles Dickens: His Tragedy and Triumph* (1953), p. 925.

8 MORNINGTON CRESCENT

1. Dickens to Wills 25 October 1858, quoted in Ada Nisbet, *Dickens and Ellen Ternan*, pp. 48–9.

2. Dickens to Miss Coutts, 28 October 1847, Pilgrim Edition, *The Letters of Charles Dickens*, Vol. V, p. 178.

3. It closed in 1862.

4. This was Eleanor Christian, the girl he had soaked in sea water on the pier at Broadstairs many years earlier, quoted here in Philip Collins, *Dickens Interviews and Recollections*, Vol. I, pp. 33ff.

5. See letter to Miss Gibson of Birmingham, 20 October 1858, printed in *The Dickensian* (1912).

6. Coutts account, 18 December 1858: 'C.D.E.T. £10'.

7. Speech in Coventry, 4 December 1858, K. J. Fielding, *The Speeches of Charles Dickens*, p. 288.

8. Forster to Dickens, 14 January 1859, R. C. Lehmann (editor), *Charles Dickens as an Editor: Being Letters Written by Him to William Henry Wills* (1912), pp. 263–4. Dickens's letter to Wills of the same day is written on the back of Forster's letter.

9. The area deteriorated when the railway cutting to Euston was enlarged but did not lose its public gardens until the 1920s. The house was inhabited by Spencer Gore, who painted the view from the back in 1912, but it was destroyed by a bomb in the Second World War.

10. Thomas Wright reported Canon Benham as saying Nelly told him Dickens took the Ampthill Square house for her, though in her mother's name. It is likely to have cost between £1,000 and £1,500, a sum quite out of the reach of the Ternans; I am indebted for information about house prices in the area at this time to Professor Eric Hobsbawm.

11. He applied these words to her in his letter of 4 July 1867 to Mrs Frances Elliot, Nonesuch Edition, *The Letters of Charles Dickens*, Vol. III, pp. 475–6 (see note 15 to Chapter 9 on misdating of this letter).

12. Information for this presentation of Nelly comes from several sources, the most important of which is the testimony gathered by Miss K. M. Longley from Helen Wickham, the daughter of Nelly's friend Rosalind Brown, some of which appears in her article 'The Real Ellen Ternan', *The Dickensian* (1985); some in her unpublished typescript 'A Pardoner's Tale: Charles Dickens and the Ternan Family'; and some is derived from private conversation with Miss Longley. See also the talk given by Constance Clinton-Baddeley, part of which appears in note 12, Chapter 15; letters by Fanny Trollope (*née* Ternan) held at Princeton and Illinois, and by Robert Cecil Esq.; the Gladys Storey papers at Dickens House; etc.

13. The story is told by Carl Dolmetsch in *The Dickensian* (1959). Watts Phillips, also inspired by Carlyle, wrote a play called *The Dead Heart* two years before Dickens wrote his *Tale of Two Cities*. Phillips's play had no Sydney Carton character, but did turn on one person substituting himself for another at the guillotine. Phillips sold his play to Ben Webster, who read it aloud to Dickens in Brighton one weekend, probably the one he spent there with Collins in March 1857. Webster delayed putting on Phillips's play, and Phillips wrote lamenting this when he began to read the Dickens serial; this provoked Webster into putting it on. Mark Lemon then attacked Phillips for plagiarism, but Webster testified to *The Dead Heart* being the earlier work and to the fact that he had read it to Dickens. The story was not taken up, and Phillips's play was killed stone dead when *A Tale of Two Cities* opened at the Lyceum in a dramatized version in January 1860, with Madame Celeste in the lead.

14. Dickens to Wills, 1 July 1859, quoted in Ada Nisbet, *Dickens and Ellen Ternan*, p. 50.

15. *A Tale of Two Cities*, Chapter 4.

16. Dickens's contemporary, Flaubert, was advised by his doctor in 1868 that he was suffering from a condition frequent among ecclesiastics, produced by not ejaculating often enough.

17. 12 June 1859, Nonesuch Edition, *The Letters of Charles Dickens*, Vol. III, p. 106.

18. 30 June 1859, Nonesuch Edition, *The Letters of Charles Dickens*, Vol. III, p. 109.

19. Dickens to James Fields, June 1859, Nonesuch Edition, *The Letters of Charles Dickens*, Vol. III, p. 108; Dickens to Arthur Smith, quoted in Ada Nisbet, *Dickens and Ellen Ternan*, p. 54, from letter in Pierpont Morgan Library; and Dickens to Forster, Nonesuch Edition, Vol. III, p. 112.

20. Sylvère Monod, 'Charles Dickens and Philoclès Régnier', *Études anglaises* (1958). Régnier and Dickens were old friends from 1845 – Macready introduced them – but after the two letters Dickens wrote him in 1859 about Fanny Ternan, the friendship lapsed; Monod believes Régnier disapproved of Dickens's separation from his wife. Later Dickens referred to him as a 'shifty little man'.

Dickens's first letter, dated Saturday, 17 September 1859, from Tavistock House, reads:

My dear Régnier, I am particularly anxious to present to you a young lady in whom I have a great interest, who comes to Paris with her mother, on a matter in which I hope your advice and experience as an artist may be of service to her.

Miss Fanny Ternan is a young lady of great accomplishments, who has been studying music – lately in Italy, under the best master – with a view, both to concert-singing and the stage. She belongs to a family of theatrical artists; and is thoroughly acquainted with her art. She has not quite decided whether she shall now come home to England, or remain in Paris for a time under such a master as Duprez. It is in the consideration of this question, and in helping her to know what kind of man Duprez is, and what hopes there may be of his being really serviceable to such a pupil, that I trust you may be able to advise Miss Ternan. And if you can help her, I am sure, you will – for my sake in the first instance, and then for your own. I cannot easily tell you how much I shall feel obliged to you.

His second letter is quoted in the text, p. 127.

21. Coutts account, 31 October 1859.

22. See John Bigelow, *Retrospections of an Active Life* (1910), in which he reports a conversation of 10 March 1860 at Thackeray's, where he

had dinner with Mrs Dickens. 'Miss Teman – I think that is the name – was the source of the difficulty between Mrs D and her husband. She played in private theatricals with D.' 'Teman' looks like an obvious misreading of his own handwriting. Bigelow says he went to see her act at the Haymarket and commented, 'She seemed rather a small cause for such a serious result – passably pretty and not much of an actress' – but it must have been Maria he saw.

23. 6 May 1860, the diary of Annie Fields, quoted in George Curry, *Charles Dickens and Annie Fields* (1988), p. 5.

24. Gladys Storey, *Dickens and Daughter*, pp. 105–6.

25. Note by Andrew de Ternant, reporting his friend Francesco Berger, *Notes and Queries* (1933).

26. Dickens to Bulwer-Lytton, 15 May 1861, Nonesuch Edition, *The Letters of Charles Dickens*, Vol. III, p. 220.

27. See 'The Old Curiosity Shop' by Robert Allbut in *The Dickensian* (1910).

28. Dickens to Mary Boyle, 28 December 1860, Nonesuch Edition, *The Letters of Charles Dickens*, Vol. III, p. 196.

29. The age of Macready's second wife, Cecile Spencer, at the time of their marriage is given as twenty-three by Macready's biographer, Alan S. Downer, though I note that Arthur A. Adrian gives it as thirty-four.

30. Edmund Wilson, *The Wound and the Bow*, p. 64.

31. These are the words of his granddaughter, Mrs Lisa Puckle, who read his diaries before they were destroyed. The published versions are known to be bowdlerized, and she was of the opinion that Dickens was 'not really so strait-laced as he made out publicly'. See account by Philip Collins, who interviewed her, in *Dickens Studies* (1966).

32. June 1862, Nonesuch Edition, *The Letters of Charles Dickens*, Vol. III, p. 297.

33. See 'Some Recollections of Mortality', *All the Year Round* (1863), reprinted as No. 19 in *The Uncommercial Traveller*; here Dickens gives the date of the incident as the winter of 1861.

9 VANISHING INTO SPACE

1. See 'A Flight' in *Household Words* (1851).

2. Dickens to William de Cerjat, October 1864, Nonesuch Edition, *The Letters of Charles Dickens*, Vol. III, p. 403.

3. Dickens to P. W. Proctor, 31 December 1864, Nonesuch Edition, *The Letters of Charles Dickens*, Vol. III, p. 407.

4. Dickens to Mary Cowden Clarke, 7 July 1862, Nonesuch Edition, *The Letters of Charles Dickens*, Vol. III, p. 299.

5. Dickens to J. Sheridan Knowles, 7 July 1862, Nonesuch Edition, *The Letters of Charles Dickens*, Vol. III, p. 299.

6. Dickens to Collins, Nonesuch Edition, *The Letters of Charles Dickens*, Vol. III, p. 333.

7. Dickens to Mamey Dickens, 1 February 1863, Nonesuch Edition, *The Letters of Charles Dickens*, Vol. III, p. 338.

8. Dickens to Collins, August 1863, Nonesuch Edition, *The Letters of Charles Dickens*, Vol. III, p. 360.

9. See Norman Page, *A Dickens Chronology* (1988), p. 115, entry for June 1864.

10. See Herbert Lottman, *Flaubert* (1989), p. 190: Flaubert made a clandestine visit to London to see Juliet, his English governess friend, in late June 1865, thus narrowly avoiding the Staplehurst accident.

11. Nonesuch Edition, *The Letters of Charles Dickens*, Vol. III, pp. 304–5.

12. Arthur A. Adrian, *Georgina Hogarth and the Dickens Circle*, p. 76–81.

13. 1 February 1863, quoted in Edgar Johnson, *Charles Dickens: His Tragedy and Triumph*, p. 1008, note 87, from letter in the Huntington Library; Johnson adds a note that the phrase was cut by Georgina and Mamey in their edition of the letters.

14. 19 February 1863, Nonesuch Edition, *The Letters of Charles Dickens*, Vol. III, pp. 342–3.

15. Dickens to Mrs Frances Elliot, 4 July 1867, Nonesuch Edition, *The Letters of Charles Dickens*, Vol. III, pp. 475–6 (the letter is misdated in the Nonesuch, as has been pointed out by many Dickens scholars). Frances Elliot was the wife of the Dean of Bristol and a friend of the Trollopes.

16. According to Gladys Storey, in her unpublished papers at Dickens House, in which she says she discussed the matter of Ellen Ternan with Sir Henry Dickens in 1928. See David Parker and Michael Slater, 'The Gladys Storey Papers', *The Dickensian* (1980).

17. Thomas Wright also stated that 'there were children' born to Dickens and Nelly in an unpublished letter written in 1935 to J. W. T. Ley and Walter Dexter, now at Dickens House; he died without substantiating his claim.

18. Madeline House to Sir Rupert Hart-Davis, 16 March 1959, letter in Dickens House, quoted by permission of Dr John House. Madeline House later wrote of a subsequent conversation with Gladys Storey: 'Gladys S's "coming baby" was uttered in a very die-away voice. I took the tone to be that of someone saying something secret, but I see now that it could have been the voice of someone saying something she wasn't confident about, i.e., though say it she did, it is not something to be unquestioningly accepted.' (This is an extract from a letter of 8 January 1968 to Miss K. M. Longley, to whom I am indebted for permission to quote it here. I have not seen the rest of this correspondence.)

19. See William M. Clarke, *The Secret Life of Wilkie Collins* (1988), pp. 122 and note 39, and p. 219.

20. Arthur Munby's diary for 10 May 1864, quoted in Philip Collins, *Dickens Interviews and Recollections*, Vol. I, p. xviii.

21. Dickens to Thomas Mitton, 13 June 1865. The letter has been printed in its uncut version only once, by A. H. Joline in *Rambles in Autograph Land*, published by Putnam's in 1913, p. 196. All other editions of Dickens's letters, and all biographies, have so far quoted the version given by Georgina Hogarth and Mamey Dickens in their edition of *The Letters of Charles Dickens* (second edition, 1880), Vol. II, p. 229, which excludes the remark by the young lady. The full text, to which Dr David Parker first drew my attention, is here given by permission of Dr Graham Storey. Georgina is known to have burned several letters to Mitton, who had been intimate with Dickens in his youth. We may assume that Dickens felt less constrained by the need for discretion with this distant and reclusive old friend than with others, without going so far as to name them.

22. She was slow to recover from the accident; she seems to be wearing a bandage over her upper arm in some subsequent photographs; and it is possible that the surgery she underwent in 1874 could have arisen from a badly set bone which needed resetting.

23. Nonesuch Edition, *The Letters of Charles Dickens*, Vol. III, p. 429.

24. 12 June 1865, Nonesuch Edition, *The Letters of Charles Dickens*, Vol. III, p. 424.

25. Quoted in Ada Nisbet, *Dickens and Ellen Ternan*, p. 57, from letter in the Huntington Library.

26. The theory has been advanced that Dickens sometimes took Nelly to Condette, near Boulogne, where he used a small country house belonging to his French landlord, Ferdinand Beaucourt, and is said to have

spent holidays in 1864. See William J. Carlton, 'Dickens's Forgotten Retreat in France', *The Dickensian* (1966).

10 FANNY AND MARIA GET MARRIED

1. 10 July 1857, Edgar Johnson (editor), *Letters from Charles Dickens to Angela Burdett-Coutts*, p. 343.
2. Dickens to Webster, 9 September 1861, Nonesuch Edition, *The Letters of Charles Dickens*, Vol. III, p. 235; and Dickens to Edmund Yates and Charles Fechter, Nonesuch Edition, Vol. III, p. 291.
3. Tom Trollope to Bice, 7 May 1865, asking her to tell her uncle (Anthony) 'that it seems to me putting the cart before the horse, to ask how much I should be content to pay for Miss Ternan's instructions as he proposes. But it seems to me, that for a run down to Waltham every other Saturday, so as to give you three lessons, one on Saturday, one on Sunday, and one on Monday, £2 would be about the mark – and I should be very willing to pay it. But I know little of the prices of such services; and it may be that is too little.' Letter quoted by kind permission of Robert Cecil Esq.
4. See N. John Hall (editor), *Letters of Anthony Trollope*, Vol. I (1983), p. 321n, for the comments of Lady Rose Fane, who admired Trollope's work but regretted meeting him in person.
5. Another example of Trollope's kindness is found in a letter of 12 July 1865, in which he asks Samuel Laurence to advise him in the matter of helping a poor girl, Miss Hughes of Camden Town, who is trying to earn her living by copying lithographs; see N. John Hall (editor), *Letters of Anthony Trollope*, Vol. I, p. 310.
6. I am grateful to Professor Eric Hobsbawm for information about rents in the area. Nelly's tenant, who paid the rates from then on, was Walter McGee: information provided by Miss K. M. Longley, from Camden Libraries. Nelly kept the house until 1901; see below, Chapter 15.
7. See T. E. Pemberton, *Dickens and the Stage*, p. 235.
8. Dickens to Ernest Hart, Secretary of the Association for the improvement of Infirmaries and London workhouses, Nonesuch Edition, *The Letters of Charles Dickens*, Vol. III, p. 462.
9. Dickens's friend George Augustus Sala, who lived at Slough in 1862, notes its speedy train service from Slough in his memoirs, and Felix Aylmer gives the details about the other stations in his *Dickens Incognito* (1959); see Chapter 11.

10. Miss K. M. Longley points out that Mrs Mary Tringham was the name of Dickens's tobacconist at 2 Brydges Street; he gave her a cheque for £50 on his Coutts account on 13 June 1862, just before setting off for France. Miss Longley also notes that there was a humorous poem by Thomas Hood, possibly known to Dickens, about the dangers of gossip, set in a village called Tringham.

11. Felix Aylmer cites the *Windsor Express* for 11 May 1889. Reporting on a fire that destroyed Elizabeth Cottage, it states that 'Charles Dickens lodged for some time' there. Note also a letter to *The Dickensian* in 1968 from J. C. Reid, quoting Gerald Dunn, a New Zealander, whose father Henry worked as a carpenter in Slough. He remembered working for Mr Tringham about 1866 and being told that Tringham was, in fact, Charles Dickens.

12. See Alfred Austin, *Autobiography* (1911).

13. Percy Fitzgerald, *Memories of Charles Dickens* (1913), pp. 220 and 312.

14. Dickens to George Dolby, 2 August 1866, Nonesuch Edition, *The Letters of Charles Dickens*, Vol. III, p. 480. For the diary, see Chapter 11.

15. This is confirmed by her daughter Mrs Gladys Reece, in an unpublished letter to T. Hill, held at Dickens House, dated 13 June 1950, which says 'Jane first went into the service of Mrs Ternan (my grandmother) at *Slough* in *1866*. Mrs Ternan and my mother were then living there together.' Jane later worked for Maria and also for Georgina Hogarth, and returned to Nelly's service in the later years of her life.

16. The sums totalled £128 in January 1867, and the end of the entries may mean only that they were then noted in a more private account. They are found in Dickens's accounts with Messrs Coutts, discussed by Veronica Stokes in *The Dickensian* (1972).

17. According to Muriel Trollope, daughter of Henry, Bice adored Fanny as a governess, but 'war broke out' for a time when she became her stepmother; see 'What I was Told', *The Trollopian* (1948).

18. 2 November 1866. This letter was among the papers left by Mrs Gladys Reece to Miss Helen Wickham, and undoubtedly came to her through her mother, who inherited it from Fanny Trollope. Miss Wickham gave the letter to Miss K. M. Longley, who generously gave me a photocopy, and has in turn presented the original to Robert Cecil Esq.

19. Letter in possession of Robert Cecil Esq. and quoted here by his permission.

20. Dickens to Collins, 10 July 1866, Nonesuch Edition, *The Letters of Charles Dickens*, Vol. III, p. 477.

21. Dickens to Mrs Frances Elliot, 4 July 1867, Nonesuch Edition, *The Letters of Charles Dickens*, Vol. III, pp. 475–6.

11 THE YEAR OF THE DIARY

1. December 1867, Nonesuch Edition, *The Letters of Charles Dickens*, Vol. III, p. 601.
2. Felix Aylmer was the first to make sense of much of it in his *Dickens Incognito*, a brilliant deciphering of most of the diary.
3. Information on the history of the diary from Francis O. Mattson, Curator of the Berg Collection.
4. On Wednesday, 8 May, he wrote to Georgina saying he could not get down to Gad's Hill until the following Monday because of pressure of work; in fact, he was at the Lyceum with 'N' in the evening and spent more time at Slough than at the office during the next few days. On Friday, 2 August, he wrote to Georgina from Liverpool, saying he would not come to Gad's Hill until Monday on the 12.10 train, because of his bad foot; the diary shows he spent the weekend at Peckham. To confuse things further, he used Gad's Hill headed paper for the letter he wrote from his office on the Monday.
5. Dickens to Mrs Frances Elliot, 4 March 1867, Nonesuch Edition, *The Letters of Charles Dickens*, Vol. III, p. 513. He instructed her to reply to him at his office, marking her letter 'Private'.
6. So the diary notes on 9 October.
7. Dickens to George Russell, 14 December 1866, unpublished letter quoted by permission of the editors of Pilgrim Edition of *The Letters of Charles Dickens*.
8. The existence of the second cottage was established by Miss K. M. Longley from the rate books. It may have been a separate working establishment for Dickens or simply an overflow when more space was needed; either way it may give credence to the assertion by the sisters of Nelly's maid Jane that she had never 'lived' with 'Mr Dickens' in answer to a written question put by Nelly's daughter in 1936.
9. *Tallis's Illustrated London* (1850).
10. It has been suggested that 'Loss' refers to bleeding caused by Dickens's piles; possibly, but there is no similar entry for February, when he was so worried by them that he wrote to his doctor and Georgina on the subject. (New information makes this suggestion superfluous.)

11. Information from the papers of Madeline House in Dickens House.

12. See *Dickens Incognito*. The conclusive rebuttal made by Graham Storey in the *Sunday Times*, 13 December 1959, of its suggestion that Dickens and Nelly had a child *which was given for adoption*, has tended to obscure the originality and cleverness of the other part of Aylmer's detective work. It was he who saw the meaning of the abbreviated names of the railway stations in the diary, who worked out how Dickens must have used them to avoid being recognized too often, who found the entries relating to 'Charles Tringham' in the local rate books, and who pointed to local newspaper references to the fact that Charles Dickens had 'lodged' in Slough for a time.

For those who are unfamiliar with Aylmer's book, here is an extract from p. 15:

An entry which closes the account of many days in the first half of the year is: 'to Sl:'. That these letters represent a place and not a person is made plain by the slightly less frequent entry: 'At Sl:'. There are also recorded various routes by which Dickens travelled between Sl: and London. On the mornings following his visits we find him usually going 'to off:' (which we may reasonably take to be his office) not from S.:, but from either 'W' or 'P'. The return journey is on one occasion made by the route: 'To D from Wat. (for Sl:)'; and on two others: 'To W from V'. There cannot be many places which satisfy all these conditions at once, and I was able to think of only one: Slough, in Buckinghamshire [Slough was moved into Berkshire after Aylmer wrote his book].

Slough, two miles from Windsor, is on the main line of the former Great Western Railway, of which the London terminus is Paddington. A branch line takes passengers the further distance to Windsor. Windsor is also served by the old London and South-Western Railway, with London termini at Waterloo and Victoria. On this line the station next before Windsor is Datchet and, owing to the curve in the railway, this station is little further from Slough than Windsor itself. Dickens could, therefore, either take the train from Slough to Paddington, and find himself with three miles of crowded London between himself and his office . . . or he could walk or drive two miles to Windsor, take the train to Waterloo, and reach his office in a ten-minute walk over Waterloo Bridge. If he found himself at the end of the day near Victoria Station, he could still travel to Windsor from there, probably changing at Clapham Junction. If he felt like a walk at the end of his journey, he could alight at Datchet, whence his way would be by country lanes and fields, and he would be home in less than forty-five minutes. Identifying these stations by their initial letters, and reading for 'W' sometimes Waterloo, and sometimes Windsor, we find the diary routes all fall neatly into place.

On p. 38 Aylmer explains a further point of interest:

The diary record of his journeys suggests a regular precaution. Journeys to Slough were commonly made direct to Slough station; those to London usually from Windsor. Making all allowance for his love of walking, one cannot ignore the fact that arrival after dark at a station from which the alighting crowd make a quick exit to their homes, involves much less chance of recognition than the daylight wait upon the up-platform for the morning train that is so often late. Strangers who identified the famous man during his journeys would be likely to infer that his quarters were in the town of Windsor rather than the small village of Slough.

13. See Pilgrim Edition, *The Letters of Charles Dickens*, Vol. XI, p. 357.

14. This is clear from a comparison of the diary and the Trollope letters.

15. Quoted in Ada Nisbet, *Dickens and Ellen Ternan*, p. 57, from letter in the Huntington Library.

16. 4 July 1867, Nonesuch Edition, *The Letters of Charles Dickens*, Vol. III, pp. 475–6.

17. Windsor Lodge was built between 1860 and 1862. It was knocked down and replaced by a council estate soon after the Second World War, but some of the villas built at the same time are still standing, and, although they are now dilapidated, you can see what fine, solid houses they were. There is an interesting description of the house known as Windsor Lodge in Linden Grove, given by Ernest J. Marshall, who lived there from 1926 to 1937, in a letter to Felix Aylmer held at Dickens House Museum, dated 17 January 1960. The house was called 'Holmdene' during his occupancy: the name is clearly visible in the only known photograph. He left it after a compulsory purchase by the LCC in 1937.

Mr Marshall describes it as a detached house with a large garden and stables on one side, prompting the thought that Nelly may have kept a horse, since she was a keen rider. There was also a covered glass sideway. The house was on four floors: a semi-basement, with four rooms, pantry and coal cellar; a first floor with three rooms; a second floor with three rooms, bathroom and WC; and an attic floor with two more rooms.

Mr Marshall was visited by Thomas Wright in 1935, and told him in a letter dated 14 December of that year (also held at Dickens House Museum) that he 'had heard' that Dickens was associated with the property.

Two other letters are also worth recording here. Both were printed in the *Sunday Times* of 22 March 1953, following two long articles by Earl Jowitt in which he discussed the forthcoming publication in England of both Edgar Johnson's biography of Dickens and Ada Nisbet's *Dickens and Ellen Ternan*. The first is from Gladys Storey:

Sir, My book, *Dickens and Daughter* (1939), was written in fulfilment of a promise I made to Charles Dickens's younger daughter Kate, Mrs Perugini, who, suffering intense remorse, revealed to me the facts of her father's intimacy, until his death, with Ellen Ternan – to tell the truth from her own lips to vindicate her mother of false accusations.

Earl Jowitt says, 'Miss Storey . . . accepts the "Peckham" version,' a pronouncement he bases on the data he takes from Mr Wright's autobiography – which I have neither seen nor read.

I asked Mrs Perugini very few questions, but when she was telling me that her father made a settlement on Ellen Ternan, and kept her in a house with two servants, I did ask her – where? She immediately replied, 'Peckham.' I yet recall her tone of voice as she said it.

Lord Jowitt goes on to say that I finally record that 'Mrs Perugini said the association of Dickens and Nelly resulted in the birth of a son who died in infancy. This fact – if fact it be – is plainly outside Mrs Perugini's personal knowledge . . .'

On what grounds but that of supposition and almost, it would appear, wishful belief could Lord Jowitt have written those last few words? Mrs Perugini could not help knowing about the child, being as she was in the centre of things.

The second letter is from a Mr H. J. Chilton of West Bridgford:

Sir, The second of Earl Jowitt's most interesting articles recalls a story my grandmother used to tell. She lived in a house immediately opposite Peckham Rye, and employed Mrs Goldring, referred to by Lord Jowitt, for several years in the late eighties and early nineties. [Jowitt was dismissive of some evidence Thomas Wright derived from another employer of Mrs Goldring.]

Mrs Goldring told my grandmother that she was employed by Dickens at the time of his death, but was totally unaware of his identity. When she saw his portrait reproduced in a newspaper, she was taken completely by surprise, and said to her husband, 'Well, if it isn't the master!' This story has always rather puzzled me, but now it appears that there may be a simple explanation of the reason she did not know she was working for Dickens.

Since the assumption is often made that Dickens's fame meant that everyone recognized him whenever he appeared in public, it is worth citing a story of his manager, Dolby. Dolby was present when Dickens took a party, including his American publisher James Fields, through Rochester – his local town – in two post-carriages with scarlet-liveried postilions; they stopped for a while in the centre of town, and a man in the crowd that collected to observe the very striking equipages confidently pointed to Fields, saying, 'That's Dickens.'

18. These rate entries were found by Thomas Wright when he was researching his *Life of Charles Dickens*; the rate books were subsequently destroyed.

19. Quoted in Ada Nisbet, *Dickens and Ellen Ternan*, p. 55, from letter in Huntington Library.

20. All these quotations are given by Ada Nisbet, *Dickens and Ellen Ternan*, pp. 55–6, from letters in the Huntington Library.

12 'THIS LIFE IS HALF MADE UP OF PARTINGS'

1. Fanny Trollope to Bice, letter quoted by permission of Robert Cecil Esq.

2. These remarks from the diary of Annie Fields for 2 May 1868 are quoted in George Curry, *Charles Dickens and Annie Fields*, p. 27.

3. These are the words of Anthony Trollope, written just after Dickens's death, in July 1870, in *St Paul's* magazine. The article is reprinted in *The Dickensian* (1910).

4. This is Annie Fields's description of Kate Perugini dancing with her father all evening, when Annie visited Gad's Hill in the autumn of 1869, quoted in George Curry, *Charles Dickens and Annie Fields*, p. 4.

5. Thomas Trollope wrote to his publisher William Blackwood on 15 October 1869, sending a story which he said could be returned if unsuitable c/o Mrs Ternan, 32 Harrington Square, Hampstead Road; the following January, Trollope wrote to Bentley, asking him to send some numbers of the *Temple Bar* magazine c/o Mrs Ternan, 305 Vauxhall Bridge Road.

6. Dickens to Plorn, 26 September 1868, Nonesuch Edition, *The Letters of Charles Dickens*, Vol. III, p. 667.

7. Dickens's purchase of silk stockings from Mr Long made such an impression on him that it has been remembered in his family to the

present day, as well as forming the main feature of his obituary notice in the Hull *Daily Mail* at the time of his death in 1927.

A Hull link with the famous author, Charles Dickens, was broken by the death of Mr Ed. Simpson Long, on Thursday of last week . . . Mr Long, who was a son of Mr Simpson Long, farmer, was born at Gateforth, near Selby in 1842. When about 25 years of age, he came to reside in Hull, and became an assistant to Mr Henry Dixon, silk mercer, of Whitefriargate. It was while Mr Long was employed with this firm that he had a red-letter day in his life.

Mr Charles Dickens, the famous novelist, who came to Hull to give some readings on his own works at the Assembly Rooms, called at Messrs Dixon's shop and asked to see some ladies' hosiery. Mr Long, unaware of the customer's identity, went forward to serve Mr Dickens, and while the latter was making his choice, the following conversation took place:

Mr Dickens: What do you do with yourself, young man, in an evening?

Mr Long: Well, I sometimes go to the theatre, if there is a good Shakespearean play on, or dramatic readings, same as tonight. But it is by subscription, so I shall not be able to go.

Mr Dickens: Why, have you read of Dickens's books?

Mr Long: Yes, I have read most of Dickens's books, and can find many characters to fit them.

Charles Dickens then asked Mr Long which of his books he liked best, and when the latter had given several titles, the novelist asked him if he would like to go to the reading, and thereupon wrote on one of his cards 'Please Admit Bearer'. One can imagine Mr Long's surprise when he turned over the card and saw that it bore the name of one of the most famous writers of the day.

When Mr Long went to his seat, he found that it was on the platform, close to the reading desk from which Dickens delivered his reading. During his performance the novelist kept turning round to see how Mr Long was enjoying himself, and purposefully chose passages from Mr Long's favourite books.

Thus ended one of Mr Long's most enjoyable days. But one thing he was never able to understand: why Dickens was buying ladies' stockings.

Mr Long's granddaughter, who remembers him well, says the stockings were black; but it was not thought quite suitable to mention this in the obituary.

8. Quoted in N. John Hall (editor), *Letters of Anthony Trollope*, Vol. I, p. 423n, from letter in the Free Library of Philadelphia.

9. Diary of Annie Fields, 8 June 1869, quoted in George Curry, *Charles Dickens and Annie Fields*, p. 42.

10. Philip Collins, 'William Charles Macready and Dickens: Some Family Recollections', *Dickens Studies* (1966).

11. See p. 201 for Forster's letter about 'Provident sums' for Miss T.

12. This information is derived from unpublished papers by Mrs Madeline House at Dickens House.

13. See William C. Clarke, *The Secret Life of Wilkie Collins*, p. 122 and notes.

14. It has been suggested by Michael Slater in his *Dickens and Women* that the story Dickens wrote at Peckham, *George Silverman's Explanation*, in which an old man narrates his unhappy life story, and in particular describes how he rejected the love of a girl he also loved, because he felt she would do better to marry another man, reflects Dickens's anxieties about Nelly's situation. There is, however, no indication that Dickens sought to weaken the ties between himself and Nelly at any point.

15. 4 November 1868, quoted in L. Szladits, *A Dickens Anthology* (New York, 1970), from letter in Berg Collection, New York Public Library.

16. 23 January 1870, quoted in Ada Nisbet, *Dickens and Ellen Ternan*, p. 57, from a letter in the Huntington Library.

17. 26 February 1870, R. C. Lehmann (editor), *Charles Dickens as an Editor: Being Letters Written by Him to William Henry Wills*, p. 396.

18. Speech to Royal Academy, 30 April 1870, K. J. Fielding (editor), *The Speeches of Charles Dickens*, p. 421.

19. See account by Constance Cross, who visited him in April 1870 at Hyde Park Place, quoted in Philip Collins, *Dickens Interviews and Recollections*, Vol. II, p. 345.

20. See Philip Collins, *Dickens Interviews and Recollections*, Vol. II, pp. 246–7, which gives Charles Kent's account of this conversation, first written down in 1872 in his *Charles Dickens as Reader*.

21. 29 March 1870, Nonesuch Edition, *The Letters of Charles Dickens*, Vol. III, p. 769.

22. Dickens to Mrs E. T. Dallas 2 May 1870, Nonesuch Edition, *The Letters of Charles Dickens*, Vol. III, p. 773.

23. Gladys Storey, *Dickens and Daughter*, pp. 133–4.

24. Nonesuch Edition, *The Letters of Charles Dickens*, Vol. III, p. 784.

25. See Una Pope-Hennessy, *Charles Dickens* (1945), p. 464: the author had her information from Gladys Storey, who was told by Kate Perugini. On the other hand Walter Dexter wrote to the Comte de Suzannet (22 February 1939, letter in Dickens House) that Gladys

Storey told him on Mrs Perugini's authority that it was Georgina who sent for Nelly: 'Mrs P. said she would never have allowed it had she been there.' Malcolm Morley also states that Gladys Reece told him her mother was present; see *The Dickensian* (1960).

26. See P. H. Ditchfield and G. Clinch, *Memorials of Old Kent* (1907), p. 251.

13 ANOTHER LIFE BEGINS

1. Fanny Trollope to Bice, 28 June 1870, letter quoted by permission of Robert Cecil Esq.

2. Georgina Hogarth to Frederic Ouvry, letters held by Messrs Farrer. It is perhaps worth noting that Farrers filed letters from other beneficiaries of the will, but there is no letter from Nelly filed.

3. The cheque book is in a box of papers held by Messrs Farrer.

4. Letter held by Messrs Farrer.

5. Letter held by Messrs Farrer.

6. See Edward C. McAleer (editor), *Dearest Isa: Letters of Robert Browning* (1951), p. 349.

7. Diary of Annie Fields, August 1870, quoted in George Curry, *Charles Dickens and Annie Fields*, p. 58.

8. Careful researches conducted by Miss K. M. Longley have turned up nobody bearing either of these names among the deaths recorded in England during this period.

9. Information from Miss K. M. Longley, who had it from Rosalind Brown's daughter Helen Wickham.

10. All material from the commonplace books is transcribed from Miss K. M. Longley's 'A Pardoner's Tale: Charles Dickens and the Ternan Family', unpublished typescript.

11. Claire Clairmont, Shelley's friend and the model for James's *The Aspern Papers*, was still living in Italy at this point; she died in 1879, and he wrote the story in 1888.

12. The letters were first printed in *The Dickensian* for January 1965, transcribed by its then editor, Leslie C. Staples, to whom the originals were given by a friend who found them in a packet inserted into a book purchased from a second-hand stall in the Farringdon Road; Staples does not say when, simply that it was a few years earlier. All Nelly's letters are originals, her writing attested to by her daughter Gladys Reece, who was consulted by Staples. The two letters from

George Smith are, however, copies, which indicates that it was he who preserved the letters, for reasons of his own, apart from the firm's files; and this suggests in turn that he knew of their curiosity value, and knew the history of 'Nelly Ternan'. Smith died in 1901, while Austin was serving as poet laureate; but the *DNB* had its crack at Austin later, suggesting that he got his position chiefly as a reward for his journalistic services to the party of Lord Salisbury.

13. The author has seen the books, inscribed by Mrs Ternan to Nelly, and now in private possession.

14. Ibsen wrote *A Doll's House* in 1879; the first English version appeared in 1884.

15. All quotations from letters in possession of Robert Cecil Esq. and quoted by his permission.

16. The following year Anny Thackeray came in for her disapproval when she married her cousin, eighteen years her junior: 'Very risky,' she pronounced, 'even a *few* years disparity on the *wrong* side is dangerous – because a woman is always *older* than a man, even if they are the same age.' Georgina Hogarth to Annie Fields, quoted in Arthur A. Adrian, *Georgina Hogarth and the Dickens Circle*, p. 200, from letter in the Huntington Library.

17. 23 July 1876, Anne Procter to Nina Lehmann, quoted in Miss K. M. Longley, 'A Pardoner's Tale: Charles Dickens and the Ternan Family', by permission of the late John Lehmann.

18. Fanny Trollope to Bice, June 1876, letter quoted by permission of Robert Cecil Esq.

14 THE SCHOOLMASTER'S WIFE AND THE FOREIGN CORRESPONDENT: MARGATE, ROME, AFRICA

1. Information from letter from Georgina Hogarth to Annie Fields, 30 October 1877; I am indebted for it to Miss K. M. Longley, who had it from Arthur A. Adrian. Miss Hogarth's presentation of prizes at the school in the summer of 1879 is reported in *Keble's Margate and Ramsgate Gazette*.

2. Told by Fanny Trollope in an unpublished collection of family anecdotes which she kept between 1879 and 1890, now in UCLA Library.

3. William Wetmore Story to J. R. Lowell, 11 February 1853, quoted in Henry James, *W. W. Story and His Friends* (1903), p. 255.

4. The story of Maria and the fishermen appears in Fanny's book of family anecdotes in the UCLA Library.

5. The album is now the property of Mrs Lillah Fields, who kindly let me see it and reproduce from it.

15 NELLY TELLS

1. See Gladys Storey papers held at Dickens House, also Walter Dexter to Comte de Suzannet, 22 February 1939, letter in Dickens House: 'It is confirmed by Miss S. that the children of Henry D and of E.T. used to play together on the sands at Boulogne.' Other information for this chapter comes from letters of Fanny Trollope in possession of Robert Cecil Esq.; the *Thanet Guardian* and *Keble's Margate and Ramsgate Gazette*; and the archivist at Margate Public Library.

2. See report in *Thanet Guardian* 1 November 1879. The preacher G. J. Everest was almost certainly a member of the Church and Stage Guild, founded in 1879 by Revd Stewart Headlam, after he'd been sacked by the Bishop of London as a result of lecturing in favour of theatre and music halls in 1877. The Guild faded out, but its ideas were taken up by the Actors' Church Union in 1898, founded by the Revd Donald Hole, whose wife had been a child actress. Information from Michal Sanderson, *From Irving to Olivier*, pp. 146–8. Soon after the sermon at St John's a group of Margate ladies and gentlemen formed an amateur dramatic society. More important, in 1885 a dramatic school was opened by Sarah Thorne, the lessee of the Margate Theatre Royal; this attracted many pupils, including Ellen Terry's children and Irene and Violet Vanbrugh.

3. The words are those of Helen Wickham, the daughter of Rosalind Brown, to Miss K. M. Longley quoted in 'The Real Ellen Ternan', *The Dickensian* (1985).

4. Thomas Adolphus Trollope, *What I Remember* (1887–9), Vol. II, pp. 113ff.

5. This was Julia Clara Byrne, wife of the editor of the *Morning Post*, in her book of reminiscences, *Gossip of the Century* (1892), Vol. I, pp. 225–6.

6. *Manchester Evening News*, 16 September 1893, quoted in Miss K. M. Longley, 'A Pardoner's Tale: Charles Dickens and the Ternan Family'.

7. Wright gives this information in his autobiography *Thomas Wright of*

Olney, published in 1936; he says Hughes wrote to him 18 April 1893, telling him about the letters; Hughes died in 1899.

8. Kate Perugini to George Bernard Shaw, letter in British Library.

9. Eliza Lynn Linton, *My Literary Life* (1899).

10. *Mabel's Progress* was translated into German and continued to sell well enough in England for there to be a new edition from Chatto & Windus in 1884. There is even a passing favourable mention of Fanny as a 'novelist of no mean ability' in the (unsigned) entry under her brother-in-law Anthony in the 1911 *Encyclopaedia Britannica*.

11. This description comes from Muriel Trollope, the granddaughter of Anthony, and appears in 'What I Was Told', *The Trollopian* (1948).

12. Constance Clinton-Baddeley gave a BBC Third Programme talk entitled 'Recollections of Thomas Adolphus Trollope' on 9 May 1947, in which she recalled her friendship with the family. This is part of it:

I was a grown-up woman when, on retiring from his work in Rome as correspondent of the *Morning Post*, Mr Trollope came to live the last years of his life in Budleigh Salterton, the Devon village where we had our home. It had been the Trollopes' plan to remain 'Incog:' for a little – but on the first walk they took, they encountered one of their oldest friends, Mr Edward Pigott, then Controller of Theatres in Great Britain: – that ended their period of retirement. Before long the Trollopes knew everybody and had started weekly receptions which were always crowded.

Mr Trollope's appearance in and outside his house was remarkably different. Outside he seemed insignificant, a short, somewhat shrunk old man. Inside, where he was generally seated, you enjoyed the sight of a large head covered with a shock of white hair, and the merriest blue eyes I ever saw; – and he used them to add to the sparkle of his conversation, – for he was full of jokes and puns and tales worth listening to, – tales of his early days when as a boy he accompanied his parents on their ill-planned journey to America; tales of his life in Florence where he had lived with his mother in the days of her triumph; tales of his own later life in Rome, and tales of his younger brother Anthony, of whom he was a devoted admirer. He had been a friend of so many people, George Eliot and Charles Dickens among them. Indeed Dickens had introduced him to his second wife. His first wife had died young, leaving a little daughter. Dickens had recommended a Miss Frances Eleanor Ternan as a companion for the child, and in due course Mr Trollope married her.

She was the sister of Dickens's friend Ellen Ternan, – and Ellen, now Mrs Robinson, often used to stay in the house on the cliff at Budleigh Salterton. She was very charming and very pretty, and I knew her well.

But I was talking about Mr Trollope's 'At Homes'. After we had all squashed into the first reception room, we were sent out into the long, big room where there was always a resplendent spread, and Mr Trollope would move around talking to everyone. Sometimes we returned to the drawing-room for music, and I recall 'Nellie' Robinson – Ellen Ternan – giving a long recitation, – I forget what, but something famous and historical. But Mrs Trollope was always very careful to see that no one performed at her 'At Homes' who could not do whatever it was well. Indeed I think she was inclined to find the Devon society a bit stupid; – but Mr Trollope loved the 'At Homes', and talked hard.

13. Helen Wickham died in 1982 at the age of ninety-eight. Miss K. M. Longley knew her from 1968: see 'The Real Ellen Ternan', *The Dickensian* (1985).

16 SOUTHSEA

1. Kate Perugini to George Bernard Shaw, 19 December 1897, letter in British Library. Her sister Mamey had died the previous year, after publishing a memoir that entirely supported the view of Dickens as a perfect father and family man.

2. These papers are held in the Morris L. Parrish Collection of Victorian Novelists, Princeton University Library.

3. See her letter to Annie Fields, who was in favour of votes for women, and to Sir Nevil Macready, 6 February 1913, both quoted in Arthur A. Adrian, *Georgina Hogarth and the Dickens Circle*, p. 257.

4. From a speech made by Kate Perugini in April 1910 at the Lyceum Club for Women Artists and Writers, reported in *The Dickensian* (1910).

5. Nelly to Geoffrey, 26 June 1913, quoted by permission of Mrs L. Fields.

6. Nelly to Charles Stuart-Wortley (Bice's widower and the father of her child, now remarried; the Stuart-Wortleys had kept in touch with Fanny and 'lent' her small sums of money from time to time), September 1913, quoted by permission of Robert Cecil Esq.

7. ibid.

17 GEOFFREY

1. The Imperial War Museum contains both printed and manuscript accounts of the experiences of the British expedition led by Major General Dunsterville; it's an extraordinary story.

2. His sister, Gladys Reece, insisted that their mother told them that *her* mother had been altogether unwilling to allow any of her daughters to follow her on to the stage professionally.

3. For instance, a playbill for the Manchester production of *The Frozen Deep*, with the names of Mrs Ternan, Maria and Ellen, had been reproduced in T. E. Pemberton's *Dickens and the Stage* in 1888.

4. Gladys Storey papers at Dickens House, 18 February 1923. A later note adds Sir Henry's confirmation in 1928. See also note in Comte de Suzannet papers at Dickens House in which Walter Dexter tells Comte de Suzannet that she told him on this date that Ellen's son 'Once called on H.F.D. with some letters and asked him point blank, "Was my mother your father's mistress?" To which H.F. had to reply, "Yes."'

5. Gladys Storey to George Bernard Shaw, 23 July 1939, letter in British Library: 'Poor Miss Ternan, I know more about her than I put in my book. Nearly all her married life she lived in perpetual fear of her association with Dickens being revealed to her children. They did not know of it until after her death, when owing to some discovery, her son took a courageous and dramatic step to learn the truth.'

6. The story was told by Mrs Thomas Whiffen (Blanche Galton) in *Keeping off the Shelf* and was denied by J. W. T. Ley in *The Dickensian* in 1930, quoting Sir Henry saying Ellen was not D.'s god-daughter, and that the accident story was pure invention. Mrs Whiffen was the daughter of Madame Pyne Galton who lived in Margate and sometimes accompanied Nelly at concerts.

7. For O'Connor's statement, which appeared 29 September 1928, see Ada Nisbet, *Dickens and Ellen Ternan*, p. 30.

8. On pp. 196 and 216.

9. An unpublished letter from Gladys Reece to Leslie Staples in Dickens House, dated 18 November, says of Geoffrey: 'knowing him as I do, I am sure that few things would upset him more than being asked to discuss this matter of Dickens and our mother. When I have once or twice slightly approached the matter, merely speaking of the fact of the friendship between them, my brother has shut up like a clam.' Malcolm Morley, whose pioneering series of articles *The Theatrical Ternans* in *The Dickensian* from 1958 to 1961 used a good deal of information supplied by Gladys Reece, notes in his papers at Dickens House that both she and Leslie Staples put pressure on him to present Nelly as 'innocent'.

10. Gladys Storey's book is not the work of a professional writer, but it is

by no means negligible as testimony. Whenever she appears to be quoting Kate Perugini's words directly, it carries particular conviction. Of course it can be argued *ad infinitum* that she and Wright were both sensationalists and scandalmongers, but it is hard to see what these two elderly people, both of whom waited for many years before publishing what they had been told, had to gain by inventing evidence, almost all of which has subsequently been corroborated from quite independent sources. Bernard Shaw, defending Gladys Storey, wrote, 'The facts of the case may be in bad taste. Facts often are' (*TLS*, 29 July 1939).

11. The editor of the Nonesuch Edition was Walter Dexter; Dexter was the recipient of a good deal of private information, including the statement by C. E. S. Chambers that his aunt, Nina Lehmann – herself the niece of Mr and Mrs Wills – told him that Dickens 'had actually lived for some twelve years with a well-known actress, I forget the name' (Chambers to Dexter, 21 January 1934, Storey papers in Dickens House).

12. The author has seen unpublished letters between Gladys Reece and several Dickens scholars, now in private possession. There are also unpublished letters at Dickens House from her to J. W. T. Ley, in which she makes the remark about love being the only possible reason for her mother to have become Dickens's mistress.

18 MYTHS AND MORALS

1. Miss K. M. Longley's unpublished typescript and notes have been a valuable source to many recent scholars and writers, among them Michael Slater, George Curry, Fred Kaplan, Peter Ackroyd and the editors of the Pilgrim Edition of the letters.

2. From a letter to Lady Emily Lytton, later Lutyens, written in 1891 and printed in *A Blessed Girl: Memoirs of a Victorian Girlhood* (1953), p. 59.

3. G. K. Chesterton, *Charles Dickens* (1906), p. 19.

4. Kate Perugini's account is given in a lecture to the Dickens Fellowship, reported in *The Dickensian* for 1918; she writes of 'garden parties, long walks, drives and rides . . . occasional rather dull dinner parties, dances and . . . opera and theatre parties . . . mornings occupied with the usual small domestic worries . . . a large amount of letter writing, embroidery and reading'. She also mentions charitable work.

5. G. K. Chesterton, *Charles Dickens*, p. 136; and John Carey, *The Violent Effigy: A Study of Dickens's Imagination* (1973), p. 71.

6. Dickens to Mrs Dickinson, 19 August 1860, Nonesuch Edition, *The Letters of Charles Dickens*, Vol. III, p. 172, and Dickens to Georgina Hogarth, 27 November 1860, Nonesuch Edition, Vol. III, p. 792.

7. Dickens to De la Rue, 23 October 1857, letter in Berg Collection, New York Public Library.

8. Charles Eliot Norton said Dickens told him a story along these lines at Gad's Hill in the summer of 1868; it appeared in the extracts from Norton's journals printed in *Scribner's Magazine* in 1913.

Bibliography

I UNPUBLISHED SOURCES

Manuscript letters held by Dr Graham Storey for the Pilgrim Edition of *The Letters of Charles Dickens*

Letters and 1867 diary of Charles Dickens held at the Berg Collection, New York Public Library

Letters of Charles Dickens held at Pierpont Morgan Library, New York

Papers held at the Morris L. Parrish Collection of Victorian Novelists, Princeton University Library

Trollope family papers in the Department of Special Collections, University of California, Los Angeles

Trollope papers held in the Rare Book and Special Collections Library, University of Illinois at Urbana-Champaign

Papers of Malcolm Morley held at Victoria and Albert Museum, Theatre Library

Letters of Helen Taylor about her provincial stage career 1856–8, held in Vol. 51 of the Mill–Taylor correspondence at the British Library of Political and Economic Science.

Papers held by Messrs Farrer & Co.

Papers held at Dickens House Museum, Doughty Street

Private collection of Robert Cecil Esq.

Private collection of Mrs Lillah Fields

Private collection of Mrs Ayres

Miss Katharine M. Longley, 'A Pardoner's Tale: Charles Dickens and the Ternan Family' (typescript)

Collections of playbills held at Minster Library, York, and Newcastle upon Tyne Central Library; also newspaper cuttings at Newcastle upon Tyne Public Library and the Colindale Newspaper Library

2 WORKS OF DICKENS

Household Words (periodical under his editorship), 19 vols. (1850–59)

All the Year Round (periodical under his editorship), 23 vols. (1859–70)

Memoirs of Grimaldi by 'Boz' (1838)

Dexter, Walter (editor), Nonesuch Edition of *The Letters of Charles Dickens*, 3 vols. (1938)

Fielding, K. J. (editor), *The Speeches of Charles Dickens* (1988)

House, Madeline, Tillotson, Kathleen and Storey, Graham (editors), Pilgrim Edition of *The Letters of Charles Dickens*, Vols. I–VI (1965)

Hutton, Laurence (editor), *Letters of Charles Dickens to Wilkie Collins 1851–1870*, selected by Miss Georgina Hogarth (1892)

Johnson, Edgar (editor), *Letters from Charles Dickens to Angela Burdett-Coutts 1841–1865* (1953). (US edition called *The Heart of Charles Dickens*, 1952)

Lehmann, R. C. (editor), *Charles Dickens as an Editor: Being Letters Written by Him to William Henry Wills* (1912)

3 PUBLISHED SOURCES

Adrian, Arthur A., *Georgina Hogarth and the Dickens Circle* (1957)

Austin, Alfred *Madonna's Child* (1873)
  Autobiography (1911)

Aylmer, Felix, *Dickens Incognito* (1959)

Berger, Francesco, *Reminiscences, Impressions and Anecdotes* (1913)
  97 (1931)

Bredsdorff, Elias, *Hans Andersen and Charles Dickens: A Friendship and Its Dissolution* (1956)

Carey, John, *The Violent Effigy: A Study of Dickens's Imagination* (1973)
  Thackeray: Prodigal Genius (1977)

Chesterton, G. K., *Charles Dickens* (1906)

Clarke, William M., *The Secret Life of Wilkie Collins* (1988)

Collins, Philip, *Dickens Interviews and Recollections*, 2 vols. (1981)

Collins, Wilkie, *The Frozen Deep* (editor R. L. Brannan; 1966)

Cowden Clarke, Mary, *My Long Life* (1896)

Curry, George, *Charles Dickens and Annie Fields* (1988)

Dickensian, The (periodical; 1905–). See Notes for individual articles

Dolby, George, *Dickens as I Knew Him* (1885)

Downer, Alan S., *The Eminent Tragedian: William Charles Macready* (1966)

Fitzgerald, Percy, *Memories of Charles Dickens* (1913)

Forster, John, *Life of Charles Dickens*, 3 vols. (1874)

Hall, N. John (editor), *Letters of Anthony Trollope*, 2 vols. (1983)

Johnson, Edgar, *Charles Dickens: His Tragedy and Triumph*, 2 vols. (1952)

Kaplan, Fred, *Dickens: A Biography* (1989)

Kingsmill, Hugh, *The Sentimental Journey: A Life of Charles Dickens* (1934)

Lindsay, Jack, *Charles Dickens* (1950)

Linton, Eliza Lynn, *My Literary Life* (1899)

Mackenzie, Norman and Jeanne, *Dickens: A Life* (1979)

Nisbet, Ada, *Dickens and Ellen Ternan* (with a Foreword by Edmund Wilson; 1952)

Page, Norman, *A Dickens Chronology* (1988)

Pemberton, T. E., *Dickens and the Stage* (1888)

Pope-Hennessy, Una, *Charles Dickens* (1945)

Roberts, C. E. Bechhofer, *This Side Idolatry* (fictionalized version of life of Dickens to 1858; 1928)

Sala, George Augustus, *Life and Adventures* (1895)

Schlicke, Paul, *Dickens and Popular Entertainment* (1985)

Slater, Michael, *Dickens and Women* (1983)
    (with Nicolas Bentley and Nina Burgis), *The Dickens Index* (1988)

Spiers, Edward M., *The Army and Society 1815–1914* (1980)

Storey, Gladys, *Dickens and Daughter* (1939)

Taylor, Maria Susanna, *Some Old Letters from North Africa* (1889)

Taylor, Robert H., *Certain Small Works* (1980)

Terry, Ellen, *The Story of My Life* (1908)

Trollope, Frances Eleanor, *Aunt Margaret's Troubles* (1867)
    Mabel's Progress (1867)
    The Sacristan's Household (1869)
    Veronica (1870)
    Anne Furness (1871)
    A Charming Fellow (1876)
    Black Spirits and White (1877)
    Like Ships upon the Sea (1883)
    That Unfortunate Marriage (1888)
    Among Aliens (1890)
    Madame Leroux (1890)
    That Wild Wheel (1892)
    Frances Trollope: Her Life and Literary Work from George III to Victoria, 2 vols. (1895)
    (with Thomas Adolphus Trollope), *Homes and Haunts of the Italian Poets* (1881)

Trollope, Thomas Adolphus, *What I Remember*, 3 vols. (1887–9)

Wharton Robinson, George (with W. T. Jeffcott and G. J. Tossell), *Helps for Latin Students* (1883)

Wilson, Edmund, *The Wound and the Bow* (1941; revised edition 1952)

Wright, Thomas, *The Life of Charles Dickens* (1935)
  Thomas Wright of Olney (autobiography; 1936)

4 THEATRICAL BOOKS

Anon., *Memoirs of Madame Vestris* (1839)

Aspinall, A., *Mrs Jordan and Her Family* (1951)

Baynham, Walter, *The Glasgow Stage* (1892)

Boaden, James, *Life of Mrs Jordan*, 2 vols. (1831)
  Life of Mrs Siddons, 2 vols. (1827)

Bunn, Alfred, *The Stage: Both Before and Behind the Curtain*, 3 vols. (1840)

Dickens, Charles, Junior (editor), *Life of Charles James Mathews*, 2 vols. (1879)

Donaldson, Walter A., *Fifty Years of Green-room Gossip* (1881)

Doran, Dr J., *Their Majesties' Servants* (1864)
  Annals of the English Stage, 3 vols. (1887)

Francis, Basil, *Fanny Kelly of Drury Lane* (1950)

Genest, Revd J., *History of the Stage*, 10 vols. (1832)

'Griffinhoofe, A.', John Duncombe's edition of the *Memoirs of the Life, Public and Private Adventures of Madame Vestris* [n.d.]

Hawkins, F. W., *The Life of Edmund Kean*, 2 vols. (1869)

History of the Theatre Royal, Dublin (1870), reprinted from *Saunders' Newsletter*

Holman, L. E., *Lamb's Barbara S.* (Fanny Kelly; 1935)

Kelly, Michael, *Reminiscences* (1826)

Kemble, Frances Ann, *Record of a Girlhood*, 3 vols. (1878)

Marshall, Dorothy, *Fanny Kemble* (1977)

Marshall, Frances (editor), *A Travelling Actress in the North and Scotland* (1984, which reprints the *Memoirs of Mrs Charlotte Deans 1768–1859*, 1837)

Mathews, Anne, *Memoirs of Charles Mathews*, 4 vols. (1838–9)

Morley, Malcolm, *Margate and Its Theatres* (1966)

Pearce, Charles E., *'Polly Peachum' Being the Story of Lavinia Fenton* [Duchess of Bolton] *and 'The Beggar's Opera'* (1913)
  Madame Vestris and Her Times [n.d.]

Price, W. T., *A Life of Charlotte Cushman* (1894)

Raby, Peter, *Fair Ophelia* (1982)

Rede, Leman Thomas, *The Road to the Stage* (1827)

Reeves, J. Sims, *Life and Recollections* (1888)

Stirling, Edward, *Old Drury Lane: Fifty Years' Recollections of an Author, Actor and Manager*, 2 vols. (1881)

Wilkinson, Tate, *The Wandering Patentee; or, A History of the Yorkshire Theatres from 1770 to the Present Time* (1795)

Williams, Michael, *Some London Theatres* (1883)

Wyndham, H. S., *Annals of Covent Garden Theatre* (1906)

Index

CLAIRE TOMALIN

CHARLES DICKENS: A LIFE

A major biography of our greatest novelist

Charles Dickens was a phenomenon. A demonically hardworking journalist, the father of ten children, a tireless walker and traveller, a supporter of liberal social causes, but most of all a great novelist – the creator of characters who live immortally in the English imagination: Sam Weller, Mr Pickwick, the Artful Dodger, David Copperfield, Little Nell, Lady Dedlock, Mrs Gamp, Pip, Miss Havisham and many more.

At the age of twelve he was sent by his affectionate but feckless parents to work in a blacking factory. By the time of his death in 1870 he drew adoring crowds to his public appearances, had met princes and presidents on both sides of the Atlantic, and had amassed a fortune. He was truly 'the inimitable', as he jokingly described himself. When he died, the world mourned, and he was buried – against his wishes – in Westminster Abbey.

Charles Dickens: A Life is the examination of Dickens we deserve. It gives full measure to his heroic stature - his huge virtues both as a writer and as a human being - while observing his failings in both respects with an understanding but unblinking eye. Claire Tomalin has written a full-scale biography of the writer, a story worthy of Dickens' own pen: a comedy that turns to tragedy as the very qualities that made him great, his indomitable energy, boldness, imagination, showmanship and enjoyment of fame, finally destroyed him. The man who emerges is one of extraordinary contradictions, whose vices and virtues were intertwined as surely as his life and art.

CLAIRE TOMALIN

THOMAS HARDY: THE TIME-TORN MAN

The definitive life of the great Dorset novelist.

Paradox ruled Thomas Hardy's life. His birth was almost his death; he became one of the great Victorian novelists and reinvented himself as one of the twentieth-century's greatest poets; he was an unhappy husband but a desolate widower; he wrote bitter attacks on the English class system yet prized the friendship of aristocrats. In the hands of Claire Tomalin, Thomas Hardy the novelist, poet, neglectful husband and mourning lover all come intensely alive.

'An extraordinary story, beautifully told' *Mail on Sunday*

'Outstanding, brilliant, another tour de force' Richard Holmes, *Guardian*

'Painfully gripping, acute and original' *Literary Review*

CLAIRE TOMALIN

MRS JORDAN'S PROFESSION:
THE STORY OF A GREAT ACTRESS AND A FUTURE KING

The story of the love between a prince and a famous actress.

Acclaimed as the greatest comic actress of her generation, Dora Jordan played a quite different role offstage as the mistress of one of the sons of George lll. Dora bore him ten children, and they lived in quiet happiness in Bushy Park on the Thames until the unexpected news arrived of his ascendancy to the throne as William lV at which point he was forced to abandon her.

Claire Tomalin vividly recreates the political, theatrical and royal worlds of the late eighteenth century. The story of how Dora moved between stage and home, of how she battled for career and family, makes for a classic tale of royal perfidy and womanly courage.

'Wonderfully readable. As gripping as the best fiction' Jan Dalley, *Independent*

'The strangest and most sensational story Tomalin has written so far' Hilary Spurling, *Daily Telegraph*

'A compelling story and Tomalin tells it with clarity and warmth' Lucy Hughes-Hallett, *Sunday Times*